Examining Education around the World

Examining Education around the World

FRED M. SHELLEY

Global Viewpoints

BLOOMSBURY ACADEMIC
NEW YORK • LONDON • OXFORD • NEW DELHI • SYDNEY

BLOOMSBURY ACADEMIC
Bloomsbury Publishing Inc
1385 Broadway, New York, NY 10018, USA
50 Bedford Square, London, WC1B 3DP, UK
29 Earlsfort Terrace, Dublin 2, Ireland

BLOOMSBURY, BLOOMSBURY ACADEMIC and the Diana logo
are trademarks of Bloomsbury Publishing Plc

First published in the United States of America by ABC-CLIO 2022
Paperback edition published by Bloomsbury Academic 2025

Cover photo: Indian village school, Uttar Pradesh, India.
(Dinodia Photos/Alamy Stock Photo)

Library of Congress Cataloging-in-Publication Data
Names: Shelley, Fred M., 1952- author.
Title: Examining education around the world / Fred M. Shelley.
Description: Santa Barbara, California : ABC-CLIO, [2022] | Series: Global Viewpoints |
Includes bibliographical references and index.
Identifiers: LCCN 2022034309 (print) | LCCN 2022034310 (ebook) |
ISBN 9781440864476 (Hardcover : acid-free paper) | ISBN 9781440864483 (eBook)
Subjects: LCSH: Education—Cross-cultural studies. | Education—Encyclopedias.
Classification: LCC LB17 .S424 2022 (print) | LCC LB17 (ebook) | DDC 370.9—dc23/eng/20220727

LC record available at https://lccn.loc.gov/2022034309
LC ebook record available at https://lccn.loc.gov/2022034310

ISBN: HB: 978-1-4408-6447-6
PB: 979-8-2161-9486-6
ePDF: 978-1-4408-6448-3
eBook: 979-8-2161-8515-4

Series: Global Viewpoints

To find out more about our authors and books visit www.bloomsbury.com
and sign up for our newsletters.

Contents

Series Foreword

We are living in an ever-evolving world, one that is rapidly changing both in terms of society and in terms of our natural environment. Hot-button topics and concerns emerge daily; the news is constantly flooded with stories of climate change, religious clashes, educational crises, pandemic diseases, data security breaches, and other countless issues. Deep within those stories, though, are stories of resilience, triumph, and success. The Global Viewpoints series seeks to explore some of the world's most important and alarming issues and, in the process, investigate solutions and actionable strategies that countries are taking to better our world.

Volumes in the series examine critical issues, including education, war and conflict, crime and justice, business and economics, environment and energy, gender and sexuality, and Internet and technology, just to name a few. Each volume is divided into 10 chapters that focus on subtopics within the larger issue. Each chapter begins with a background overview, helping readers to better understand why the topic is important to our society and world today. Each overview is followed by eight country profiles that explore the issue at a global level. For instance, the volume on education might have a chapter exploring literacy, honing in on literacy rates and advocacy in eight nations. The volume on war and conflict might dedicate a chapter to women in the military, examining women's military roles in eight countries. The volume on crime and justice might include a chapter on policing, focusing on police infrastructure in eight countries. Readers will have an opportunity to use this organization to draw cross-cultural comparisons; to compare how Brazil is grappling with renewable energy amid a booming economy versus India, for instance, or how Internet access and control differs from Cuba to the United States.

Readers may read through each chapter in the volumes as they would a narrative book or may pick and choose specific entries to review. Each entry concludes with a list of further reading sources to accommodate additional research needs. Entries are written with high school and undergraduate students in mind but are appropriate and accessible to general audiences.

The goal of the series is not to make stark comparisons between nations, but instead to present readers with examples of countries that are afflicted by various issues and to examine how these nations are working to face these challenges.

Introduction

This book analyzes education as practiced in countries throughout the world. It considers issues involving diversity, gender, literacy, religion, and several other issues that are addressed in different countries.

Education can be defined as the process of providing or obtaining systematic, organized instruction that provides those receiving this instruction skills needed to participate meaningfully in society. Education takes place throughout the life cycle, beginning with infancy and continuing into adulthood. In this book, we focus on the education of children and teenagers. In the United States, the term "K-12 education" is used commonly to describe the process of teaching these young people. "K-12" refers to formal schooling beginning with kindergarten and continuing through the completion of 12 grades after kindergarten and culminating with the completion of high school. Although specifics vary, this structure is used in developed countries and an increasing number of less developed countries worldwide.

Ancient and Medieval Education

The process of education dates back thousands of years. In all cultures, parents and other adults provided children skills needed to survive and succeed within these cultures as adults. This training predated the invention of writing, which is believed to have emerged in various civilizations more than 5000 years ago.

The invention of writing likely coincided with the development of agriculture. In contrast to hunting and gathering, farming allowed people to settle in one place rather than being forced to move constantly from place to place in search of game or edible plants and other foodstuffs. As people settled in one place and grew crops in that place, populations increased rapidly. Towns and cities developed, and people had the opportunity to accumulate property because they were no longer forced to move all of their possessions as they had while hunting and gathering. However, people also needed a means by which property ownership, including land ownership and amounts of crops produced, could be known unambiguously. Some anthropologists believe, in fact, that writing was developed and used initially so that people could keep records of crop production and distribution.

As it became necessary for people to keep records and to be able to understand these records, it became necessary for them to learn to read and write. However, in most societies in ancient times only a small minority of people were taught these skills. Recording the levels of production of crops and other goods and interpreting these records was important to government officials who used this information in order to levy taxes, for example. Literacy was important also to religious officials, and this became particularly important as various religious traditions became reliant on written texts such as the Bible, the Quran, and the sayings of Confucius. Other people including peasants were seldom taught to read and write. Through the Middle Ages, most people in agricultural societies were farmers who learned their farming skills through observation or training from parents or experienced farmers, outside systematic education.

With the invention of agriculture and writing came the development of systematic formal instruction. Schools where children were taught to read and write were established. Of course, education provided at such schools often went far beyond reading and writing. Students were also taught subjects such as arithmetic, art and music, and geography. By the Middle Ages, many students in Europe were taught the seven liberal arts. These included the trivium including grammar, rhetoric, and logic or dialectic along with the quadrivium including arithmetic, geometry, astronomy, and music. The term "liberal arts" continues to be used to describe these components type of formal education even today.

Education was often intertwined with religion, and students in ancient and medieval schools were taught the principles of the religions associated with the societies where they lived. Many teachers were themselves priests, monks, or other religious officials. In medieval Europe, education was generally the responsibility of the Roman Catholic Church. Religious instruction was a dominant component of the curriculum. Teaching was done in Latin, which was the language of the Church and the educated population in general. Many of the students were members of the aristocracy and/or were being trained to become priests or Church officials themselves. In medieval China, young men who wished to become officials in the Chinese government were required to learn, memorize, and recite Confucian texts in order to qualify for such positions.

The Printing Press

The transition from the Middle Ages to the modern world coincided with the invention of the printing press. Although printing was known and used in East Asia long before the end of the Middle Ages in Europe, Johannes Gutenberg (c. 1400–1468) is generally credited with the invention of the printing press in Europe beginning around 1440.

The invention and use of printing had profound effects on European and global society in general. Its effects on education were especially profound. Prior to the invention of the printing press, all documents had to be produced individually. Printing allowed the mass production of written material so that large numbers of people could have access to this material simultaneously. Although printing was first used to produce copies of the Bible and other religious texts, it soon came to be used in secular contexts as well.

Most likely, the invention of the printing press contributed as well to the rise of Protestantism in Europe. A fundamental tenet of Protestant belief is "sola scriptura," or the idea that the Bible, rather than sacred tradition, represented the highest authority of religion. Believers could approach God through Christ directly, rather than through mediation by priests. The view that the Bible represented the highest authority of Christian belief required that believers learn to read it. Hence, education of entire populations as opposed to limiting education to the nobility and the clergy became important in Protestant societies. As Protestantism spread throughout northern Europe, rates of literacy increased. And as more and more people learned to read and write, the communication of information—both religious and secular—was facilitated. Hence, people could become more involved in the process of governance and commerce, as well as in the practice of religion.

Printing also facilitated the development of learning materials and textbooks. An entire class could read from the same book at the same time, and large numbers of people could obtain the same messages via books, newspapers, and other print media. Printing also resulted in standardization of spelling and grammar, and by the nineteenth century, standardized dictionaries had been prepared in many languages.

From Church to State in the Educational Process

For several centuries after the invention of the printing press and the rise of Protestantism, religious officials remained in charge of formal education in many places. Beginning in the eighteenth and nineteenth centuries, and continuing to the present day, governments began to replace religious authority as the primary provider of education. In many countries today, education is recognized as a fundamental right for all citizens and is often included in these countries' constitutions.

Transition from religion-oriented to government-provided education was sometimes accompanied by conflict. As might be expected, religious principles were often an important part of education provided by churches and other religious authorities. As governments began to play a more and more significant role in the educational process, education tended to become more secular in orientation. In some countries, religion was eliminated from curricula entirely.

Religious authorities often objected to this de-emphasis on the teaching of religious principles to children. In many countries, those religious officials and parents who had had strong concerns about the role of religion in school established private schools that retained religious instruction. Relationships between private and public education vary from country to country, although in general religious and private schools are obligated to conform to standards established and enforced by secular governments. In some countries, however, state-mandated curricula do include instruction in religious principles. This is especially the case in countries that have official state religions. In Greece, for example, students are required to study the principles of the Greek Orthodox faith. However, in Greece and many other countries that require religious instruction, parents have the right to opt their children out of these religious classes. Religious instruction in many countries, including the United States, is provided on an optional basis by individual religious communities or congregations and outside of normal school hours.

The Practice of Education Today

In most countries today, schooling is free and supported by taxes levied on the general population, regardless of whether these people have children. However, in some countries, parents are required to pay various fees and/or for textbooks and school supplies. In countries where students are required to wear uniforms to school, parents might also be required to pay for these uniforms. Especially in less developed countries, these fees and additional costs can represent a significant financial hardship. This hardship can keep children away from school, especially at the secondary level. Governments have also established requirements that education is compulsory for children within specified age ranges. Almost every country now maintains compulsory education laws, although especially in less developed countries such laws may not be enforced. Many children leave school long before completing the number of years of school required by law for a variety of reasons, including poverty and the need for children to work in order to support their families.

Relationships between national and subnational governments within individual countries also vary among countries throughout the world. In the United States, the Constitution specifies that power is shared formally by the federal government and the governments of the individual states. This relationship is spelled out in the Tenth Amendment, which states, "The powers not delegated to the United States by the Constitution, nor prohibited by it to the States, are reserved to the States respectively, or to the people." Because the Constitution does not mention education specifically, the Tenth Amendment implies that education is the responsibility of the individual states. Thus, specific requirements regarding the provision of education vary from one state to another.

Countries such as the United States where power is shared formally between the national government and subnational governments are known as federal states. Other federal states throughout the world include Canada, Mexico, Germany, Brazil, India, and Nigeria. Those countries where all authority is centered in the national government are known as unitary states. In unitary states, the primary function of local or subnational governments is to administer and enforce laws and policies that are established at the national level. In general, federal states are large and contain diverse populations whereas unitary states tend to be smaller and more homogeneous, although large countries such as Japan, China, Indonesia, and France are unitary states. Because education is the responsibility of local governments in U.S. states, Canadian provinces, and other federal states, specific details about the educational process vary among these local governments. In unitary states, however, governments manage education directly, usually via the administration on the part of a national ministry or government institution. This difference is often reflected in the degree to which educational practice varies from place to place within a country, although even in universal states, the availability and quality of education varies and is often lower in poor, rural, and/or isolated areas.

In many countries, one or more languages have been chosen as the language or languages of instruction. Usually, languages of instruction are a country's official language or languages—the United States is one of few countries in the world that has not identified an official language. In some former European colonies, the language of the colonial power has become the language of instruction. Indigenous peoples in such countries have expressed concern that the imposition of an official language, and its mandatory use in schools, has contributed to the destruction of their cultures. Such concerns are not limited to less developed countries. For example, the use of Gaelic and Irish has declined steadily as English has dominated education in Scotland and Ireland, respectively, although efforts are now being made to restore the use of these languages in such places.

Education in the United States

This book includes 10 chapters, each of which addresses a significant issue associated with education today throughout the world. Each of the 10 chapters contains an entry about the United States. Here, we provide a brief overview of education in the United States in historical context.

Education in Early America

Formal education in the United States originated during colonial times, long before American independence. Public schools were established initially in the New England colonies. New England was settled initially by Puritans and other Protestants who stressed the importance of the ability to read the Bible. In 1647, the colony of Massachusetts enacted a law that required each town whose population contained at least 50 families to establish a primary school. Public schooling spread throughout New England before the American Revolution. It has been estimated that by that time more than two-thirds of New Englanders were literate. However, few public schools were established south of New England during the seventeenth and eighteenth centuries. Children from wealthy families were educated at home by parents or private tutors, and some were sent to private schools. However, most residents of the Southern colonies remained illiterate.

During the nineteenth century after the American Revolution, public schools were established throughout the then independent United States. Tax-supported public schools had been opened in every state by 1870. American public education during this period continued to be influenced by circumstances in New England. During the early nineteenth century, the concept of common schooling was developed under the leadership of Horace Mann (1796–1859), who served as Secretary of the Massachusetts Board of Education from its establishment in 1837 until he was elected to the U.S. House of Representatives in 1848. In 1838, Mann articulated six principles of common schooling, arguing that the public should be educated, that education should be paid for by the public, that schools should include children of varying economic backgrounds, that education should be non-sectarian, that it should emphasize American values, and that it be provided by rained and qualified teachers.

The "American values" that Mann promoted in advocating common schooling, however, reflected a relatively narrow perspective emphasizing a white, Protestant worldview. Some of Mann's contemporaries were highly critical of Mann's view that education should be nonsectarian. However, Mann believed that Christian values and ethics should become part of the educational process more indirectly. For example, reading and other skills were taught using textbooks with religious orientations or moralistic themes. Curricula used in common schools often emphasized moral lessons associated with the worldview promoted by Mann. In many schools, for example, children were required to read from the King James version of the Bible, which was used by Protestants but not by Roman Catholics.

Mann's view was that common schools should be attended by pupils of all economic and social classes living in a community. In practice, however, many common schools excluded non-white persons. Although some efforts were made to educate Native Americans, in some textbooks and learning materials Native Americans and other non-white persons were referred to routinely as "primitive people" or as "savages." This view linked the common school movement to the concept of Manifest Destiny or the belief that Americans of European ancestry were destined by God to settle and spread Western civilization throughout the entirety of North America. This, in turn, was used as justification to evict Native Americans from their ancestral lands and relocate them forcibly to reservations, most of which remain mired in poverty today.

Also, most African Americans were excluded from public schools in the South. Prior to the Civil War, it was illegal in some Southern states to teach slaves to read and write. Even after the war, law and custom segregated African American children and white children in public schools until the U.S. Supreme Court ruled that segregated public education policies were unconstitutional in *Brown v. Board of Education of Topeka, Kansas* (347 U.S. 483) in 1954. In some areas, meaningful integration did not occur for an additional 15–20 years or more after the *Brown* decision had been handed down by the Court.

The Progressive Era into the Twentieth Century

The period from the 1890s until World War I is known as the Progressive Era. Progressives focused on societal reform at a time when American society became more and more diverse, industrialized, and urbanized. Progressive Era reformers emphasized limiting the power of large corporations and corrupt political bosses and political machines. Reforms included antitrust legislation, regulation of labor conditions including limiting working hours, and oversight of trade. During the Progressive Era, the Sixteenth, Seventeenth, Eighteenth, and Nineteenth Amendments were added to the U.S. Constitution. The Sixteenth Amendment allowed the federal government to levy and collect income taxes. The Seventeenth Amendment called for the direct elections of U.S. Senators. The Eighteenth Amendment (which was repealed later via the Twenty-First Amendment) called for prohibition of alcoholic beverages, and the Nineteenth Amendment granted women the right to vote in all elections.

The Progressive Era resulted in several significant reforms in American education. Public schools had been established throughout the country by the 1870s. In most places, however, public education in the nineteenth century was managed locally under the auspices of locally elected school boards of education. Many teachers were poorly qualified and poorly trained. Many were young local women who were often fired upon marriage. However, Mann's strong support for improved teacher preparation was instrumental in the founding of normal schools in most states by the end of the nineteenth century.

In addition to improved teacher preparation, the Progressives pushed for reform of school governance of administration. Recognizing that each state had primary responsibility for supplying education, they encouraged the imposition of professional standards for educators. They also advocated reducing the power of local school boards, many of whose members were local residents and politicians who had little or no knowledge of the educational process. They advocated reforms that required superintendents and principals, as well as teachers, to hold appropriate professional credentials. They emphasized the value of regarding education as a profession that should be managed by professionals inside and outside of the classroom. Also, the Progressives supported inclusion of teaching skills needed for everyday life, such as teaching industrial skills to boys at a time when more and more Americans were living in cities and working at industrial jobs and teaching "domestic" skills such as sewing, cooking, and home economics to girls.

During this period also, states began to impose compulsory education laws. Massachusetts had been the first state to make education compulsory when it did so in 1852. By 1918, every state had made education compulsory at least through completion of elementary school. By the end of World War II, education had become compulsory until the age of 16 in most states. By that time, the separation of elementary school from secondary school had become universal.

The Progressive Era coincided with a period of large-scale immigration into the United States from eastern and southern European countries such as Russia, Poland, Hungary, and Italy. Many of these immigrants settled in cities where they took jobs in factories and other industries, and many spoke little or no English upon arrival. Public schooling came to be regarded as a means by which their children learned to speak English and to be assimilated into mainstream American culture. Children were required to learn to speak, read, and write in English. In some places, children who spoke to one another in languages other than English were punished. As is discussed in greater detail in the chapter on language, however, in many places English-only education is no longer practiced, and immigrant children, at least in the early years, are taught in their first languages. Whether children who do not speak English at home should be required to speak English only in school remains a controversial question today.

Into the Late Twentieth Century and the Early Twenty-First Century

After the Progressive Era, relatively few changes were made in the structure of American education until after World War II. During the Cold War, however, many Americans became concerned that the United States might become unable to keep up with the Soviet Union. Educators became concerned that schooling was becoming antiquated. Many children continued to be educated in very small school systems with few pupils. Consolidating these districts into fewer, larger districts came to be regarded as a means of providing more efficient and effective education. Even more significantly, concern was raised about the teaching of science and mathematics. More and more engineers and scientists were needed, and so improvements in the teaching of science became viewed as necessary and were developed and implemented. Memorization gave way to the scientific method, and the "new math," which de-emphasized calculation and placed more emphasis on understanding the general principles of mathematical reasoning, was put into place.

New educational technologies were also developed and adapted for educational use. Calculators and later computers replaced slide rules. Typewriters had come into general use well before World War II, but keyboarding skills became essential as more and more students and adults used mainframe and later personal computers. As computer use became universal, people relied more and more on the reading and writing of printed documents. Hence, cursive writing, which had long been regarded as a basic educational skill, became seen as outmoded and is no longer taught in many American schools today. Hence, teaching students how to use these and other new technologies became more and more central to curricula. Technology also revolutionized communication. Memorization of factual material, for example, became less necessary because students can now look up large quantities of information very quickly.

As educators began to pay more and more attention to the role of education in helping students to learn about significant social issues, the traditional organization of curricula came to be questioned. Many such issues, including environmental change and degradation, globalization, and economic development, are highly complex. Reliance on the traditional separation of curricula among English and language skills, mathematics, science, social studies, and art and music came to be regarded as ineffective in teaching students about how to understand and address such problems. For example, understanding environmental degradation requires the integration of the natural and physical sciences with history, geography, economics, and political science.

Organization of the Book

This book contains chapters involving 10 contemporary issues associated with education. Each chapter includes 8 entries—1 for the United States and 1 for each of 7 other countries—to best represent the issue to readers. Chapter topics cover literacy, gender, religion, multiculturalism, difference, special education, school violence, STEM, arts and humanities, and sustainability. Entries focus on countries that are representative of all world regions.

Literacy, Gender, and Religion

Since ancient times, the most fundamental component of formal education has been reading and writing. The teaching of all other skills and ideas depends on the ability to read and write along with the ability to do arithmetic. Levels of literacy were very low in ancient and medieval times, but they increased steadily in recent centuries especially following the invention of the printing press and the degree to which government has supplanted religious authority in providing education. Today, literacy is virtually universal in the United States and other countries throughout the world. Literacy rates are lower in most developed countries, but in general have been increasing. Nearly all countries today report literacy rates of over 50 percent, and these rates are higher for younger people as opposed to other people.

In most countries where significant numbers of adults remain illiterate, literacy rates are higher among men than among women. Historically, formal education had been regarded as of little value to women, who would learn farming, food preparation, childrearing, and household management skills from their mothers and other adult women. This labor was needed to support the family, and therefore, attendance at school came to be regarded as a waste of time and money. Moreover, in many societies, women left the family home at marriage and moved into their husbands' homes so that their labor benefited the husband's family rather than the birth family. Under such circumstances, raising daughters became an economic burden on the birth family, which would be very reluctant to spend money and time in providing their daughters with any formal education. On the other hand, sons who were educated could be expected to contribute their additional earnings to support their families as adults and to help to care for their parents in their old age.

Although literacy is universal among both men and women in the United States and other developed countries, gender differences in the educational process remain. Even in developed countries, until recently girls were expected to study skills such as cooking and sewing in order to prepare themselves to be stay-at-home mothers as adults. Girls were discouraged and some were prevented from taking advanced classes in science and mathematics, and they were often excluded from male-dominated professions such as medicine, law, and engineering. Girls in some secondary schools, especially in less developed countries, remain subject to sexual harassment and assault by teachers and administrators as well as by fellow students.

The degree to which religion should inform curricula, and how religious aspects of education should be conducted, has long been a controversial issue. Historically, schooling was provided by churches and other religious institutions. Over time, of course, government has become the primary provider of education, and this has led to the question of whether religion should be included in the curriculum.

As we have seen, countries with official religions such as Greece mandate religious instruction in schools although parents who do not practice these official religions are often allowed to opt out of this requirement. And in some countries, religious principles affect education even outside of formal religious classes. For example, students in some American public schools were required to recite Christian prayers in classrooms until this practice was declared unconstitutional by the Supreme Court in *Engel v. Vitale* (370 U.S. 421) in 1962.

Questions of religion in schooling have been especially controversial in countries whose populations contain significant numbers of adherents to different religions. For example, Nigeria contains a roughly equal percentage of Christians and Muslims. Although Nigeria is officially a secular state, leaders of both religions have made ongoing efforts to introduce principles of their respective religions into school curricula. And in former Communist countries, the degree to which religion should be introduced into curricula that had once been operated by the officially atheistic Soviet Union has become an issue of discord.

Multiculturalism, Difference, and Special Education

Many countries, especially large countries and those that contain significant numbers of people who practice different religions, can be considered multicultural. In such countries, governments must balance the need to recognize different cultures, including their different languages and religions, with the overall goal of providing educations to each of their citizens.

In some countries, governments dominated by majority populations have attempted to force these dominant cultures on their countries' entire population. For example, the Soviet Union promoted what it called Russification. All citizens, regardless of nationality, were to be educated in Russian. Traditional values of non-Russian cultures within the Soviet Union were downplayed. In some cases, the Soviet government attempted to eliminate these traditional values, including religious traditions, entirely. Members of different national groups were encouraged to move to other areas, while ethnic Russians were given strong incentives to migrate to areas dominated by non-Russian people. After the breakup of the Soviet Union, now-independent former Soviet republics have had to address the aftermath of the Russification policy, including the presence of substantial numbers of non-Russians in their populations, as they began to develop their post-Soviet educational policies and systems.

In Myanmar, similarly, the post-independence government was dominated by ethnic Burmans who make up nearly two-thirds of the population. The Burman-dominated government attempted to impose Burmese culture on the entire country, including requiring that all education be conducted in Burmese and that all government business be transacted in Burmese. As a result, secessionist movements have sprung up throughout non-Burmese areas of the country. After India became independent, the country's original goal was to make Hindi, which is spoken by about 40 percent of the population, its official language. However, the imposition of Hindi was resisted fiercely by those who spoke other languages, and as a result, this original policy was abandoned.

Multiculturalism has been intensified in the United States and Europe by large-scale immigration. International migrants are much more likely to move from less developed countries of origin to developed destination countries in search of economic opportunity, and in order to escape political turmoil and in some cases religious or political persecution. Many arrive illegally. In recent years, there has been considerable backlash against immigrants. The United States and other countries have been building walls to keep illegal immigrants out. Immigration has increased the degree to which societies become more diverse, but it has also generated more and more controversy with respect to education.

Multiculturalism is often linked to differences within a country's population—differences in culture, language, religion, and economic organization among these populations, for example. Groups of people often perceive themselves as unique relative to other groups of people. The term "tribalism" has been used to describe recognition of these differences, and some groups look down upon or exclude those people who are not part of their tribes. Such discrimination is known as "othering," and throughout the world, othering has been used as justification for discrimination against such people. Indigenous peoples such as Native Americans in the United States and First Nations people in Canada have been "othered" since North America was first colonized by Europeans, for example. Similarly, the Roma in eastern Europe remain excluded from the mainstream of society, and this exclusion has been intensified via these countries' educational systems. The examples of the Soviet Union and Myanmar are examples of what have been largely unsuccessful attempts to wipe out such differences. Other countries have been more tolerant of difference but continue to discriminate against "different" people indirectly, even when such discrimination is prohibited by law.

Differences exist even within small groups of people who share common cultures. In all societies, many children have disabilities or special needs. Some of these disabilities are physical disabilities that are recognized easily, such as vision impairments, hearing impairments, and crippling diseases. Other students have disabilities that are more difficult to recognize physically and include people who have autism, clinical depression, and/or learning disabilities that prevent or impede their progress through the educational systems of their countries. But each of these children requires some form of special education.

Historically, children with special needs were often isolated from society, and few had the opportunity to obtain any sort of special education whatsoever. Even when educated, these children were generally separated from their peers and in some cases from their families. Today, the right of special-needs students and of children with disabilities to education is now recognized by the United Nations. These rights are recognized formally by many countries. In practice, however, it has been difficult to balance the needs of students with disabilities with the overall goal of providing education to all children. In some countries, resources needed to provide adequate special education are lacking. For example, some countries face a lack of qualified special education teachers and insufficient resources to provide these teachers with adequate training. Societal discrimination against the disabled also plagues efforts to provide special education. Such is particularly a problem in various parts of West Africa, where disability continues to be recognized in some cultures as a curse or punishment upon the family of a disabled person.

Violence and the Threat of Violence

Special-needs children have often been subjected to bullying and other forms of violence. Yet by no means is violence in schools confined to special-needs children. In recent years, mass shootings of students in American schools have been given worldwide attention. Teachers and school officials as well as students have been victimized by such violence. In some countries, violence has been linked to civil war and armed conflict. Terrorist groups such as Boko Haram in Nigeria, for example, have attacked schools and killed or abducted hundreds of children. In other countries, school violence has been linked to the activities of drug cartels and organized gangs. Students have not only been killed or wounded but have also been kidnapped, raped, or captured and sold into slavery.

The impacts of school violence go far beyond violent acts themselves, as horrific as they may be. Faced with the threat of violence, parents are often unwilling to send their children to school. And in some countries, endemic violence has made it difficult to recruit qualified teachers who are willing to live and work in violence-prone areas. For these and other reasons, some schools have been closed entirely. Bullying can also be a form of violence, and students who have been subjected to repeated bullying by their peers may refuse to go to school. Some have even considered or committed suicide.

STEM, Arts and Humanities, and Sustainability

Curricula evolve, of course, in response to changes in society. In today's globalized world, more and more emphasis has been laid on the development and use of technology. Such technology benefits individuals themselves within any given country, and it is often a key to a country's economic development. These considerations have placed greater and greater emphasis on the teaching and learning of science, technology, engineering, and mathematics. Collectively, the acronym STEM has been used to describe these disciplines.

Relatively little attention has been paid to STEM disciplines in education over the course of history. Arithmetic, geometry, and astronomy were components of the liberal arts in medieval Europe, but these subjects were not taught scientifically. Today, however, STEM teaching emphasizes the understanding and application of scientific method, which includes direct observation of various phenomena and the testing of hypotheses based on such observations. Hence, science curricula today include opportunities for students to investigate phenomena directly through observation, logic, and analysis of data drawn from these observations.

Memorization of scientific information, for example, chemical formulas and mathematical tables, has given way to understanding of the scientific process. Scientific method is applied also to the teaching of technology and engineering via which scientific understanding is applied to practical problems and can be used in the development and implementation of new products of value to society. STEM teaching has become emphasized more and more in less developed countries that are making efforts to transition their economies from reliance on agricultural, natural resources, and manufacturing toward the development of more lucrative technologies.

With greater emphasis on STEM, however, it is important to recognize that the arts and humanities should not be neglected. The arts and humanities—including the visual arts, literature, and music—are forms of cultural expression. Through the arts and humanities, cultural values and insights are passed on from one generation to the next.

In the past, the arts and humanities were taught outside systems of formal education. Elements of folk culture were transmitted informally from parents and other adults to children. Those who prepared to become professional artists and musicians often learned their skills through being apprenticed to masters of their crafts. The diffusion of artistic expression outside of local contexts often relied on the support of the nobility within a society, and visual artists and musicians depended on commissions provided to them from the wealthy, and such commissions could disappear when a new ruler who was uninterested in the arts came to power.

Today, of course, arts and humanities are recognized as a significant component of formal education. K-12 curricula used in most countries include instruction in the visual arts and music. The study of the arts and humanities also takes into consideration an understanding of how cultures borrow from one another. Thus, American students study not only American literature, art, and music, but they also study the literature, art, and music of other Western and non-Western cultures. Through such study, students can also gain an understanding of values associated with cultures other than their own.

The contemporary world faces many challenges. These include climate change and other forms of environmental degradation, poverty, the impacts of rapidly growing human populations, the effects of globalization, and many others. The students of today are set to become the leaders of tomorrow, and it will fall on them to develop and put into practice effective methods to address contemporary problems. The principles of sustainability underlie these many issues. Sustainability refers to the potential that a system can operate effectively over time. These principles have been applied to relationships between human society and the natural world.

Is long-running environmental sustainability possible? Can society as we know it today survive and prosper in the future? Recognizing these questions, educators throughout the world are making efforts to implement and teach understanding of questions associated with sustainability. Such understanding links the STEM disciplines with the arts and humanities as well as with the study of economics, governance, history, and geography. Thus, understanding of sustainability is coming to be associated with the breakdown of traditional disciplinary boundaries within the educational process. For example, biology, geography, and economics are usually taught separately, in isolation from one another. However, integrated knowledge of all of these subjects, and others, is necessary to promote meaningful understanding of questions associated with environmental change and degradation. Only through the integration of knowledge can we expect to maintain sustainability.

Chapter 1: Literacy

OVERVIEW

Education has many purposes. But the most fundamental goal of education in societies throughout the world is the achievement of literacy or the ability to read and write. Numerous studies have demonstrated that illiterate persons have far fewer opportunities, lower life expectancies, higher rates of poverty, and greater exposure to diseases as compared with literate persons even within individual countries. Although a large majority of persons throughout the world today are literate, illiteracy remains a significant problem in many countries.

Although it is not known where and when writing first developed, societies throughout the world invented systems of writing several thousand years ago. Many anthropologists believe that writing was invented in conjunction with the development of agriculture. Prior to the development of agriculture, people survived by hunting and gathering. Hunters and gatherers were nomads who were forced to move from place to place constantly. However, agriculture allowed people to establish settled communities. The practice of agriculture created a need to record information about crop production and distribution, and some believe that writing first developed as a means to create and maintain these records. Writing allowed people to preserve such records and other information. With the invention of paper and other lightweight materials, written records could be transported over long distances, and hence, information transmission no longer necessarily required face-to-face communication.

Historians believe that in most ancient and medieval societies only a small minority of persons were literate. For example, in medieval Europe literacy was generally restricted to the clergy and the nobility, with most peasants unable to read and write. This began to change in Europe with the invention of the printing press in the late fifteenth century. Printing allowed mass production of books, newspapers, pamphlets, and other written documents. Thus, many people could read printed documents simultaneously. The Protestant Reformation, with its emphasis on individual interpretation of the Bible, also encouraged literacy.

At the outset of the nineteenth century, the majority of people in northern and western Europe and in the United States could read and write. However, only a small percentage of people in other parts of the world were literate. At that time, not all languages existed in written form, precluding literacy in these languages. Some Indigenous languages spoken outside Europe and North America were written only after Europeans introduced alphabets and scripts. For example, the

Khasi language spoken in northeastern India was not written until the early nineteenth century, when English missionaries began to write the language using both the Latin and the Bengali scripts. The original intention of such activities was to encourage understanding of the Bible and other religious works, but secular documents were soon written and published as well. Thus, the percentage of people who were able to read and write in their native languages increased steadily during the nineteenth and twentieth centuries.

By the mid-twentieth century, education including literacy became recognized as a fundamental human right. In 1948, the United Nations issued the Universal Declaration of Human Rights, in which education was recognized explicitly as a human right. Literacy was recognized as an essential component of education. In 2006, the United Nations Educational, Scientific, and Cultural Organization (UNESCO) stated, "The human benefits from literature are related to factors such as the improved self-esteem, empowerment, creativity and critical reflection that participation in adult literacy programmes and the practice of literacy may produce. Human benefits are intrinsically valuable and may also be instrumental in realizing other benefits of literacy: improved health, increased political participation and so on." Another UNESCO website contains the words that "education is a powerful tool by which economically and socially marginalized adults and children can lift themselves out of poverty and participate fully as citizens" (https://en.unesco.org/themes/right-to-education). The constitutions of the majority of countries throughout the world specify that education is a fundamental right and therefore literacy is a fundamental right.

Despite recognition that literacy is a fundamental human right, many people throughout the world continue to lack the ability to read and write. According to a 2017 report from UNESCO, more than 750 million people aged 15 years of age or more, or about 14 percent of the world's adult population, are illiterate. Many are older adults, but in many places, illiteracy among the young remains a significant problem. In examining literacy rates, it is important to recognize that the concept of literacy considers the degree to which people can understand and derive meaning from written texts and to which they can write effectively to communicate meaning. Literacy has been linked also to numeracy, or the ability to understand and use basic mathematical concepts.

Various countries use different definitions of literacy. The most basic definition, as used in the CIA World Factbook's entry on literacy, is "the ability to read and write at a specified age." Based on this definition, levels of literacy vary considerably throughout the world. In developed countries, literacy is universal. Within the European Union, for example, every country, except Greece with 95.3 percent, had reported a literacy rate of at least 98 percent by the first decade of the twenty-first century. Norway, with an adult literacy rate of 99.0 percent as of 2014, typifies literacy in western Europe and other highly developed countries. Literacy is universal in most countries in the Caribbean region such as Trinidad and Tobago. Rates of literacy are considerably lower in less developed countries, however. As of 2013, 9 of the 10 countries having the lowest reported literacy rates were located in sub-Saharan Africa. Typical of these countries with low rates of literacy is Niger, whose adult literacy rate in 2018 was only 35 percent. Somalia, which is recognized as a failed state and has been embroiled in civil war since the early 1990s, also has a very low rate of literacy.

However, the United States and other countries distinguish between pure illiteracy and functional illiteracy. Pure illiteracy is the complete inability to read and write. This is the basis for international comparison of literacy rates. However, many people who are able to read and write at a basic level are considered to be functionally illiterate. A person who is functionally illiterate is someone who is unable to read and write at a level needed for everyday life. For example, a functionally illiterate person knows the basics of reading and writing, but may be unable to read newspapers, advertisements, road signs, or directions for the use of medications. In 1978, UNESCO defined functional literacy: "A person is functionally literate who can engage in all those activities in which literacy is required for effective functioning of his [sic] group and community and also for enabling him [sic] to continue to use reading, writing and calculation for his own and the community's development. One who is not able to undertake these functions is regarded as functionally illiterate."

More recently, the Program for the International Assessment of Adult Competencies, which operates for the United Nations Organization for Economic Co-operation and Development, has defined literacy as "understanding, evaluating, using, and engaging with written text to participate in society, to achieve one's goals, and to develop one's knowledge and potential."

Generally, literacy levels are linked to economic development. However, some countries are exceptions to the general pattern of correlation between literacy and economic development. For example, Armenia and Mongolia have achieved universal literacy despite relatively modest per capita gross domestic products. On the

---

International Literacy Day

In 1966, the United Nations Education, Scientific, and Cultural Organization (UNESCO) declared September 8 of each year as International Literacy Day. The purpose of International Literacy Day is to "remind the public of the importance of literacy as a matter of dignity and human rights, and to advance the literacy agenda towards a more literate and sustainable society." In 2015, International Literacy Day became linked to the United Nations' sustainable development goals. Each year, a different theme is identified. For example, the 2017 theme was Literacy in the Digital World, and the theme for 2018 was Literacy and Skills Development. The 2019 theme was Literacy and Multilingualism. Throughout the world, special events in recognition of International Literacy are held, reinforcing understanding the critical importance of literacy in today's world.

Source: https://en.unesco.org/commemorations/literacyday.

other hand, Egypt's per capita gross domestic product of about $12,500 is about the same as that of Mongolia and higher than that of Armenia, but only 75 percent of Egyptian adults are literate. Above and beyond economic development, linguistic uniformity often promotes literacy. More than 90 percent of people in Norway, Armenia, and Mongolia speak Norwegian, Armenian, and Mongolian, respectively, as their first languages, whereas many different languages are spoken by substantial numbers of people in Niger and Somalia.

In most countries where literacy rates are relatively low, there is a significant gender gap between literacy rates among males and females. According to UNESCO's 2013 estimate, two-thirds of the world's illiterate adults are women. This is evident also when comparing literacy rates among male adults (88.6%) and female adults (79.7%). The question of gender and illiteracy is covered in more detail in the chapter titled "Gender and Education" in this volume.

Further Reading

Kristina Chew, "10 countries with the worst literacy rates in the world," care2.com, September 8, 2013, http://www.care2.com/causes/10-countries-with-the-worst-literacy-rates-in-the-world.html. Retrieved on April 27, 2017.

UNESCO, Education for All Global Monitoring Report, "Five decades of literacy work," 2015, https://en.unesco.org/themes/literacy-all/five-decades. Retrieved on July 21, 2022.

UNESCO, "International Literacy Day 2013" (infographic), http://www.uis.unesco.org/literacy/Documents/Intl-literacy-day/literacy-infographic-2013-en.pdf. Retrieved on April 29, 2017.

UNESCO, Literary Statistics Metadata Information Table, retrievable via the UNESCO website at http://www.unesco.org/new/en/education/themes/education-building-blocks/literacy/resources/statistics/. Retrieved on April 29, 2017. Updated periodically.

UNESCO, "Literacy," n.d., https://en.unesco.org/themes/literacy. Retrieved on July 21, 2022.

ARMENIA

The Republic of Armenia is located in the Caucasus Mountains of southwestern Asia between the Black Sea to the west and the Caspian Sea to the east. Armenia's land area is about 11,484 square miles, slightly larger than Maryland. Its population in 2022 was about 2.9 million.

Present-day Armenia is believed to have been settled at least 6,000 years ago, and Armenia's capital city of Yerevan is believed to have been founded in 782 BC. The area was ruled by the Kingdom of Armenia from about 600 BC until 66 BC, when it was made a protectorate of the Roman Empire. After about 400 AD, control of Armenia was contested among the Byzantine Empire and kingdoms and empires based in Turkey, Persia, and the Middle East. It became part of the Ottoman Empire in the fifteenth century. In the early nineteenth century, Russia also became interested in Armenia, which was divided between the Ottomans and the Russians after a war between the two empires was fought in the 1820s.

During the early twentieth century, the Ottomans massacred more than a million Armenians in what became known as the Armenian Genocide or the Armenian Massacre. Hundreds of thousands of other Armenians were forced out of the country as refugees. Those who survived the massacre moved in large numbers to Russia, other parts of Southwest Asia, Europe, or the United States in what became recognized as the Armenian diaspora. The Armenian Genocide and its impact on Armenia's population continue to affect relationships between Armenia and Turkey even today.

Armenia declared independence as the Democratic Republic of Armenia in 1918, but the Democratic Republic was soon destroyed by the Soviet forces. In 1922, Armenia became annexed to the Soviet Union as part of the Transcaucasian Soviet Federated Socialist Republic (TSFSR), along with Azerbaijan and Georgia. In 1936, Armenia was separated from the TSFSR and became the Armenian Soviet Socialist Republic. Armenia declared its independence in 1990, and its independence was recognized fully by the international community after the Soviet Union broke up in 1991. Today, about 98 percent of Armenia's residents are ethnic Armenians. In 301 AD, Armenia became the first country in the world to adopt Christianity as its state religion, and even today, nearly 95 percent of Armenians belong to the Armenian Apostolic Church.

Armenian is an Indo-European language, but it is not related closely to other Indo-European languages. It is written using a distinctive alphabet that contains 39 letters. The Armenian alphabet was developed and introduced in about 406 AD by Mesrop Mashtots (362 AD–440 AD), who is venerated as a saint in Armenia. The Armenian alphabet continues to be used today and is regarded by many Armenians as an important component of their cultural identity. However, many Armenians are fluent in spoken and written Russian, which was used as the primary means of instruction during the nearly 70 years of Soviet hegemony and remains a required subject in Armenian public schools today.

Education in Armenia

Ever since the Armenian alphabet was introduced, literacy and education have been regarded as significant components of Armenian culture. Even before and during the Middle Ages, many Armenian peasants learned at least the rudiments of reading and writing. Thus, a long tradition of literacy has persisted throughout Armenian history.

The educational system of Armenia as it exists today was developed initially by the government of the short-lived Democratic Republic of Armenia and was modified first by the Soviets and more recently by the independent Armenian government. Today, education in Armenia is managed by the Ministry of Education and Science. Public education in Armenia includes three levels: primary school, secondary school, and higher education. Primary school begins at the age of three and continues until the child is seven or eight. After completing primary school, students move on to secondary school, which includes five years of basic school and two years of high school.

The primary school curriculum includes basic literacy and numeracy skills such as knowing the alphabet and counting, along with social development and behavioral skills. Basic school pupils study science, geography, Armenian history, Russian, and at least one additional foreign language. Chess is also taught, and the Armenian Tigran Petrosian (1929–1984), who represented the Soviet Union and who was the world's chess champion from 1963 until 1969, remains a national hero. High school students continue to study these subjects while specializing in natural sciences or the humanities. Primary and secondary education in Armenia is free, and completion of secondary school is compulsory. However, parents are responsible for providing textbooks and some other school supplies, putting children from lower-income backgrounds at a disadvantage.

As was the case elsewhere in the Soviet Union, education in Armenia was controlled and managed tightly by the Soviets during Armenia's seven decades of Communist control. After Armenia became independent, the system was decentralized and reformed. Whereas many classes in Soviet Armenia were conducted in Russian, Armenian became the sole language of instruction after independence. More and more Armenian children also study English. More emphasis has been placed also on the teaching of Armenian history and culture.

Literacy in Armenia

With a gross domestic product of about US$9,000 per capita, Armenia remains a relatively poor country. Yet for a variety of reasons, Armenia has maintained virtually universal literacy since the middle of the twentieth century.

A key factor in Armenian literacy has been Armenian culture. The Armenian alphabet, which is used nowhere else in the world, remains an important cultural marker for Armenians. Since its inception more than 1,600 years ago, it has inspired a rich literary tradition. Even before the contemporary Armenian educational system was implemented in the early twentieth century, many Armenian peasants could read and write the Armenian language. Literacy has been facilitated by cultural uniformity in that more than 98 percent of Armenia's people speak Armenian as their first language. Living in a small country with a unique language, a unique alphabet, and a long-standing literary tradition, many Armenians today see knowledge of reading and writing as crucial to the preservation of Armenian culture.

This literary tradition facilitated the development of modern Armenian education in that the development of literary skills remained important in Armenian culture. The Soviet reforms reinforced this emphasis on reading and writing, mandating formal education. In 1960, the Soviets announced that Armenia had achieved nearly 100 percent literacy. Universal literacy has characterized Armenia ever since.

Further Reading

Naruk Manukyan, "How literate is Armenia?" EVN Report, January 21, 2020, https://evnreport.com/raw-unfiltered/how-literate-is-armenia/. Retrieved on May 8, 2022.

Anna Mkhoyan, "Soft power, Russia and the former Soviet states: A case study of Russian language and education in Armenia," *International Journal of Cultural Policy*, 23 (2017), pp. 690–704.

Shelley Terzian, *Curricular reform in post-Soviet Armenia: Balancing local and global context in the Armenian secondary schools.* Frankfurt, Germany: VDM Verlag, 2010.

EGYPT

The Arab Republic of Egypt is located in the northeastern corner of Africa, and it also includes the Sinai Peninsula of southwestern Asia. Egypt's land area is about 390,000 square miles, of which more than 90 percent is in Africa. With a population of over 106 million as of 2022, Egypt is the largest country by population in the Middle East and the third largest on the African continent following Nigeria and Ethiopia. Egypt's land area is nearly 400,000 square miles, about two-thirds the size of Alaska. However, most of Egypt is located in the very sparsely populated Sahara Desert. More than 90 percent of Egyptians live within 10 miles of the Nile River. Thus, the inhabited portions of Egypt are very densely populated.

Water from the annual floods along the Nile has been used to irrigate crops for more than 5,000 years, and Egypt has been unified politically since about 3150 BC. After more than 2,500 years of rule by its own pharaohs, Egypt became controlled by foreign powers during the sixth century BC. It was absorbed into the Roman Empire in 30 BC. It became part of the Islamic Caliphate during the seventh century AD and became part of the Ottoman Empire in 1517.

Given its strategic location between the Mediterranean Sea and the Red Sea, the European colonial powers began to take a strong interest in Egypt during the nineteenth century. The Suez Canal was constructed and opened to maritime traffic in 1869 under French control. The British took control of the canal in 1882. After that, Egypt was a nominally independent monarchy. However, its rulers had little actual power, and Egypt's government was controlled effectively by the United Kingdom until 1922. In 1952, the monarchy was overthrown, but it has been governed for most of its recent history by authoritarian rulers.

Although it lacks the natural resources that contribute to wealth in Saudi Arabia and other Middle Eastern countries, Egypt is more prosperous than many other Middle Eastern states that lack substantial wealth from petroleum and natural gas production. Trade via the Suez Canal and in the Mediterranean Sea has stimulated Egypt's economy, along with manufacturing, information technology, and tourism. In 2016, the International Monetary Fund estimated that Egypt's per capita income was approximately $12,554 annually. On the African continent, only Gabon, Botswana, and South Africa were estimated to have had higher per capita incomes.

Education in Egypt

Education in Egypt is highly centralized, and it is managed by the Ministry of Education. Schooling is free and compulsory for children between 4 and 14 years of age. Egyptian children attend kindergarten for 2 years, followed by 6 years of primary school and 3 years of what is known as preparatory school. In combination, this progression is known as basic education.

Basic education is followed by three years of secondary or high school. Secondary school is not compulsory, although in 2013 it was estimated that about 70 percent of Egyptian youths who had completed basic education were enrolled in secondary school programs. As of 2015, about 16 million Egyptian children were enrolled in school, and the education system employed more than 1.5 million teachers, administrators, and other personnel. Arabic, which is the official language of Egypt, is the language of instruction.

Literacy in Egypt

Literacy rates in Egypt have increased consistently over time and are higher among young adults than among older people. In 2013, UNESCO estimated that 93.7 percent of men and 90.2 percent of women between the ages of 15 and 24 were literate, with literacy being defined as the percentage of people "who can both read and write with understanding a short simple statement about their everyday life." In 2015, Egypt's literacy rate for the entire adult population was estimated by the United Nations Educational, Scientific, and Cultural Organization (UNESCO) to be 75.2 percent, including 83.2 percent for males and 67.3 percent for females. According to Egyptian authorities, the literacy rate is about 79 percent. However, Egypt's literacy rates remain low relative to other countries with similar economic and development status. By point of comparison, Mongolia's per capita income was estimated by the International Monetary Fund at $12,275 annually, or approximately the same as that of Egypt, whereas Armenia's per capita income is substantially less than that of Egypt. Yet Mongolia and Armenia, unlike Egypt, have achieved universal literacy.

The interpretation of estimates of literacy rates in Egypt must take into account that the government has calculated literacy rates on the basis of enrollment in literacy programs, rather than on the basis of successful completion of these programs. Educational observers have noted that many children and young adults are enrolled in schools but are functionally illiterate, in part because they attend schools of very poor quality with large class sizes, poorly trained teachers, and a lack of adequate classroom facilities.

In addition, according to one estimate more than 10 percent of children who according to Egyptian law should be attending school do not attend school or have dropped out. Dropout and nonattendance rates are highest among children from impoverished backgrounds and among those living in sparsely populated areas distant from the Nile Valley. Among such populations, compulsory education laws are not as likely to be enforced by government authorities. Some parents, especially in rural areas, see little value in formal education and expect their children to go to work at an early age to support their families, as children who attend school do not contribute to the household's income. Parents who are illiterate themselves are less apt to recognize the economic and social value of literacy.

These factors are reflected in the geographic differences in rates of literacy among the 27 governorates or provinces within Egypt. In 2014, government authorities estimated that about 7 percent of people living in the Red Sea governorate of southeastern Egypt were illiterate. However, this region has a population of less than 400,000. By contrast, more than 30 percent of the residents of the Asyut governorate, south of Cairo in central Egypt, could not read and write. In the governorates comprising the Cairo metropolitan area, the government estimated that about 16 percent of the population was illiterate.

According to this estimate, 11.3 percent of males in the Cairo metropolitan area were illiterate as compared to 20.5 percent of females. Nationwide, it was estimated that 15 percent of men were illiterate, as compared to 28.5 percent of women. These figures illustrated a strong gender difference in literacy rates.

Gender differences in illiteracy are especially noticeable in rural areas. These differences have been attributed to the influence of expected traditional gender roles. Some young girls are expected to help with household chores, taking care of younger siblings, or other work and are discouraged from or forbidden by their parents from attending school. In addition, early marriage for women and girls remains commonplace in Egypt, especially in rural areas where women are expected to maintain the household and bear and raise children. Moreover, girls often move out of their parental households upon marriage, and their labor is valuable to their husbands' families rather than their own birth families. Because of these differences in gender roles, parents and husbands may regard literacy for their daughters or wives as unnecessary, and thus the problem of female illiteracy in Egypt continues.

Further Reading

Albawawa.com, "Illiteracy in Egypt reaches 16 million," September 16, 2013, https://www.albawaba.com/editorchoice/egypt-illiteracy-female-520546. Retrieved on August 27, 2017.

Cairo Post, "More than 25% of Egypt's population 'illiterate'," September 9, 2014, https://egyptianstreets.com/2014/09/09/more-than-25-of-egypts-population-illiterate/. Retrieved on August 27, 2017.

Nick Clark and Sulaf Al-Shaikhly, "Education in Egypt," *World Education News and Reviews*, November 4, 2013, https://wenr.wes.org/2013/11/education-in-egypt. Retrieved on February 18, 2018.

Mohamed M. Ghoneim Sywelem, "Literacy and adult education in Egypt: Achievements and challenges," *American Journal of Educational Research*, 3 (2015), pp. 793–799, http://pubs.sciepub.com/education/3/7/1. Retrieved on August 27, 2017.

Irin—Inside Story on Emergencies, "Illiteracy still rife among rural women," March 8, 2006, http://www.irinnews.org/report/26179/egypt-illiteracy-still-rife-among-rural-women. Retrieved on February 18, 2018.

MONGOLIA

Mongolia is a landlocked country in central Asia, sandwiched between Russia to the north and China to the south. It has a land area of about 600,000 square miles, making it slightly larger than Alaska. Its population as of early 2022 was about 3.1 million, and thus Mongolia is one of the most sparsely populated countries in the world. Although Mongolia is one of Asia's poorer countries, it has achieved near-universal literacy. Thus, Mongolia represents an exception to the general relationship between development levels and literacy rates.

For several thousand years, present-day Mongolia was occupied by nomads who traveled long distances on horseback. In the late twelfth century, Genghis Khan (1160?–1227) united the scattered Mongol tribes and established the Mongol Empire. At its height, the Mongols controlled territory from China and Siberia westward Eastern Europe. Mongol power waned eventually, however, and China's Qing Dynasty incorporated present-day Mongolia into the Chinese empire.

Mongolia declared its independence in 1911, after the Qing dynasty collapsed. However, after World War I, Bolshevik troops invaded Mongolia and established a Communist government. The Communists retained control of Mongolia until after the Soviet Union collapsed in 1991. Since then, Mongolia has transitioned into a multiparty democracy with a market economy. About 95 percent of Mongolians speak the Mongolian language, which is known also as Khalkha Mongol. Khalkha Mongol is the most widely spoken language in the small Mongolic language family. Mongolian was written historically with its own script that is believed to have been developed by Genghis Khan, but during the 1940s, the Communist government of Mongolia introduced the Cyrillic alphabet that continues to be used to write Mongolian today.

Mongolia is one of the world's last strongholds of pastoral nomadism, which is a form of subsistence agriculture oriented to the herding of livestock. The animals are used for food, clothing, and transportation and/or are sold or traded in exchange for fruits and vegetables, tools, weapons, and other commodities. Pastoral nomadism is well suited to dry climates in which there is insufficient rainfall to permit settled crop agriculture, as is the case with much of Mongolia.

In Mongolia, pastoral nomadism has been practiced for thousands of years. Nomadic culture in Mongolia is highly oriented to the horse, and Mongolian horses are considered symbolic of the country's culture. Mongolian pastoral nomads also raise and care for cattle, sheep, goats, and camels. Cashmere from the wool of goats raised by nomads is one of Mongolia's leading exports and provides income to the nomads who raise and care for the goats.

Today, Mongolia's nomads are dealing with problems such as drought, desertification, overgrazing, and poaching. Many have given up their traditional nomadic lifestyles and have instead moved to cities and towns to work for wages. Some have encouraged their children to obtain formal education in order to better their opportunities in life as adults. Others practice nomadism at only certain times of the year. However, it is believed that more than a million Mongolians, or more than a quarter of the population, still practice pastoral nomadism.

Education in Mongolia

Education in Mongolia has evolved in conjunction with changes in Mongolian society from pre-Communist to Communist to post-Communist rule. Until the twentieth century, formal education in Mongolia was provided primarily to Buddhist monks in schools associated with monasteries. Government officials and wealthy citizens hired private tutors to teach their children to read and write. However, the large majority of Mongolians were illiterate. It is believed that at the beginning of the twentieth century less than 10 percent of Mongolians could read and write.

In Mongolia, education has been provided traditionally by Buddhist monks such as this one. Many Mongolians are nomads who move frequently from place to place, relying on these monks and secular teachers to provide formal education to their children. (Chiakto | Dreamstime.com)

After seizing power in the 1920s, Mongolia's Communist government began to establish secular public schools although many children continued to attend religious schools. As late as the 1930s, less than half of Mongolia's Communist Party members were able to read and write. After World War II, the government devoted more resources to education, and literacy rates began to increase rapidly. The literacy rate exceeded 50 percent in the late 1940s, and the government claimed that 98 percent of Mongolians were literate by the late 1960s. Mongolia's success in eliminating illiteracy rapidly has been attributed to emphasis on education by the Communist regime and the introduction of the Cyrillic alphabet. That most Mongolians speak Khalkha Mongol has also facilitated improved literacy in that educational resources could be concentrated on teaching a single language throughout the country.

Post-Communist Mongolia has maintained the Communist government's emphasis on literacy. During the first few years of transition to a market economy, school dropout rates increased. Many of these dropouts were boys who left school in order to help their parents care for livestock that were now owned privately rather than collectively. Herders began to question the value of formal education, claiming that it was unnecessary for a lifestyle oriented to herding livestock. By the mid-1990s, however, dropout rates had declined to previous levels. Literacy in Mongolia has remained virtually universal ever since.

The structure of education in contemporary Mongolia remains based on the Soviet model that was implemented during Communist times. Mongolian law calls for eight years of compulsory education beginning at the age of six. The system provides for four years of primary education, four years of "lower secondary" education, and four years of high school or "upper secondary" education. Most pupils attend public schools, although some students in the larger cities attend private schools. In some sparsely populated areas, public schooling is provided only through eight years, and students who wish to obtain additional education must attend boarding schools. Levels of government investment in education in Mongolia are high. The percentage of the country's budget spent on education exceeds that of the United States, Germany, the United Kingdom, Australia, and other developed countries.

Literacy in Mongolia

In its efforts to promote education and maintain universal literacy, the Mongolian government has identified several criteria defining levels of literacy. The government defines literacy as "the ability to read and write a short simple statement in Mongolian or any other language with understanding." A person over 15 years of age who is unable to "read and write a short simple statement" is defined as illiterate. In between these definitions, a neo-literate person is one "who is able to perform very basic tasks like to read a sentence word by word and to make a copy of what is written without fully understanding of its meaning. In other words, this is a person who got acquainted with the basic principles of reading, writing, and numerating techniques, but is unable to continue further training without teacher or instructor." These principles guide primary and lower secondary education in Mongolia.

Although Mongolia has been very highly successful in maintaining high rates of literacy, some populations within Mongolia remain less able to attend school and become literate. Those children who are less likely to have the opportunity to learn to read and write include children of nomads, children living in sparsely populated rural areas, and children of members of the small minority groups that do not use Khalkha Mongol as their primary language.

The Mongolian government has faced particular challenges in providing education to children of nomads. Because nomads in Mongolia and elsewhere have no fixed residences, their children are often unable to attend traditional schools. Even herders who do not move their herds from place to place often live in isolated places that are distant from cities or towns where schools are located and which may be inaccessible by paved roads. In order to alleviate this problem, the United Nations International Children's Emergency Fund (UNICEF) has worked with local Mongolian authorities to provide schooling in temporary structures. Some of these schools operate in yurts, which are known as "ger" in Mongolia. Traditional ger are large, portable tents made with animal skins or felt and supported by beams made from wood or bamboo. Today, many ger are constructed with canvas and supported by wooden or metal frames. These temporary schools operate primarily in the spring and the fall, because the ger are unheated during Mongolia's intensely cold winters. Young children attend these schools in order to achieve basic literacy and numeracy skills as well as to have the opportunity to socialize with other children.

Distance education is also being implemented in Mongolia and is directed at older students and adults. Because of nomads' mobility and of lack of access to the internet, much of this distance education is provided using radio communication. These programs provide further instruction in literacy skills, and those students who have not been able to finish primary school can earn certificates of completion by completing these courses. Temporary schooling, distance education, and other technologies are helping Mongolia maintain its high level of literacy despite its modest level of economic development and its sparse population.

Further Reading

Bolorchimeg Bor, "Writing a bright future: Literacy rates in Mongolia," United Nations International Children's Emergency Fund, September 22, 2014, http://unicefmongolia .blogspot.com/2014/09/writing-bright-future-literacy-rates-in.html. Retrieved on June 3, 2017.

Andy Brown, "Rolling stone: Helping Mongolian families with a mobile kindergarten," United Nations International Children's Emergency Fund, July 17, 2013, https://blogs.unicef. org/east-asia-pacific/rolling-stone-helping-herder-families/. Retrieved on June 3, 2017.

Hannah Reyes, "Mongolia: Nomads in transition," *The Diplomat*, October 16, 2014, http:// thediplomat.com/2014/10/mongolia-nomads-in-transition/. Retrieved on June 3, 2017.

Clinton D. W. Robinson and Chultem Otgonbayar, "Surch Amidarya: Learning for life—Nonformal basic distance education in Mongolia," United Nations Educational, Scientific and Cultural Organization, 2003, http://unesdoc.unesco.org/images /0014/001448/144849e.pdf. Retrieved on June 3, 2017.

Batchuluun Yembuu and Khulan Munkh-Erdene, "Literacy country study: Mongolia," United Nations Educational, Scientific and Cultural Organization, 2005, http://unesdoc .unesco.org/images/0014/001462/146207e.pdf. Retrieved on June 3, 2017.

NIGER

The Republic of Niger is located in north-central Africa, with a land area of about 489,000 square miles and a population of about 25 million as of early 2022. Northern Niger is covered by the Sahara Desert, and the large majority of Niger's people live in the southern and western parts of the country in the Sahel region where rainfall, although sometimes erratic, is more plentiful.

The territory comprising present-day Niger was contested among various tribal and ethnic groups for hundreds of years prior to the arrival of the European colonial powers. Niger became a French colony when the European colonial powers divided Africa in the late nineteenth century. In the early twentieth century, it became part of French West Africa, which included several other French colonies, and was administered from the city of Dakar in present-day Senegal. Niger became independent in 1960. Since then, Niger's government has alternated between democratic and authoritarian regimes.

Niger is one of the world's poorest countries with a per capita gross domestic product of $500 per year. More than two-thirds of Niger's labor force consists of farmers. Many are subsistence farmers whose crop production has been affected by recurring droughts in the Sahel. However, Niger is a major producer of uranium, which provides well over half of the country's export income. Thus, the health of Niger's economy depends on world market prices for uranium. Niger's poverty has been exacerbated not only by drought but also by its very high rate of population growth associated with its high birth rates.

French is Niger's primary official language, used in governmental administration, business, and the media. French is also the language of instruction in Niger's schools. However, Arabic and nine African languages are spoken in various parts of the country and also have official status in Niger. Of these languages, Hausa is the most prevalent and is spoken as a first language by about half of the population. The diversity of languages in Niger has proven to be an impediment to literacy, especially in comparison to countries such as Armenia, Mongolia, and Norway where nearly every citizen speaks a common language.

Education in Niger

Formal education in Niger is based on the French educational system that was imported during the colonial period. Students in Niger attend primary school for six years, followed by four years in the first cycle of secondary school and three years in the second cycle of secondary school. The French model emphasizes academic knowledge, although more efforts are being made to teach agriculture and other vocational skills that are of more immediate value to local communities.

Education is free through both cycles of secondary school, and it is compulsory from ages seven through fifteen, or through completion of the first cycle of secondary school. However, compulsory education laws are seldom enforced, especially in rural areas. In sparsely populated rural regions, secondary schools are often unavailable. According to one estimate, only 54 percent of Niger's children actually complete primary school and only 10 percent complete secondary school.

In part because so few children in Niger attend school, Niger has one of the lowest rates of literacy in the world. According to statistics compiled by the United Nations Educational, Scientific, and Cultural Organization (UNESCO) in 2015, only about 27 percent of men and 11 percent of women could read and write. However, illiteracy is more common among older citizens of Niger relative to younger persons.

Improving Literacy in Africa

How can literacy rates in Africa's poorest countries be increased in a meaningful way? The Global Partnership for Education has been active in promoting literacy throughout Africa. But the partnership realizes that literacy is more than simply the ability to read and write. Rather, the partnership recognizes that literacy today "needs to be based on a new and clear vision of literacy in our changing world. The principle behind this improvement is the 'contextualization' of literacy. This means listening to individuals' growing real needs and legitimate expectations while ensuring that they tie in with the visions and values accepted at continental level, if not worldwide." New and innovative technologies are important to carrying out this vision.

Source: Remy Habou, "Improving literacy in Africa," Global Partnership for Education, September 8, 2017, https://www.globalpartnership.org/blog/improving-literacy-africa. Retrieved on March 7, 2020.

Literacy in Niger

Illiteracy is associated with a variety of impediments including poverty and lack of access to schools. Many subsistence farmers also see little value in education. Rather than attending school, their children are expected to provide farm labor, especially during the planting and harvest seasons. In addition, many people who live in the northern part of Niger, which has a dry climate and is located near the edge of the Sahara Desert, are nomads who move constantly and are therefore unable to send their children to schools in settled communities.

Language diversity has also impeded increased literacy in Niger. Although French has historically been the language of instruction in Niger's schools, many children who begin school are unable to speak French. Rather, they speak one of Niger's nine official Indigenous languages at home. The problem is compounded in that some teachers are fluent in French and unable to speak the local language. Beginning in 2008, Niger's Ministry of Education began to experiment with a program by which children would be taught in the local language as they begin going to school, with French introduced gradually as they progress through primary school. French then would become the exclusive language of instruction only in secondary school. Assessment of students' progress has shown that students graduating from primary school after having attended these bilingual schools tend to perform better than do those children who are taught in French only.

Gender differences in literacy rates are also prevalent in Niger, with girls and women considerably less likely to attend school or achieve literacy relative to boys and men. While slightly more than half of all of Niger's children of primary school age attend school, less than half of girls of primary school age go to school. Illiteracy is reinforced by early marriage, and it has been estimated that more than 30 percent of Niger's women are married by the age of 15.

Overall, Niger is caught in a dilemma with respect to literacy, and with respect to education more generally. Widespread illiteracy impedes development, but the lack of development has stunted the development of literacy programs and has discouraged Niger's poorer citizens from investing in the education of their children. However, Niger's government continues to undertake efforts to improve education and reduce literacy. In 2014, the government issued a 10-year plan to promote education. This plan, written in French, can be accessed via https://www.global-partnership.org/fr/content/niger-plan-secteur-education-2014-2024.

Further Reading

Global Partnership for Education, "Piloting mother-tongue curriculum to improve literacy in Niger," October 2, 2017, https://www.globalpartnership.org/blog/piloting-mother -tongue-curriculum-improve-literacy-niger. Retrieved on February 8, 2018.

Kaitlin Hocker, "Top three causes of poverty in Niger," borgenproject.org, August 2, 2017, https://borgenproject.org/top-3-causes-of-poverty-in-niger/. Retrieved on January 29, 2018.

Eleni Lentz-Marino, "Education in Niger," Borgen Magazine, August 22, 2014, http://www .borgenmagazine.com/education-niger/. Retrieved on January 29, 2018.

United States Agency for International Development, "Education: Niger," April 19, 2017, https://www.usaid.gov/niger/education. Retrieved on June 12, 2017.

NORWAY

Norway occupies the western half of the Scandinavian peninsula, which it shares with Sweden. It is long, narrow, and mountainous, and it has an overall land area of about 149,000 square miles and a population of about 5.5 million as of 2022.

The ancestral home of the Vikings or "Northmen" between the eighth and eleventh centuries AD, Norway was united politically with Sweden and Denmark during the late Middle Ages. The three countries formed the Kalmar Union in 1396. Sweden left the Kalmar Union in 1523, but Norway remained under Danish rule until 1814, when it became part of Sweden after the Napoleonic Wars. In 1905, Norway became a fully independent country.

Today, Norway is one of the most prosperous countries in the world. In 2016, the International Monetary Fund reported that Norway has the second highest per capita gross national product in Europe, following the much smaller Luxembourg. Norway joined the North Atlantic Treaty Organization (NATO) in 1949. However, Norway declined invitations to join the European Union in 1972 and 1994.

Norway owes much of its present prosperity to natural resources, especially oil and natural gas. Although it is a capitalist country, it is also recognized as a social democracy with substantial government management of the country's economy and infrastructure, including education. Norway ranks very high on global comparison of environmental awareness and policy and on income equality. The Norwegian language is spoken as a first language by about 95 percent of Norway's people. Norwegian has been a written language for more than 2,000 years, and the Latin script came to Norway and the rest of Scandinavia in the early eleventh century in conjunction with the arrival of Christianity. The Sami language, which is spoken by the Sami people of northern Scandinavia, is also an official language in Norway.

Education in Norway

Organized education in Norway dates back to the Middle Ages, but at first, it was confined primarily to the training of the clergy. In the early eighteenth century, the large majority of Norwegian peasants were illiterate. With the support of the state-sponsored Evangelical Lutheran Church, the government implemented the Education Act in 1739. This law required all citizens to be taught to read and to be taught the principles of Christianity, although this law was not enforced throughout the country until the nineteenth century. Primary schools known as folkeskole were established in the early nineteenth century. The curriculum included writing, arithmetic, and singing as well as reading and religion. In 1889, a compulsory attendance law requiring Norwegian children to attend folkeskole for seven years was implemented. However, many children in rural areas attended folkeskole for only a few weeks each year.

In 1936, Norway amended its 1889 law to require a minimum length of the school year. In 1997, Norway extended the law to require children between 6 and 16 to attend school, which is free. Today, more than 90 percent of Norwegian primary and secondary students attend public schools, and more than 80 percent of Norwegians have graduated from the country's equivalent of high school.

Literacy in Norway

As is the case throughout western and northern Europe, Norway enjoys universal literacy in that virtually all native-born Norwegians can read and write. In Norway, as in other highly developed countries, concern about literacy goes beyond the simple ability to read and write. Rather, it also considers the degree to which persons who are able to read and write can interpret what they have read effectively.

How proficient adults are in the ability to interpret written texts varies both within Norway and between Norway and other countries. A survey of literacy conducted by the Organisation for Economic Co-operation and Development (OECD) and published in 2012 showed that adults in Norway scored above the European average in literacy, which it defined as "the ability to understand and respond appropriately to written texts." The survey also address numeracy, or "the ability to use numerical and mathematical concepts," and problem-solving in technology-rich environments, or "the capacity to access, interpret and analyse information found, transformed and communicated in digital environments." According to the OECD study, Norwegian adults score high relative to other countries with respect to literacy, numeracy, and problem-solving in technology-rich environments. Norway ranked seventh among 30 countries in surveys on literacy and fifth in numeracy. It was seventh in the percentage of persons who were capable of problem-solving.

Literacy in Norway is lower among immigrants than among native-born Norwegians. As of early 2017, nearly 17 percent of Norway's people consisted of immigrants or Norwegian-born children of immigrant parents. Of these, more than 80 percent came from outside western and northern Europe. The Norwegian language is unique to Norway and is related most closely to other Germanic languages including Danish, Swedish, Icelandic, German, and English. However, relatively few immigrants into Norway come from European countries in which these languages are spoken. The leading countries of origin of immigrants into Norway today include Poland, Sweden, Somalia, Lithuania, Pakistan, and Iraq with more than 10 percent of these immigrants coming from Poland alone. Except for Sweden, the primary languages of these countries of origin are quite different from Norwegian. These differences may contribute to relatively low levels of literacy proficiency among these immigrants and their offspring as compared to those of native-born Norwegians.

Levels of literacy proficiency in Norway vary also between younger and older adults. While older Norwegian adults score higher than the European average in literacy proficiency, numeracy proficiency, and problem-solving, younger adults scored lower than the European average in both literacy proficiency and numeracy proficiency. The fact that younger adults do not score as well as older adults in these areas has raised concern among Norwegian educational specialists and government officials. According to one study comparing Norway, Canada, and the United States, illiterate immigrants in Norway have had much more difficulty in being successful in the labor force as compared to those in North America. This difference has been attributed to high levels of government investment in education at the folkeskole level in Norway. This investment benefits native-born Norwegians and young children of immigrants, but does not benefit older immigrants who move to Norway as teenagers or adults. Most of these adult immigrants are literate in their first languages, but they are not proficient in Norwegian.

Literacy levels are high, however, among the Sami people of northern Norway. Historically, the Sami were known as "Lapps," but that term is regarded today as derogatory. Traditionally, the Sami were nomadic reindeer herders, and many subsisted also on fishing, fur trapping, and sheepherding. Today, some Sami continue to work in these traditional occupations, but the majority live in cities and towns. An estimated 55,000–60,000 Sami people live in northern Norway today, with others living in northern Sweden, northern Finland, and the northwestern corner of Russia. They are the only recognized Indigenous population group in Norway. The Sami language is a Uralic language that is related to Finnish and Estonian, although some experts dispute the idea that Sami and Finnish have a common linguistic ancestry. The Sami language has existed in written form since the early seventeenth century. Today, it is written throughout Scandinavia using a standardized Latin alphabet.

Historically, the Sami were victims of discrimination by the majority Norwegian population. In the late nineteenth century, the Norwegian government initiated a

This picture of a Sami family in traditional dress was taken in northern Norway in the early 1900s. Historically, Sami people were known by the derogatory exonym "Lapps." Sami people were traditionally nomads and often were not taught in formal school settings. (Library of Congress, Prints and Photographs Division. http://hdl.loc.gov/loc.pnp/ppmsc.06257)

program known as *fornorsking av samur*, or "Norwegianization" of the Indigenous Sami population. Under the fornorsking program, all schooling throughout the country was conducted in Norwegian. Some Sami children were separated from their families and sent to be educated at boarding schools where they were taught in Norwegian and where teachers were expected to force Sami students to assimilate Norwegian culture.

The fornorsking program was ended in the 1980s, at which time the Sami were recognized formally as an Indigenous population within Norway. In 1989, the Constitution of Norway was amended to recognize Sami rights with the words "it is the responsibility of the authorities of the State to create conditions enabling the Sami people to preserve and develop its language, culture and way of life," although mining activities, logging, climate change, and military activity continue to intrude upon the Sami homeland. However, the 1989 amendment guaranteed the right of Sami children living in majority-Sami regions of northern Norway to be educated in the Sami language. As a result, literacy rates among the Sami are comparable to those throughout Norway, and most young Sami are literate in both Sami and Norwegian.

Further Reading

Nina Berglund, "Sami still battling discrimination," *News in English.no*, March 24, 2016, http://www.newsinenglish.no/2016/03/24/sami-still-battling-discrimination/. Retrieved on May 9, 2017.

Bernt Bratsberg, Torbjorn Haegeland, and Oddbjorn Raaum, "Immigrant skills and employment: Cross-country evidence from the Adult Literacy and Life Skills Survey," Statistics Norway Research Department, Discussion Paper 730, January 2013, http://www.ssb.no/a/publikasjoner/pdf/DP/dp730.pdf. Retrieved on May 9, 2017.

Jonas Jakobsen, "Education, recognition, and the Sami people of Norway," in *Writing postcolonial histories of intercultural education*, edited by Heike Niedrig and Christian Ydesen. New York: Oxford, 2011, http://www.academia.edu/1488801/Education_Recognition_and_the_Sami_People_of_Norway. Retrieved on May 9, 2017.

Organisation for Economic Co-Operation and Development, "Survey of adult skills—First results," Country Note: Norway, 2012, http://www.oecd.org/skills/piaac/Country%20note%20-%20Norway.pdf. Retrieved on April 29, 2017.

The Oslo Times, "History of education in Norway," September 1, 2015, http://www.theoslotimes.com/article/history-of-education-in-norway. Retrieved on April 29, 2017.

Statistics Norway, "Immigrants and Norwegian-born to immigrant parents, 1 January 2014," April 24, 2014, http://www.ssb.no/en/befolkning/statistikker/innvbef/aar/2014-04-24. Retrieved on April 29, 2017.

Sverre Tveit, "Testing and assessment in Norway," *International Education News*, February 11, 2016, https://internationalednews.com/2016/02/11/testing-and-assessment-in-norway/. Retrieved on April 29, 2017.

SOMALIA

Somalia, which is known formally as the Somali Republic, is located in the Horn of Africa with long coastlines on the Indian Ocean and the Arabian Gulf. Somalia's land area is approximately 246,000 square miles, making it slightly smaller than Texas. It has a population of about 17 million as of 2022. Somalia consists of the former European colonies of British Somaliland and Italian Somaliland. Italian Somaliland became the Trust Territory of Somaliland after World War II and was administered by Britain. The Trust Territory and British Somaliland merged and became the independent country of Somalia in 1960.

Although a majority of Somalia's people are ethnic Somalis, the country is regarded as a failed state and has been embroiled in civil war for more than 25 years. Warlords and factions including the radical Islamic group Al-Shabaab continue to fight for control of the country. Somalia is one of the poorest countries in the world, and ongoing civil war along with a succession of droughts has resulted in higher levels of poverty. As is the case with many less developed countries, Somalia has a high birth rate and a very young population. Its median age is about 16.6 years. However, the civil war has also impeded education. Many Somali youths have been denied the opportunity to become educated, and rates of illiteracy in Somalia remain among the highest in the world.

Education in Somalia

Somali law provides for eight years of compulsory education including instruction in reading and writing the Somali language, which is written with a Latin script, and in reading and writing English. However, the compulsory education law is not enforced effectively, especially in rural areas. According to a 2011 estimate by the United Nations International Children's Emergency Fund (UNICEF), only 30 percent of Somali children of school age were attending school. Gender is an ongoing issue in Somalia's schools. In 2002, it was estimated that only 36 percent of primary school students in Somalia were girls. Somalia's status as a failed state has meant that government authorities in some areas have been unable to establish and maintain schools. Instead, most of Somalia's schools are operated privately, by local or international NGOs, or by local authorities in the more stable and prosperous areas of the country. Many are madrassas operated by Islamic religious authorities.

Lack of opportunity to obtain schooling is an especially acute problem in central and southern Somalia, which are the poorest areas of the country and where the most fighting has taken place during the continuing civil war. Opportunities for education have been reduced further by internal displacement, due to which many persons have been forced to leave their homes because of the wars. Many of these internally displaced persons have moved to the capital city of Mogadishu, where there are insufficient resources to provide educational facilities for the city's increasing refugee population. Throughout the country, it has been estimated that there is only 1 teacher for every 33 primary school students. In addition, some Somalis living in rural areas of the drought-stricken country are pastoral nomads who are unable to send their children to schools located in fixed places.

Literacy in Somalia

All of these factors contribute to Somalia's low rate of literacy. In 2002, it was estimated that only about 20 percent of Somalis were literate. Literacy rates have increased, but according to estimates by the United Nations Educational, Scientific, and Cultural Organization (UNESCO), less than 40 percent of Somali citizens are literate today. According to these UNESCO data, there is a large gender gap with respect to literacy in about half of Somali men, but only a quarter of Somali women are literate. This high rate of illiteracy is of particular concern because Somalia's population is young and because many Somali children have not had the opportunity to attend school.

Efforts to combat illiteracy in Somalia have been undertaken, especially in the regions of Somaliland and Puntland in northern Somalia. Somaliland, located along the Arabian Gulf coast, includes the former British Somaliland and had a population estimated at 5.7 million in 2021. Somaliland has sought independence from Somalia itself. Although its independence is not recognized by other countries, Somaliland has an autonomous relationship with the rest of Somalia including its own military forces, currency, and legal institutions. Somaliland has largely been spared the lawlessness and violence associated with the rest of the country.

The relatively peaceful landscape of Somaliland has allowed the Somaliland Ministry of Education to promote education. In 2012, the ministry adopted a five-year plan that called for the provision of free public education through the eighth grade, with the goal that 75 percent of Somaliland's children would be attending these schools despite the fact that less than a third of children throughout the Somali Republic attend school. The plan also called for training of teachers to keep up with the demand for public schooling, for encouraging gender balance in education, and for providing water, sanitation, and other services facilitating the schooling process.

The Ministry of Education has also partnered with several nongovernmental organizations (NGOs) including Save the Children, CARE International, and the Norwegian Refugee Council. This project, known as Horumarinta Elmiga, has also been supported with funds supplied by the European Union. Horumarinta Elmiga has promoted literacy and numeracy by constructing schools and providing text-books and other learning materials. Mobile schools are being established to serve children of pastoral nomads. Efforts are also being made to encourage girls to attend school and to provide educational services to children with special needs. In 2015, it was reported that Horumarinta Elmiga was successful in providing educational services to nearly 50,000 children in Somaliland. Education in Somaliland has been provided in a relatively decentralized fashion, with facilities maintained and operated by the government, the private sector, and NGOs. However, critics have claimed that the decentralized approach to education in Somaliland, along with the activities of various organizations from outside the country, has made Somaliland's youth susceptible to radical Islamic influences.

Puntland, meanwhile, is located east of Somaliland and has coastlines on both the Arabian Gulf and the Indian Ocean. Its population was estimated at 4.3 million in 2021. Puntland also maintains a semiautonomous relationship with the Somali Republic. With a thriving petrochemical industry and abundant marine resources, Puntland's per capita gross domestic product is considerably higher than is the case in other parts of the country. Puntland's economy has been augmented through piracy. Pirate crews operating out of Puntland's coast have seized many ships on the high seas in the Arabian Gulf and the Indian Ocean, and the lack of a function-ing central government in the Somali Republic has facilitated pirate operations. Many pirate crews include young Somali men who see piracy as a means to escape poverty. In recent years, however, international cooperation spearheaded by the International Maritime Bureau has reduced the number of pirate attacks off the Puntland coast.

As is the case with Somaliland, Puntland's relative prosperity and peacefulness has facilitated efforts to provide education and reduce illiteracy. The region's Min-istry of Education has the responsibility for providing educational services in Punt-land. The ministry's educational goals are to "cultivate national consciousness and unity in the minds of the children at an early age and enhance a spirit of patriotism for Somalia in general and Puntland in particular as well as a desire for its sustained integration, stability and prosperity" and to "promote the acquisition of attitudes and skills in Somalis in such a way as to make Somalia an active and effective member of the international community, which contributes to human progress and development." Government planning has emphasized effective teacher training and early childhood education. These efforts have been relatively successful, especially in Somaliland where 50 percent of children had completed primary school as of 2013 and only 13 percent were fully illiterate. In Puntland, 35 percent completed primary school and 28 percent were fully illiterate.

Success in reducing illiteracy in Somaliland and Puntland has illustrated the potential for tackling problems associated with illiteracy elsewhere in Somalia as well as in other less developed countries throughout the world. Additional discussion of literacy in Somalia can be found on the Somali Literacy Project's website at https://thesomaliliteracyproject.com/. This website includes stories about Somali expatriates, some of whom have contributed to reducing literacy in their native country. However, the successful reduction of illiteracy in Somaliland and Puntland is associated also with relative peace, stability, and prosperity in these portions of Somalia in comparison with the rest of the country. War, poverty, and drought have impeded efforts to promote literacy in much of the country, and this trend is likely to continue.

Further Reading

Afrol News, "Some 80% of Somalis now illiterate," 2003, http://afrol.com/articles/10890. Retrieved on May 20, 2017.

Lee Cassanelli and Farah Sheik Abdikadir, "Somalia: Education in transition," *Bildhaan: An International Journal of Somali Studies*, 7 (2007), http://digitalcommons.macalester .edu/cgi/viewcontent.cgi?article=1066&context=bildhaan. Retrieved on May 19, 2017.

Nashon Tado, "Challenging illiteracy in Somaliland," Norwegian Refugee Council, September 8, 2016, https://www.nrc.no/news/2016/september/challenging-illiteracy-in-somaliland/. Retrieved on May 20, 2017.

United Nations International Children's Emergency Fund, "UNICEF warns of education crisis in Somalia," 2011, https://www.unicefusa.org/press/releases/unicef-warns -education-crisis-somalia/8062. Retrieved on May 19, 2017.

Emily Walthouse, "Primary education in Somalia and the U.S.," borgenproject.org, 2014, https://borgenproject.org/primary-education-somalia-u-s/. Retrieved on May 19, 2017.

TRINIDAD AND TOBAGO

The Republic of Trinidad and Tobago consists of the islands of Trinidad and Tobago in the southern Caribbean Sea near the coast of Venezuela on the South American mainland. The country has an overall land area of 1,981 square miles and a population of nearly 1.4 million as of 2022. The larger island of Trinidad contains more than 90 percent of the country's land area and of its population. The population is highly diverse, including many people of African, Asian, European, and Indigenous ancestry.

Trinidad was settled by Native Americans from the South American main-land for thousands of years before it was visited by Christopher Columbus, who claimed the island for Spain, in 1498. In 1797, Spain ceded Trinidad to Britain. Meanwhile, Tobago changed hands among the United Kingdom, the Netherlands, France, and Courland (present-day Latvia) throughout the sixteenth, seventeenth, and eighteenth centuries and became a permanent British colony in 1814. The two islands were combined into a single colony in 1889. The colony became part of the independent Federation of the West Indies including Jamaica and Barbados in 1958. The Federation collapsed, and Trinidad and Tobago became fully indepen-dent in 1962.

Sugar cultivation was a mainstay of both islands' economies throughout the seventeenth, eighteenth, and nineteenth centuries. Many sugar plantations were worked by slaves. As was the case elsewhere in the Western Hemisphere, slaves were discouraged or forbidden from learning to read and write, and hence most were illiterate. After slavery was abolished throughout the British Empire in 1834, the British paid former slaves and brought in contract laborers to work on sugar plantations on Trinidad. Later in the nineteenth century, many of these contract laborers were brought to Trinidad from present-day India, Bangladesh, and Paki-stan. Today about 40 percent of the population is of Asian ancestry.

Oil was first discovered in Trinidad in the late nineteenth century, and the petro-chemical industry became and remains central to Trinidad and Tobago's economy. Today, oil accounts for more than a third of Trinidad and Tobago's gross national product and nearly 80 percent of its exports. The country's per capita income ranks fourth in the Western Hemisphere after only the United States, Canada, and Barbados. In contrast to most Caribbean islands, tourism has had little impact on Trinidad and Tobago's economy.

Education in Trinidad and Tobago

The government of Trinidad and Tobago has explicitly linked education to achiev-ing the goal of developed country status. In 2004, the government's Ministry of Education stated that "heavy investment of the government in the education system is critical if Trinidad and Tobago is to reach developed country status by the year 2020." Trinidad and Tobago's educational system is based on the British model of education that was introduced after the British assumed control of the islands. However, not until the twentieth century, several decades after emancipa-tion, were efforts made to promote basic education for all residents. The literacy rate increased slowly, and by 1946, the literacy rate in Trinidad and Tobago had increased to nearly 75 percent. The country's literacy rate reached 95 percent by 1980 and 99 percent by 2015.

Schooling in Trinidad and Tobago is free and compulsory for children between the ages of 5 and 15. Most children attend free public schools, although parents may choose to pay tuition to send their children to private or religious schools. The curriculum, which is administered at the national level, includes 5 years of primary school followed by 5 years of secondary school. After completing these 10 years of schooling, students may continue in school to obtain vocational and technical training. Other students remain in school for an additional 2 years, after which they complete examinations analogous to the O-level and A-level examinations administered in the United Kingdom. Those who succeed in these examinations are eligible to attend universities such as the University of the West Indies, the University of Trinidad and Tobago, or the University of the Southern Caribbean. Undergraduate education at these universities is also free to Trinidad and Tobago's citizens. Recently, the government has expanded programs to provide additional financial aid to students at these universities. Some observers regard Trinidad and Tobago's educational programs as a model for other former European colonies in the Caribbean region.

Literacy in Trinidad and Tobago

In particular, given that virtually all citizens of Trinidad and Tobago are able to read and write, the government's view of literacy goes far beyond these basic skills. Rather, the government's perspective on education encompasses numeracy, problem-solving, and communications skills. Education in Trinidad and Tobago is managed by the Ministry of Education, which has identified

> six essential learning outcomes which help to define standards of attainment for all secondary school students—aesthetic expression, citizenship, communication, personal development, problem solving, and technological competence. Curriculum design therefore facilitates the attainment of these learning outcomes, and prepares students for further study or for entry into the world of work. The national curricula should also provide all students with the maximum opportunity to develop their potential and should therefore reflect ad support our national ideals; be flexible and responsive to the developmental needs, life experiences and unique abilities of each individual; provide learners with the resources to construct knowledge that is relevant to their needs and interests; and equip all learners with the knowledge and skills to attain a good quality of life.

With respect to literacy itself, these goals have been articulated in government's primary school syllabus for language arts, adopted in 1999. The learning outcomes associated with this syllabus state that pupils completing this program will be able to "listen with a high degree of understanding to instructions, descriptions, explanations and narration in Standard English, in a familiar accent and in the vocabulary and sentence structure appropriate to his/her age, speak, using words exactly and precisely for his [sic] age, to communicate thoughts and feels; demonstrate spontaneity in speaking in a variety of situations, think creatively, critically and constructively, respond sensitively to varied and meaningful literature and other forms of art at the appropriate level, read effectively, and for different purposes, a variety of print or electronic media, express himself or herself in the following forms of writing, explanations, narratives, descriptions, letters writing and do so legibly, [and] use various forms of visual literacy to interpret and gain information."

Most residents of Trinidad speak what is called the Trinidad dialect or Trinidad creole, which differs somewhat from standard English. Because the language is influenced considerably by French, the language is sometimes called Trinidad French creole. The creole language is influenced strongly by French because many slaves were brought to Trinidad from the French-speaking islands of Guadeloupe and Martinique. Some residents of the more isolated interior regions of Trinidad, many of whom have descended from runaway slaves, continue to speak a French-based dialect or patois as their primary language.

Much of the vocabulary of Trinidad creole comes from standard English, but some of its vocabulary comes from French, African languages, languages of India, and other origins. Examples of words unique to Trinidad creole include "bonmatin" (good morning), "lime" (to hang out), and "pothound" (a mongrel dog). A slightly different creole language is spoken on Tobago. In Trinidad and Tobago's educational system, emphasis is placed on literacy in written and spoken standard English, although the primary syllabus recognizes that most residents of Trinidad and Tobago who remain in the country as adults will speak creole throughout their lives.

The role of creole languages in Trinidad and Tobago can be linked with observations about the country's educational system itself. Critics of Trinidad and Tobago's educational system have argued that the system is more elitist than egalitarian. Such criticism recognizes that the British model upon which Trinidad and Tobago's educational system is based emphasizes meritocracy at the expense of providing for the needs of the majority of the population. Even today, critics point out, the system privileges children of the elite. Many of these children of the elite have educated parents who are most fluent in standard English, which is emphasized in the curriculum. From this viewpoint, children from poorer families then are victims of low expectations and are less likely to be provided with the guidance, resources, or encouragement to achieve optimum success in Trinidad and Tobago's school system.

Further Reading

Raiesa Ali, "Trinidad and Tobago: Education reform and social mobilization," Council on Hemispheric Affairs, August 7, 2015, http://www.coha.org/trinidad-and-tobago-education-reform-and-societal-mobilization/. Retrieved on May 29, 2017.

Barbara Joseph, "Communication, language, and literacy in Trinidad and Tobago," *Connexions*, 2011, https://cnx.org/exports/56aa32ab-c366-48f9-89ff-3cc0f7c757ac@19.1.pdf/communication-language-and-literacy-in-trinidad-and-tobago-19.1.pdf. Retrieved on May 29, 2017.

Jerome De Lisle, Harrilal Seecharan, and Aya Taliba Ayodike, "Is the Trinidad and Tobago education system structured to facilitate optimum human capital development?," 2011, http://sta.uwi.edu/conferences/09/salises/documents/J%20De%20Lisle.pdf. Retrieved on June 3, 2017.

Republic of Trinidad and Tobago Ministry of Education, "Primary School Syllabus: Language Arts," September 1999, http://homeschoolerstt.weebly.com/uploads/5/3/9/3/53938319/2_curriculum_guide_ela.pdf. Retrieved on June 3, 2017.

Saturday Express, "Paramin keeping patois alive high in the hills," July 31, 2011, http://www.trinidadexpress.com/news/Paramin_keeping_patois_alive-126497818.html. Retrieved on June 3, 2017.

United Nations Educational, Scientific, and Cultural Organization, International Bureau of Education, "World Data on Education—Trinidad and Tobago," 2011, http://www.ibe.unesco.org/fileadmin/user_upload/Publications/WDE/2010/pdf-versions/Trinidad_and_Tobago.pdf. Retrieved on May 29, 2017.

UNITED STATES

Throughout the history of the United States, rates of literacy have been high, and many political and religious leaders have placed high priority on ensuring that Americans are able to read and write. The history of literacy in the United States is linked closely to the history of American education at the elementary school level.

The United States has a long history of literacy. Prior to the American Revolution, residents of the Thirteen Colonies were more likely to have been literate than Europeans. It has been estimated that about 70 percent of adults living in the Thirteen Colonies were literate in 1700, as compared to about 40 percent in England and 30 percent in France. The relatively high literacy rates in the Colonies have been attributed in part to religion. Puritans and other Protestant denominations stressed the importance of individual interpretation of the Bible, requiring members of these churches to be able to read.

Literacy rates in the American colonies were the highest in New England, with its large population of Puritans and other Dissenters. In 1647, Massachusetts enacted a law requiring each town of a minimum population to maintain a public school where children were taught reading, writing, and arithmetic as well as the basic principles of the Puritan faith. Thus, by 1700 nearly every adult resident of Massachusetts was literate. Literacy rates were lower in the South, however, because the South was a more rural society, whereas many New Englanders lived in villages and towns. In addition, the colonial South had substantial populations of slaves and indentured servants. The leaders of the Southern colonies were associated often with the established Church of England (today's Episcopalian Church), which placed less emphasis on individual knowledge and interpretation of Scripture. At that time, children of wealthier families were often taught to read and write by their parents or private tutors, whereas children from poor families had little or no opportunity to achieve literacy skills. Most slaves were also illiterate, and in some Southern states teaching slaves to read and write was regarded as a criminal offense.

Literacy in the colonial period was reinforced by the requirement in many of the colonies that citizens were required to pass tests of literacy in order to be granted the right to vote. This requirement continued in some areas until the middle of the twentieth century. After the Revolution, leaders of the newly independent United States believed that literacy promoted the free exchange of ideas and reduced the possibility that the United States would descend into tyranny. The importance of literacy is illustrated by the First Amendment to the U.S. Constitution, which guarantees freedom of the press.

The Common School movement, described in more detail elsewhere in this volume, helped to promote literacy. As public education in the United States became universal during the late nineteenth and early twentieth centuries, rates of illiteracy defined as the inability to read and write in any language declined steadily. It has been estimated that in 1870 about 20 percent of the U.S. adult population was illiterate. This percentage dropped to 10.7 percent in 1900 and to 3.2 percent in 1950.

Foreign-born adults moving to the United States were more likely to be illiterate as compared to native-born Americans. In 1900, for example, 12.9 percent of foreign-born Americans were illiterate in any language, as compared to 4.6 percent of native-born Americans. Rates of illiteracy were historically much higher among Blacks. In 1870, nearly 80 percent of Blacks were unable to read and write. This very high rate of illiteracy was a by-product of the slavery system in that the majority of Blacks after the Civil War were former slaves. Illiteracy rates dropped sharply after that. By 1900, well over half of Black adults were literate, and many who were illiterate were older persons who had been born and raised as slaves.

As is the case with developed countries throughout the world, the United States has achieved virtually universal literacy for the past several decades. However, the distinction between basic literacy and functional literacy remains considerable. Today, a substantial number of Americans remain functionally illiterate, or unable to read and write at a level needed to engage in day-to-day life. Many functionally illiterate people are unable to read books and newspapers, use social media, fill out applications for jobs or government services, or understand written directions such as those on road signs and dosages for medications.

According to a study conducted in 2013, about 32 million American adults, or about 14 percent of the U.S. adult population, were considered functionally

---

Literacy Volunteers

It has been estimated that about 35 million American adults are unable to read at a fourth-grade level. Many illiterate adults are embarrassed by their inability to read and write, and some believe that they are unable to learn these skills. Others have learning disabilities. But with the help of volunteer teachers and tutors, some are willing to make efforts to overcome the stigma of illiteracy. One such group is the Literacy Volunteers of Bangor, Maine. Since 1969, the Literacy Volunteers have matched illiterate adults with tutors who not only teach reading and writing skills but also work to build self-confidence in their students' learning abilities.

Source: Melissa Block and Marisa Penaloza, "Casting aside shame and stigma, adults tackle struggles with literacy," *NPR*, April 26, 2018, https://www.npr.org/sections/ed/2018/04/26/602797769/casting-aside-shame-and-stigma-adults-tackle-struggles-with-literacy. Retrieved on March 7, 2020.

A literacy class being taught at Fort Valley Normal and Industrial School (now Fort Valley State University), a historically Black college in Fort Valley, Georgia. Throughout the world, people have been taught literacy skills in such settings—sometimes in indoor classrooms and at other times outdoors or in temporary classrooms or even tents. (Schomburg Center for Research in Black Culture, Photographs and Prints Division, The New York Public Library. "Fort Valley Normal and Industrial School literacy class." New York Public Library Digital Collections. Accessed February 18, 2022. https://digitalcollections.nypl.org/items/85e70e60 -2500-0134-7e26-00505686a51c)

illiterate although many of these functionally illiterate people have completed several years of formal schooling and some have graduated from high school. Adults who are functionally illiterate may be embarrassed by or ashamed of their inability to read and write and may therefore be unwilling to seek help to improve their literacy skills. Some functionally illiterate people may have learning disabilities such as dyslexia or ADHD, which impede their ability to master literacy skills.

On the basis of results of literacy tests, the U.S. National Assessment of Adult Literacy (NAAL) has classified American adults into four categories—below basic, basic, intermediate, and proficient. People who were classified in the "below basic" category were considered functionally illiterate. In general, a functionally literate person is able to read and write at a fourth grade to sixth grade level. According to NAAL, nearly half of these persons were living at or below the poverty line. Several studies have demonstrated that functionally illiterate Americans are more likely to be impoverished or to become incarcerated. For example, according to one study, more than half of American adults who are in the U.S. prison system, along with more than 80 percent of juvenile inmates, were unable to read or write above a fourth-grade level.

Within the United States, rates of functional illiteracy among English-speaking adults varied from more than 20 percent in California, Florida, and New York to 6 percent in Minnesota, New Hampshire, and North Dakota and to 7 percent in six other states. Of course, many people who are functionally illiterate in English and who live in states such as California, Florida, and New York are immigrants for whom English is a second language, although these people may not be literate in their first languages either.

Further Reading

Marilyn Binkley and Trevor Williams, "Reading literacy in the United States," U.S. Department of Education, Office of Educational Research and Improvement, 1996, https://nces.ed.gov/pubs/96258.pdf. Retrieved on February 7, 2018.

Daniel Lattier, "32 million U.S. adults are 'Functionally Illiterate' . . . what does that mean?" *Intellectual Takeout*, August 26, 2015, https://www.educationviews.org/32-million-u-s-adults-functionally-illiterate-mean/. Retrieved on February 7, 2018.

National Center for Education Statistics, "120 Years of literacy," 1993, https://nces.ed.gov/NAAL/lit_history.asp. Retrieved on February 7, 2018.

Chapter 2: Gender and Education

OVERVIEW

Ever since formal education was first developed and implemented thousands of years ago, questions about gender in education in the educational process have arisen. What formal education was needed for boys and for girls as they prepared for adulthood? Such questions have affected education throughout the world ever since. In most traditional societies, gender roles were defined very clearly. Boys and girls were taught skills that were associated with these gender roles that they would assume as adults. In the more complex world of today, these gender roles have become much less rigid. It has come to be recognized that girls as well as boys need formal education above and beyond training in activities associated with their traditional gender roles. Such is evident with respect to literacy. As is discussed in detail in the chapter on literacy, developed countries are characterized by universal literacy. However, in most societies that continue to face substantial levels of illiteracy, literacy rates among boys and men exceed those among girls and women. Thus, in many countries today there remains substantial gender inequality with respect to education.

As formal education developed, in many societies this formal education was provided only to boys. Few girls were given the opportunity to obtain formal educations. Girls were taught domestic skills informally by their mothers, grandmothers, and other female relatives. As a result, most women remained illiterate in part because knowledge of reading and writing was seen as unimportant to taking care of the home and family. This was true especially among peasants and lower-class people, as formal education in many societies was restricted largely to children of the elite.

Prior to the Renaissance, most formal education was provided by religious institutions or by private tutors. Even after governments began to provide and manage formal public education, in many countries only boys received this formal education. Formal education was often regarded as unnecessary for girls, whose roles in many societies were restricted to taking care of home and family. In addition, in the past women were seen as intellectually incapable of understanding mathematics, science, and other subjects taught to boys and men.

The Protestant Reformation in Northern Europe brought attention to the importance of literacy for both sexes. Because Protestantism stressed individual knowledge of the Bible, both women and men had to learn to read the Bible. Thus, both boys and girls were taught to read and write. It has been estimated that by 1800,

Equestrian Portrait of Cornelis and Michiel Pompe van Meerdervoort with Their Tutor and Coachman was painted by the Dutch artist Aelbert Cuyp (1620–1691) in the early 1650s. At that time, wealthy families relied on private tutors to educate their children while children of peasants and other poor people received little or no formal education. During the nineteenth and twentieth centuries, governments took over the management of education and began to make it available to all children regardless of social and economic status. (The Metropolitan Museum of Art, New York. The Friedsam Collection, Bequest of Michael Friedsam, 1931)

the majority of adults in Prussia, England, and Scotland were literate, although literacy rates were higher among men than among women. However, beyond reading and writing, formal education for girls, especially those from noble or wealthy families, focused on what were often called "the feminine arts," including sewing, cooking, music, and preparation for future marriage and childbearing.

Although in these societies a majority of women were now able to read and write, writing for a public audience continued to be regarded as unfeminine and unladylike especially with respect to serious works of literature. Female writers were expected to restrict themselves to writing romances and light poetry. Women who wrote more serious works of literature often published them under masculine pseudonyms. Thus, Mary Anne Evans (1819–1880) became George Eliot, and the Bronte sisters, Charlotte (1816–1855), Emily (1818–1848), and Anne (1820–1849), published their novels under the names of Currer, Ellis, and Acton Bell, respectively.

By the twentieth century, it had become acceptable for women to publish their writings under their own names. Such acceptance coincided generally with transition from agricultural to industrial to postindustrial society. However, women were often forbidden from attending colleges and universities until into the twentieth century. Even in the United States, many medical schools and law schools refused to admit women until after World War II. In developed countries today, however, women have been granted equal opportunity to enter professions that require formal education.

Gender inequality in access to education has been eliminated in developed countries today, although there remain other issues that contribute to more subtle inequalities on the basis of gender. By contrast, gender inequality in education remains a significant issue in many less developed countries. Boys are likely to attend school and graduate from school for several reasons. Cultural norms play a significant role, in some cases continuing traditions that have existed for hundreds or thousands of years. In many traditional societies, women are expected to maintain the household and perform such duties as cleaning, cooking, and raising children. Even young girls are expected to take part in these activities, including caring for younger siblings. Formal education beyond the rudiments of reading, writing, and arithmetic continues to be regarded in such societies as unnecessary for girls who are preparing to assume these traditional roles as adults. And in some less developed countries, girls who are having their periods are not allowed to attend school on those days.

Although public education is usually free, in many countries parents are expected to pay for uniforms, textbooks, and other supplies. Regarding formal schooling as unnecessary, parents may keep their daughters at home. In addition, in some societies it is considered inappropriate for girls, especially teenagers, to be taught by male teachers and/or in mixed-sex classrooms. Sexual harassment and sexual assaults on teenage girls by teachers and school officials are a significant problem in some countries, especially in those less developed countries that maintain traditional patriarchal cultures. Safety concerns also affect girls' access to formal education in countries throughout the world as discussed in chapter 7.

This chapter contains profiles of education with a focus on gender-related issues in seven countries in addition to the United States. In developed countries including the United States and Australia, all children are given formal education, and compulsory education laws are enforced. Here, analysis of gender and education is focused not so much on gender inequality with respect to access to education as on how education can be provided in such a way to provide the best learning opportunities for all children. Concern is also raised about ensuring that schools are safe spaces, away from bullying and sexual harassment.

In the majority of less developed countries, however, gender-related equality remains considerable. Literacy rates and school attendance rates continue to be lower among girls and among boys. Malawi, which is one of the 20 poorest countries in the world on the basis of per capita income, is a good example. The Malawian government is well aware of gender inequality and has been taking steps to rectify this problem. However, cultural traditions continue to keep girls away from school. Poverty also means that for many families, formal education especially for girls is seen as a luxury item rather than as a necessity. The problem is exacerbated by insufficient classroom space, a shortage of teachers, and a lack of textbooks and learning materials.

Although Malawi was a dictatorship for most of its first three decades following independence from the United Kingdom, it has been a functioning democracy for nearly 25 years, and it has experienced neither civil war nor wars with any neighboring countries. However, other less developed countries have experienced or continue to experience sometimes catastrophic civil or international war. Three such countries are Afghanistan, Liberia, and Yemen. Afghanistan has been the scene of war since the late 1970s, when it was invaded by Soviet forces. After the collapse of the Soviet Union in 1991, various factions struggled for control of the government until it was taken over by the radical Islamist Taliban in 1996. Essentially, the Taliban forbade the education of girls and women. The United States ousted the Taliban in 2001, and since then, Afghanistan has worked to rebuild its educational system and give girls and women the opportunity to catch up to compensate for their missed schooling. However, many obstacles to gender equality remain.

Liberia faced two devastating civil wars in the 1990s, following a struggle between Americo-Liberians who had controlled the government for more than 100 years and other factions representing Indigenous Africans. These wars drained Liberia of resources that might otherwise have been devoted to education. Poverty and insufficient funds have made it very difficult for Liberia to achieve gender inequality. Yemen has also experienced civil war, which is linked in part to conflict between Sunni and Shiite Muslims. Saudi Arabia, whose residents are almost all Sunni Muslims, has intervened on behalf of the government that was displaced from Yemen's capital city of Sanaa by Shiite Houthi rebels. Thousands of school buildings in Yemen have been bombed, burned, or otherwise destroyed or damaged heavily while others have been converted to military installations.

Two significant exceptions to gender inequality with respect to education in less developed countries include the Philippines and Namibia. The Philippines, although regarded as a less developed county, does not experience the degree of dire poverty associated with countries such as Malawi. However, as compared to many less developed countries, gender inequality in education is lacking in the Philippines. This has been attributed to the general expectation in Filipino society that daughters are expected to care for their parents in their old age. Many Filipino parents recognize the value of education in that their daughters will be able to earn more money to support themselves in the future. Namibia is one of few African countries in which literacy rates for women are higher than those for men. This difference has been explained in part on the basis of government commitment to gender equality in education, including a government office with specific responsibility for gender-related issues. Namibia is a stable democracy with a per capita income higher than the per capita incomes of many other African countries, and its stability and relative wealth contribute also to Namibia's success in overcoming gender inequality in education.

AFGHANISTAN

The Islamic Republic of Afghanistan is a landlocked country in central Asia, with a land area of approximately 250,000 square miles. As of 2022, Afghanistan's population was approximately 39 million. The population is highly diverse. The Pashtun, most of whom live in southern and central Afghanistan, comprise about 42 percent of the population. The next largest national groups are the Tajiks, with approximately 25 percent, and the Uzbeks and Hazaras with about 10 percent each.

Present-day Afghanistan has been contested among various empires, kingdoms, and regimes from East Asia, Central Asia, South Asia, the Middle East, and Europe for thousands of years. More than 2,000 years ago, it was ruled by the Persian-based Achaemenid Empire for several hundred years before being taken over by Alexander the Great in approximately 340 BC. In the seventh century AD, it was invaded by forces from the Umayyad Caliphate, which was headquartered in Damascus in present-day Syria. The Umayyads brought Islam to present-day Afghanistan. After the collapse of the Umayyad Caliphate, parts of Afghanistan were governed by Mongols, Persians, Indians, and Central Asians.

During the nineteenth century, European colonial powers began to move into what is now Afghanistan. Russia expanded from the north and Britain from the south. The two countries recognized Afghanistan's role as a buffer state and established its boundaries, which with minor adjustments remain in place today. In 1979, Soviet troops invaded Afghanistan. The invasion was resisted by many Afghans who were supplied with money and weapons from the United States, Pakistan, and Saudi Arabia. As many as 1 million Afghan military personnel and civilians lost their lives as war continued over the next 10 years before Soviet troops were withdrawn as the Soviet Union collapsed.

After the Soviets left, a civil war between various factions struggling over control of the Afghan government began. War has continued without interruption to the present day. In 1996, the Taliban seized control of the country. The Taliban regime became known for its very harsh interpretation and imposition of Islamic Sharia laws, including the suppression of women. This suppression of women has affected gender-related issues with respect to education ever since. The Taliban also provided support to the radical Islamic terrorist organization known as Al Qaeda, which used Afghanistan as its base of operations. After a terrorist attack on the United States initiated by Al Qaeda on September 11, 2001, claimed 3,000 lives, the United States began military operations in Afghanistan with the intent of toppling the Taliban regime. American forces have remained in Afghanistan ever since. Although the Taliban regime was ousted and democratic elections were held, the Taliban remained a significant force. In 2021, the Taliban regained control of the government and American troops were withdrawn from the country.

Education in Afghanistan

Formal education in Afghanistan dates back to the early twentieth century. However, Afghanistan's long history of civil war has had a profound impact on the provision of education throughout the country. These impacts continue today, and they affect girls in particular. Afghanistan maintains one of the highest birth rates in the world, and as a result, it has a very low median age. More than half of Afghans are less than 18 years of age. Thus, the need for education remains high. Afghanistan faces a shortage of classrooms and learning materials, and some children attend school in tents.

Education in Afghanistan is managed by the state's Ministry of Education. A 2008 law mandated that nine years of formal schooling was compulsory. The structure of education includes six years of primary education followed by three years of lower secondary education and three years of high school. High school students can choose between an academic track that prepares students for college and a vocational track that prepares them for direct entry into the labor force. The languages of instruction include English along with Pashto and Dari, which are the two most frequently spoken languages throughout the country.

Although education in Afghanistan is compulsory for nine years, in fact large numbers of children do not attend school for a variety of reasons. As is the case in many less developed countries, many Afghan families rely on their children's labor especially in the agricultural sector. Girls are often expected to perform household duties, including taking care of younger siblings. Some parents regard formal schooling as a waste of their children's time. Access to education is also impeded by geographical factors in rural areas. Much of Afghanistan is mountainous, and there are relatively few schools located within walking distance of many rural villages. The threat of natural disasters including earthquakes and floods has also been a concern.

Safety is a major concern as well. Violence in Afghan schools has been commonplace for many years. Many students, as well as many teachers, have been killed or injured while attending school. Afghanistan has also experienced a shortage of teachers, in part because of the large number of children relative to the overall population living in the country. Moreover, since the civil war began in Afghanistan many teachers have left the country, many as refugees. Thousands of teachers in Afghanistan have been murdered over the past 40 years. Given the frequency of armed conflict, some parents fear that their children are in danger of being kidnapped or victimized by violence while attending school or while traveling between home and school. For these and other reasons, literacy rates in Afghanistan remain low. As of 2015, only about 39 percent of male Afghan adults and about 24 percent of female Afghan adults were literate. Post-Taliban governments made efforts to remedy this situation, but with only partial success.

Gender and Education in Afghanistan

Major differences in literacy rates between females and males reflect the ongoing issues with respect to the education of girls and women in Afghanistan. Even in 2019, nearly two decades after the Taliban government had been initially ousted by U.S. forces, it was estimated that only about one-third of Afghan girls of school age were actually attending school.

In the late 1990s, the Taliban government of Afghanistan placed severe restrictions on the formal education of girls. After the Taliban regime was ousted, girls such as these began returning to classrooms although female literacy rates in Afghanistan remain well below those of males. (U.S. Agency for International Development)

By the time the Taliban took power in 1996, the educational structure of Afghanistan was already very fragile in light of more than 15 years of civil war. After taking control of the government, the Taliban issued policies that forbade girls from attending school. The regime closed schools for girls, for whom formal education was no longer permitted. Female students attending colleges and universities were also expelled. Some of the schools for girls that remained open were bombed, burned, or attacked using firearms or poisoned gas. Teachers who tried to keep these schools open were faced with death threats, with some killed outright. By 2001, it has been estimated that only about 3 percent of Afghan girls of school age were actually attending school.

After the Taliban were ousted, post-Taliban governments initiated efforts to once again provide access to education for girls. However, these efforts were not fully successful, as is evidenced by the two-thirds of Afghan girls of school age who are not attending school. Many of the pressures that Afghan education faces in general have particularly strong impacts on girls and women. Afghanistan remains a highly traditional society. Not only do some parents rely on the labor of their daughters as well as their sons, but some believe also that formal education diverts girls away from their traditional roles as wives and mothers. Afghanistan's high birth rate is linked to the prevalence of early marriage, with more than half of Afghan women married before reaching the age of 18.

Between 2003 and 2021, the Taliban remained strong in some areas of Afghanistan, especially in the southern part of the country, and these pressures have been particularly prevalent in these areas. In some places, girls who are allowed to go to school at all are permitted only to attend religious schools or madrassas where the curriculum is limited largely to the study of Islamic principles. Also, religious traditions sometimes do not allow girls to go to school unless they are taught by female teachers. The shortage of female teachers, exacerbated by Taliban policies, has meant that large numbers of Afghan girls remain away from school.

The United Nations, the United States, and other developed countries have invested considerable effort in addressing the profound gender inequalities that plague the educational process in Afghanistan. However, there remain considerable barriers to overcoming these issues, and there is much progress still to be made. How this might be affected by the Taliban's recapture of the government remains to be seen.

Further Reading

Human Rights Watch, "'I won't be a doctor, and one day you'll be sick': Girls' access to education in Afghanistan," October 17, 2017, https://www.hrw.org/report/2017/10/17/i-wont-be-doctor-and-one-day-youll-be-sick/girls-access-education-afghanistan#. Retrieved on January 8, 2018.

Zafar Shayan, "Gender inequality in education in Afghanistan: Access and barriers," *Open Journal of Philosophy*, 5 (2015), pp. 277–284, https://www.researchgate.net/publication/276167701_Gender_Inequality_in_Education_in_Afghanistan_Access_and_Barriers. Retrieved on January 8, 2019.

Theirworld, "Changing attitudes is key to getting more Afghan girls in school," November 27, 2017, https://reliefweb.int/report/afghanistan/changing-attitudes-key-getting-more-afghan-girls-school. Retrieved on May 1, 2022.

Camille Wilson, "10 facts about girls' education in Afghanistan," The Borgen Project, July 3, 2018, https://borgenproject.org/facts-about-girls-education-in-afghanistan/. Retrieved on January 8, 2019.

AUSTRALIA

The Commonwealth of Australia includes the entire continent of Australia, along with the island of Tasmania and several smaller islands. Its land area is nearly 3 million square miles. The population of Australia as of 2022 was about 26 million. Most Australians live along its coastlines, especially in the major metropolitan areas of Adelaide, Brisbane, Melbourne, Perth, and Sydney. Much of interior Australia consists of very dry desert terrain that is uninhabited or sparsely populated.

Anthropologists believe that the ancestors of today's Indigenous Australians, who were often referred to as "Aborigines," first settled in Australia between 40,000 and 60,000 years ago. Today, the term "Aborigine" is regarded as derogatory. Instead, descendants of the original inhabitants of Australia are referred to as Aboriginal Australians or Indigenous Australians. Between 500,000 and 1,000,000 Indigenous Australians are believed to have lived in Australia at the time of European contact in the late eighteenth century. Captain James Cook (1728–1779) claimed Australia for the United Kingdom in 1770. The British established a penal colony near the site of present-day Sydney in 1788. This penal colony eventually became the colony of New South Wales. Australia's other major cities were founded over the next several decades, and each became the political and financial center of its colony. Many Indigenous Australians died from exposure to European diseases, and many of those who survived were driven into less hospitable territory in the interior.

By the end of the nineteenth centuries, the colonies of New South Wales, Queensland, South Australia, Tasmania, Victoria, and Western Australia had been established. These six colonies united in 1901 to form the Commonwealth of Australia, which became a Dominion within the British Empire. Australia became completely independent in 1942 but remains part of the British Commonwealth of Nations. Each of the six former colonies became one of Australia's states, each of which has considerable autonomy as is the case in the United States. Australia also includes the sparsely populated Northern Territory along with the Australian Capital Territory that contains the capital city of Canberra.

Education in Australia

In Australia, each of the six states along with the territory of Northern Australia and the Australian Capital Territory has formal responsibility for the provision of education. Specifics of the educational process vary slightly between the states. Education is compulsory between the age of 5 in Tasmania and the age of 6 in the other states until age 15 through 17, depending on the state. About two-thirds of Australian students attend public schools. The remainder are enrolled in Roman Catholic schools or "independent" schools, some of which are operated by other religious denominations. Public schooling is free, although parents or guardians are required to pay fees for uniforms, school supplies, and textbooks.

In general, education in Australia begins with seven or eight years of primary school, starting with kindergarten. Primary school is followed by three or four years of secondary school and two years of senior secondary school. English is the language of instruction, although bilingual education is provided in some areas where substantial numbers of Indigenous Australians or non-English-speaking immigrants live. As is the case with most highly developed countries, literacy is nearly universal in Australia. In recent years, however, there is concern that the general quality of Australian education has been declining. In particular, critics have noted a decline in enrollment in STEM disciplines, especially among girls. In addition, Australia is the only developed country in the world that does not require high school graduates to have completed courses in mathematics.

Gender and Education in Australia

The history of education of girls in Australia parallels the history of education in many other developed countries. Historically, formal education and especially higher education was limited largely to boys. During the late twentieth and early twenty-first centuries, gender equality in access to formal education has been achieved largely. However, several issues associated with gender and education remain.

The various colonies that comprised present-day Australia began to establish public schools in the nineteenth century. Both boys and girls attended school. Once both sexes achieved basic literacy and numeracy, however, boys were often taught higher mathematics, geography, and science. On the other hand, girls were taught domestic skills such as sewing, knitting, and cooking. Girls generally received little instruction in more advanced academic subjects until the twentieth century.

The Australian government issued its first formal plan for gender equity in education in 1984 and updated this plan in 1996. The plan was developed into a Framework for Action on Gender Equity in Schooling, which can be accessed at http://www.curriculum.edu.au/verve/_resources/genderframwk1-22.pdf. It was based on recognition that gender and gender-related issues impact educational outcomes. It took into consideration gender roles in that boys tended to choose traditionally male-dominated fields and courses such as those associated with the STEM disciplines. Although many girls were steered away from these subjects, those girls who did take these subjects tended to do as well or better than boys. Despite these successes, these girls were less likely to obtain high-level jobs in the STEM fields as compared to boys and young men. As of 2018, according to government statistics only about 16 percent of jobs in STEM fields in Australia were held by women.

Cultural factors as well as the impacts of sexual harassment, bullying, and other behaviors that were contrary to the idea that school should be a safe environment for girls were also taken into consideration. Sex-segregated classrooms remain

Do Girls Need to Work Harder?

Although literacy along with access to education is universal in the United States, studies have indicated that many teachers perceive girls to be less able than boys in various aspects of learning, particularly in mathematics and science. Because they believe that girls are less capable of learning these concepts than boys, these teachers expect that in order for girls to do as well as boys in tests, the girls must work harder than the boys. As one teacher who participated in one study put it, "The girls can do just as well as the boys if they work hard enough." In the long run, such perceptions may be discouraging girls from entering the STEM fields, reinforcing the long-standing tendency for girls to be less likely to enter STEM-related professions as adults.

Source: Joseph Cimpian, "How our education system undermines gender equity," Brookings Institute, April 23, 2018, https://www.brookings.edu/blog/brown-center-chalkboard/2018/04/23/how-our-education-system-undermines-gender-equity/. Retrieved on March 14, 2020.

common in many Australian schools. This practice has been seen as reinforcing stereotypes relating gender to achievement, although some authorities have expressed the view single-sex schooling promotes rather than inhibits general inequality in schools and beyond.

Research about the life experiences of Australian girls between the ages of 10 and 17 reinforces the ongoing issues associated with true gender equality in the country's schools. These issues involved equality both in school and at home. Nearly 98 percent of girls surveyed indicated that they experienced gender inequality at school, at home, in sports, and/or in the media. Schools were criticized for failure to respond to or encourage girls' educational aspirations. Girls felt that they were not given the same opportunity as boys to achieve leadership roles. In response, some educators have advocated elimination of gender-based school uniforms and sex-segregated classrooms. However, many see that the larger issue is gender inequality in the workplace, and it is argued that promoting gender equality in school will be key to reducing gender inequality later in life.

Further Reading

SBS News, "Up to 98 per cent of Australian girls feel gender inequality, survey suggests," October 11, 2017, https://www.sbs.com.au/news/up-to-98-per-cent-of-australian-girls -feel-gender-inequality-survey-suggests. Retrieved on January 12, 2019.

Deborah Towns, "Sexism needs to be challenged in schools; not just workplaces," the-conversation.com, March 7, 2018, http://theconversation.com/six-ways-australias -education-system-is-failing-our-kids-32958. Retrieved on January 12, 2019.

The Uni Tutor, "What impact does gender have on education in Australia?" n.d., https:// www.theunitutor.com/impact-gender-education-australia/. Retrieved on January 11, 2019.

Rachel Wilson, Bronwen Dalton, and Chris Baumann, "Six ways Australia's education is failing our kids," theconversation.com, March 15, 2015, http://theconversation.com /six-ways-australias-.education-system-is-failing-our-kids-32958. Retrieved on January 12, 2019.

LIBERIA

The Republic of Liberia is located along the Atlantic Coast of West Africa. It has a land area of about 43,000 square miles and a population of 5.3 million as of 2022.

In 1816, the American Colonization Society was founded. The purpose of the Society was to establish a homeland for freed slaves of African ancestry living in the United States. The society purchased Cape Mesurado on the African coast in 1821 and began shipping freed slaves to the area. Over the next 40 years, about 20,000 freed slaves from the United States and the European colonies in the Caribbean moved to Africa. In 1847, Liberia declared its independence. Liberia and Ethiopia are the only African countries that have never been a formal colony of one or more European powers.

Descendants of these freed slaves, who are known as Americo-Liberians, make up only about 5 percent or Liberia's population today. However, Americo-Liberians have dominated Liberia's government and economy for most of the country's history. In 1980, the government of Liberia that had long been dominated by Americo-Liberians was overthrown in a coup d'état led by Samuel K. Doe (1951–1990). Subsequently, various Indigenous factions fought for control of the government. More than 200,000 Liberians were killed in civil wars that lasted throughout most of the 1990s and into the early twenty-first century. Thousands of other Liberians fled the country as refugees.

Democracy returned to Liberia in 2005, when the Harvard-educated Ellen Johnson Sirleaf (1938–) was elected President and in doing so became the first woman elected as head of state in Africa. After serving two six-year terms, Sirleaf was succeeded by the internationally recognized soccer star George Weah (1966–).

Education in Liberia

The Ministry of Education is responsible for overseeing formal education throughout the country in Liberia. In doing so, the ministry has had to respond to challenges associated with the Liberian civil wars and their aftermath. The civil wars caused great destruction to Liberian education, with the result that Liberia's literacy rate today is only about 60 percent.

The educational structure in Liberia includes three years of preprimary school for children aged three to five. Children then attend primary school for nine years. This includes six years of lower basic or primary school followed by three years of upper primary school. These nine years of schooling are compulsory. Students may then continue to high school and can choose between academic and vocational tracks. Upon completion of the upper primary school and again after completing high school, students must pass standardized examinations to move on to the next level. English is the language of instruction.

Liberia's educational system faces significant challenges, many of which are common to other less developed countries. As with many countries in sub-Saharan Africa, Liberia has a high birth rate and a young population. Accordingly, Liberia is experiencing a shortage of classroom space, educational facilities, and textbooks and learning materials. There is also a shortage of qualified teachers.

In part because of these problems, and in part because of the legacy of Liberia's civil wars, it has been estimated that less than half of Liberia's school-age children actually attend school. School attendance rates are especially low in rural areas, where some parents rely on the labor of their children for day-to-day survival and discourage their children from going to school. in addition, lack of availability of educational facilities in rural areas has forced some students to move temporarily to cities to be schooled. Rural parents may be reluctant to allow their children to do so and to pay for the associated expenses. In 2012, at the end of Sirleaf's first term, it was estimated that about 64 percent of girls and 87 percent of boys of school age in the capital city of Monrovia were attending school. However, school attendance rates in rural Liberia were estimated to be only 33 percent for girls and 45 percent for boys, respectively.

In 2017, the Liberian government issued a strategic plan entitled "Getting to Best Education Sector Plan: 2017–2021." Its objectives included policies and practices intended to remedy the ongoing issues with Liberian education. These included improved assessment, accountability, and quality management; improved access to formal education; the provision of quality educational materials; and improved training of teachers. Management of some schools has been turned over to private operators, some international and some local. The government is anticipating that the overall quality of education in Liberia will be improved after these private-public partnerships have been implemented.

Gender and Education in Liberia

Relative to most other countries, Liberia ranks low in general measures of gender equality. In 2013, according to the United Nations Development Programme, Liberia ranked 143rd of the 147 countries surveyed on its Gender Equality Index. Inequality has been associated with continued reliance on traditional gender roles, in which women are expected to bear and raise children, maintain the household, and perform traditional tasks such as cleaning and cooking. This is reinforced by the general expectation in Liberian society that when a girl marries, her labor contributes to her husband's family as opposed to her birth family.

Maintaining these traditional gender roles in Liberia, as is the case in other less developed countries, implies that boys are privileged over girls with respect to access to education. Many families will bear the costs, including short-term loss of labor, associated with educating their sons but not their daughters. Extended family members are also more likely to provide funds to educate boys, but not to educate girls. Accordingly, many girls who wish to attend schools must raise the costs themselves or find other sources of revenue. Sponsors may demand sexual favors in return for these tuition costs. Sexual assaults of female students and teachers have also been reported, and in some cases, teenage girls are forced into prostitution in order to afford schooling.

Recognizing these issues, one of the specific goals of the "Getting to Best Education Sector Plan" was "mainstreaming gender and school health across the education sector." The means of achieving this goal have included emphasis on recruiting and training more female teachers, given that only about a quarter of Liberia's teachers are women. Female teachers are regarded often as more effective role models for young girls in Liberian schools, and their presence can help to mitigate the impacts of ongoing inequalities and biases against women in Liberian society. International organizations such as UNICEF have been instrumental in developing programs to encourage girls to go to school and help them succeed. For example, all-female study groups have been established as safe spaces within which girls can voice their concerns about education, including dealing with sexual violence and sexual harassment. Efforts are being made also to persuade parents about the long-run economic value of educating their daughters.

Gender Parity in Education Globally

Most countries throughout the world are achieving gender parity in primary education, with approximately the same number of boys and girls enrolled in school. However, according to data compiled by the United Nations International Children's Emergency Fund (UNICEF) primary school enrollment among girls continues to lag behind that among boys in some countries, notably in sub-Saharan Africa, South Asia, and the Middle East. At the secondary school level, these disparities are more noticeable—again, in places such as sub-Saharan Africa although girls outnumber boys slightly in a few less developed countries. Gender disparities are attributed to poverty, lack of access to schooling, cultural prejudices, and early marriage and childbearing.

Source: United Nations International Children's Emergency Fund, "Gender and education," 2020, https://data.unicef.org/topic/gender/gender-disparities-in-education/. Retrieved on March 14, 2020.

Further Reading

David Woods Baysah, "Liberia launches 'getting to best in education' program," Global Partnership for Education, September 10, 2018, https://www.globalpartnership.org/blog/liberia-launches-getting-best-education-program. Retrieved on January 8, 2019.

Felicia Dahlquist, "Incredible women are fighting for girls' education in Liberia but there's a long way to go," *Huffington Post*, March 20, 2017, https://www.huffingtonpost.co.uk/felicia-dalhquist/girls-education_b_15409934.html?guccounter=1&guce_referrer_us=aHR0cHM6Ly93d3cuZ29vZ2xlLmNvbS8&guce_referrer_cs=w9eKaMn88Ivrn GrUhw4Ztw. Retrieved on January 8, 2019.

Nyamah Dunbar, "Growth of girls' education lags in Liberia," *UM News*, August 18, 2015, https://www.umnews.org/en/news/commentary-growth-of-girls-education-lags-in-liberia. Retrieved on January 8, 2017.

Macsu Hill, "Girls' education in Liberia: Challenges and opportunities," organizeforliberia.org, May 26, 2017, https://www.organizeforliberia.org/blog/girls-education-in-liberia-challenges-and-opportunities/. Retrieved in January 8, 2019.

David Laws, "Liberia's big school experiment," BBC News, January 3, 2018, https://www.bbc.com/news/business-42413639. Retrieved on January 8, 2019.

MALAWI

The Republic of Malawi, located in the highlands of inland east-central Africa, has a land area of nearly 46,000 square miles. As of 2022, its population was about 20 million.

Bantu peoples have lived in present-day Malawi for the past thousand years. The Bantu Maravi Empire (whose name inspired the name of independent Malawi) began to rule the area in the fifteenth century. During the nineteenth century, the Maravi Empire fell apart after invasions from other tribes. The British and the

Portuguese, who had established a colony in neighboring Mozambique, claimed the area, but Britain took control of the region in 1890. The colony was renamed Nyasaland in 1907.

In 1953, Britain joined Nyasaland to the neighboring Northern Rhodesia and Southern Rhodesia (present-day Zambia and Zimbabwe, respectively) to create the Federation of Rhodesia and Nyasaland. Following pro-independence agitation, Nyasaland became a self-governing colony in 1963 and a fully independent country in 1964. For the first three decades of independence, Malawi was a one-party state with a repressive regime ruled by Hastings Banda (1898–1997). In the early 1990s, international pressure and internal protests resulted in the elimination of Banda's autocratic rule, and Malawi transitioned successfully to become a multiparty democracy. However, Malawi remains one of the poorest countries in the world, with over half of Malawians living on less than US$1.25 per day.

Despite Banda's rigid, autocratic, and socially conservative regime, Malawi during that period was regarded as a somewhat progressive country with respect to gender-related issues. Banda encouraged education and promoted family planning at a time when many Malawian women were expected to raise large families while contributing in other ways to their families' well-being.

Education in Malawi

The formal educational structure in Malawi includes eight years of primary school followed by four years of secondary school. The Revised Education Act of 2012 also made eight years of primary school compulsory. It is free although parents are expected to pay various fees such as the cost of school supplies. Parents are also responsible for transportation. Because access to education is often absent in rural areas, some students attend secondary schools in cities. In addition, many youths are expected to provide their labor to help support their families. For these reasons, many Malawian children do not actually attend school. In 2007, it was estimated that about 75 percent of Malawi's children of primary school age were actually enrolled in primary school, although the majority do not complete the full eight-year course. And, as of 2013, only about a quarter of students who had completed compulsory primary school continued on to secondary school.

Malawi is a multilingual society. English is the country's official language, but most Malawians speak one of several Indigenous languages at home. Chichewa is spoken at home by about half of the population, with many other languages spoken by significant numbers of people. During the first four years of primary school, Malawian children are taught in their local Indigenous language. English becomes the official language of instruction in the fifth year of primary school and beyond.

In 2016, the United Nations estimated that about 66 percent of Malawians were literate, including 73 percent of men and 59 percent of women. Literacy rates are higher among young Malawians, indicating that the school system has done at least a reasonable job in providing education. However, education in Malawi faces many problems that are common in less developed countries including shortage

These students are attending Kande Beach Primary School in Malawi. Malawi is one of many less developed countries where girls are less likely to be educated than boys. Some Malawian parents believe that they cannot afford to educate their daughters, who are needed to help take care of the household and who may not need formal education after marriage. (Martin Mwaura | Dreamstime.com)

of facilities, high ratios of pupils to teachers, corruption in school funding and administration, and a lack of accountability with respect to individual schools. As of 2016, it was reported that there were more than 80 pupils per teacher in Malawi. In rural areas, the absence of schools means that children have to travel long distances to school. This becomes almost impossible during the rainy season when unpaved roads become all but impassable.

Recognizing ongoing problems with education and as a follow-up to the Revised Education Act, in 2013 the Malawian government issued its Education Sector Implementation Plan II. Several of the plan's objectives were in response to these problems. These responses included building more classrooms, supplying more textbooks and learning materials, and preparing "motivated and high-performing" teachers.

Gender and Education in Malawi

Ongoing issues with gender inequality associated with Malawian education are evident through comparing male and female literacy rates even today. Although the Revised Education Act and the Education Sector Implementation Plan recognize issues associated with gender inequality in education in Malawi, significant issues remain as the Ministry of Education, Science, and Technology makes efforts to address this inequality.

Girls are less likely to attend school or, if enrolled, drop out for several reasons. The gender gap in school attendance is particularly high for teenagers of secondary school age. An important factor is parental need for their daughters' labor. Young girls are often responsible for maintaining the household, including caring for younger brothers and sisters.

Early marriage followed soon by pregnancy generally ends school attendance of teenage girls. According to a 2015 study, nearly half of girls in secondary schools in Malawi who dropped out did so because of marriage or and/or pregnancy. In 2017, however, the legal minimum age of marriage was raised from 15 to 18 years via constitutional amendment. In addition, as in other less developed countries, girls of secondary school age are subject to sexual assaults and sexual harassment on the part of male fellow students and teachers.

In 2017, recognizing the problems in education that affected girls especially, the government of Malawi issued a plan directed specifically at addressing issues of gender inequality in education. Priorities associated with this plan included making concerted efforts to reduce dropout rates, training more female teachers who can serve as role models for young girls who do attend school and emphasizing more coordination and efficiency in developing and implementing policies associated with gender inequality in education.

Further Reading

Jill Filipovic, "In 2014, it's unacceptable for girls in Malawi to be unable to go to school," *The Guardian*, January 1, 2014, https://www.theguardian.com/commentisfree/2014/jan/01/malawi-girls-education-poverty-aid-corruption. Retrieved on January 10, 2019.

Sally Robertson, "Improving girls' education in Malawi," Australian Council for Educational Research, October 10, 2017, https://rd.acer.org/article/improving-girls-education-in-malawi. Retrieved on January 10, 2019.

Rachel Williams, "The struggle to finish school in Malawi," *The Guardian*, March 12, 2012, https://www.theguardian.com/education/2012/mar/12/education-school-malawi-girls-millennium. Retrieved on January 10, 2019.

NAMIBIA

The Republic of Namibia is located in southwestern Africa, north of South Africa, and borders the Atlantic Ocean. Its land area is approximately 319,000 square miles. With a population of about 2.7 million as of 2022, Namibia is the most sparsely populated country in sub-Saharan Africa. Much of the country is arid, and it includes portions of the Namib Desert along the coast and the Kalahari Desert inland.

The first inhabitants of Namibia were the San people. The San were called "Bushmen," which is regarded today as a derogatory exonym, by Europeans. About 2,000 years ago, other people migrated to Namibia from the north, east, and south. European mariners began to visit the Namibian coast during the fifteenth and sixteenth centuries. However, in light of the dry climate and lack of arable land, the Europeans did not begin to penetrate inland areas until the nineteenth century. In 1884, Germany claimed present-day Namibia and named the colony German Southwest Africa. When the Treaty of Versailles that was signed after World War I forced Germany to give up its overseas colonies, the League of Nations placed German Southwest Africa under a South African mandate. The South Africans renamed the colony Southwest Africa. After South Africa achieved control of Southwest Africa, many white farmers moved northward into Southwest Africa. Following World War II, South Africa applied the principle of "apartheid" to its Southwest African colony, privileging whites who made up about 14 percent of the colony's population as of 1960 but controlled most of its land and natural resources.

While colonies throughout Africa were gaining independence in the 1950s and 1960s, South Africa refused to grant independence to Southwest Africa. In 1971, the International Court of Justice ruled that the continued occupation of Southwest Africa by South Africa was in violation of international law. However, South Africa ignored this decision and continued to support Southwest Africa's white-dominated colonial government. Negotiations about independence took place in the 1970s and 1980s, and the former colony was granted independence under its current name in 1990. Namibia has substantial mineral resources, making it one of the wealthier countries in sub-Saharan Africa. The country has been successful also in establishing and maintaining a multiparty democracy after having become independent.

Education in Namibia

In most less developed countries that lack universal literacy, boys are more likely to have attended or completed school than have girls. As a result, literacy rates in these countries are generally higher among males than among females. In Namibia, the reverse is true. During the 2008–2012 period, the literacy rate among boys and young men aged 15–24 was 83.2 percent, whereas the literacy rate among girls and young women aged 15–24 was 90.6 percent.

Education in Namibia is managed centrally by the Ministry of Education, Arts, and Culture. Schooling is compulsory for 10 years, from the ages of 6 through 16. Public education is free, although parents or guardians are expected to pay for school uniforms, textbooks, and other supplies. Prior to independence, schools in Southwest Africa were managed in accordance with the principles of "apartheid," and the white minority received the most educational resources. Many non-whites received little or no formal education. After independence, the new government of Namibia initiated efforts to redress these disparities by instituting a unified system of providing education. The primary language of instruction was changed from Afrikaans to English. In support of this goal, about 20 percent of the Namibian government's budget is devoted to education. By 2005, about 95 percent of Namibian children between 6 and 16 were enrolled in school. In 2013, the government reinforced its policy of ensuring that public elementary schools were free to all Namibians, citing that many poor Namibians could not afford to pay the various fees that were charged by public schools.

Gender and Education in Namibia

Despite government efforts and commitment to public education, by the second decade of the twenty-first century some observers both within and outside Namibia began to question the government's success especially after educational outcomes were audited. Some critics went so far as to label the policy a failure, citing high dropout rates, low standardized test scores in English and mathematics, and a shortage of qualified teachers. One explanatory factor cited is the lack of diversity of Namibia's economy, which is dependent considerably on mining and agriculture. These economic sectors are dependent on global markets, and price declines result in substantial reductions in revenue available to the government for education and other purposes. In addition, many of Namibia's farmers are subsistence farmers and food for urban residents must be imported, further making the country dependent on worldwide markets for consumer products.

The audit also indicated that boys were considerably more likely to drop out of school as compared to girls, helping to explain the unusual gender differences in literacy rates in Namibia. This difference has been noted by the government, which via a series of policy statements since independence has committed itself to gender equality although women continue to be underrepresented in government and business and victimized by sexual assaults. Thus, although literacy rates among women exceed literacy rates among men, gender inequality in education in Namibia continues. The government regards education as a key to gender equality, and the government ministry that deals with gender-related issues is known as the Ministry of Gender Equality and Child Welfare. Strategies included in the ministry's plans include ensuring that pregnant adolescents or those with infants and small children can continue in school. Efforts are being made also to remove gender bias from textbooks and to encourage young women to pursue education in science, technology, education, and mathematics. However, the government's report also cited regional differences in female literacy rates and ongoing cultural bias against the education of young women. Despite Namibia's success in achieving success in female literacy, the consensus of observers and government officials is that there is much more to be done.

Further Reading

Brian Faust, "The unique history of education in Namibia," borgenproject.org, December 25, 2016, https://borgenproject.org/history-of-education-in-namibia/. Retrieved on October 23, 2018.

Government of Namibia, Ministry of Gender Equality and Child Welfare, "National Gender Policy (2010–2020)," March, 2010, http://www.africanchildforum.org/clr/policy%20 per%20country/namibia/namibia_gender_2010-2020_en.pdf. Retrieved on October 23, 2018.

Catherine Sasman, "Education under spotlight," *The Namibian*, June 8, 2011, https://web
.archive.org/web/20120531123130/http://www.namibian.com.na/news/full-story
/archive/2011/june/article/education-under-spotlight/. Retrieved on October 23, 2018.
United States Agency for International Development, "Namibia: Quality primary education," August 28, 2006, https://web.archive.org/web/20080816151933/http://www
.usaid.gov/na/so2.htm#39/. Retrieved on October 23, 2018.

PHILIPPINES

The Republic of the Philippines is located in the western Pacific Ocean, about
500 miles at its closest point off the coast of mainland Southeast Asia. It consists of
more than 7,500 islands, of which about 2,000 are inhabited. The total land area is
about 116,000 square miles. Its population was estimated at 112.5 million in 2022.

Archaeologists believe that the Philippines archipelago has been inhabited for
at least 50,000 years. Many kingdoms and chiefdoms arose beginning before 1000
BC, although at no time did any one kingdom control the entire archipelago. In
1521, however, Ferdinand Magellan visited the islands and claimed them for
Spain. In the late sixteenth century, Spain established political control over the
Philippines.

Spain remained in control of the Philippines until 1898, when sovereignty was
transferred to the United States after the Spanish-American War. The Americans
put down a pro-independence insurgency, and its control over the islands was
recognized in 1901. Japan invaded the Philippines in 1942, but the United States
regained control over the territory toward the end of World War II. The Philippines
became an independent country in 1946.

Education in the Philippines

Formal education in the Philippines was first introduced by the Spaniards in the
late sixteenth century. It was provided initially by the Roman Catholic Church. In
1863, the Spanish issued the Educational Decree of 1863. This policy mandated
that at least one primary school for boys and at least one primary school for girls be
established in each town. Schooling was free. Maintenance of these schools was the
responsibility of the local government, although the Roman Catholic Jesuit order
was responsible for the training of teachers.

Free public education continued during the period of American rule and again
after independence. A new constitution came into effect in 1987. Article XIV of
this constitution affirmed education as a fundamental right. Section 1 of Article
XIV reads: "The State shall protect and promote the right of all citizens to quality
education at all levels and shall take appropriate steps to make such education
accessible to all." As stipulated in Section 3(2), "[Schools] shall inculcate patriotism and nationalism, foster love of humanity, respect for human rights, appreciation of the role of national heroes in the historical development of the country,
teach the rights and duties of citizenship, strengthen ethical and spiritual values,

develop moral character and personal discipline, encourage critical and creative thinking, broaden scientific and technological knowledge, and promote vocational efficiency." Free primary education was made compulsory for all Filipino children. Today, education is compulsory from kindergarten through high school, although it remains difficult for the government to provide formal education in remote and isolated islands and other places. Nevertheless, the Philippines has obtained nearly universal literacy, with nearly 98 percent of the population able to read and write.

K-12 education in the Philippines is organized and managed at the national level, with the curriculum organized by the State Department of Education. Public education includes three levels: seven years of primary school from kindergarten through the sixth grade, four years of junior high school, and two years of senior high school. Tagalog (Filipino) and English are the primary languages of instruction. However, as of 2014 early primary education was also imparted in 19 regional languages that are spoken in various parts of the country, with a gradual transition to Filipino and English by the end of primary school. In areas with large Muslim populations in the southern part of the country, the Arabic language and "Islamic values" are also taught in public schools.

As is the case with other relatively less developed countries, the Philippines has struggled to implement these policies fully. Many children within the rapidly increasing Philippines population face overcrowded classes and a shortage of classrooms, teachers, and textbooks and other learning materials. These shortages are especially acute in the Philippines' growing cities. However, rates of school completion are higher in metropolitan areas relative to rural areas. In rural areas, in particular, education may not be affordable to parents who depend on their children's labor to make ends meet. The government must also deal with problems associated with lack of access to children living in isolated places, including small islands and remote regions even in the largest islands. For example, some rural villages or "barangays" can be accessed only by unpaved dirt roads that are impassable during the rainy season, or even only on foot.

Gender and Education in the Philippines

The Philippines is recognized as one of the most successful countries in the world with respect to gender equality in education. According to the World Economic Forum in 2016, the Philippines ranked fourth among the countries in the world with respect to gender equality in education behind only the far more developed Finland, Slovenia, and Ireland. What accounts for the Philippines' conspicuous success in this area?

Part of the explanation involves history. Formal education has been available to girls as well as to boys since the nineteenth century. For many years, literacy rates among men and women have remained nearly identical. Another key factor involves the intersection among education, the labor market, and Filipino culture. The Philippines is distinctive among other semideveloped countries in that many parents give considerable value to educating daughters as well as sons.

Standardized test scores generally confirm that girls do better in school than do boys. They are less likely to drop out and, on average, spend more years in school.

However, as in many countries young women who graduate from high school or college earn considerably less income than do young men. A substantial number of educated Filipinos move to more developed countries to practice their professions. In addition, many young Filipino women work abroad temporarily. Many work as domestic servants, factory workers, or in other low-status, low-wage occupations in more developed and higher-income countries such as Singapore, Australia, and the United Arab Emirates. Many parents encourage their daughters to remain in school and, if possible, continue to college in hopes that after graduating they can remain in the Philippines to earn higher salaries while working. This emphasis on educating young women may be related also to Filipino cultural norms in which daughters, rather than sons, are expected to support their parents and other relatives in their old age. This emphasis on educating girls seems to be particularly strong within relatively poor families, which are more dependent on female labor force participation as a form of social security.

Recognizing the concerns of this sort, in 2017 the Department of Education stated formally that it "commits to integrate the principles of gender equality, gender equity, gender sensitivity, nondiscrimination and human rights in the provision and governance of basic education." This policy specified that education in the Philippines was to be based on a gender-responsive framework, including issues of gender equality, human rights, and gender sensitivity across the K-12 curriculum. Gender-related differences in learning styles between girls and boys have also been investigated and taken into consideration in implementing these new policies.

Further Reading

Sara Gustafson, "In the Philippines, a school program shows diverging results for male and female students," International Food Policy Research Institute, IFPRI Blog: Research Post, March 13, 2018, http://www.ifpri.org/blog/philippines-school-program-shows -diverging-results-male-and-female-students. Retrieved on January 7, 2019.

Thessa A. Hernandez and Mario A. Cudiamat, "Integrating gender and development in the classroom: The case of Lucsuhin National High School, Department of Education-Philippines," *Knowledge E: Engaging Minds, Fourth Annual Research Conference on Higher Education*, (2018), pp. 1135–1141, https://knepublishing.com/index.php/Kne-Social /article/view/2430/5338. Retrieved on January 7, 2019.

Jurgette Honculada and Rosalinda Pineda Ofreneo, "The National Commission on the role of Filipino women, the women's movement, and gender mainstreaming in the Philippines," Manchester Open Hive, July 30, 2018, https://www.manchesteropenhive.com /view/9781526137494/9781526137494.00017.xml. Retrieved on January 7, 2019.

Republic of the Philippines, Department of Education, *Gender-Responsive Basic Education Policy*, http://www.deped.gov.ph/wp-content/uploads/2017/06/DO_s2017_032.pdf. Retrieved on January 7, 2019.

United Nations Educational, Scientific, and Cultural Organization, *World Data on Education: Philippines*, 2011, http://www.ibe.unesco.org/fileadmin/user_upload/Publications /WDE/2010/pdf-versions/Philippines.pdf. Retrieved on January 7, 2019.

YEMEN

The Republic of Yemen includes the southern and southwestern Arabian Peninsula in southwest Asia. Including more than 200 islands in the Gulf of Aden and the Arabian Sea south of the mainland, Yemen's land area is slightly over 200,000 square miles. Its population as of 2022 was approximately 31 million, more than 99 percent of whom live on the mainland.

With the Red Sea to the west and the Gulf of Aden and the Arabian Sea to the south, present-day Yemen has been an area of strategic importance and a major center for trade for thousands of years. The region has been contested among kingdoms based locally, elsewhere in the Middle East, and in Africa since ancient times. As Europeans began to colonize other parts of the world, they recognized Yemen's strategic and economic value. In 1838, the Sultan of Lahej ceded a territory along the coast of about 75 square miles to the British, who established the port of Aden. In order to protect its interests in Aden and to regulate trade through the Gulf of Aden and the Red Sea, the British worked to maintain naval control of these offshore areas. In 1872, Britain negotiated an informal agreement with the Ottoman Empire. This informal agreement, which granted the British control over coastal areas and the Ottomans control of the interior, was formalized by a treaty in 1904.

After the collapse of the Ottoman Empire during World War I, Yemenis in the Ottoman-controlled area declared independence. This area became known as North Yemen, which was a kingdom until the royal family was deposed in a coup d'état in 1962 and the country was renamed the Yemen Arab Republic. To the south, the British administered Aden as part of British India until the two areas were separated in 1937. Aden became independent in 1967. A Marxist regime took power in 1970 and renamed the country the People's Democratic Republic of South Yemen. North Yemen and South Yemen united as a single independent country in 1990, although civil war between northern and southern forces has broken out on several occasions since unification. Religious differences between Shiite and Sunni Muslims, who represent about 42 and 58 percent of the population, respectively, have contributed to ongoing civil war and political instability.

In 2015, civil war broke out once again between the government and Houthi rebels, who are known formally as Ansar Allah. The Houthi are based in northwestern Yemen, and many of its members belong to the Zaidi sect, which is an offshoot of the Shia branch of Islam. The Houthi took control of Yemen's capital city, Sanaa, and ousted the existing government from that city in 2015. In doing so, the Houthi assumed de facto control of the western portion of the country, including much of what had been North Yemen. Saudi Arabia intervened on behalf of the government, which was dominated by Sunni Muslims, against the Houthi, and war has continued ever since then. It has been estimated that more than 10,000 military personnel and civilians lost their lives between 2015 and 2018. In part because of the civil war, widespread famine broke out, and thousands of Yemeni citizens have perished as a result of starvation. International observers have estimated that millions more Yemenis are likely to be affected by and are at risk of starvation because of the ongoing famine. Civil war and famine have resulted in major disruptions in education in Yemen, making it difficult for authorities to manage the country's educational system.

Education in Yemen

Prior to unification, North Yemen and South Yemen implemented distinctive approaches to education. In North Yemen, emphasis was placed on religious instruction, and relatively few girls had access to formal schooling. Education in South Yemen was conducted only in haphazard fashion before independence was granted in 1967. By the 1970s, both countries had developed educational systems that included primary, lower secondary, and upper secondary schooling. These systems were merged, with greater instruction placed on secular subjects, after unification.

Today, education in Yemen is supervised by the government's Ministry of Education. K-12 education consists of six years of primary school, three years of lower secondary school, and three years of upper secondary school or high school. Arabic is the language of instruction. Primary and lower secondary schools are compulsory, although in practice many Yemeni children do not attend school. The percentage of children in Yemen who do attend school has dropped since civil war broke out in 2015. As of 2018, according to United Nations estimates, about 70 percent of Yemenis were literate. However, male literacy rates remain much higher among men than among women. According to the United Nations' 2018 estimates, 85 percent of men and 55 percent of women were literate. This gap was even higher outside Sanaa, Aden, and other major cities.

Schooling in Yemen is beset by problems common to less developed countries, including a shortage of classroom facilities, learning materials, and teachers and parental resistance to formal education on short-term economic grounds. Yemen made considerable progress in improving its educational system during the first decade of the twenty-first century. By 2013, government officials estimated that more than 95 percent of Yemeni children of school age were enrolled in school. However, civil war has devastated education in Yemen since the outbreak of civil war in 2015, making these ongoing problems more acute. By late 2018, the United Nations International Children's Emergency Fund (UNICEF) estimated that as many as 80 percent of Yemeni children had become dependent on international humanitarian aid.

Another impact of the war has been an even more acute shortage of teachers. Many Yemeni teachers were not paid for at least two years after war broke out, forcing them to leave the country or to seek alternative employment to support themselves and their families. More than 2,000 school buildings have been heavily damaged or destroyed during the war. Other schools have been closed so that the buildings can be converted into military installations or shelters for people displaced by the conflict. Moreover, boys attending school run the risk of being conscripted as child soldiers while children of both sexes risk being killed, robbed, or kidnapped while traveling to and from school.

Gender and Education in Yemen

That there remains a large gap in rates of literacy between men and women in Yemen illustrates the gender inequality associated with Yemeni society and culture. These inequalities have become accentuated as a result of the civil war, which has had a particularly devastating impact on women and children.

Yemeni society is highly patriarchal, with women expected to care for children and maintain households rather than work outside the home. As in other countries, Yemen's patriarchal norms have discouraged the education of girls. This has been reinforced by the prevalence of child marriage. Since war has broken out, the percentage of Yemeni girls who are married before reaching 18 has increased considerably. Between 2017 and 2018 alone, this rate increased from 52 percent to 66 percent. This increase has been attributed to war and resulting famine—a family that marries off a daughter has one less mouth to feed. Other cultural factors have also been recognized as contributing to low rates of school attendance among Yemeni girls. For example, traditional cultural norms discourage or forbid girls from being taught by male teachers or to attend mixed-sex classes in school, and some parents have refused to send their daughters to schools that are not sex-segregated.

Since the outbreak of the civil war, thousands of Yemeni men have been killed or have died from diseases and other war-related causes. This has meant that large numbers of Yemeni women have been forced to become heads of their households. Lacking education and often illiterate, these women often find it very difficult to earn enough money to support themselves and their children. In general, Yemen's educational system faces a crisis in that residents of this war-torn country must put aside long-running educational goals in the interest of present survival. Whether Yemen will resume progress in its educational sector if and when the current civil war winds down remains to be seen.

Further Reading

Merna Ibrahim, "8 facts about girls' education in Yemen," The Borgen Project, December 10, 2019, https://borgenproject.org/girls-education-in-yemen/. Retrieved on January 23, 2022.

Jayendrina Singha Ray, "Breaking down cultural barriers to girls' education in Yemen," The Borgen Project, June 10, 2018, https://borgenproject.org/breaking-down-cultural -barriers-to-girls-education-in-yemen/. Retrieved on January 9, 2019.

Lisa Schlein, "UNICEF: Education a major casualty of Yemen's civil war," *VOA News*, September 16, 2018, https://www.voanews.com/a/education-a-major-casualty-of-yemen -s-war/4573629.html. Retrieved on January 9, 2019.

Mareike Transfeld, "Yemen's education at a tipping point: Youth between their future and present survival," *Project on Middle East Political Science*, January 12, 2018,

https://pomeps.org/2018/01/12/yemens-education-system-at-a-tipping-point-youth
-between-their-future-and-present-survival/. Retrieved on January 9, 2019.
Neha Wadekar, "A man-made war paid for by women and children," *Washington Post*,
December 13, 2018, https://www.washingtonpost.com/graphics/2018/world/yemen
-civil-war-women-children/?utm_term=.d0af88734b46. Retrieved on January 9, 2019.

UNITED STATES

The history of relationships between gender and education parallels the experience of many developed countries, including Australia. Since colonial days, the United States has experienced a long history of inequality and discrimination against women with respect to education. Gender inequality in access to education and in educational outcomes has largely been eliminated. However, various factors continue to contribute to various gender-related inequalities in American education.

As indicated elsewhere in this volume, and as was the case in Protestant northern Europe, the Puritans and other Dissenters who first settled in colonial New England placed great emphasis on literacy for both men and women. The ability to read and write was considered essential for everyone so as to be able to read and interpret the Bible. Towns throughout New England were required to provide common schools for children of both sexes. Beyond basic literacy, however, there were few opportunities for women to continue their education. Some New England communities provided what were then known as "grammar schools" that were established in order to prepare boys for college and eventual careers in the ministry, law, or medicine. However, girls were not permitted to attend these grammar schools. Outside New England, tax-supported public schools were not established until the nineteenth century.

In the late nineteenth and early twentieth centuries, some women began to advocate equality in the public sphere for women. Of particular concern was the women's suffrage movement, which culminated in the enactment of the Nineteenth Amendment that granted women the right to vote in 1919. However, many of these women also demanded greater access to education for women and girls. By the 1930s, high schools had been established throughout the United States. Both boys and girls attended these schools although boys did so at a higher rate. However, curricula at most of these schools were still gender-based. Girls were taught domestic skills such as home economics, sewing, and cooking under the assumption that they would become homemakers as adults, but they were given relatively little training in skills needed for entry into the workforce outside the home.

Thus, curricula at American high schools in the early twentieth century were focused on women's traditional roles as wives and mothers. The majority of women entering the workforce during this period were employed as teachers, nurses, or in office work. Until the late 1960s, classified advertisements were divided between "Help Wanted—Female" and "Help Wanted—Male." During this period also, women were routinely denied admission to medical school, law school, or various other professional programs. Underlying these trends was the traditional view that women were expected to choose between a career and a family, whereas men were expected to have both. Indeed, in some school districts, married female teachers were forced to give up their teaching positions.

These traditional barriers began to break down after World War II, and they did so at a more accelerated pace during and after the feminist movement of the late 1960s. A key development in the development of gender equality in American education was Title IX, which was part of the Education Amendments of 1972. The Amendments were passed by Congress and signed into law by President Richard Nixon (1913–1994). The text of Title IX reads: "No person in the United States shall, on the basis of sex, be excluded from participation in, be denied the benefits of, or be subjected to discrimination under any education program or activity receiving Federal financial assistance." In effect, Title IX extended federal protection on the basis of race, class, or national origin to gender. Because K-12 schools as well as most colleges and universities received federal financial aid, Title IX applied to elementary and secondary schools as well as to institutions of higher education.

Once implemented, Title IX had many important implications for American public education. It required schools, colleges, and universities to implement sports programs and field teams for girls and women as well as for boys and men. This requirement helped to dispel the archaic belief that participating in sports and athletic activities was unfeminine, unladylike, and therefore inappropriate for girls and women. After Title IX was implemented, the number of girls participating in school-sponsored athletic activities increased dramatically. Rising levels of sports participation among girls after the implementation of Title IX impacted other aspects of gender inequality in schooling indirectly in that it helped to contradict the traditional view that education for women should emphasize domestic skills and that women were less capable of mastering scientific and technical concepts than men.

The impacts of Title IX have gone far beyond sports. Title IX coincided with a dramatic increase in the number of women going on to higher education. The percentage of women who earned bachelor's degrees at American colleges and universities nearly tripled between 1970 and 2010. Women today also earn more than half of all graduate and professional degrees conferred in the United States. Degrees in the STEM fields are a conspicuous exception, however, as discussed in more detail in the chapter on STEM education in this volume.

Title IX also affected the impacts of marriage and pregnancy on access to education. Typically, high school girls who became pregnant were forced to leave school, and many never returned to complete their high school educations. At the college level, many female students dropped out upon becoming engaged, married, or pregnant. Female teachers were also subject to suspension or termination when they became pregnant. However, Title IX made such discrimination against married or pregnant female students and teachers illegal.

More recently, issues of sexual assault and sexual harassment have come to the fore with respect to Title IX. Female victims of sexual assaults have filed lawsuits

---

Gender, Violence, and Education

Girls are disproportionately likely to be affected by school-related violence. Some such violence occurs at a school-wide level. Between 2000 and 2014, for example, girls' schools were three times more likely to be targeted by terrorist groups than boys' schools. Yet much of this violence, including threat of violence, affects girls individually. Many girls, especially at the secondary level, are subject to bullying, sexual harassment, and sexual assaults on the part of fellow students, teachers, and school administrators. Thus, girls may find that schools are neither safe nor supportive environments, and therefore, they are more prone to drop out of school. This leads to a dilemma in that school violence tends to be less prevalent in societies where girls and women have more formal education.

Source: Megan O'Donnell, "Girls' education and gender-based violence: Current risks and future opportunities," ONE.org, November 27, 2017, https://www.one.org/us/blog /violence-gender-education/. Retrieved on March 14, 2020.

---

under the auspices of Title IX. As a result of these lawsuits, it became recognized that schools, colleges, and universities must bear the responsibility to address issues of sexual harassment, intimidation, and violence. The right to a safe educational environment has come to be recognized as an implication of Title IX. Recently, Title IX has also been invoked in cases involving transgender students.

Other issues continue to affect questions of gender equality in education throughout the United States. Recognition of different learning styles between men and women has called attention to a shortage of female teachers at the college level, especially in the STEM fields. Most elementary school teachers are women, as has been the case throughout U.S. history. Although the percentage of full-time university faculty members who are women has been increasing, a majority of these faculty members are men. This is particularly true in the STEM disciplines. Young women may be discouraged from pursuing careers in science, engineering, or technology because they face a lack of role models and institutional support for their ambitions.

Research has shown that teachers of young children tend to believe that their male students are better at science and mathematics than are their female students, even in cases in which test scores and other measures of achievement are identical. In such cases, some teachers attributed boys' successes to their natural ability whereas they believed that girls were successful only because of hard work. Such attitudes can reinforce girls' perceptions that they are intellectually inferior to boys in scientific and technical subjects and that they lack boys' innate abilities in these areas.

Some critics, however, have made arguments that aside from mathematics and science elementary schooling is biased toward girls rather than away from them. Reasons given in support of these arguments often center around the preponderance of female elementary school teachers. Because most elementary teachers are women, young girls have more role models. In addition, girls mature faster than boys. Elementary school also rewards docile behavior rather than rough play, and it places emphasis on fine motor skills, in which girls are also more likely to excel. Curricula are sometimes viewed as privileging girls. For example, chapter books read by elementary school children tend to focus on subjects that are usually of more interest to girls than boys, whose interests are more likely to center on science, technology, and sports. However, some respond to these arguments by pointing out that these qualities are an outgrowth of a culture of masculinity, as opposed to innate differences between boys and girls.

All of these factors highlight that whereas gender equality in American schools has been achieved on the surface, there are still many nuances with respect to gender and education that remain to be addressed. The landscape of gender equality in education has changed dramatically over the course of American history, but much more research and implementation is needed.

Further Reading

Joseph Cimpian, "How our education system undermines gender equity," Brookings Institute, April 23, 2018, https://www.brookings.edu/blog/brown-center-chalkboard/2018/04/23/how-our-education-system-undermines-gender-equity/. Retrieved on January 12, 2019.

Thomas A. DiPrete and Claudia Buchmann, "The growing gender gap in education and what it means for American schools," Council on Contemporary Families, September 22, 2014, https://thesocietypages.org/ccf/2014/09/22/the-growing-gender-gap/. Retrieved on January 13, 2019.

Kelley Taylor, "Evaluating the varied impacts of Title IX," Insight Into Diversity, July 5, 2016, http://www.insightintodiversity.com/evaluating-the-varied-impacts-of-title-ix/. Retrieved on January 13, 2019.

Barbara Winslow, "Title IX's positive impact on education life before Title IX," Everfi, October 15, 2018, https://everfi.com/insights/blog/title-ix-positive-changes/. Retrieved on January 13, 2019.

Chapter 3: Religion and Education

OVERVIEW

Religion, which deals with fundamental questions of human existence, has been central to human experience since the dawn of civilization. People throughout the world have had and continue to have very different religious beliefs, but every culture throughout history and today maintains a set of religious principles, doctrines, beliefs, and practices.

Religion and governance have been linked closely since ancient times. Over time, religious practice changed as new rulers took power. For example, Christians during the first three centuries of the Roman Empire were persecuted, and some who persevered in the practice of Christianity under threat of persecution or execution became recognized as saints or martyrs. Some of these individuals continue to be recognized as saints or martyrs as such even today. However, Emperor Constantine (272 AD–337 AD) became a Christian in 313 AD, and he ended officially the persecution of Christians. In 380 AD, Nicene Christianity became the official religion of the Roman Empire.

In the seventeenth century, the foundations of the modern global state system were developed. A key event was the Thirty Years' War, which was fought in central Europe including present-day Germany and Austria between 1618 and 1648. It has been estimated that as many as eight million Europeans died as a direct or indirect result of the war. Some were soldiers or victims of violence, but many other persons succumbed to disease and famine during this period. One cause of the Thirty Years' War was the response to an effort by the Holy Roman Emperor Ferdinand II (1578–1637) to impose Roman Catholicism on the entire Empire, which was populated by numerous Protestants as well as Catholics. Protestants living in various kingdoms and principalities within the Empire resisted these efforts and rebelled against them. Gradually, the great powers of continental Europe including France and Sweden were drawn into the conflict.

During the 1640s, the rulers of the major powers involved in the Thirty Years' War initiated efforts to end the conflict. These efforts resulted in the Peace of Westphalia, which was a series of treaties among the great powers. The two major treaties were the Treaty of Munster and the Treaty of Osnabruck, named for the German cities in Westphalia in which they were negotiated. Under the terms of these treaties, the Holy Roman Emperor could no longer attempt to impose a particular religion on the entire empire. Instead, each individual ruler within the empire could determine the religion of his or her own kingdom or principality, selecting among Roman Catholicism, Lutheranism, or Calvinism. However, people who preferred to practice a faith other than the religion chosen by the ruler were free to do so without fear of persecution. Most importantly, the Peace of Westphalia included the provision that rulers of individual kingdoms and principalities could not interfere with one another's choice of an official religion.

Within each sovereign territory, rulers could and often did determine, and in some cases impose, a state religion. For example, the Church of England was recognized as the state religion of England, and Evangelical Lutheranism became the state religion of the Scandinavian countries. Although many of these states respected the rights of individuals to practice alternative religions, the state church was privileged over other denominations. State funds were used to construct churches and other religious buildings and to train and pay members of the clergy. In support of these efforts, individual countries imposed and collected taxes on their citizens, who were required to pay these taxes whether or not they belonged to the state church or practiced that religion. In some cases, rulers and other officials were required to belong to the state church. For example, the ruler of England and later the United Kingdom was required to be a Protestant, and this requirement remains in place today. Similarly, the king of Thailand is required to be a Theravada Buddhist although the Thai constitution guarantees freedom of worship.

Since ancient times, religious instruction has been a very important component of the educational process. In many cultures, religious rites and ceremonies are regarded as an essential component of the maturation process from infancy to adulthood. As part of this process, children are taught essential doctrines, principles, rituals, and customs associated with their religious traditions.

Atheism, Agnosticism, and Skepticism in UK Education

Generally, religious education presupposes the existence of religion. Education in the state religion is mandatory in some countries. In other countries, parents have the right to exempt their children from classes in the state religion. But should the absence of religion—the ideas of atheism, agnosticism, and skepticism—be taught in countries other than those in which atheism is official state policy? It has been proposed that schools in the United Kingdom should include curricular content in "different traditions within Christianity, Buddhism, Hinduism, Islam, Judaism and Sikhism, non-religious worldviews and concepts including humanism, secularism, atheism and agnosticism." Advocates argue that such a change will help students learn respect for alternative philosophical viewpoints, but opponents see this change as "teaching less religion" and therefore undermining the quality of "religious instruction."

Source: Harriet Sherwood, "Call for atheism to be included in religious education," *The Guardian*, September 9, 2018, https://www.theguardian.com/education/2018/sep/09/religious-education-schools-overhaul-reflect-diverse-world. Retrieved on March 14, 2020.

Over time, religious instruction became intertwined with secular education. For example, in northern Europe during and after the Protestant Reformation it was regarded as important for people to learn to read and write, because Protestant theology emphasized direct personal relationships between individuals and God via the Bible. People needed to be able to read the Bible in order to develop such relationships. As a result, before the nineteenth century the countries of Protestant northern Europe had the highest rates of literacy in the world. In some places outside Europe, alphabets and systems of writing were introduced by Christian missionaries with the idea of providing the local Indigenous people with the opportunity to read the Bible. However, as more people learned these scripts they came to be used for secular as well as religious purposes.

Historically, church officials and members of the clergy were more likely to be literate and well educated than were members of the general population. Among the duties associated with these religious officials was education. Churches and religious institutions were frequently responsible for providing children with education, both religious and secular. Children would be taught the principles of religious theology and practice as well as skills that could be used also in the secular world including reading, writing, and arithmetic.

During the nineteenth and twentieth centuries, governments began to take over the provision of education. Today, in countries throughout the world the state is responsible for providing education. Churches, synagogues, mosques, and other religious institutions provide religious instruction to children being brought up in their respective faiths. Thus, in most countries secular education has been separated from religious education. However, the degree to which religion and education are or should be intertwined is a matter of controversy throughout the world.

These controversies are illustrated in the individual vignettes presented in this chapter. In the United States, of course, separation of church and state is a core value. This is articulated via the First Amendment to the Constitution, which guarantees freedom of religion and therefore prevents the establishment of a state church. By the end of the nineteenth century, each U.S. state made free public education a requirement and had established a system of public schools. However, curricula used during the nineteenth century were influenced heavily by a Protestant worldview and included instruction in principles of Christianity. These traditions were challenged over the course of the twentieth century, for example, with the elimination of mandatory prayer in public schools and upholding the teaching of the scientific theory of evolution.

Saudi Arabia is an absolute monarchy where Sunni Islam is the state religion. Here, instruction in the principles of Islam is mandatory and is an integral part of the Saudi educational system. Large majorities of the populations of Turkey and Malaysia are also Muslims, but these states are officially secular. In both countries, tension between the religious communities and the state with respect to education is evident, and some in the Islamic communities in both countries have argued for greater integration of Islam into the public school curriculum for both Muslims and non-Muslims. Thailand has a primarily Buddhist population, but faces

---

Religion and Education in Ireland

In Ireland, most primary schools are operated by the Roman Catholic Church although all primary schools, whether religious or secular, receive state funding. Irish law upholds "the right of any child to attend a school receiving public money without attending religious instruction at that school." In practice, however, those children whose parents want them to opt out of mandatory religion classes are often separated from their peers and moved to the back of their classrooms. As Ireland becomes a more secularized society, it has been argued that religious instruction should be made optional and held outside of normal school hours—in other words, to shift from an "opt-out" to an "opt-in" policy.

Source: David Graham, "Religion is a choice—not an obligation. Let's make religious classes opt-in," *The Journal*, February 5, 2020, https://www.thejournal.ie/readme/religious-education-ireland-4973515-Feb2020/. Retrieved on March 14, 2020.

---

issues associated with conflicts between Buddhists and Muslims in the southern part of that country. The government is currently trying to address this conflict via education.

The populations of both Austria and Mexico are dominated by Roman Catholics, although both are also secular states. The government of Austria is dealing with questions associated with its large numbers of Muslim immigrants from Turkey and the Middle East. Here, education is seen as a means of integrating these immigrants and their descendants into Austrian society. Although more than 80 percent of Mexicans are Roman Catholics, the constitution of Mexico explicitly limits the role of the Church in secular matters, including education. Russia is a distinct case in that the Soviet Union, of which Russia was an integral component between 1918 and 1991, was an officially atheistic state. Prior to the Russian Revolution, the majority of Russians were associated with the Russian Orthodox Church, which has experienced a renewal since the collapse of the Soviet Union. Today the Russian government faces questions of the role of religion in public education following the Soviet Union's explicit embrace of atheism.

AUSTRIA

The Republic of Austria, located in central Europe, has a land area of 32,377 square miles and a population estimated at 9 million in 2002. The high and rugged Alps cross western and southern Austria, while northern Austria is crossed by the Danube River and contains much of Austria's fertile, arable land.

Present-day southern Austria was part of the Roman Empire for several centuries. After the collapse of the Roman Empire and throughout the Middle Ages, many different principalities governed various parts of the region until the rise of the Habsburg dynasty after 1000 AD. The Habsburgs controlled most of present-day

Austria and Slovenia by the fifteenth century, and between 1438 and 1740, all of the Holy Roman Emperors were members of the Habsburg family.

The Holy Roman Empire was dissolved formally in 1804, and the last Holy Roman Emperor, Francis II (1768–1835), then declared himself to be the Emperor of Austria. The empire of Austria included not only present-day Austria itself but also the present-day Czech Republic, Slovakia, Hungary, and Slovenia along with parts of what are now Italy, Croatia, and Romania. In 1867, the Austrian Empire became the Austro-Hungarian Empire, which was allied with Germany during World War I. After World War I ended, the German-speaking regions of the western portions of the empire became the independent country of Austria. After World War II, Austria was divided into Soviet, British, French, and American spheres of influence, but this division was dissolved in 1955 on the condition that Austria remain neutral during the Cold War. After the Cold War ended, Austria joined the European Union and became associated increasingly with Western Europe.

German, which is spoken as a first language by nearly 90 percent of the population, is Austria's official language. Many Austrians speak a dialect of German similar to that spoken in Bavaria across the border in Germany. About 10 percent of Austria's residents are immigrants, many of whom come from Turkey or the former Yugoslavia and who speak the languages of their home countries. More than half of the residents of present-day Austria are Roman Catholics with smaller communities of Protestants, Eastern Orthodox Christians, and Muslims.

Education in Austria

Like the United States and Canada, Austria is a federal state consisting of nine federal states, which are known in German as *bundeslander*. However, the bundeslander have less authority than is the case with American states or Canadian provinces. Authority over education is shared between the federal and state governments, but the system throughout the country is highly centralized.

Education in Austria is free and compulsory for nine years, including four years of elementary school and four years of lower secondary school. Those students who wish to prepare for higher education attend upper secondary school for four years. Other students attend a polytechnic institute for a year, followed by three years of vocational education accompanied by an apprenticeship. About 90 percent of Austrian children attend public schools. The remaining 10 percent attend private schools, most of which are run by the Roman Catholic Church. Kindergarten is offered, but it is not compulsory.

Religion and Education in Austria

The history of education in Austria is intertwined with the history of the Roman Catholic Church. Prior to the late eighteenth century, schooling was provided only by convents within the Church. In 1775, however, Holy Roman Empress Maria

These children are on their way to attending Mass at a Roman Catholic church in Vienna, Austria. Approximately two-thirds of Austria's people are Roman Catholics. The degree to which religious principles should be integrated into state-sponsored school curricula in Austria remains controversial, especially as more and more non-Christian immigrants move into the country. (Radiokafka | Dreamstime.com)

Theresa (1717–1780) made it a requirement that all children, both boys and girls, between the ages of six and twelve attend school. As a result, by the nineteenth century the Austrian Empire had one of the highest literacy rates in Europe. During the nineteenth and twentieth centuries, independent Austria became involved more and more in education, and public school attendance increased consistently in comparison to attendance at Church-run schools.

Religious or "confessional" education is required in Austrian schools for children under the age of 14. While this requirement derives from the influence of the Church within Austria, according to contemporary Austrian law, education is regarded as "neutral, implying respect for philosophical, ideological or religious beliefs of parents and students." Although the majority of Austrians are Roman Catholics, religious education for children of parents of other faiths including Protestantism, Eastern Orthodoxy, and Islam is also provided. A total of 13 religious communities are recognized, and teachers charged with providing religious instruction in all of these faiths are paid by the state.

Given Austria's recent history of in-migration from outside Europe and the high birth rates in immigrant communities, Islam is now the second most frequently practiced religion in Austria. An estimated 8–10 percent of Austrian residents

Banning Headscarves in Austria's Primary Schools

Many religious traditions are associated with particular types of clothing. For example, in most Islamic societies, women are expected to wear headscarves to cover their hair in public. Recently, several European countries have enacted laws forbidding girls to wear headscarves in primary schools. In 2019, Austria became the latest country to enact such legislation. Opponents of the new law argued that the law was a direct attack on Muslims, who make up about 8 percent of Austria's population, and against immigrants in general. After the law was passed, Muslim leaders made efforts to challenge the legality of this headscarf ban in court.

Source: Francois Murphy, "Austrian Muslims to challenge school headscarf ban in court," reuters.com, May 16, 2019, https://www.reuters.com/a ia-politics-headscarves Vaustrian-muslims-to-challenge-school-headscarf-ban-in-court-idUSKCN1SM22Z. Retrieved on March 15, 2020.

today are Muslims. In the capital city of Vienna, where these immigrant communities are concentrated, it has been estimated that Muslim children in elementary school now outnumber Roman Catholic children.

In 2015, the government of Austria enacted and implemented a "Law on Islam." The law forbids Muslim organizations within Austria from accepting funding from overseas. It also requires that Muslim groups in Austria use a standard German-language translation of the Quran. This policy was put into place to restrict influence of countries of origin of immigrants over Austria's Muslim communities. In particular, Turkey's Diyanet, or state religious organization, had sent Turkish-speaking imams to Austria to work with Austria's large Turkish-speaking Muslim immigrant community, but the Law on Islam banned this practice. Proponents of the Law on Islam claimed that many Turkish imams were unqualified as teachers and that their teaching was at odds with the "neutral" orientation associated with Austria's educational system.

Some within Austria's Muslim communities have regarded the Law on Islam as discriminating against Muslims, especially given that other religious communities have not been subjected to analogous restrictions. The rise of anti-immigrant political parties in recent years has intensified such concerns. In 2017, the Österreichische Volkspartei or Austrian People's Party gained power in coalition with the Freiheitliche Partei Österreichs or Freedom Party of Austria. Both parties, and in particular the Freedom Party, have stood for significant restrictions on immigration into Austria in part with the goal of retaining Austria's cultural identity. In 2018, the government announced that girls in kindergartens and primary schools would no longer be permitted to wear headscarves at school, and teachers are now longer allowed to wear them in the classroom.

Further Reading

Jenny Berglund, "Publicly funded Islamic education in Europe and the United States," The Brookings Project on U.S. Relations with the Islamic World, 2015, https://www .brookings.edu/wp-content/uploads/2016/06/Final-Web-PDF.pdf. Retrieved on June 28, 2018. See especially pages 13–15.

Soeren Kern, "Turkey's growing influence over Islam in Austria," Gatestone Institute International Policy Council, June 30, 2016, https://www.gatestoneinstitute.org/8352/austria -islam-turkey. Retrieved on June 28, 2018.

Alison Lesley, "Austria passes a controversial law on Islam," *World Religion News*, March 4, 2015, https://www.worldreligionnews.com/religion-news/islam/austria-passes-controversial -law-islam. Retrieved on June 28, 2018.

Shadia Nasralla, "Austria passes 'Law on Islam' requiring Austrian Muslim groups to use German-language Qurans," *Huffington Post*, April 28, 2015, https://www.huffingtonpost .com/2015/02/26/austria-law-on-islam_n_6754012.html. Retrieved on June 28, 2018.

MALAYSIA

Malaysia includes the southern portion of the Malay Peninsula on the Southeast Asian mainland along with most of the northern third of the island of Borneo, which it shares with Indonesia and Brunei, and includes the Malaysian regions of Sarawak and Sabah. Malaysia's overall land area is approximately 127,720 square miles with a population of about 34 million as of 2022. The mainland portion of Malaysia, known as Peninsular Malaysia, contains about 40 percent of Malaysia's land area but is home to more than three-quarters of Malaysia's people. Peninsular Malaya became independent from Britain in 1957. In 1963, Malaya was joined with Sarawak, Sabah, and Singapore as the Federation of Malaysia, but Singapore left the federation and became an independent country in 1965.

Malaysia is a multicultural society. About half of Malaysia's population is made up of Malay people, who are sometimes known as *bumiputras* or "sons of the soil." More than 20 percent of Malaysians are of Chinese ancestry, with smaller populations of Indians, Indigenous peoples, and people associated with other cultural groups. Historically, Malaysia's economy was based on natural resources including tin, palm oil, and rubber. In recent years, manufacturing, financial services, tourism, and high-technology industry have become important components of the Malaysian economy. Today, Malaysia's per capita gross domestic product is the third highest in Southeast Asia, following only Singapore and Brunei.

Education in Malaysia

Prior to British colonization of the Malay Peninsula, schooling was provided largely in Islamic religious schools. The British introduced secular education, but when first introduced, education in these secular schools was imparted in English. Later, various Roman Catholic and Protestant denominations established schools, but instruction in most of these schools was also imparted in English.

As Malaya prepared for independence in the 1950s, the government established a national system of public schools. Primary-level instruction was to be conducted in Malay, English, Chinese, or Tamil with secondary instruction in Malay or English. The same syllabus is used for every course in secondary school, regardless of whether that course is conducted in Malay or in English. Both these languages are the required subjects for study at the secondary level.

Today, education is compulsory for only six years. However, as of 2014 about 79 percent of eligible children in Malaysia were attending secondary schools. As of 2009, Malaysia's literacy rate for both men and women exceeded 95 percent. In 2013, the government issued a National Blueprint for Education in Malaysia, in which it advocated increasing the compulsory education requirement from 6 years to 11 years, with the intention that all Malaysia children should have access to and be enrolled in preschool, primary school, or secondary school by 2020.

Religion and Education in Malaysia

Islam is practiced by about 60 percent of Malaysia's citizens. To profess Islam is a requirement according to the Constitution of Malaysia for identification as a bumiputra or Malay. However, the majority of non-Malays do not practice Islam. About 20 percent are Buddhists and about 10 percent are Christians, with the rest practicing other religions or not practicing religion at all.

Article 3 of the constitution states that "Islam is the religion of the Federation; but other religions may be practised in peace and harmony in any part of the Federation." Article 11 specifies in part that "every person has the right to profess and practice his [sic] religion." Since independence, Malaysia has faced controversy regarding the degree to which the country is to be considered a secular state as opposed to an Islamic state. The state maintains both secular and Sharia law, which is applied only to Muslim litigants, but the division of authority between the secular court system and Sharia law remains an issue of controversy. Given that Malays must profess Islam, this tension carries over also into the realm of cultural identity. For decades, Malaysia's leaders have grappled with the question of how Malaysia can remain a nationally integrated society while respecting and preserving the cultural identities of its citizens without regard to their religions and languages.

This controversy has carried over into the realm of education. This tension is evident in Article 12 of the constitution, which states in part that "every religious group has the right to establish and maintain institutions for the education of children in its own religion, and there shall be no discrimination on the ground only of religion in any law relating to such institutions or in the administration of any such law; but it shall be lawful for the Federation or a State to establish or maintain or assist in establishing or maintaining Islamic institutions or provide or assist in providing instruction in the religion of Islam and incur such expenditure as may be necessary for the purpose."

In 1988, the government issued an education plan, the preamble of which reads in part that "education in Malaysia is an on-going effort towards further developing the potential of individuals in a holistic and integrated manner, so as to produce individuals who are intellectually, spiritually, emotionally and physically balanced and harmonious, based on a firm belief in and devotion to God. Such an effort is designed to produce Malaysian citizens who are knowledgeable and competent, who possess high moral standards and who are responsible and capable of achieving a high level of personal well-being as well as being able to contribute to the betterment of society and the nation at large." As with other Malaysian institutions, this preamble reflects the ongoing tension between Islamic and secular principles.

Although all schools in Malaysia are required to follow the same curriculum, this curriculum is delivered in several types of schools. Many students attend public schools, while others attend religious schools, ethnic schools that are attended primarily by Chinese and Indian students, or private schools. The national primary school curriculum includes Islamic studies, which is compulsory for Muslim pupils. Muslim secondary school students must also take classes in Islamic studies, whereas non-Muslim students must take classes in "moral education and history." Courses in Islamic Sharia law and in Arabic are also elective subjects at the secondary level. Malaysia's Ministry of Education maintains a separate division of religious education, which was established in 1973 and renamed the Bahagian Pendidikan Islam dan Moral (BPIM) or Islamic and Moral Education Division in 1995.

BPIM is responsible for creating the religious education syllabi that are part of the Malaysia's required national educational curriculum. The underlying principles of Islamic education, as quoted in a report by Ahmed Fauzi Abdul Hamid, are that "Islamic Education is a continuous effort to deliver knowledge, skill and emotional experience based on al-Qur'an and al-Sunnah in order to build behaviour, skill, personality and a view of life as the servant of Allah, responsible for self development, the community, the environment and the nation for the sake of prosperity and salvation in this world and the hereafter." At the secondary level, some of the learning outcomes associated with BPIM's program include the expectation that students should be able to read selected verses from the Koran, memorize other verses "to increase the reading of daily prayers and religious practices," and understand verses from the Koran and the Hadith to "appreciate the lessons learned as well as the source of the law and guide believers" and to "strengthen the confidence of the Islamic faith and [in] turn holding the concept of conscious faith in the whole practice and religious bulwark."

Centralization of education has characterized Malaysian education since the time of independence. The Islamic studies curriculum in particular has been subject to ongoing centralization. However, critics have argued that this centralization of the Islamic curriculum privileges upper-class Muslims at the expense of the poor and also emphasizes conformity at the expense of any questioning of authority. Also, critics have argued that the curriculum is constructed in such a way as to prioritize training of Malays, who by law are entitled to a particular percentage of positions in government service, for these positions rather than promoting Islamic values. As Hamid wrote (p. 84), "By stripping Islamic education of its pristine ideals, noble purposes and praiseworthy practices, the Malay-Muslim ruling establishment has transformed it into yet another area vulnerably bound to its largesse and patronage."

In general, Malaysia's approach to religion in its educational system represents an ongoing effort to reconcile tension between conceptualizing the country as an Islamic state and as a secular state in a country in which Islam is the official state religion but in which only slightly over half of the people practice Islam. The government and the Ministry of Education are engaged in efforts to promote Islamic values within the context of Malay culture while recognizing the rights of non-Muslims and recognizing the value of multiculturalism in promoting the development of Malaysia.

Further Reading

Nick Clark, "Education in Malaysia," *World Education News and Reviews*, December 2, 2014, http://wenr.wes.org/2014/12/education-in-malaysia. Retrieved on May 28, 2017.

Ahmed Fauzi Abdul Hamid, "Islamic Education in Malaysia," S. Rajaratnam School of International Studies Monograph #18, 2010, http://www.rsis.edu.sg/wp-content/uploads/2014/07/Monograph1813.pdf. Retrieved on May 28, 2017.

Rozita Ibrahim, "Multiculturalism and education in Malaysia," *Culture and Religion*, 8 (2007), pp. 155–168.

Mohammed Shuhaimi bin Haji Ishak and Osman Chuah Abdullah, "Islamic Education in Malaysia: A Study of History and Development," *Religious Education*, 108 (2013), pp. 298–311.

Ezad Azraai Jamsari, Adibah Sulaiman, and Azizi Umar, "Religious education in Malaya-Malaysia: A lesson from the Indian modernization," *Australian Journal of Basic and Applied Sciences*, 7 (2013), pp. 500–506, http://ajbasweb.com/old/ajbas/2013/August/500-506.pdf. Retrieved on May 28, 2017.

MEXICO

The United Mexican States, usually referred to as Mexico, is located in the southern portion of North America between the United States to the north and Central America to the south. Mexico has a total land area of 761,606 square miles, making it three times the size of Texas. As of 2022, its population was about 131 million.

Archaeologists believe that human settlement in present-day Mexico dates back more than 13,000 years. More recently, several large and distinctive Native American civilizations developed in the region. The first of these were the Olmecs, whose civilization arose approximately 1500 BC in and near the present-day Mexican state of Tabasco adjacent to the Gulf of Mexico. Around 200 AD, the Mayan civilization arose and came to dominate the Yucatan Peninsula and the neighboring areas of southeastern Mexico along with parts of present-day Guatemala and Belize. For unknown reasons, the Mayan civilization collapsed between 900 and 1000 AD, although millions of people of Mayan ancestry continue to live in the region and speak the ancestral Mayan tongue as their first language today.

The Aztec civilization arose in the Valley of Mexico near present-day Mexico City in the fourteenth century. The Aztecs conquered substantial territory across central and southern Mexico between the Gulf of Mexico and the Pacific Ocean. However, the Aztec Empire was overthrown by Spanish conquistadors in the early sixteenth century. Mexico became part of the Spanish Viceroyalty of New Spain, which also included the present-day southwestern United States, the islands of Cuba and Puerto Rico, and much of Central America.

After three centuries of Spanish rule, Mexico became independent in 1821 following the Mexican War for Independence. Between 1821 and 1853, Mexico gave up its claims to present-day Texas and the American Southwest, all of which became part of the United States. For much of the first hundred years following independence, Mexico was ruled by dictators. Since the 1920s, however, Mexico has been a democracy although its politics were controlled by one party, the Partido Revolucionario Institucional (Institutional Revolutional Party or PRI), until 2000, when opposition candidate Vicente Fox Quesada (1942–) was elected as Mexico's president.

The majority of Mexicans are Roman Catholics. According to a survey conducted in 2014, about 81 percent of Mexican citizens identify themselves with the Roman Catholic Church. For most of Mexico's history, well over 90 percent of Mexicans practiced Roman Catholicism. However, this number has declined in recent years because some young people have renounced the Church and because many Mexicans have become evangelical Protestants or Mormons. Roman Catholicism was the state religion of Mexico throughout its three centuries of Spanish rule. After independence, the Church retained a dominant and privileged position within independent Mexico. Until 1856, membership in the Church was a requirement for citizenship. However, the Constitution of 1857 limited the influence of the Church by abolishing practices that had in effect placed the Church above the law and by guaranteeing freedom of religion.

The anticlerical principles contained within the Constitution of 1857 were reinforced by Mexico's present constitution, which took effect in 1917. The Constitution of 1917 restricted the activities of religious orders and prohibited churches from owning property. Also, it prevented the Church and members of the clergy from participating in political activities, including outlawing comments on political matters by clergymen from the pulpit. The Constitution of 1857 specified also that education would be secular and "free from religious orientation." In the early 1990s, some of the anticlerical provisions in the Constitution of 1857 were repealed and Mexico restored diplomatic ties with the Vatican. However, in 2010 another amendment was introduced into Mexico's Congress that would formally declare the country to be *laica* or secular.

Education in Mexico

Under the Mexican educational system, students attend six years of primary school followed by three years of secondary school and three years of high school. Public schools are free, and primary and secondary education are compulsory. Education is managed by the Secretariat of Public Education, which establishes educational standards in use throughout the country. Spanish, which is not an official language of Mexico but is spoken or understood by more than 90 percent of the population, is the primary language of instruction. Instruction is provided in Mayan and other Indigenous languages in some areas where populations are dominated by non-Spanish speaking populations. However, rates of school attendance are lowest in southern Mexico, whose population has the highest percentage of people of Indigenous ancestry. Here, literacy rates are also lower than in other parts of the country. In 2005, for example, the literacy rate among children aged 8–14 was 90 percent in the southern state of Chiapas as opposed to nearly 99 percent for the same age group of children in Mexico City.

Education in colonial Mexico was provided primarily by the Church. Generally, only the sons of the elite were educated, along with young men preparing for the Roman Catholic priesthood. The large majority of Mexicans at that time did not attend school and were unable to read and write. After independence, the government created the Ministry of Public Education in 1833. After the Constitution of 1857 established the principle of separation of church and state, the government took charge of public education. Although education became compulsory after 1867, compulsory education rules were seldom enforced. The Mexican Census of 1960 revealed that less than 10 percent of Mexico's people had completed more than 6 years of schooling. By 2015, however, more than 96 percent of Mexico's children aged from 6 to 14 were enrolled in school in compliance with the country's compulsory education laws. Even today, however, state-run public education in Mexico has been criticized frequently for corruption, inefficiency, and lack of student performance. This has been recognized as a particular problem in areas with impoverished and/or Indigenous populations. Standardized test scores of Mexican students are among the lowest in Latin America.

Religion and Education in Mexico

Conflict between those supporting a stronger role for organized religion in public life and those wishing to maintain Mexico as a secular state has been ongoing since the 1850s, and it remains a significant issue today. Such debates have been articulated within the larger context of the nature of Mexican society and culture. The provisions of the Constitution of 1917 with respect to education were tilted in favor of secular management of public education. Curricula in public schools exclude any form of religious instruction. Although the Constitution of 1917 strictly forbade the establishment of religious schools, this provision was reformed in the early 1990s. Today, students may attend schools run by the Church and other religious organizations, but these private religious schools are ineligible for government funding.

Above and beyond the establishment of private religious schools, some leaders of the Roman Catholic Church continue to advocate a greater role for religion in Mexico's public schools. Church officials have argued that Roman Catholicism is intertwined closely with Mexican culture. Catholic traditions such as drawing a

The Basilica of Our Lady of Guadalupe in Mexico City is the most frequently visited Roman Catholic shrine in the world. Many Mexicans regard the Basilica not only as a religious shrine but also as a symbol of Mexican culture and national identity. (Rodrigolab | Dreamstime.com)

cross with one's hand when passing a church are ingrained in Mexican culture, even among non-Catholics. The Basilica of Our Lady of Guadalupe, also known as the Virgin of Guadalupe, in Mexico City is the most frequently visited Catholic shrine in the world. It is regarded throughout Mexico as symbolic of Mexican culture and national identity. Images of Our Lady of Guadalupe were used by supporters of Mexican independence from Spain in the early twentieth century.

However, according to a 2013 survey a majority of Mexicans believe that religious leaders should not have a say in politics and that religion should not influence public policy.

In addition, many Mexican Protestants, Mormons, and those practicing other religions, oppose reducing separation of church and state on the grounds that doing so could reinforce the historically dominant position of the Church in Mexican public life. Such concerns have intensified as numbers of non-Catholics in Mexico have continued to increase. Whether Mexico's long-standing tradition of secular education and governance will continue to be challenged in the years ahead remains to be seen.

Further Reading

David Agren, "The religious right begins to flex its muscles in secular Mexico," *Washington Post*, October 8, 2016, https://www.washingtonpost.com/world/the_americas/the -religious-right-begins-to-flex-its-muscles-in-secular-mexico/2016/10/07/1e551cd2

-88f5-11e6-8cdc-4fbb1973b506_story.html?noredirect=on&utm_term=.
2b8d1ffb80b5. Retrieved on August 20, 2018.

Luke Goodrich, "Mexico's separation of church and state," *Wall Street Journal*, March 1,
2010, https://www.wsj.com/articles/SB100014240527487037407045750957040653
65166. Retrieved on August 20, 2018.

Rebecca Janzen, "The Virgin of Guadalupe is more than a religious icon to Mexican Catholics," Interfaith Youth Core, June 11, 2020, https://ifyc.org/article/virgin-guadalupe
-more-religious-icon-mexican-catholics. Retrieved on January 14, 2022.

Cruz Ocano and Luis Ernesto, "Secular education and religious education in Mexico:
Reflections on the students' attitudes and beliefs towards religion and interreligious
dialogue," *Religious Education Journal of Australia*, 31 (2015), pp. 25–30.

RUSSIA

The Russian Federation, usually referred to as Russia, is by far the largest country by land area in the world. Its land area of more than 6.5 million square miles is nearly twice that of the United States and is 60 percent larger than that of Canada, which ranks second in the world in overall land area. However, relative to most other countries with large land areas, Russia is sparsely populated. Its population was estimated at 146 million in 2022. Russia spans northeastern Europe and northern Asia, but the large majority of Russians live in the European portion of Russia. Asiatic Russia has a much smaller population, and large areas of this region are uninhabited.

The ancestors of European Russians today had descended from members of Slavic tribes who migrated northward from eastern and southern Europe and from Scandinavians who moved westward more than a thousand years ago. Russia derives its name from the Rus people, who were among the Scandinavian immigrants and who were the first to establish a significant kingdom in the area. The Rus kingdom was centered on the city of Kyiv or Kiev, the capital city of present-day Ukraine.

The Rus kingdom was overrun by Mongol invaders from Asia in the thirteenth century AD. In the fourteenth century, the Grand Duchy of Moscow was established, centered upon that city. The Grand Duchy expelled the Mongols and consolidated power throughout European Russia. It evolved into the Russian Empire, in which Ivan IV or Ivan the Terrible (1530–1584) was crowned the first tsar in 1547. Over the next three centuries, the Russian Empire expanded to the west, east, and south. By the late nineteenth century, the empire controlled most of the territory that today is part of the Russian Federation.

In 1917, the Russian monarchy was deposed, and the empire was eliminated in the Russian Revolution. In the early 1920s, the Communist Bolshevik regime took control of the country. The new Soviet regime expanded to include Estonia, Latvia, Lithuania, Belorussia (present-day Belarus), and Ukraine in eastern Europe; Armenia, Georgia, and Azerbaijan between the Black and Caspian Seas; and five present-day countries in Central Asia. The former Russian Empire became the Russian Soviet Federative Socialist Republic (RSFSR), which contained more than three-quarters of the Soviet Union's land area and more than half of its population. In 1991, the Soviet Union was dissolved, and the RSFSR became the present-day Russian Federation.

Historically, the majority of Russians were affiliated with the Russian Orthodox Church, which took hold in Russia under the Rus during the tenth and eleventh centuries AD. Orthodox churches are autocephalous, with each church organization linked closely to the state in which it was located. The Russian Orthodox Church was established formally in 1448, and it was linked closely with the Russian Empire until its collapse during the Russian Revolution. The tsar of the Russian Empire was regarded by many Russians as God's chosen ruler who was expected to promote the values and principles of the Church.

After the Russian Revolution and the rise of the Soviet Union, however, the Bolsheviks took aggressive steps to limit the power of the Church and to promote atheism among the Russian population. The Soviet regime eliminated state subsidies to the Church, and it confiscated and, in some cases, destroyed church property. It has been estimated that more than 100,000 Russian Orthodox priests were executed between 1917 and the outbreak of World War II in 1939. Many other priests were imprisoned or sent to forced labor camps in Siberia by the Soviet regime. Although nearly all Orthodox churches were shut down by the Communist government, there remained a strong undercurrent of clandestine support for Russian Orthodoxy and other religions during the Soviet period.

After the Soviet regime collapsed, Russia experienced a religious revival. Today, about two-thirds of Russian citizens regard themselves as Russian Orthodox. Nine percent are Muslims, some practice other forms of Christianity, and only 13 percent regard themselves as atheists. The history of religion in Russia has had a strong impact on relationships between religion and education in Russia throughout history and continues to have this impact today.

Education in Russia

As in many other countries, education in pre-Soviet Russia was limited largely to the children of the nobility and the elite. Most schooling was provided by the Russian Orthodox Church, augmented in some cases by private tutoring. It has been estimated that more than 80 percent of Russians, including most of Russia's peasants, were illiterate in the early twentieth century.

The Soviets placed much higher value on public education, with the result that the large majority of Soviet citizens born after 1917, including those living in the RSFSR, were literate by the 1950s. The Soviets also emphasized technical education in comparison to other countries. However, the Soviet Union's underlying philosophy of centralized planning carried over into education. The Soviet educational system was very centralized and rigid. At all levels, curricula emphasized Marxist-Leninist ideology, including its underlying philosophy of atheism. Religious schools were banned. The Soviet-era curriculum was based also on the principles of Russification, through which the Russian language and culture were imposed on children throughout the country regardless of nationality.

In 1992, the new post-Soviet Russian government enacted the Law on Education, whose intent was to reduce centralized state control of schooling. Local authorities were granted more leeway to develop curricula that were linked to local historical, cultural, and linguistic traditions, and the dominance of Marxist-Leninist ideology was eliminated. The following year, the new Russian constitution specified that Russian citizens have a fundamental right to education. This relative decentralization has characterized Russian education ever since.

Today, the Russian educational system includes four years of primary education, five years of lower secondary education, and two to three years of upper secondary education. Primary and lower secondary education are free and compulsory. Upper secondary education is free but not compulsory, although the large majority of Russian teenagers attend upper secondary schools. Russian is the language of instruction in secondary schools and most primary schools, but primary education in other languages is available.

Religion and Education in Russia

The most significant issue with respect to the relationship between education and religion in Russia involves the role of the Russian Orthodox Church in the process of education. Since the collapse of the Soviet Union, Church officials, government officials, and educators have grappled with the question of the extent to which religion should be part of the public school curriculum in Russia. Some Church officials are committed to introducing religion into all Russian classrooms. On the other hand, many government officials—some of whom remain in positions that they had held during the atheistic Soviet period—remain skeptical of this goal.

In 2010, the Russian Ministry of Education initiated efforts to introduce religion into school curricula. The ministry established a pilot project in 19 Russian regions in which students in the fourth grade, or the final year of primary school, would be required to take a class on religion as part of their curriculum for that grade. Although some Church leaders would have preferred that this class be based on Russian Orthodoxy for all students, the ministry decided to give parents and students a choice among Orthodox Christianity and five alternatives: Islam, Judaism, Buddhism, World Religious Cultures, and Secular Ethics. The majority of parents selected the Secular Ethics class for their children. Although many of these parents were themselves members of the Russian Orthodox Church, some remained concerned about the degree to which religion should be part of public, otherwise secular education. Others have stated that exposure to other religions and ethical traditions will strengthen, rather than weaken, their children's commitment to Orthodoxy. Two years later, however, the ministry deemed the pilot project to be a success and decreed the religion class mandatory for all fourth graders nationwide.

Some officials of the Church, however, believe that the required religion class does not go far enough. Some have advocated for the inclusion of classes on Orthodox culture throughout primary and lower secondary schooling. Supporters of the Church's position on religion in public schools regard Russian Orthodoxy as a pillar of Russian nationalism, identifying the Church with the Russian state and with Russian culture.

Critics of stronger relationships between Russian Orthodoxy and the Russian government have argued that the Church's position and its emphasis on nationalism promote autocracy rather than democracy. These critics have pointed out that Russia was an autocratic state throughout its history, both during the rule of the Russian Empire and during the Soviet period. Only since the collapse of the Soviet Union has democracy been practiced in Russia, and some regard the current Russian government as increasingly autocratic. These criticisms have been amplified since Vladimir Putin (1952–) first became the president of Russia in 2000. Observers have noted close linkages between the Church's view and Putin's view of Russian national identity, in which the Church plays a highly important role. Thus, a strengthened role of the Church in public education might be regarded as a means by which concepts of Russian national identity—an identity distinct from the identities of Western Europe and of Asia—can be developed and reinforced.

Further Reading

Matthew Brunwasser, "Russia's new required religion class for 4th graders," pri.org, December 26, 2012, https://www.pri.org/stories/2012-12-26/russias-new-required-religion-class-4th-graders. Retrieved on August 20, 2018.

Paul Coyer, "Un(Holy) alliance: Vladimir Putin, the Russian Orthodox Church, and Russian exceptionalism," *Forbes*, May 21, 2015, https://www.forbes.com/sites/paulcoyer/2015/05/21/unholy-alliance-vladimir-putin-and-the-russian-orthodox-church/#3ca94d9d27d5. Retrieved on August 20, 2018.

Natalya Yakovleva, "Teaching orthodoxy in Russian schools," opendemocracy.net, December 4, 2014, https://www.opendemocracy.net/od-russia/natalya-yakovleva/teaching-orthodoxy-in-russian-schools. Retrieved on August 20, 2018.

SAUDI ARABIA

The Kingdom of Saudi Arabia includes about 80 percent of the Arabian Peninsula in southwestern Asia. The kingdom has a land area of about 830,000 square miles and a population of about 36 million as of 2022. Of these, several million are foreign expatriates drawn to Saudi Arabia because of its wealth and employment opportunities. Saudi Arabia contains the city of Mecca, the home of the Prophet Muhammad and the holiest city of Islam.

During the nineteenth and early twentieth centuries, Saudi Arabia was part of the Ottoman Empire. After World War I, what is now Saudi Arabia included the kingdoms of Nejd in what is now eastern Saudi Arabia and Hejaz, which included Mecca, in the west. At the time of unification, the majority of Saudis were nomads who lived in rural areas. The current Saudi royal family united the two kingdoms in 1932. Oil was discovered in Saudi Arabia during the 1930s, and petroleum extraction and export transformed Saudi Arabia from a rural backwater to one of the wealthiest countries in the world.

Saudi Arabia is an absolute monarchy controlled tightly by its royal family, which has held power since the country was first unified. Islam is the state religion, and all Saudi citizens are required to practice Islam. Saudi Arabia's legal institutions are based on the principles of Islamic Sharia law as interpreted by the conservative, fundamentalist Wahhabi doctrine. Violators of these strict Islamic principles are often subject to corporal punishment and sometimes to capital punishment.

Saudi women are subject to severe restrictions. For example, women going out in public must be accompanied by their husbands or male relatives, and women were not not permitted to drive automobiles until 2018. In 2011, women were granted the right to vote in local elections but could do so only with the permission of their husbands or male guardians. Because of the frequency of corporal and capital punishment and because of restrictions on the rights of women, international observers and organizations have often ranked Saudi at the bottom of the list of world's countries with respect to human rights.

Education in Saudi Arabia

The dominance of conservative interpretations of Islam within Saudi culture and society has had a major impact on the country's educational system. Prior to the unification of Saudi Arabia and the discovery of oil, education in Saudi Arabia was usually limited to Islamic studies. During the nineteenth century, some children were taught to memorize the Koran in religious classes associated with mosques. Emphasis on memorization meant that the teaching of reading and writing were not considered vital to education. In 1970, it was estimated that only 15 percent of Saudi men and 2 percent of Saudi women were literate.

Public schools in Saudi Arabia were first established for boys in 1951 and for girls, over the opposition of some conservative clerics, in 1960. As the government expanded its role in public education, literacy rates rose rapidly. In 1990, the literacy rate was estimated at 73 percent for men and 48 percent for women. Today, more than 95 percent of Saudis of both genders are able to read and write.

Saudi law requires six years of compulsory education, and education in Saudi Arabia is supervised at the national level by the Ministry of Education. After completing six years of primary school, most Saudi students attend intermediate school for three years, followed by three years of secondary school. More than 90 percent of Saudi children attend intermediate and secondary school following completion of primary school. Arabic, which is the official language of the country, is the medium of instruction although English is taught at the intermediate and secondary levels as well. Education at the primary, intermediate, and secondary schools is free to all Saudi citizens. Strict gender separation is practiced in most schools, with female students taught by women in separate classrooms and sometimes in separate buildings.

Religion and Education in Saudi Arabia

At the primary, intermediate, and secondary levels, curricula are dominated by instruction in Islamic principles. The study of Islam is required at all levels of Saudi public education, and according to estimates, more than a third of time spent in school is devoted to religious studies. The religion curriculum emphasizes memorization of the Koran and other Islamic religious texts, and religion-related training encompasses as much as half of the curriculum. Little attention is paid to teaching about non-Muslim cultures and societies. Memorization and rote learning characterize secular aspects of the curriculum as well.

Much of the Islamic curriculum is guided by the principles of the Wahhabi interpretation of Islam. Wahhabism is much more conservative and less tolerant of alternative interpretations of the faith as compared to mainstream Sunni Islam. The dominance of Wahhabism in Saudi Arabia dates back to the eighteenth century, when its founder Muhammad ibn Abd al-Wahhab (1703–1792) formed a protective alliance with Muhammad ibn Saud (??–1765), a local Nejd leader who became the progenitor of what is today the Saudi royal family. The alliance between Wahhabism and the Saudi royal family has been maintained ever since. The Wahhabi interpretation rejects not only non-Muslim theology, but it is also highly critical of Shi'ites and non-Wahhabi Sunni Muslims. According to some textbooks, practitioners of these forms of Islam are regarded as heretics.

In recent years, education as practiced in Saudi Arabia has been criticized both within the country and internationally for its emphasis on rote memorization and on religious training at the expense of secular studies. Critics have argued that the Saudi education system does an inadequate job of preparing students for employment after graduation, especially in the technical sector of the economy. From this viewpoint, emphasis on memorization and learning by rote discourages creative thinking that is seen as vital to economic development in the long run. Even today, many technical and professional jobs are held by highly skilled foreign expatriates, especially in the private sector. Concern about low-quality education is especially acute among those working to prepare Saudi Arabia for transition to an economy less dependent on fossil fuels.

Education based on religious principles and Saudi cultural traditions has sometimes come into conflict with efforts to promote teaching and learning in science and technology. For example, Saudi educational authorities have recognized the value of information and communications technology in the educational process. However, the Saudi government censors access to the internet strictly on the grounds that access to many internet sites would interfere with its efforts to maintain and preserve Islamic values. Thus, it has sometimes been difficult for educational officials to implement web-based educational material in Saudi curricula.

Although the government has initiated some reform efforts, critics claim nevertheless that many Saudi university graduates are unprepared for professional positions. In response, the government has provided more funds to allow Saudi students to study at the undergraduate or graduate levels in the United States, the

United Kingdom, and other foreign countries. The King Abdullah University of Science and Technology was established in 2009 and is authorized to offer graduate degrees in various science and engineering disciplines.

Further Reading

Ali al-Ahmed, "The medieval Saudi educational system must be reformed," *The Guardian*, November 26, 2010, https://www.theguardian.com/commentisfree/belief/2010/nov /26/saudi-arabia-religious-education. Retrieved on June 11, 2016.

Sultan Albugami and Vian Ahmed, "Effects of culture and religion on the use of ICT in the Saudi education system," Proceedings of the IRES 25th International Conference, January 24, 2016, http://usir.salford.ac.uk/38040/1/175-145473407225-27.pdf/. Retrieved on June 11, 2016.

Ursula Lindsey, "Saudi Arabia's education reforms emphasize training for jobs," *Chronicle of Higher Education*, October 3, 2010, http://www.chronicle.com/article/Saudi-Arabias -Education/124771/. Retrieved on June 11, 2017.

World Education News and Reviews, "Education in Saudi Arabia," 2001, http://wenr.wes .org/2001/11/wenr-nov-dec-2001-education-in-saudi-arabia. Retrieved on June 11, 2017.

THAILAND

The Kingdom of Thailand is a constitutional monarchy located in mainland Southeast Asia. It has a land area of nearly 200,000 square miles and a 2022 population of approximately 67 million. Most of Thailand's people live in the valley of the Chao Phraya River, which flows through Thailand's capital and major city of Bangkok before emptying into the Gulf of Thailand. The hilly areas to the west, north, and east of the Chao Phraya valley are more sparsely populated and separate Thailand from neighboring Burma, Laos, and Cambodia, respectively. To the south, Thailand includes a long, narrow strip of territory along the eastern portion of the Malay Peninsula. The majority of Thailand's people are of full or partial ethnic Thai ancestry and speak the Thai language or related languages. Most non-Thai people in Thailand live in the outlying areas.

Present-day Thailand has been settled for thousands of years. The ancestors of the Thai people who occupy much of Thailand today are believed to have moved southward from what is now southwestern China more than 1,000 years ago. Most of Thailand, including the Chao Phraya valley, has been ruled by a succession of Thai-based kingdoms and empires since the thirteenth century AD. While most of Southeast Asia was governed as British and French colonies from the late nineteenth century until after World War II, Thailand retained its independence throughout the colonial era and is the only Southeast Asian state with no colonial history.

Education in Thailand

It is believed that formal education in Thailand began with the creation of the Thai alphabet, which some believe was invented by King Ram Khamhaeng the Great (1237 or 1247–1298) during the late thirteenth century. Using this alphabet,

These children are in class in an elementary school in Thailand. Although about 90 percent of Thailand's citizens are Theraveda Buddhists, freedom of worship is guaranteed by law. All students, regardless of faith, take a course called "Social, Religion, and Culture Studies." Muslim students can pursue an Islamic-oriented curriculum. (Patryk Kosmider | Dreamstime.com)

instruction in reading and writing was provided to children of the royal family and the nobility. Buddhist monks provided education to some other Thai people, but by the late nineteenth century, the government recognized that this education was insufficient to prepare Thai citizens for careers in government service, trade, and business. The Ministry of Education was established in 1887, and girls were permitted to attend public schools that began 10 years later. The ministry continues to manage education in Thailand today.

Today, the public educational system in Thailand includes nine years of "basic" education, which is divided into six years of primary or elementary school followed by three years of lower secondary education. Basic education is free and compulsory, and children begin their basic education at the age of six. According to recent estimates by the United Nations Education, Scientific, and Cultural Organization (UNESCO), nearly 99 percent of Thai children complete primary school, but only about 85 percent complete lower secondary school. The government also provides three years of preschool and three years of upper secondary education before and after compulsory basic education, respectively. This education is also free, but it is not compulsory. Thai is the language of instruction, placing non-Thai people at a disadvantage with respect to standardized testing. However, English is also taught widely in Thailand's public schools.

Despite Thailand's prosperity compared to its neighbors, some critics have claimed that the quality of Thailand's education is very low. These critics have attributed problems with the quality of Thai education to insufficient funding, low salaries for teachers, large class sizes, poorly managed bureaucracy, and indifference on the part of teachers and students. Critics also point out that education often emphasizes memorization, with little or more effort spent on teaching and using critical thinking skills.

Religion and Education in Thailand

More than 90 percent of Thailand's people are Theravada Buddhists. About 5 percent are Muslims, with small minorities of Christians, Jews, Hindus, Sikhs, and people of other religious faiths. The constitution of Thailand guarantees religious freedom, although Thai law requires that the king be a Theravada Buddhist. The state provides financial support to the Theravada Buddhist community. However, four other religions—Islam, Christianity, Hinduism, and Judaism—are recognized by the state.

The Ministry of Education has made religious education a requirement in public schools. Beginning in 2003, students were required to take a course entitled "Social, Religion, and Culture Studies." This course provides students information about all five of Thailand's recognized religious traditions. Students can elect Buddhist or Muslim faith-based curricula, and those who do so take standardized national examinations tailored specifically to these curricula.

Issues associated with religion and education in Thailand have become particularly noteworthy in the southern part of the country. Although only about 5 percent of Thailand's people are Muslims, the Islamic community is highly concentrated geographically in this region. Muslims form a majority of the population in far southern Thailand, in the coastal strip of the Malay Peninsula west of the Gulf of Thailand. This region, known as Pattani, was conquered originally by Thailand in the late eighteenth century.

Conflict between Buddhists and Muslims in Pattani and throughout southern Thailand has been ongoing for decades. The conflict has occasionally erupted into violence in Thailand and neighboring countries. Several thousand Thai citizens of both faiths have lost their lives as a result of this violence, which has become tantamount to civil war, since the start of the twenty-first century. Some Pattani activists continue to demand independence or at least greater autonomy for this Muslim-majority region.

In part to alleviate ongoing conflict between Buddhists and Muslims in southern Thailand, the Thai government has initiated several accommodations in support of the local Islamic community. Students in many public schools in southern Thailand may elect to pursue a curriculum based on Islamic studies. The curriculum is developed and administered by the Central Islamic Committee of Thailand, although its implementation requires approval by the government. Many Muslim students attend private Islamic schools. Some pursue the government-approved

Islamic curriculum. Upon completion of this curriculum, a student receives the equivalent of a high school diploma and becomes eligible for higher education.

Other Muslim students attend private Islamic schools known as *pondoks*. Pondoks receive only limited government funding, but their curricula are monitored strictly by the government. Students graduating from these pondoks are not recognized automatically as high school graduates, but they can achieve this recognition by passing a government-administered equivalency examination. Despite Thailand's constitutionally recognized freedom of religion, most believe that it is not likely that religious conflicts experienced in the country today will alleviate in the foreseeable future despite government efforts to recognize and accommodate religious issues and principles in the Thai educational system.

Further Reading

Austin Bodetti, "Thailand's forgotten insurgency," *The Diplomat*, June 15, 2017, https://thediplomat.com/2017/06/thailands-forgotten-insurgency/. Retrieved on August 2, 2018.

Rachel Michael and Stefan Trines, "Education in Thailand," *World Education News and Reviews*, February 6, 2018, https://wenr.wes.org/2018/02/education-in-thailand-2. Retrieved on August 2, 2018.

Karim Raslan, "Looking within: What's behind Thailand's Buddhist-Muslim divide?," *This Week in Asia*, March 29, 2018, https://www.scmp.com/week-asia/society/article/2139389/looking-within-whats-behind-thailands-buddhist-muslim-divide. Retrieved on August 2, 2018.

Bruno Marshall Shirley, "Buddhist-Muslim violence in South and South-east Asia: The local becomes regional, or a clash of civilizations?," *International Policy Digest*, June 29, 2016, https://intpolicydigest.org/2016/06/29/buddhist-muslim-violence-in-south-and-south-east-asia-the-local-becomes-regional-or-a-clash-of-civilizations/. Retrieved on August 2, 2018.

Sivarnee, "Education system in Thailand: A terrible failure in S.E. Asia," *CNN iReport*, June 8, 2013, http://ireport.cnn.com/docs/DOC-985267. Retrieved on August 2, 2018.

TURKEY

The Republic of Turkey is located in western Asia and southeastern Europe. About 97 percent of Turkey's total land area of 302,535 square miles is located in Asia. The European portion of Turkey, with the remaining 3 percent of the country's land area, contains about 14 percent of the population. The country's largest city, Istanbul, is located on both sides of the Bosporus Strait that separates Europe from Asia. Nearly two-thirds of Istanbul's people live on the European side of the Strait. As of 2022, Turkey's population was about 85.5 million.

Given its location at the crossroads between Europe and Asia, and with its coastlines on the Mediterranean and Black Seas, Turkey has been an area of strategic importance and a cultural and economic crossroads for thousands of years. Most of present-day Turkey was part of the Persian Empire in the sixth and fifth centuries BC, and it was conquered by Alexander the Great in about 334 BC. By the first century BC, all of present-day Turkey had become part of the Roman Empire.

In the fourth century AD, the Roman Empire became divided administratively between the Western Roman Empire, which was centered on Rome, and the Eastern Roman Empire, which was centered on Constantinople (present-day Istanbul). The Western Roman Empire was dissolved in 476 AD, but the Eastern Roman Empire or Byzantine Empire continued to rule present-day Turkey until it also collapsed in the eleventh century AD. After present-day Turkey experienced several centuries of political fragmentation, the Ottoman dynasty conquered Constantinople in 1453. By the early sixteenth century, the Ottoman Empire controlled Turkey as well as many parts of southeastern Europe and territories on the east coast of the Mediterranean Sea.

After World War I, the Ottoman Empire was dissolved. The international community recognized present-day Turkey as the successor state to the empire in 1923. In exchange for this recognition, the Republic of Turkey gave up all claims to Ottoman territory elsewhere. The first president of the republic, Mustafa Kemal Ataturk (1881–1938), declared Turkey to be a secular state and implemented reforms intended to westernize the country. He regarded the practice of traditional Islam, which was practiced by the large majority of Turks, as having a detrimental impact on efforts to modernize the country. Ataturk's government provided women with rights equal to those of men, including the right to vote. He also introduced the use of a Roman alphabet, which replaced the old Ottoman script that had been similar to those used to write Persian and other Asian languages.

Ataturk also pushed policies intended to create a unified Turkish identity. Turkish became the country's official language, and today about 85 percent of Turks speak Turkish as a first language. However, the majority of people in southeastern Turkey are ethnic Kurds who speak a distinct language. Many Kurdish speakers support greater autonomy or outright independence for the Kurdish-speaking area, which extends into neighboring Iran, Iraq, and Syria.

Turkey remains a secular state, with no official religion. As of 2016, about 82 percent of Turks, including most Kurds, identified themselves as Muslims. However, people who do not identify themselves with any other religion are registered as Muslims.

The role of religion in public life, including education, has been a matter of controversy in Turkey for many years although Turkey remains a secular state. In 2003, Recep Tayyip Erdogan (1954–) became the prime minister of Turkey. Erdogan's political party, the Adalet ve Kalkinma Partisi or Justice and Development Party (AKP), has been described as "Islamist" although party leaders reject this label. Its critics claim that AKP is promoting an Islamist orientation and a return to the religious-oriented policies of the Ottomans, as opposed to the secular orientation of Ataturk and his successors.

Since AKP first took power, in several elections it has been strongest in Asian areas of Turkey, especially in rural areas. Opposition parties, often referred to as Kemalist parties in the legacy of Ataturk's vision of Turkey as a modern secular state, is strongest in European Turkey and in coastal areas along the Mediterranean and Black Seas. Pro-secession Kurdish nationalist parties dominate the Kurdish-speaking southeast.

Education in Turkey

Ataturk's reforms included the provision of free, state-supported, and compulsory public education. Ataturk believed that education was critical to the westernization and development of Turkey as a modern state. Shortly after independence, the Ministry of Education (currently the Ministry of National Education) was established. Education became highly centralized under the auspices of the ministry. The ministry implemented an educational curriculum that was based on practice in Western Europe.

In 2012, the Turkish government mandated 12 years of compulsory education between the ages of 6 and 18. The system includes 4 years of primary school, 4 years of upper-level primary school, and 4 years of secondary school. For the last 2 years of secondary school, students may choose academic or vocational tracks, with those students aspiring to college-level education selecting an academic track.

Religion and Education in Turkey

Under Ataturk's regime, public education was to be secular, and it remained so during Ataturk's lifetime. However, after World War II, religion became part of Turkish education. Religious classes during the fourth and fifth grades of public primary school became compulsory in 1950, although parents had the right to opt their children out of this requirement. The number of years in which curricula included classes in religion increased over time. In 1982, classes in religion and ethics became mandatory in all 12 grades of public school, and parents could no longer opt their children out of these classes. The principles taught in these classes are, for the most part, based on the Sunni Islam that is practiced by most Turks. Children are taught Sunni prayers and religious practices. Erdogan's Islamist-oriented government is strongly supportive of further integrating Islamic principles into Turkish public education.

Although Erdogan's government has retained solid support among the majority of Turkey's voters, there remains significant opposition to its educational objectives and policies. Among the most controversial issues is the establishment of Imam Hatip schools at the secondary school level. These schools are intended to train imams to minister to Turkey's Muslim communities, and in some cases to minister to Turkish people living in other countries.

The number of students enrolled in Imam Hatip schools has increased from about 60,000 in 2002 to over one million in 2017, or more than 10 percent of all secondary school students in the country. As of 2018, nearly a quarter of Turkey's budget for the support of secondary school education went to Imam Hatip schools. The development of Imam Hatip schools has impacted national curricula at all levels. For example, in 2017 the government eliminated the teaching of the theory of evolution from the science curriculum in all secondary schools in Turkey.

Parents and educators are divided over the impacts of Imam Hatip schools on Turkish lives. Those who express concern about the expansion of these schools point out that students and graduates of Imam Hatip schools do not do as well in standardized tests as students and graduates of other secondary schools. Graduates of Imam Hatip schools are also less likely to succeed at the university level. In addition, non-Muslims and those who practice alternative interpretations of Islam are concerned about the increasing integration of Sunni Islam into Turkish public life. However, government officials and many parents and educators see Imam Hatip schools to be important for the maintenance and development of Turkish identity. Supporters of the schools also see them as a means to reconcile Turkey's Islamic culture with the goals of economic development in a globalized world. The debate over these schools may be reflective of the ongoing debate about religion in Turkey in general, as is evident in levels of support for and opposition to the Erdogan government.

Further Reading

Darin Butler, "With more Islamic schooling, Erdogan aims to reshape Turkey," *Reuters Investigates*, January 25, 2018, https://www.reuters.com/investigates/special-report/turkey-erdogan-education/. Retrieved on July 9, 2018.

Fatma Gok, "The history and development of Turkish education," in *Education in multicultural societies—Turkish and Swedish perspectives*, edited by Marie Carlson, Annika Rabo, and Fatma Gok, Swedish Research Institute in Istanbul, *Transactions*, 18 (Stockholm 2007), pp. 247–255, https://www.semanticscholar.org/paper/The-History-and-Development-of-Turkish-Education-G%C3%B6k/c39369f1af4654da98c930534737df8a-f246e7c5. Retrieved on July 9, 2018.

Abdurrahman Hendek, "Religious education in Turkey," *World Bulletin*, August 30, 2013, http://www.worldbulletin.net/haber/116510/religious-education-in-turkey. Retrieved on July 9, 2018.

Constanze Letsch, "Turkish parents complain of push toward religious schools," *The Guardian*, February 12, 2015, https://www.theguardian.com/world/2015/feb/12/turkish-parents-steered-religious-schools-secular-imam-hatip. Retrieved on July 9, 2018.

UNITED STATES

Throughout the history of the United States, the role of religion in American public education has been a matter of controversy. Religion-related issues have influenced the history of American education, and they continue to do so today.

During colonial times, the New England colonies began to establish public schools. Massachusetts, which was established by the Puritans, was the first colony to require towns to establish public schools when it passed such a law in 1647. At these public schools, children were taught reading, writing, and arithmetic, but they were also given religious instruction in the Puritan interpretation of Christianity. In 1690, the New England Primer was published. It was used in New England primary schools for more than a hundred years. The Primer used Puritan and

Calvinist principles to instruct children in the alphabet and to read. For example, a poem used to teach the alphabet began with "In Adam's fall, we sinned all; Thy life to men, God's Book attend."

As described elsewhere in this volume, during the nineteenth century public schools were established throughout the United States. The establishment of these schools was an outgrowth of the Common School movement. The founder of the Common School movement, Horace Mann (1796–1859), was concerned primarily with education as a foundation underlying a functioning democracy. However, Mann's interpretation of common school education was based on a Protestant worldview. Curricula were linked closely with these Protestant values. For example, the school day usually began with a reading from Scripture and a prayer. Textbooks such as the well-known McGuffey's Readers included numerous references to religion, although the Readers did not include direct reference to Christian doctrine as had been the case with the New England Primer.

As American society began to industrialize and diversify, this approach to education became more controversial. By the late nineteenth century, more and more immigrants were coming to the United States from eastern and southern Europe. Many were Roman Catholics or Jews who objected to their children being required to recite or read passages from the King James version of the Bible. In Wisconsin, for example, in 1890 the state Supreme Court ruled in the case of *Weiss v. District Board* (76 Wis. 177). The *Weiss* decision overturned a state requirement that the school day begin with a reading from the King James version. However, several later federal and state court decisions reinforced the prevailing view that the United States was a Christian nation. These were summarized by the U.S. Supreme Court in the case of *Church of the Holy Trinity v. United States* (143 U.S. 457) in 1892.

Relationships between religion and public education in the United States were informed also by various interpretations of the First Amendment to the U.S. Constitution, which reads in part that "Congress shall make no law respecting an establishment of religion, or prohibiting the free exercise thereof." For many jurists, this first or Establishment Clause of the First Amendment implies that no religion can be privileged in comparison to others. As indicated in Holy Trinity, however, nineteenth-century courts indicated consistently that the United States is a Christian nation. Issues associated with interpretation of the First Amendment are complicated in that public education in the United States is under the control of the individual states, and not the federal government. The Tenth Amendment to the Constitution reads that "the powers not delegated to the United States by the Constitution, nor prohibited by it to the States, are reserved to the States respectively, or to the people." Because the Constitution does not mention education, the states rather than the federal government have legal responsibility for the provision of public education.

Issues of this sort were discussed and litigated throughout the twentieth century. In 1962, the Supreme Court ruled on the issue of prayer in public schools in *Engel v. Vitale* (370 U.S. 421). In 1955, the Board of Regents for education in the state of New York drafted a prayer reading "Almighty God, we acknowledge our dependence on Thee, and we beg Thy blessings upon us, our parents, our teachers, and our country." The Regents encouraged local districts strongly to adopt this prayer and have pupils recite it at the beginning of the school day. Parents who objected to this prayer filed suit, arguing that this prayer violated the establishment clause of the First Amendment. In the *Engel* decision, the Court ruled that the recitation of government-mandated prayers was in violation of the establishment clause and was therefore unconstitutional. A year later, in the follow-up case of *Abington School District v. Schempp* (374 U.S. 203), the Court extended this argument by ruling that the recitation of the Lord's Prayer and readings from the Bible in public schools were also unconstitutional. Later cases extended and modified this basic principle.

Another ongoing controversy has involved the teaching of evolution in public schools. In 1859, Charles Darwin (1809–1882) and Alfred Russel Wallace (1823–1913) developed simultaneously the theory of evolution. By the early twentieth century, the idea that humans and other species had evolved over millions of years through the process of natural selection had become accepted universally by the scientific community. The discovery and analysis of fossil dinosaurs and other animals was further evidence in support of the theory of evolution, and further research has established that the earth is about 4.5 billion years old. However, the idea that humans evolved from "lower" animals is inconsistent with the language of the Book of Genesis in the Bible, in which it is stated that each species was created independently by God and that the Earth was created only about 6,000 years ago. Thus, many Christians objected not only to the concept of evolution itself but also to it being taught in public schools.

The issue came to national attention in 1925 in what became known popularly as the Scopes "monkey trial." At that time, a Tennessee law prohibited the teaching of evolution in public schools. John Scopes (1900–1970), a science teacher in Dayton, Tennessee, taught a lesson on human evolution in violation of the law. A jury found Scopes guilty and fined him $100, but his conviction was overturned later on a technicality.

The Tennessee statute remained on the books until 1967. In the following year, in *Epperson v. Arkansas* (393 U.S. 97) the Supreme Court overturned an Arkansas law that prohibited instructors in any school "supported in whole or in part from public funds derived by state or local taxation" to teach evolution or use any textbook that "teaches the doctrine or theory that mankind ascended or descended from a lower order of animal." This law was overturned also on the grounds that the Arkansas law violated the Establishment Clause.

After *Epperson* was decided, those opposed to teaching evolution in public schools attempted to ensure that alternatives were presented to pupils. Some who did not accept the theory of evolution developed what they call "creation science," basing these ideas on a literal interpretation of the Book of Genesis. In 1981, a law requiring that teaching evolution must be accompanied by teaching "creation science" was enacted in Louisiana. This law was overturned also by the U.S. Supreme Court in *Edwards v. Aguillard* (482 U.S. 578) in 1987. More recently, other states have enacted various laws dealing with the issue of teaching "creation science" in such a way as to not violate the *Edwards* decision.

Further Reading

Sam Blumenfeld, "Religion and early American education," New American, October 18, 2012, https://www.thenewamerican.com/reviews/opinion/item/13262-religion-in-early -american-education. Retrieved on February 9, 2018.

Philip C. Chinn, "Religion, culture, and education in the United States," in *Encyclopedia of diversity in education*, edited by James A. Banks. Thousand Oaks, CA: Sage Publications, 2012.

Bruce Dierenfield, *The battle over school prayer: How Engel v. Vitale changed America*. Lawrence: University Press of Kansas, 2007.

Suzanne Rosenblith, "Religion in schools in the United States," in *Oxford Research Encyclopedia of Education*, 2017, http://education.oxfordre.com/view/10.1093/acrefore /9780190264093.001.0001/acrefore-9780190264093-e-46?print=pdf. Retrieved on February 9, 2018.

Chapter 4: Multicultural and Multilingual Education

OVERVIEW

Literacy is a basic goal of educational systems throughout the world. But what languages should be taught? Decisions concerning what languages should be taught have been highly controversial, in that language is a primary means by which cultural values are transmitted to future generations. Failure to teach particular languages, and especially those spoken by only small numbers of people, can contribute to the extinction of these languages as the last Indigenous speakers of these languages die. With the extinction of these languages can come the extinction of the cultures associated with them.

An estimated 5,000–10,000 languages are spoken around the world. Some such as English, Chinese, Spanish, and Hindi are spoken by hundreds of millions of people. Others are spoken by only a thousand people, or even fewer. As a result of colonialism, the languages of the European colonial powers including English, French, Spanish, Dutch, and Portuguese have become the dominant languages of their countries' former colonies.

Most countries throughout the world have designated official languages. The United States is one of a small minority of countries that does not have an official language. In some countries, more than one language has official status. For

---

Why Should Indigenous Languages Be Preserved?

Anthropologists have estimated that between 6,000 and 8,000 languages are spoken throughout the world. However, more than 2,000 of these languages, or nearly a third, are spoken by fewer by a thousand people. These languages are considered highly endangered, and most are spoken by Indigenous people who live in remote areas of the world. By analogy with biology, when the last speakers of a language die the language becomes extinct. The extinction of a language means the loss of the culture with which that language is associated. In many areas, efforts are being made to preserve these endangered languages. These efforts include ensuring that these languages are taught in schools and by less formal means.

Source: Anastasia Riehl, "Why are languages worth preserving?" *Sapiens*, November 8, 2019, https://www.sapiens.org/language/endangered-languages/. Retrieved on March 21, 2020.

example, English and French have official status in Canada, and French and German are the official languages of Luxembourg. In some countries, various languages have official status in some regions but not in others. For example, Belgium is divided into language communities, and Dutch, French, and German are official within these communities. In India, each state has the right to identify its own official language or languages. Twenty-two languages have official status in one or more of India's 28 states.

Decisions about making a language official are often controversial, as in the United States where there has been considerable debate about whether to make English the country's official language. These decisions are controversial for several reasons. Historically, in many countries there has been overt discrimination against users of nonofficial languages. People who did not speak or use the official language were subject to punishment. Even today, people who cannot speak or read the official language may not have access to important services.

Many of these controversies over official languages involve education, including what languages are or are not taught in schools. Should children of linguistic minorities be required to learn to speak and read the official language? Are students who do not speak the official language at home at a disadvantage as they proceed through school, and if so, how can such disadvantages be rectified? Concerns of this sort, and decisions as to how these issues should be addressed, are significant especially because of the role of education in transmitting culture and cultural values to future generations.

Issues involving language in education are linked closely to concerns about cultural diversity. In addition to linguistic diversity, many countries are characterized by great diversity in culture, including religious differences. With cultural diversity often comes cultural conflict. Language has been identified as a means of unifying highly diverse countries, but for many the imposition of a common exogenous language is regarded as a threat to the preservation of existing languages and cultures. In addition, English in particular is seen as a world language, and fluency in English is regarded by many as essential to become successful in the contemporary world economy. For many countries, decisions about multilingual and multicultural education involve efforts to balance competing objectives—competitive advantage in the world economy, national integration, and preservation of local culture.

The seven countries that are profiled in this chapter are all characterized by language conflict and/or very high levels of linguistic and cultural diversity. Belgium includes Dutch-speaking Flanders and French-speaking Wallonia, along with a small area in eastern Belgium where German is spoken. Tensions between the Flemish and the Walloons have reached the point that some predict that Belgium will become divided eventually into two separate countries.

Canada's language and cultural issues date back to its initial settlement by Europeans, with French settlers colonizing present-day Quebec while present-day Ontario and parts of the present-day Atlantic Provinces were settled by English speakers from the British Isles. In addition, northern Canada's population includes many people of Native American or First Nations ancestry, who have their own linguistic history and cultural traditions. In South America, Spanish conquistadors ousted the Inca rulers of much of present-day Peru in the sixteenth century. However, millions of Peruvians living in the Andes Mountains are of Inca ancestry and speak Quechua or Aymara, both of which are derived from the language of their ancestors. Other Peruvians live in the Amazon basin and speak completely unrelated languages.

While Belgium, Canada, and Peru achieved independent status during the nineteenth century, the other four countries did not achieve independence until after World War II. All four were colonies of English-speaking countries. India, Nigeria, and Tanzania were British colonies and Papua New Guinea was administered as a colony of Australia until it became independent in 1975. All four are characterized by sometimes bewildering cultural diversity, and no ethnic or linguistic group dominates any of their populations. Although its population is only about 9.3 million, about 800 distinct languages are spoken in Papua New Guinea. Papua New Guinea is unique in that a pidgin language known as Tok Pisin—that is, an artificial language whose vocabulary is drawn from many different languages and that was developed initially to promote trade between people speaking different languages—has become a full-fledged national and official language.

In Tanzania, which has perhaps more cultural diversity relative to its size than any other African country, the government announced recently that Swahili, which is called Kiswahili in Tanzania, would replace English as the country's official language. Thus, Tanzania has become the first African country where an African language has been chosen as its official language, as opposed to a European language. Kiswahili has been viewed as a means toward unifying Tanzania in light of its cultural diversity. Supporters of Kiswahili have pointed out that Tanzania has experienced far less conflict over language, culture, and religion relative to neighboring countries. Nevertheless, some remain concerned that emphasis on Kiswahili and English in education may accelerate the decline and possible extinction of some of the more than 100 local languages spoken throughout Tanzania.

Nigeria, which is Africa's largest country by population, has even more linguistic diversity than Tanzania. More than 500 different languages are spoken in Nigeria, although more than two-thirds of Nigerians speak Hausa, Yoruba, or Igbo. Nigerian educational policy is intended to promote literacy and economic development while balancing efforts to promote cultural diversity. However, rapid population growth coupled with religious warfare and a lack of infrastructure has made it very difficult for Nigeria to achieve its educational objectives.

Issues regarding language and culture in India parallel those in Nigeria. In addition, India has experienced ongoing turmoil over the choice of its official language since it became independent in 1947. Hindi, which is spoken by about 40 percent of India's population, was slated to have become India's official language by 1965. However, massive protests on the part of non-Hindi speakers forced the government to back down, and the provision in the Indian constitution declaring Hindi to become the official language of India was repealed. Today, each of India's states can identify its own language or languages of instruction although some Indians continue to express concern that Hindi will eventually become a dominant language throughout the country.

BELGIUM

Belgium is located in northwestern Europe on the North Sea, adjacent to the Netherlands and between France and Germany. The country has a land area of 11,787 square miles, slightly larger than the state of Maryland, with a population of about 11.7 million as of 2022. Thus, Belgium is one of the most densely populated countries in Europe.

The two major regions of Belgium are Flanders in the north and Wallonia in the south, with Dutch and French being the predominant languages of these regions respectively. About 58 percent of the overall native-born population of Belgium speaks Dutch, and about 40 percent are French speakers. A small number of German speakers live in eastern Belgium near the boundary between Belgium and Germany. Dutch, French, and German are recognized as official languages of Flanders, Wallonia, and eastern Belgium, respectively.

Present-day Belgium has been contested among the European powers for hundreds of years. Belgium along with neighboring Luxembourg and the Netherlands became independent in 1815, after the Napoleonic Wars, as the United Kingdom of the Netherlands. However, the kingdom soon became fragmented because of these linguistic differences, as well as religious differences between Protestant Flanders and Roman Catholic Wallonia. In 1830, leaders in present-day Belgium supported by Roman Catholic clergy declared independence, and the Belgian Revolution began. Britain and France recognized Belgium as an independent state in 1831. The revolution ended in 1839, when the Netherlands recognized Belgian independence.

After independence, tension between the Flemish and the Walloons within Belgium developed and intensified. These tensions involved language and culture. After independence, the government decreed that French would be the dominant language of education and government throughout the country. In 1873, however, the government passed a law that allowed government business to be conducted in Dutch as well as French. Both languages were recognized as official languages of Belgium in 1899, after the Law on Equality was enacted.

In 1962, Belgium established Dutch, French, and German cultural communities. In 1970, the Belgian constitution was amended to confirm the existence and rights of the cultural communities. Each language became official in its community. However, the capital city of Brussels was recognized officially as a bilingual city because it is located within Flanders, but more than three-quarters of its residents speak French. Brussels is the headquarters of the European Union, and its population includes many people from outside of Belgium as well as French-speaking Belgians. Recently, the Brussels metropolitan area has expanded, and many French-speaking persons who work in Brussels have moved to suburban areas that have been established within the borders of the Flemish Cultural Community. Observers have detected tension between the newcomers and longtime residents of these areas who are concerned that the influx of these residents will compromise Flemish culture.

A further bone of contention between Flanders and Wallonia involves economic disparities. For several decades, Flanders has enjoyed higher per capita incomes and considerably lower unemployment relative to Wallonia. In 2013, Flanders' gross domestic product per capita was more than 25 percent greater than that of Wallonia. Cultural and economic tensions between Flanders and Wallonia have led some to predict that Belgium will eventually be divided into two independent countries, and pro-independence parties play important roles in the politics of both regions.

Education in Belgium

Public education in Belgium is managed by each of its cultural communities. The federal government does not play a major role in the provision of education, although it has mandated that education be free and compulsory from the age of 6 until a child reaches the age of 18 or graduates from secondary school.

The basic structure of education in each cultural community is similar. Education begins with preschool, which children as young as two years and six months of age are eligible to attend. Although preschool is not compulsory, well over 90 percent of children between three and six years old are enrolled in preschools. At six years of age, students begin attending primary school, which lasts for six years. The language of instruction is the language of the cultural community, while instruction in a second language begins in the fifth year of primary school. In bilingual Brussels, children are taught either Dutch or French as a second language beginning in the third year of primary school.

Primary school in Belgium is followed by six years of secondary school. There are four basic categories of secondary schools—general or humanities, technical, artistic, and vocational. Graduates in the first three programs usually proceed to higher education, whereas graduates of the vocational category generally move directly into the workforce. Alternative educational programs are also available for children with special needs. A third language, usually English, is also taught in secondary schools.

Whereas Dutch and French are the languages of instructions in Belgium's Flemish and French cultural communities, respectively, Belgium has a large population of immigrants, and both communities provide instruction to immigrant children in their first languages. As of 2016, nearly 500,000 immigrants from non-European Union countries, or more than 4 percent of Belgium's population, were living in Belgium. Many of these migrants come from the Middle East, with the largest numbers of immigrants to Belgium arriving from Morocco and Turkey. To accommodate children of these migrants, schools in which the primary language of instruction is Arabic, Turkish, and Chinese have been established.

Residents of any European Union (EU) country are free to migrate to any other EU country, and schooling is also conducted in Spanish, Italian, Romanian, and the languages of other EU countries that are sending significant numbers of migrants to Belgium.

Language, Multiculturalism, and Education in Belgium

In general, the quality of education in Belgium has been seen as comparable to other wealthier European Union countries. A 2017 survey by the Organisation for Economic Co-operation and Development ranked Belgium third among 35 highly developed countries worldwide, behind only Australia and Canada and ahead of all other EU countries included in the survey.

However, assessment of Belgian education must consider Belgium's language divide and its impacts on Belgian educational outcomes. For example, comparison of standardized test scores across the three cultural communities have indicated that Dutch-speaking children do considerably better in standardized tests than do French-speaking children, with the German-speaking children getting average scores in between. This increasingly controversial distinction between test scores has been attributed not only to differences in wealth between Flanders and Wallonia but also to differences in the secondary school curriculum between the two communities in that the Flemish curriculum places more emphasis on science and mathematics. Flanders' cultural community government also spends a higher percentage of its revenues on education as compared to the French cultural community.

Despite these disparities, some observers have suggested that the long-standing division of Belgium on the basis of language is beneficial, rather than detrimental, to Belgium. Because many Belgians are fluent in three or more languages, Belgian employees are seen as valuable to companies that do business in many different countries. According to one survey conducted in 2012, more than a third of all Belgians speak or read a language other than their first language on an everyday basis. This is particularly true in cosmopolitan, multilingual Brussels. The future of education in Belgium, especially with respect to language, is very likely to depend on Belgium's political future including the possibility that Flanders and Wallonia may eventually become separate independent countries.

Further Reading

Organisation for Economic Co-operation and Development, "Education at a glance 2017," 2017, http://www.oecd.org/education/education-at-a-glance-19991487.htm. Retrieved on March 2, 2018.

Organisation for Economic Co-operation and Development, "Education policy outlook: Belgium," September 2017, http://www.oecd.org/education/Education-Policy-Outlook-Country-Profile-Belgium.pdf. Retrieved on March 2, 2018.

Duncan Robinson, "Tough choices for Wallonia, a region desperate to reinvent itself," *Financial Times*, November 2, 2015, https://www.ft.com/content/c4765a3a-7349-11e5-bdb1-e6e4767162cc. Retrieved on February 26, 2018.

Ian Traynor, "The language divide at the heart of a split that is tearing Belgium apart," *The Guardian*, May 8, 2010, https://www.theguardian.com/world/2010/may/09/belgium -flanders-wallonia-french-dutch. Retrieved on February 26, 2018.

CANADA

Canada, which is the second largest country in the world by land area, occupies the northern portion of North America north of the United States and south of the Arctic Ocean. The large majority of Canada's approximately 38 million people as of 2022 lives within 100 miles of the U.S. border, while much of northern Canada is very sparsely populated or uninhabited.

Native Americans, who are known in Canada as First Nations people, have lived in present-day Canada for at least 12,000 years. The first permanent European settlements in Canada were established in the early seventeenth century. Both France and Britain were active in the settlement of Canada. The cities of Quebec City and Montreal in the St. Lawrence River valley were founded by French settlers in 1608 and 1642, respectively. France claimed the St. Lawrence Valley and named this region New France. To the east, the French also claimed the colony of Acadia. Acadia included the present-day provinces of Nova Scotia and Prince Edward Island, which at that time were known as Acadia and Ile St. Jean, respectively. Meanwhile, Britain claimed Rupert's Land, or present-day northern Ontario, Quebec, and Manitoba. The British also claimed Newfoundland, which became part of Canada in 1948.

France and Britain fought over control of Acadia during the first half of the eighteenth century. With the aid of British colonists in the present-day United States, Britain conquered Acadia in 1710. However, a treaty signed in 1713 returned Prince Edward Island and the northeastern portion of Nova Scotia to France. Beginning in 1756, Britain and France began a protracted struggle throughout the world known as the Seven Years' War and in North America as the French and Indian War. The war ended with the signing of the Treaty of Paris in 1763. Under terms of this treaty, France agreed to give up all of its territorial claims in North America with the exception of the two small islands of St. Pierre and Miquelon off the coast of Newfoundland. However, colonists of French ancestry were allowed to retain the use of the French language and their Roman Catholic religion.

After the Treaty of Paris came into effect, many colonists moved into present-day Canada from Britain or from the Thirteen Colonies. British settlement was augmented by the arrival of many loyalists from the Thirteen Colonies who had opposed the American Revolution. In addition, a substantial number of French speakers left the region, including Acadians or "Cajuns" who moved from Nova Scotia to present-day southern Louisiana. Thus, by the nineteenth century a large majority of residents of what was then called British North America were of British descent and spoke English, with the exception of the remnants of New France, which was now known as Quebec, and the majority of whose residents spoke French. Canada, including Quebec and the English-speaking colonies, became independent in 1867. Originally consisting of the provinces of Quebec, Ontario,

Nova Scotia, and New Brunswick, Canada today includes 10 provinces along with three sparsely populated territories located north of the 60th parallel of north latitude.

Since independence, Canada has remained a highly diverse country. Not only is Quebec overwhelmingly Francophone, whereas large majorities of people living in its other provinces speak English, but also many Canadians come from other cultural traditions and speak other languages. In particular, in many parts of northern Canada First Nations people form the majority of the population. Large numbers of immigrants from China and their descendants live in and near Vancouver, and many immigrants and their descendants from eastern Europe inhabit the central Canadian provinces of Manitoba and Saskatchewan. The ongoing diversity of Canada's population has had considerable impact on Canadian education.

Education in Canada

In Canada, public education is the responsibility of each province's government. The structure of education in each province is similar, although details vary. For example, education is compulsory through the age of 16 in every province, but in Manitoba, New Brunswick, Ontario, and the territory of Nunavut it is compulsory until the age of 18 or until the student has completed secondary school. As in other countries, public education in Canada is divided between primary and secondary schooling.

Although details vary by province, Canadian public education includes kindergarten for one or two years followed by eight years of "elementary education" and four years of secondary education. According to the Canadian Charter of Rights and Freedoms, citizens have the right to have their children educated in public schools in a "minority" language if there are a sufficient number of children speaking that minority language in the area. In practice, this means that English-speaking parents in the province of Quebec can choose to have their children educated in English rather than in French. Public schools are free, but parents may choose to send their children to private schools for which they must pay tuition. As of 2015, about 6 percent of Canadian 15-year-olds were enrolled in private schools.

Language, Multiculturalism, and Education in Canada

Language and culture play important roles in Canadian education. Both English and French are official languages in Canada. Section 16 of the Canadian Charter of Rights and Freedoms, adopted in 1982, contains the words "English and French are the official languages of Canada and have the equality of status and equal rights and privileges as to their use in all institutions of the Parliament and government of Canada." Based on the charter, government business is conducted in both languages. For example, all government documents are published in both French and English, all government services to the Canadian public are available in both languages, and government employees must be fluent in both languages.

This principle applies also to public education. In Quebec, public schooling at the primary and secondary levels is conducted in French with the exception that students have the right to free public education in English. However, English as a second language is taught beginning in primary school. Elsewhere, Canadian citizens have the right to public schooling in French "where numbers warrant." Thus, communities of French-speaking Canadians outside of Quebec maintain publicly funded schools in which French is the language of instruction, although English is the language of instruction in the large majority of Canadian public schools outside Quebec. In these schools, French is usually taught as a second language. For example, students in English-speaking schools in the province of Ontario begin the study of French as a second language beginning in the fourth grade of elementary school.

Language, including the role of language in public education, remains an issue of controversy across Canada. Controversy is particularly intense within Quebec, which is overwhelming Francophone in contrast to the rest of the country. Many Quebecois support more autonomy or outright independence, and French outside of federal government services has become a stronger and stronger marker of cultural identity within Quebec. Because many English-speaking residents of Quebec have left for other provinces, the size of the Francophone majority has continued to increase, and conflict has intensified.

Moreover, some students in Quebec are enrolling in English-speaking postsecondary junior colleges, which are not subject to Quebec's law mandating primary and secondary education in French. Some have done so under the rationale that English, much more than French, is a global language of commerce and business and that the ability to speak English is essential for a successful career. However, members of Quebec's Parti Quebecois, which supports Quebec independence, have tried to eliminate funding for these English-speaking junior colleges in part because they are attracting larger and larger numbers of French-speaking students.

Controversy over language and multiculturalism continues also in areas of Canada containing significant numbers of people who do not speak either English or French as a first language, or what the Canadian government calls their "mother tongue." For example, some children among the more than 400,000 persons of Chinese ancestry in and near Vancouver, British Colombia, now attend schools in which either Mandarin or Cantonese Chinese is the primary language of instruction. Many others attend English-language public schools where Chinese is taught as a second language. However, Vancouver's school board rejected a proposal by some Chinese-Canadian parents to establish a school to be run on principles more characteristic of China and East Asia, including more in-school discipline and more homework than in other public schools in the city.

Controversy is evident also in the territory of Nunavut, which is located north of the 60th parallel in northeastern Canada. Nunavut was separated from the Northwest Territories in 1999. The division was motivated by the goal of creating an Inuit-majority territory, and more than two-thirds of its 40,000 residents as of 2021 are of Inuit ancestry. The Inuit language Inuktitut has official status in

This school bus is on a dirt road in Clyde River in the territory of Nunavut, Canada. Sparsely populated Nunavut has only about 40,000 residents, of whom about 80% are Inuit. The Inuit language, Inuktitut, has equal status with English and French. Many Inuit are pushing for complete bilingual education in order to preserve Inuit culture. (Rpianoshow | Dreamstime.com)

Nunavut along with English and French. As of 2006, only about 25 percent of Nunavut's secondary school students completed high school diplomas.

In part in order to increase this percentage and also in an effort to maintain Inuit cultural identity, in 2008 the government of Nunavut enacted a law that called for complete bilingual education in both English and Inuktitut. The law stated that the implementation of this system would be completed by 2019. However, more recently the government announced its desire to delay this commitment for an additional 10 years. Critics of this decision stated their concern that the delay would cause a loss in the use of Inuktitut and would therefore imperil Inuit culture in Nunavat and throughout northern Canada.

Further Reading

Hillary Brenhouse, "Quebec's war on English: Language politics intensify in Canadian province," *Time*, April 8, 2013, http://world.time.com/2013/04/08/quebecs-war-on-english -language-politics-intensify-in-canadian-province/. Retrieved on March 26, 2018.

CBC Radio, "Nunavut's delay of bilingual education a threat to Inuit language, critic says," March 29, 2017, http://www.cbc.ca/radio/thecurrent/the-current-for-march -29-2017-1.4044278/nunavut-s-delay-of-bilingual-education-a-threat-to-inuit -language-says-critic-1.4044376. Retrieved on March 26, 2018.

Joseph Dicks and Fred Genesee, "Bilingual education in Canada," in *Bilingual and multilingual education. Encyclopedia of Language and Education*, 3rd ed., edited by O. Garcia, A. Lin, and S. May. Cham: Springer.

Giuseppe Valiante, "Controversy in Quebec as more French students choose English colleges," *The Star*, September 8, 2017, https://www.thestar.com/news/canada/2017/09/09/controversy-in-quebec-as-more-french-students-choose-english-colleges.html. Retrieved on March 26, 2018.

INDIA

The Republic of India is located in South Asia, and it occupies most of the Indian subcontinent. With a land area of nearly 1.3 million square miles, India is the seventh largest country in the world by land area. India is the second largest country in the world by population, with more than 1.4 billion residents as of 2022. About 80 percent of India's people are Hindus, and about 14 percent are Muslims.

Portions of present-day India were ruled by various dynasties for more than 2,000 years before the Mughals, who originated in Central Asia before invading northern India, established the Mughal Empire in 1526. The Mughals ruled most of the Indian subcontinent for more than 200 years. Although the Mughal rulers were Muslims, the majority of the Empire's residents were Hindus. During the eighteenth century, the British East India Company began to establish port cities on the Indian coast, enabling the company to control trade between India and England.

In 1858, the British government placed the Indian subcontinent under its control, replacing the company. Direct British control under the auspices of what became known as the British Raj continued into the twentieth century. The area controlled by the British Raj included the present-day countries of India, Pakistan, Bangladesh, and Myanmar. The latter was then known as Burma and was separated from the Raj in 1937. After World War II, the British agreed to grant independence to the British Raj. The area was divided along linguistic lines. Predominantly Hindu areas were placed in the independent state of India, while predominantly Muslim areas in the northwest and northeast became the separate state of Pakistan, which split between present-day Pakistan and present-day Bangladesh in 1971.

As with Nigeria, Tanzania, and Papua New Guinea, India experiences great linguistic diversity. It has been estimated that more than 750 distinct languages are spoken throughout India. Only Papua New Guinea among the world's countries has more languages. The most widely spoken language of India is Hindi, which is spoken by about 40 percent of the population. Hindi is spoken primarily in densely populated northern India.

Hindi and other languages of northern India that are related to Hindi are Indo-European languages and thus are part of the same language family that includes English, Spanish, French, German, and many other languages. In addition to Hindi, major Indo-European languages of northern India include Bengali, Assamese, Punjabi, and Marathi. These and other Indo-European languages are

---

Regional Languages and Education in India

India is a highly diverse society, with hundreds of languages spoken throughout the country. Since India became independent in 1947, the choice of an official language or languages has been controversial. The original Constitution of India specified that Hindi, which is spoken by about 40 percent of the population, would become the official language. However, objections and protests resulted in repealing of this provision. Each state can select one or more languages as official, but English remains understood throughout the country. English is the language of instruction in many schools throughout India, but some experts believe that more attention should be paid to teaching in regional languages.

Source: Nilesh Gaikwad, "Why is education in regional language considered low standard?" *India Today*, August 20, 2019, https://www.indiatoday.in/education-today /featurephilia/story/why-is-education-in-regional-language-considered-low-standard -1582650-2019-08-20. Retrieved on March 21, 2020.

---

spoken by about three-quarters of the population. However, most residents of southern India speak Dravidian languages, which belong to a separate language family. The major Dravidian languages include Telugu, Tamil, Kannada, and Malayalam. Together, these languages are spoken by about 20 percent of the population.

Conflict over language has characterized India since its independence. The original Constitution of India, which came into effect in 1950, specified that Hindi, using the Devanagari script in which it is written generally, would become the official language of India within 15 years, with the words "fifteen years from the commencement of the Constitution, the English Language shall continue to be used for all the official purposes of the Union for which it was being used immediately before such commencement." However, this provision was opposed bitterly by non-Hindi speakers, especially in South India where Dravidian languages were spoken. In 1963, the Official Languages Act was adopted. The Official Languages Act allowed for the continued use of English for official purposes. The Eighth Schedule to the Constitution identified 14 Indian languages, along with English, to having status within the country. Such status implies the government's responsibility for enhancing the development of each of these languages. Subsequent constitutional amendments have identified 8 additional languages as having such status.

Each of India's 28 states (whose status within India is roughly equivalent to the status of the states in the United States or the provinces in Canada) has the right to declare one or more languages as official within its boundaries. Currently, 22 languages, most but not all of which are identified as having national status according to the amended Constitution, are official in one or more states. English is official in 10 states, and Hindi is official in 7 states including Uttar Pradesh, Bihar, and Madhya Pradesh, which are three of India's five largest states by population. In the National Capital Territory (Delhi), which contains the capital city of New Delhi, both English and Hindi along with the closely related Urdu have official status.

Education in India

In India, education is compulsory between the ages of 6 and 14. The system includes 6 years of primary school followed by 6 years of secondary school. Private schools play a significant role in the provision of education, although about 80 percent of children between 6 and 14 attend public schools. The national government proposes and determines educational policies, but it is up to the state governments to implement them.

The Right of Children to Free and Compulsory Education Act of 2009 specified education as a fundamental right. The act also stipulated that public schooling for children between 6 and 14 would be free. Secondary school curricula prepare students for nationwide examinations that are taken upon completion of the tenth and twelfth grades. This system has been criticized on the grounds that preparation for the examination privileges rote memorization at the expense of critical thinking and that students' mental and physical health is affected because they spend so much time preparing for the examinations.

As is the case with other developing countries, Indian education suffers from a lack of resources needed to educate India's large and growing population. Many schools suffer from high pupil-to-teacher ratios; a lack of qualified teachers; and shortages of buildings, textbooks, and other learning materials. These problems have encouraged many parents who can afford to do so to send their children to private schools, which are generally assumed to provide better education as compared to public schools.

Overall, according to 2011 statistics about 93 percent of children of appropriate ages were enrolled in primary school and 69 percent were enrolled in secondary school. However, in general student performance in tests of educational competence has been generally poor. This is a particular issue in rural India, in part because of conservative cultural attitudes and because rural farm families depend on child labor. Despite government policy as articulated in the Right of Children Act, many children remain functionally illiterate. Gender differences in literacy remain a matter of concern.

Language, Multiculturalism, and Education in India

Policy concerning languages of instruction varies across India. After the original mandate to phase out English by 1965 was eliminated, the government promoted the idea that students graduating from secondary school should demonstrate fluency in three languages—English, Hindi, and the local language. Those students living in Hindi-speaking areas would be taught another Indian language other than Hindi. Opponents of this idea expressed concern that the three-language policy

These children are studying Hindi in a school in northern India. Hindi is spoken by about 40 percent of India's population, but speakers of other languages have resisted efforts to make Hindi the country's national language. Rather, each state can identify one or more languages as official, and education in that state is conducted in its official language. (Koscusko | Dreamstime.com)

represented an indirect means of imposing Hindi on the entire country. Over time, some states rejected the three-language policy. For example, in the southern state of Tamil Nadu the government announced in 2010 that by 2016 all instruction would be undertaken in Tamil or English only, while the study of Hindi would no longer be compulsory.

In some states, concern has been raised about the status of Indigenous peoples, known as Adivasis. For example, about half of the population of the small north-eastern state of Manipur are members of the Meitei ethnic group. The Meitei speak the Meitei language, which is known also as Manipuri and is the official language of the state. However, many non-Meitei in Manipur are Adivasis, many of whom live in isolated rural areas and speak distinct languages that are unrelated to Meitei. A lack of qualified teachers and textbooks has made it very difficult to provide early primary schooling in these languages, putting these Adivasi students at a disadvantage as they progress through the educational system.

Debate continues about the desirability of English as the language of instruction in India's schools, as opposed to instruction in other official languages (including Hindi) of the respective states. As in other culturally diverse countries, this debate involves how to balance the competing objectives of economic development in a global society with cultural preservation and continuity. Proponents of

English-language instruction also point out that English, rather than Hindi, can be considered a unifying force within the entire country. In recent years, increasing numbers of parents have sent their children to English-language schools, believing that English fluency would be very important to their children's career success and income potential as adults. In India's largest city of Mumbai, some teachers explain concepts in Marathi, which is the official language of the state of Maharashtra where Mumbai is located. However, students read from English-language textbooks and take examinations in English.

Further Reading

Niruba Sarath Jayasundara, "The development of language education policy: An Indian perspective; a view from Tamil Nadu," *International Journal of Scientific and Research Publications*, 4 (2014), pp. 1–4, http://www.ijsrp.org/research-paper-1114/ijsrp-p3530.pdf. Retrieved on June 18, 2018.

Pushpa Pai, "Multilingualism, multiculturalism, and education: Case study of Mumbai City," in *ISB4: Proceedings of the 4th International Symposium on Bilingualism*, edited by James Cohen, Kara T. McAlister, Kellie Rolstad, and Jeff MacSwain. Somerville, MA: Cascadilla Press, 2005, pp. 1794–1806, http://www.lingref.com/isb/4/141ISB4.PDF. Retrieved on June 18, 2018.

Maseeh Rahman, "Language exodus reshapes India's schools," *The Guardian*, May 15, 2012, https://www.theguardian.com/education/2012/may/15/india-schools-english. Retrieved on June 18, 2012.

NIGERIA

The Federal Republic of Nigeria, located in west-central Africa, is by far the largest country in Africa by population. With more than 216 million people as of 2022, Nigeria is the seventh largest country in the world by population. With a land area of about 357,000 miles, Nigeria's population density is more than 500 people per square mile. Only Rwanda and Burundi among Africa's mainland countries have a higher population density.

Not only is Nigeria heavily populated, but it also contains great cultural, linguistic, and environmental diversity. Southern Nigeria has a rainy climate and was originally covered in forest, although humans have cut down many of Nigeria's forests. By contrast, northern Nigeria is semiarid and often subject to drought. Nigeria's population contains many different ethnic groups who speak numerous distinct languages. The largest of these ethnic groups are the Hausa and Fulani in the north, the Yoruba in the southwest, and the Igbo in the southeast. The population is also divided by religion, with the north dominated by Muslims and the south dominated by Christians. Most Hausa and Fulani are Muslims; most Igbo are Christians, and the Yoruba population is divided between the two religions. Violent conflict between Christians and Muslims has plagued Nigeria for many years.

Prior to European colonization, parts of present-day Nigeria were ruled at times by various empires, kingdoms, and city-states. Europeans began to assume control of the Nigerian coast in the eighteenth century. Lagos, which is by far the largest city in Nigeria today, was incorporated into the British Empire in 1861 as the Lagos Colony. In the late nineteenth century, the British established a presence in the interior and created the Niger Coast Protectorate including most of the remaining portions of present-day southern Nigeria. Meanwhile, what is today northern Nigeria was placed under a British sphere of influence via the Treaty of Berlin, which divided most of African into spheres of influence dominated by the European colonial powers. Northern and Southern Nigeria were united as the colony of Nigeria in 1914. In 1960, Nigeria became independent. However, the intense cultural, ethnic, and religious differences within the country have hindered efforts to create a national identity and have also affected education.

Education in Nigeria

Education in Nigeria has been based historically on the British system, but over time, government educational policy and practice have been modified in accordance with changes in the country. The current system was established under the Universal Basic Education Act, which took effect in 1999. Under the act, nine years of education including six years of primary school and three years of junior secondary school are compulsory. Education at these levels is free, although parents are required to purchase school supplies and uniforms. Junior secondary school is followed by three years of senior secondary school, which is not compulsory.

Rapid population growth, lack of resources, and high population densities in many parts of the country have caused severe overcrowding in many of Nigeria's schools. Class sizes of more than 60 pupils are not unusual, and a shortage of classroom buildings has forced teachers in some schools to hold their classes outdoors. However, it has been estimated that a third or more of Nigeria's children of primary school age are not actually enrolled in school. This lack of enrollment is associated with several factors. Many parents cannot afford uniforms and school supplies. Other families, particularly farming families in rural areas, depend on their children's labor and regard school as a waste of their children's time. For similar reasons, and especially because of family dependence on children as sources of labor, only about a third of students who do complete primary school go on to secondary school. Thus, only a minority of school-age students in Nigeria follow the University Basic Education Act's policies.

Also, school attendance has been affected by religious factors, especially in the northeast where some areas are controlled by the radical Islamic group Boko Haram. On several occasions, Boko Haram has taken responsibility for kidnapping schoolchildren. In 2014, for example, Boko Haram operatives kidnapped 276 schoolgirls in Chibok, which is a Christian-majority community within the area under Boko Haram control. Threats of kidnapping and violence have discouraged parents from sending their children, particularly girls, to school. Boko Haram's actions have also displaced many families as refugees, further impacting enrollment in schools. In part for all of these reasons, it has been estimated that as many as two-thirds of residents of northern Nigeria are functionally illiterate.

Language, Multiculturalism, and Education in Nigeria

Although more than 500 distinct languages are spoken in Nigeria, English is the country's official language and is also the language of instruction in Nigeria's schools. During the first three years of primary school, instruction is given in the local language with English taught as a school subject. Beginning in the fourth year of primary school, English is the language of instruction at all levels of education throughout the country. Some Nigerian officials see English as a unifying force in Nigeria's highly diverse, multilingual society. Also, fluency in English is viewed as important to international business, government service, trade, and industry within Nigeria.

It has been estimated, however, that only about one-third of adult Nigerians can speak, read, and write English fluently. Most of those Nigerians who are fluent in English are members of the middle and upper classes and reside in urban areas. Farmers and other rural residents are much less likely to be able to speak or understand English. Thus, some Nigerians regard English as the language of the elite and have called for greater recognition of Indigenous languages, with more emphasis on teaching these languages as well as English to students. It has been argued that Hausa, Yoruba, Igbo, and perhaps other languages should become the languages of instruction beyond the early primary school level in those areas in which these languages predominate.

Thus, Nigerian educational policy is based on balancing the goal of national unity with the goal of preserving Nigerian cultural diversity. According to the national education policy that is based on the Universal Basic Education Act, "Government appreciates the importance of language as a means of promoting social interaction and national cohesion; and preserving cultures. Thus every child shall learn the language of the immediate environment. Furthermore, in the interest of national unity it is expedient that every child shall be required to learn one of the three Nigerian languages: Hausa, Igbo and Yoruba." Also, the policy specifies that "the medium of instruction in the primary school shall be the language of the environment for the first three years. During this period, English shall be taught as a subject. From the fourth year, English shall progressively be used as a medium of instruction and the language of immediate environment and French [which is the official language of nearby West African countries that are former French colonies] shall be taught as subjects."

According to one study, only a minority of school systems in Nigeria actually follow this model. The study as reported by Oladuton Olagbajo contains the results of a survey of teachers concerning language education. Most teachers reported that students preferred to be educated in English and that parents preferred English-language instruction for their children. However, they reported that students were more interested in the subjects when these subjects were taught in

Here are school children in Nigeria, which is the largest country by population in Africa. More than 500 distinct languages are spoken in Nigeria, making it one of the most culturally diverse countries in the world. The Nigerian government is working to balance cultural diversity with national unity. (Rwhittlesey | Dreamstime.com)

the local Indigenous language and that the students understood better the material being taught. A large majority of the teachers surveyed called attention to a lack of textbooks and other learning materials, and many stated that they themselves did not understand the two Indigenous languages (that is, the local language as well as Hausa, Yoruba, or Igbo) needed for compliance with government policy.

Further Reading

Danjuli Abdullahi and John Abdullah, "The political will and quality basic education in Nigeria," *Journal of Power, Politics, and Governance*, 2 (2014), pp. 75–100, http://jppgnet .com/journals/jppg/Vol_2_No_2_June_2014/5.pdf. Retrieved on June 18, 2018.

Ifeyinwa Obiegbu, "The English language and sustainable development in Nigeria," *Open Journal of Political Science*, 5 (2015), pp. 82–86, http://file.scirp.org/pdf/OJPS _2015022711023491.pdf. Retrieved on June 18, 2018.

Morakinyo Ogunmodimu, "Language policy in Nigeria: Problems, prospects, and perspectives," *International Journal of Humanities and Social Science*, 5 (2015), pp. 154–160, http://www.ijhssnet.com/journals/Vol_5_No_9_September_2015/16.pdf. Retrieved on June 18, 2018.

Oladuton O. Olagbaju, "Multilingual education in Nigeria: Policy, practice, challenges, and solutions," *Journal of Education and Practice*, 5 (2015), pp. 66–73, http://www.iiste.org /Journals/index.php/JEP/article/viewFile/11209/11538. Retrieved on June 18, 2018.

Ushe Mike Ushe, "Religious conflicts and education in Nigeria: Implications for national security," *Journal of Education and Practice*, 6 (2015), pp. 117–129, https://files.eric .ed.gov/fulltext/EJ1083822.pdf. Retrieved on June 18, 2018.

PAPUA NEW GUINEA

The Independent State of Papua New Guinea occupies the eastern half of the island of New Guinea along with many offshore islands including Bougainville, New Britain, and New Ireland. At its closest point, Papua New Guinea is less than 150 miles north of Australia, from which it is separated by the Torres Strait. The overall land area of Papua New Guinea is about 178,703 square miles, making it slightly larger than California, and the population was estimated at 9.3 million in 2022. Papua New Guinea is one of the most rural societies in the world, with an estimated 80 percent of its people residing outside of cities.

According to anthropologists, settlers from mainland Asia first began to inhabit the island of New Guinea between 40,000 and 50,000 years ago. Europeans first sighted New Guinea in the sixteenth century and began to establish territorial claims to the island in the late nineteenth century. The western half of New Guinea, which is now part of Indonesia, was claimed by the Netherlands. Germany claimed northeastern New Guinea, and Britain claimed the southeastern portion of the island. In 1906, the British authorized Australia to administer its portion of New Guinea, which was known as Papua.

After World War I, Germany was required to give up all of its overseas colonies in accordance with the terms of the Treaty of Versailles. The League of Nations gave various countries mandates over the former German colonies, and German New Guinea was assigned to Australia. After World War II, Australia combined the former German New Guinea and Papua into a single colony known as the Territory of Papua and New Guinea. The territory became independent under its current name in 1975.

Papua New Guinea's cultural diversity is unmatched anywhere else in the world. Its 9.3 million people speak more than 800 mutually unintelligible languages. The value of cultural diversity is recognized in the country's constitution with the words "traditional villages and communities [are] to remain as viable units of Papua New Guinean society." However, cultural diversity within the country resulted in difficulties in communication. Since the arrival of Europeans, present-day Papua New Guinea has faced the question of how to facilitate communication among its diverse populations as well as with traders, settlers, and colonists from Europe, mainland Asia, and other places throughout the world. In places with high degrees of cultural diversity including Papua New Guinea, pidgin languages have been developed to promote intercultural communication. Pidgin languages include vocabularies containing words originating from many different languages. Most pidgin languages have relatively simple grammatical structures, making them easy to learn.

The pidgin language that developed in what is now Papua New Guinea became known as Tok Pisin (literally "Talk Pidgin"). Linguists estimate that about 80 percent of the vocabulary of Tok Pisin originated from European languages, especially English and German as the languages of former colonial powers. Most of the remaining vocabulary comes from the Indigenous languages of New Guinea and the offshore islands, with a few words coming from Asian languages. Words

---

Supporting Diversity in the Classroom

How can cultural diversity be supported and celebrated in schools? In many countries, children who are perceived as "different" on the basis of ethnicity, culture, race, or religion feel excluded. However, researchers have demonstrated that classroom diversity promotes critical thinking and can result in improved academic outcomes. Several strategies to promote cultural diversity in the classroom are advocated. These include promoting connections with the students' communities, critical analysis of teaching materials, and getting to know each student as an individual, recognizing his or her unique background and life experiences.

Source: Maria Kampen, "7 ways to support diversity in the classroom," prodigygame.com, April 17, 2019, https://www.prodigygame.com/blog/diversity-in-the-classroom/. Retrieved on March 21, 2020.

---

commonly used in Tok Pisin are "solwara" (the ocean, or salt water), "haus moni" (a house of money, or a bank), "haus sik" (a house for people who are ill, or a hospital), and "hukim pis" (to hook or catch a fish).

After independence, Tok Pisin developed into the national language of Papua New Guinea. The language developed in written form. Today, many books and newspapers are published in Tok Pisin, and many websites on the internet are posted in Tok Pisin. Debates in the parliament of Papua New Guinea are conducted in Tok Pisin, implying that any candidate for a seat in the parliament must be able to speak and understand the language. Tok Pisin became one of Papua New Guinea's three official languages along with English and Hiri Motu, which is based upon a widely spoken Indigenous language but has been infused with Australian vocabulary. However, the use of Hiri Motu has been declining as the use of Tok Pisin has increased in part because the former is associated with Papua New Guinea's colonial past. Thus, the ability to speak, read, and write Tok Pisin has become a cultural marker and a symbol of national identity for Papua New Guinea.

Education in Papua New Guinea

Education in Papua New Guinea is free to citizens of the country, but it is not compulsory. That education is not compulsory contributes to Papua New Guinea's relatively low literacy rate of less than 65 percent as of 2015. However, in 2009, the government's Ministry of Education established a 10-year plan, one of the goals of which was make education compulsory.

The educational process includes two years of "introductory" school followed by four years of primary school, four years of secondary school, and two years of high school. Introductory education, which begins at the age of seven, and primary education are provided in local community schools and are conducted in the local languages spoken commonly in the area. As of 2009, about 87 percent of school-age children were enrolled in introductory or primary schools although this percentage is lower in more isolated and sparsely populated areas.

In secondary schools, one of the country's three official languages becomes the language of instruction. The first two years of secondary school are also conducted locally, after which students proceed to schools provided at the provincial level via one of Papua New Guinea's 33 provinces. Because a large majority of Papua New Guinea's people live in rural areas where secondary schools are not available or accessible, many secondary school and high school students attend boarding schools. Some students are educated in schools established by churches and other religious organizations.

Language, Multiculturalism, and Education in Papua New Guinea

Papua New Guinea remains a highly rural society, with many people living in isolated areas in rugged terrain. In these areas, in particular, there remains a shortage of learning materials and qualified teachers. Government officials have found it difficult to recruit teachers who are willing to work in remote rural areas. Thus, Papua New Guinea's educational system is hindered by the country's geography, although literacy rates are increasing, and education is becoming more and more universally available.

The use of Tok Pisin as one of Papua New Guinea's official languages has helped provide a common ground for education, given the country's great cultural and linguistic diversity. Although Tok Pisin has become a more and more universal language within Papua New Guinea, some educators see Tok Pisin as primarily a vehicle for teaching English as opposed to it being a meaningful language in and of itself. In addition, a study conducted on the island of New Britain indicated that a majority of teachers surveyed believed that extensive use of Tok Pisin in the classroom interfered with the students' ability to learn English. Teachers noted that this created confusion among students in part because many words in English are very similar to the equivalent words in Tok Pisin. For example, the words "boy" and "house" in English are spelled "boi" and "haus," respectively, in Tok Pisin. However, a large majority of secondary school students surveyed agreed that knowledge of English is very important in today's society.

Some teachers and parents argued also that emphasis on Tok Pisin in schools could impede the preservation of vernacular languages within the country. This is true particularly with respect to vernacular languages that lack alphabets and are spoken but not written. Also, many of Papua New Guinea's languages are highly endangered and spoken by less than a few thousand or even a few hundred people. Moreover, many government-certified teachers do not know the local vernacular languages when they begin to teach in a place where that language is used. Thus, some Papua New Guineans are concerned that their local cultures may disappear and that they are being discriminated against or looked down upon if they continue to use the vernacular language as opposed to Tok Pisin, English, or Hiri Motu.

Further Reading

Kilala Devette-Chee, "Bilingual education in a multilingual nation: Attitudes toward Tok Pisin and Tolai in Papua New Guinea primary schools," Ph.D. dissertation, University of Canberra, 2014, https://docplayer.net/29553237-Bilingual-education-in-a-multilingual -nation.html. Retrieved on May 3, 2022.

Government of Papua New Guinea, National Executive Council, "Achieving universal education for a better future: Universal basic education plan 2010–2019," 2009, https://www.globalpartnership.org/content/papua-new-guinea-universal-basic -education-plan-2010-2019. Retrieved on March 3, 2018.

Catherine Levy, "Language research in Papua New Guinea: A case study of Awar," *Contemporary PNG Studies: DWU Research Journal*, 2 (2005), pp. 79–92, https://www .thefreelibrary.com/Language+research+in+Papua+New+Guinea%3A+A+case+study +of+Awar.-a0179978519. Retrieved on May 3, 2022.

Susan Malone and Patricia Paraide, "Mother tongue-based bilingual education in Papua New Guinea," *International Review of Education*, 57 (2011), pp. 705–720.

PERU

The Republic of Peru is located along the Pacific Ocean coast of western South America. With a land area of nearly 500,000 square miles, Peru is the third largest country in South America after Brazil and Argentina. It is the fourth largest country in South America by population, with 33 million inhabitants as of 2021. Peru includes three dramatically different environments: its arid coastal plain including its capital city of Lima to the west, the high peaks and plateaus of the Andes Mountains in the center, and rainforest lowlands that are part of the Amazon River basin east of the Andes. This geography continues to contribute to Peru's cultural diversity today.

The Inca Empire conquered and governed much of present-day western and central Peru during the fifteenth and early sixteenth centuries, ruling their empire from the Peruvian city of Cusco. In 1526, Spanish conquistadors made contact with the Incas. In 1533, the Inca empire was overthrown, and the area that had been ruled by the Incas was claimed by Spain. Present-day Peru became part of the Viceroyalty of Peru and remained under the Viceroyalty until declaring independence in 1821.

Today, about a third of Peru's people live in Lima and its surrounding suburbs. Many people from outlying areas of Peru have migrated to Lima, but the rest of the country contains a highly diverse population from many different cultural and linguistic backgrounds. Today about 84 percent of Peruvians speak Spanish as a first language. About 13 percent speak Quechua or Aymara, which are derived from the language used by the Incas prior to Spanish conquest. Quechua is an official language of Peru and is spoken primarily in the Andean highlands.

The remaining 3 percent of Peruvians speak other Indigenous languages. Peruvians who live in the Amazon basin region speak a wide variety of Indigenous languages that are unrelated to either Spanish or Quechua. According to one estimate, nearly 50 Indigenous languages are spoken in Peru. Many Peruvians, who are not native Spanish speakers, have learned Spanish as a second language, although a few tribes living in this area have had little or no contact with outsiders.

During the last two decades of the twentieth century, Peru experienced substantial levels of insurrection, civil war, and unrest. Authoritarian regimes attempted to impose Spanish on the entire country. Thousands of Peruvians, many of them from Indigenous backgrounds, lost their lives during this period of violence. Peru now enjoys more political stability, and more recent governments have relaxed previous regimes' efforts to impose Spanish culture. However, Peruvians who do not speak Spanish are at a considerable disadvantage in comparison to Spanish speakers. Non-Spanish speakers are much more likely to face poverty than are those persons who do speak Spanish and are more likely to be targets of racial and ethnic discrimination. These considerations have contributed to Peru's ongoing history of conflict over language and cultural identity, especially as these concerns affect education.

Education in Peru

Education in Peru is managed by the Ministry of Education. It is organized and administered at the national level. Local educational officials are expected to implement the policies and procedures set forth by the ministry.

Public education in Peru is free and compulsory between the ages of 6 and 16. Children between ages 3 and 6 may attend "initial" schools, but attendance at these initial schools is not compulsory. At age 6, children begin primary school, which lasts for 6 years. They then move on to secondary school for 5 years. Since 2005, according to government estimates, about 72 percent of Peruvian children of the appropriate age have been enrolled in initial school. The enrollment rates at primary and secondary schools have been estimated at 97 percent and 91 percent, respectively.

Despite high levels of school enrollment, other government estimates have indicated that about a third of Peruvian children between 5 and 17 years of age are in the labor force. This estimate suggests that many of these children are enrolled in school but do not actually attend school. This lack of actual school attendance has been observed especially in the Andean highlands and in the Amazon River basin regions, which are both inhabited by relatively large numbers of persons with Indigenous ancestry.

Language, Multiculturalism, and Education in Peru

Spanish is the language of instruction in most Peruvian schools. Until the beginning of the twenty-first century, the Ministry of Education required that all instruction be conducted in Spanish. This policy has been relaxed, however. In the Andean highlands, at some places primary schooling is conducted in Quechua with Spanish taught as a second language. Nevertheless, nearly half of Peruvian children who speak a language other than Spanish as their first language are not provided with instruction in their Indigenous languages. In part because they have difficulty in understanding Spanish, these children are more likely to drop out of school.

More generally, the overall quality of education is characterized by high levels of geographical disparity. In geographically isolated and remote areas, schools are not always available to pupils. Transportation may not be available for students even if the nearest schools are reasonably close to settlements and students must walk to school, and the long walk is difficult for younger children. Moreover, schools in rural areas suffer from a lack of qualified teachers and educational resources and materials, and teachers are often paid very poorly. Differences between educational performance in urban and rural areas have been noted, with much higher percentages of students in urban areas performing at a satisfactory level in standardized, government-administered tests in comparison to the percentages among those in rural areas.

Bilingual education has become an issue of concern for some Peruvian parents as well as for government officials and education experts. Throughout Peru, many parents want their children to learn Spanish. Knowledge of Spanish is seen as important especially for those Peruvians who migrate to cities in search of employment. Those Peruvians who cannot speak Spanish may also be victims of discrimination.

However, the importance of Indigenous languages in preserving local cultures is also recognized. As in other parts of the world, there are concerns that the loss of a language results in the loss of the culture with which that language is associated. Hence, many parents and local officials in areas dominated by Indigenous cultures have become strong advocates for bilingual education. There is some evidence that bilingual education has a positive impact on educational achievement. According to one study, Quechua-speaking children who attended schools conducted in Quechua did as well in tests of Spanish as did children educated in Spanish, and they performed much better in standardized tests on mathematics. Despite poverty, lack of accessibility, and discrimination, some have argued that rural schools throughout Peru will play critical roles in maintaining Indigenous cultures while at the same time preparing young people for Peruvian life as adults.

Further Reading

The Borgen Project, "The State of Education in Peru," June 4, 2014, https://borgenproject.org/state-education-peru/. Retrieved on April 2, 2018.

Marisol D'Andrea, "Peru: Inequality of education for indigenous groups, the neglected class," Inequality for Indigenous Groups, 2007, http://www.focal.ca/pdf/Inequality%20of%20Indigenous%20Groups%20in%20Peru.pdf. Retrieved on April 2, 2018.

Maria Luisa Fornara, "Peru: Guaranteeing education in indigenous languages," UNICEF, November 18, 2015, https://blogs.unicef.org/blog/peru-guaranteeing-education-in-indigenous-languages/. Retrieved on April 2, 2018.

Disa Hynsjo and Amy Damon, "Bilingual education in Peru: Evidence on how Quechua-medium education affects indigenous children's academic achievement," *Economics of Education Review*, 53 (2016), pp. 116–132.

TANZANIA

The United Republic of Tanzania, located in east-central Africa, includes Tanganyika on the Indian Ocean coast of the African mainland and the offshore islands of Zanzibar and Pemba in the Indian Ocean. The country's name amalgamates the names of these two territories. Tanzania's overall land area is about 365,000. The population was estimated at 62 million as of 2022 . Tanganyika on the mainland includes about 98 percent of the country's land area and about 98 percent of the country's total population.

Most of sub-Saharan Africa's countries contain highly diverse populations. The cultural and ethnic diversity of many African countries is due in part to their colonial histories, when European colonial powers delineated their boundaries with little or no knowledge of or regard for local conditions. Tanzania is no exception, and its population includes more than 100 distinct ethnic groups. Compared to its population, Tanzania is believed to have more cultural and linguistic diversity than any other country in Africa.

Zanzibar and the mainland coast have been recognized as trade centers for hundreds of years. Merchants from the Persian Gulf region and from the Indian subcontinent are known to have visited Zanzibar at least 1,500 years ago. Although nearly 99 percent of Tanzanians are of African ancestry, substantial numbers of people of Asian, Middle Eastern, and European ancestry live in Tanzania. None of Tanzania's ethnic groups dominate the country relative to others. The Sukuma, who live primarily in northwestern Tanzania, are the largest ethnic group in Tanzania, but with about 9 million members, they represent less than 20 percent of the population.

The cultural diversity of Tanzania has been enhanced by the distinct colonial histories of its two components. Vasco de Gama became the first European to visit Zanzibar in 1498, claiming the region for Portugal. The Portuguese were expelled from the area in the early eighteenth century when the sultanate of Zanzibar, whose rulers were Arabs from present-day Oman, took control of both Zanzibar and the mainland coast. In the 1880s, the sultanate was overthrown. As the European powers divided Africa into colonies, Tanganyika became a German colony while Zanzibar became a British protectorate. The Germans agreed not to interfere with British administration of Zanzibar. However, after Germany was forced to give up its overseas colonies following World War I, the League of Nations awarded a mandate over Tanganyika to the British. The two colonies were administered separately by the British until Tanganyika became independent in 1962 and Zanzibar became independent in 1963. The two united into a single country with its present name in 1964.

More than 100 distinct languages are spoken locally throughout Tanzania. Swahili, known in Tanzania as Kiswahili, is the official language of the country, and

English is used widely. Kiswahili developed initially as a trade language along the East African coast, enabling communication among African, Arab, and European traders and merchants prior to European colonization of the region. It is spoken in Kenya, Uganda, Zambia, Mozambique, and other East African countries in addition to Tanzania. Most Tanzanians speak Kiswahili, and many speak English also. However, for many Tanzanians, these languages are second and third languages. Nevertheless, within Tanzania, Kiswahili has been seen as a unifying force, with the result that Tanzania has experienced much less ethnic conflict than have most of its neighbors.

Education in Tanzania

The structure of public education in Tanzania is based largely on the British model. At the age of five, children can attend preprimary education, although participation in preprimary education is not compulsory. This is followed by seven years of primary school, which is compulsory. Tuition is free, but parents must pay for uniforms, books, and other school supplies for their children. Primary school is followed by six years of secondary education, including four years of ordinary or O-level secondary education followed by two years of advanced or A-level secondary education. Even though tuition at public schools is free, many teenagers do not attend secondary school because their families cannot afford the additional fees associated with secondary education. However, as part of a far-reaching plan the government announced plans to eliminate required fees for uniforms and school supplies.

As of 2011, about 94 percent of Tanzania's children between the ages of 7 and 13 were enrolled in primary school. This percentage has increased rapidly since 2002, when the government eliminated tuition fees for public schooling despite the other required expenses. Rapid increases in the percentage of students in school, along with a high birth rate and steady population growth, have led to overcrowding, very large class sizes, and a shortage of qualified teachers.

Language, Multiculturalism, and Education in Tanzania

Even before Tanzania achieved independence, English has been the language of instruction in most of Tanzania's secondary schools. However, critics of Tanzanian education have argued that use of English at this level privileges children from wealthy families at the expense of those from poor families and rural areas. English speakers tend to be concentrated in urban areas and among the middle and upper classes. Although Tanzanian children do well in standardized tests of proficiency in various subjects as compared to those in nearby African countries, in 2009 only about a third of Tanzania's secondary school students demonstrated proficiency in English.

Whether English or Kiswahili should be the primary language of instruction has been a matter of debate for many years. Those supportive of maintaining English as the language of instruction have argued that higher levels of proficiency in English will help students to prepare better for careers in the English-dominated global economy. Critics of English as the language of instruction argued that this practice would reinforce and increase the gap in wealth between the urban elite and poorer, rural Tanzanians. In 2015, the government announced that Kiswahili, rather than English, would become the language of instruction in public schools although English is the language of instruction in most private schools. In doing so, Tanzania became the first African country to mandate an African language as its language of instruction.

The debate over language of instruction also applies to the more than 100 Indigenous languages spoken throughout Tanzania. Tanzania has experienced considerably less ethnic conflict than has been the case in neighboring countries such as Kenya and Rwanda. Kiswahili has been seen as a unifying factor associated with the absence of ethnic conflicts in Tanzania. However, the dominance of Kiswahili and English is seen as imperiling the viability of other languages. According to one study, 48 of the 126 languages spoken in the country (not including English, Kiswahili, and languages spoken by non-African Tanzanians such as Chinese, Arabic, and Hindi) have been classified as "endangered" or "dying." Speakers of some of these languages have expressed concern that these languages will become extinct in the foreseeable future, and with the loss of these languages will come the loss of cultures that have existed for hundreds or thousands of years. Tanzanian education will likely continue to deal with conflicting pressures and objectives: English as the language of the global economy, Kiswahili as a unifying factor within Tanzania and a mark of East African identity, and local languages as means of preserving the many distinct cultural traditions throughout the country.

Plans to unite Tanzania with Kenya, Uganda, Rwanda, Burundi, and South Sudan into a single country tentatively to be called the East African Federation are under consideration. All of these countries except for Rwanda and Burundi are former British colonies. If created, the federation would become the largest country by land area in Africa. It would become the second largest country by population in Africa, following Nigeria, and the eighth largest country by population in the world. Kiswahili has been proposed as the federation's official language, with the idea of promoting national identity throughout the highly diverse federation.

Further Reading

Omar Mohammed, "Tanzania ditches English as its official language in schools, opts for Kiswahili," Quartz Media, March 5, 2015, https://qz.com/355444/tanzania-dumps-english-as-its-official-language-in-schools-opts-for-kiswahili/. Retrieved on June 15, 2018.

Huruma Luhuvilo Sigalla, "Ethnic diversity in East Africa: The Tanzanian case," *The Future of Africa*, October 16, 2009, https://thefutureofafrica.wordpress.com/2009/10/16/ethnic-diversity-in-east-africa-the-tanzania-case/. Retrieved on June 16, 2018.

Marie Yahl, "Education in Tanzania," 2015, http://www.nyu.edu/classes/keefer/waoe/webbj.pdf. Retrieved on June 13, 2018.

UNITED STATES

The population of the United States is highly diverse, including people whose ancestors originated throughout the world—in North America itself, Asia, Africa, Latin America, Europe, and many other places. Thus, the United States has one of the most diverse populations in the world. The diversity of the American population is recognized in the United States' motto, E pluribus unum.

This diversity is expressed also in the large numbers of languages spoken by Americans, past and present. Immigrants to the United States, both in the past and present, bring with them a wide variety of spoken and written languages. English is used commonly in government, private business, and education. However, English is not the official language of the United States, which differs from most countries throughout the world in not having any official language at all.

Many Americans believe that English should be the official language of the United States, and others argue for maintaining the status quo on the grounds that mandating an official language will squelch cultural diversity. This debate has focused in particular on education. Should American children be educated in English? Or should English be taught as a second language to those children who do not speak English at home? The debate about language of instruction carries over into questions of teaching about cultural diversity and the degree to which curricula should promote and emphasize cultural diversity among the American population.

The Common School Movement

Understanding of multicultural and multilingual education in the United States begins with the common school movement. In colonial New England, many early settlers were Puritans, Separatists, and other Protestants for whom personal knowledge of the Bible was very important for their religious beliefs. Hence, one had to learn to read in order to gain this personal knowledge.

Thus, the New England colonies began to establish public schools. By the end of the seventeenth century, each of them required every town to provide schools for their children. Although New England's colonial legislatures made education compulsory, in practice enrollment at these public schools was sometimes limited to white boys. Not until 1767, shortly before the American Revolution, did the New England colonies begin to establish tax-supported public schools for girls. Schools were also not free; parents were charged tuition, reducing access to education among children of the poor. Nevertheless, literacy rates in the New England colonies were substantially higher than those in the rest of the Thirteen Colonies. In these areas, children of wealthy parents were educated by private tutors or in private schools while children of the poor often had little or no opportunity to attend school or to learn to read and write.

During and after the revolutions, leaders of the newly independent United States began to promote universal public education. In 1779, for example, Thomas Jefferson (1743–1826) expressed a belief that education in these "common schools" was necessary to provide American citizens instruction in what he regarded as civic and moral virtues. Thus, proponents of universal education argued that the government should play a larger and more prominent role in providing schools for children regardless of their socioeconomic status.

The concept of the common school is associated most frequently with Horace Mann (1796–1859). Mann was appointed as the first Secretary to the Commonwealth of Massachusetts' Board of Education. As Secretary, with administrative responsibilities, Mann became the United States' leading advocate for common schooling. He believed that social progress and the maintenance of freedom and democracy depended on universal literacy and knowledge of civic rights, duties, and responsibilities. To achieve these goals, Mann argued that schools should be made available to all children, supported by taxes, and provided in schools that would be attended by all children regardless of social class and status. The idea of common schooling spread gradually throughout the United States.

Mann believed that public schooling should be "nonsectarian." However, the curricula associated with the majority of nineteenth-century common schools emphasized a white, Protestant worldview. Native Americans were seen often as "savages" who were to be removed from lands desired by Euro-American farmers and planters. In many schools, children were required to read from the King James version of the Bible. This practice offended many Roman Catholics, who were moving to the United States from Europe in increasing numbers by the middle of the nineteenth century.

Moving toward Multicultural Education

Over the course of the nineteenth century, the idea of common schooling spread gradually across the United States. Its implementation was delayed in the South until after the abolition of slavery during the Civil War, however, in part because Southern planters and other elites had imposed laws prohibiting slaves from being taught to read and write. Nevertheless, by the end of the nineteenth century public schools had been established in every state.

With the end of the Civil War and Reconstruction came recognition that African Americans, including the children of former slaves, were entitled to education. Southern states established public schools for African American children, but these children attended racially segregated schools despite Mann's belief that all children regardless of background should attend school together. In 1896, the U.S. Supreme Court upheld the constitutionality of racial segregation in *Plessy* v. *Ferguson* (163 U.S. 537). In *Plessy*, the Court ruled that laws mandating racial segregation in public facilities as long as these facilities were equivalent in quality. This ruling came to be known as the "separate but equal" principle.

Although the *Plessy* case involved segregation on railroad trains, the "separate but equal" principle was applied to public education in *Cumming* v. *Richmond County Board of Education* (175 U.S. 528) in 1899. Although *Plessy* and *Cumming* required states to provide education of "equal" quality to both whites and African Americans, in practice schools for African American children were of far lower quality.

States allocated far less money per pupil to schools attended by African American students, and many African American children attended schools in dilapidated buildings with insufficient desks, textbooks, and instructional materials and taught by poorly paid teachers. *Plessy* was overturned in 1954 by *Brown* v. *Board of Education* (347 U.S 483), in which a unanimous Court ruled that state-sponsored segregation in public schools was unconstitutional.

Especially outside of the South, the United States in the late nineteenth and early twentieth centuries was becoming an increasingly diverse society. Millions of immigrants had moved to the United States from Europe. Although the majority of immigrants during most of the nineteenth century had come from Great Britain, Ireland, Germany, or Scandinavia, by the 1890s the number of immigrants from western and northern Europe was exceeded by the number of immigrants from southern and eastern Europe including Italy, Poland, Hungary, and Russia. Most of these immigrants were Roman Catholics, Jews, or members of Eastern Orthodox churches, and many spoke little or no English upon arriving in the United States.

Many native-born Americans believed that it would be difficult to assimilate these southern and eastern European immigrants into the mainstream of American culture. Public schools came to be viewed as an important means of assimilation. Public schooling was conducted in English, forcing children to learn English in order to receive their educations. Schools were viewed as "melting pots," but in general, educational curricula continued to emphasize a Protestant-based, white-dominated interpretation of American culture and history.

Multiculturalism and Education in the Late Twentieth and Early Twenty-First Centuries

As the twentieth century drew to a close, educators and public officials began to question the dominance of public education by white Protestant viewpoints. The *Brown* decision and the subsequent Civil Rights Act of 1964 and the Voting Rights Act of 1965 brought attention to the need to bring an African American viewpoint into the teaching of history, including the history of slavery, lynchings, and Jim Crow laws.

Mexican Americans, Native Americans, Asian Americans, and other ethnic groups also argued for representation of their cultures and history. Issues involving these groups included the substandard working conditions faced by Mexican American farmworkers, the Trail of Tears, the internment of Japanese American citizens during World War II, and many others. At the same time, the women's movement brought attention to the suppression of women over the course of American history. It became evident to many American educators that curricula needed to be revised in order to incorporate these issues and concerns.

How these concerns would be addressed became a matter of considerable controversy. Textbooks used in history and social studies classes were scrutinized carefully by educators, public officials, parents, and concerned citizens who examined how various historical events were presented. For example, in 2015 the caption of a photograph in a geography textbook referred to African American slaves before the Civil War as "workers," saying, "The Atlantic Slave Trade between the 1500s and 1800s brought millions of workers from Africa to the southern United States to work on agricultural plantations." After readers became aware of this caption, the publisher issued an apology and corrected this caption on the online edition of the book. However, such a correction could not be made in the printed copies of the book, many of which were already in use. Another controversy arose in Texas, more than half of whose schoolchildren are Mexican-American, about the use of a textbook whose author stereotyped Mexicans as lazy, prone to criminal activity, and responsible for importing illegal drugs into the United States.

Bilingual and Multilingual Education

During the nineteenth century, many immigrant children were educated in their first languages, in particular in rural areas. However, strong opposition to educating children in languages other than English arose before and during World War I, and this opposition was directed against German Americans at a time when the United States was declaring war on Germany. In Iowa, in 1918 Governor William L. Harding (1877–1934) issued a proclamation that not only banned teaching languages other than English but also prohibited conversations in public places, on trains, or on the telephone in foreign languages. (Governor Harding was no relation to President Warren G. Harding (1865–1923).) Governor Harding's proclamation was opposed vigorously by non-German immigrants, especially those from countries whose governments supported the Allies during the war. Older immigrants who did not speak English well also objected on their grounds that they could no longer attend church services in which sermons were delivered in German or other foreign languages.

Meanwhile, Nebraska passed a law forbidding teaching in languages other than English to children who had not completed the eighth grade in any public, private, or parochial school. This law was challenged by a plaintiff who taught catechism in German in a parochial school to a boy who was the son of German immigrants. In *Meyer v. State of Nebraska* (262 U.S. 390), the Supreme Court ruled in 1923 that the Nebraska law, and similar anti-German laws, were unconstitutional. Nevertheless, efforts to require English-language instruction in schools coincided with limits on immigration imposed by the federal government. The Johnson-Reed Act of 1924 limited immigration by imposing quotas on a country-by-country basis. Under terms of this act, the number of immigrants allowed into the United States from each country per year could not exceed 2 percent of the total number of immigrants who had come to the United States over the course of history. The Johnson-Reed Act privileged immigration from the English-speaking British Isles along with Germany and Scandinavia because many more immigrants had come from these countries since 1790, whereas large-scale immigration from eastern and southern Europe did not begin until the 1890s.

After the 1960s, the federal government and the states began to look on bilingual education more favorably. This change coincided with the repeal of the Johnson-Reed Act in 1965. The Bilingual Education Act of 1968 specified that federal funds could be used to support bilingual education programs. Six years later, the Equal Educational Opportunity Act established that children who did not speak English as a first language had the right to special education programs. More specific guidelines, including some based on recognition of diversity, were issued in 1988.

Despite these laws and guidelines, opposition to bilingual education continues. Although efforts to establish English as the official language of the United States have been made at the federal level, none have become law. However, supporters of English as an official language have had more success at the state level. As of 2018, 31 of the 50 states had declared English as an official language, some by constitutional amendment and some by statute. Alaska has given official status to more than 20 Native American and Inuit languages, and Hawaii has given official status to Hawaiian. New Mexico and Louisiana have given "special status" to Spanish and French, respectively. In the other 27 states, English is the only official language.

Many of these statutes and constitutional amendments make specific reference to education. For example, Wyoming's Official Language Act of 1996 states that "English shall be the official language of Wyoming." However, this act specified that state agencies or officials can use other languages for several reasons, one of which is "[t]o provide instruction designed to aid students with limited English proficiency so they can make a timely transition to the use of the English language in the public schools." Identical language was used in Kansas' official language law, enacted in 2007.

The debate over the value, legitimacy, and importance of bilingual education continues. Experts on education are divided over the question as to whether students in bilingual education programs perform better in school as compared to those in English-only schools. Proponents of bilingual education point out that compared to citizens of most European countries, Americans are much more likely to be proficient in only one language. The debate is almost certain to continue, especially in light of increasing numbers of non-English-speaking immigrants moving to the United States.

Further Reading

James Crawford, *Educating English learners: Language diversity in the classroom*. Los Angeles: Bilingual Education Services, 2004.

Laura Isensee, "Texas textbook called out as 'racist' against Mexican-Americans," NPR, September 14, 2016, http://www.newsweek.com/company-behind-texas-textbook-calling -slaves-workers-apologizes-we-made-380168. Retrieved on June 11, 2018.

Zoe Schlanger, "Company apologizes for Texas textbook calling slaves 'workers': We made a mistake," *Newsweek*, October 5, 2015, http://www.newsweek.com/company -behind-texas-textbook-calling-slaves-workers-apologizes-we-made-380168. Retrieved on June 11, 2018.

Joel H. Spring, *American education: A global context from the Puritans to the Obama era*. New York: McGraw-Hill, 2011.

Chapter 5: Diversity and Cultural Differences

OVERVIEW

Humans are social creatures. Except for in a few extreme instances, people live their lives in the company of others. Yet people are also acutely aware of differences among themselves. And these differences are factors of major importance in human social organization, and therefore in the process and practice of education.

Since ancient times, people have grouped themselves based on similarities among one another. Historically, these groupings were generally based on kinship. Bands of hunters and gatherers generally consisted of people who related to one another biologically. Indeed, many such groups referred to themselves as "the people" and in doing so differentiated themselves from other bands or tribes. As societies became larger and more complex over time, groupings extended beyond kinship to encompass other similarities among their members including common languages, religions, and cultures. Even today, people tend to group themselves based on similarities such as common religious beliefs and practices, languages, or political views.

The term "tribalism" has been developed to reflect this tendency. Although the word "tribe" is used often to denote a group of Indigenous people, more generally the word refers to groups of people defined by perceived similarities among members. People are acutely aware of differences between the tribes of which they are members and people who are not members of these tribes. Perception of these differences can and often does lead to distrust and animosity. Those who are not members of the tribe are "othered"—that is, they are regarded, perceived, and treated as somehow different from the tribe. This difference usually implies a perception that these "othered" people are inferior to the tribe and therefore do not and cannot have the status associated with tribal membership.

Such othering occurs across geographical scales from the global to the local. At the global scale, Western civilization has been regarded by many Europeans as superior to non-Western civilizations. Edward Said (1935–2003) coined the term "orientalism" to describe how Europeans have "othered" civilizations and cultures in other parts of the world, notably in Asia where his research was focused. Said pointed out that many Europeans looked down upon non-Western cultures as backward, static, primitive, and uncivilized. Hence, the term "orientalism" referred to the geographical location of such societies as east of the West, which perceived itself as the center of civilized life. Indeed, people outside Europe, and especially

Indigenous peoples, were often regarded by Europeans as "savages." This perception was used to justify efforts to capture resources and territory from these "savages" and in many cases to displace, enslave, or slaughter them. In addition, some Europeans made efforts to "civilize" these "savages," although these efforts were often ruinous. In the Western Hemisphere, for example, millions of Indigenous inhabitants of North America, Central American, and South America—those who were not killed or enslaved outright—died after contracting infectious European diseases to which they had no immunity.

Tribalism has had profound effects on societal interaction since antiquity. Since ancient times, rulers of societies throughout the world attempted to expand their power by conquering other areas. This process is illustrated by the expansion of the Roman Empire from central Italy, the Mongols from central Asia, and the Mughals in present-day India. More recently, Russia and what would later become the Soviet Union expanded by taking over territories occupied previously by non-Russian cultures. Some empires, such as those of the Romans and the Mughals, lasted for several hundred years, whereas others such as that of Alexander the Great lasted for only a generation or two.

However, the process of empire building has proven throughout the world to be unstable. As empires expanded, they conquered territories that were inhabited by people whose cultures, languages, economies, and religions were very different from their own. Often, the rulers of the empires attempted to impose their own cultures upon people living in conquered territories. The rulers would also attempt to exploit these conquered territories through making taxes, payment of tribute, and/or forced labor a requirement. Naturally, local people resented and resisted such exploitation. In order to enforce this exploitation, troops from the centers of the empires were sent to these frontier areas. But, as the empires became larger, more and more resources were needed in order to maintain these exploitative relationships. Eventually, the empires became stretched too thin and collapsed.

The creation of the modern state system, which began in the early seventeenth century, contributed also to tribalism. The treaties ending the Thirty Years' War, known collectively as the Peace of Westphalia, established the principle that any ruler was sovereign over the people that he or she ruled. States could not interfere in one another's internal affairs. Implementation of the Peace of Westphalia meant that knowledge of which people were controlled by individual sovereigns was necessary. This in turn mandated the establishment of boundaries so that which kingdom or principality had control of any particular territory would be known. Since then, many wars among sovereign territories have been fought over control of contested spaces, with the side winning the war often taking territory away from the side that lost the war.

As an illustration, the European colonial powers agreed to divide most of Africa into colonies in the 1880s. However, Europeans had little knowledge of the geographies and cultures of the areas through which these boundary lines passed, especially in the interior that had not been explored by Europeans at the time that these agreements were negotiated. As a result, many of these boundaries divided the territories occupied by individual societies, or they grouped together tribes with different cultures and languages and sometimes with a history of antagonism toward one another. Most of these colonial boundaries continued to be used when countries on the African continent achieved political independence beginning in the late 1950s. Even today, many African countries contain many distinct ethnic groups, and the political history of such countries has been dominated by conflict and a struggle for control between these groups.

In most places throughout the world, formal education was at first generally the responsibility of religious institutions. As we have seen in other entries throughout this book, however, state governments took over control of education in the nineteenth and twentieth centuries. As these governments did so, they were forced to take differences in culture, language, and religion into account. This process illustrates the relationships between multiculturalism and education, as illustrated in more detail elsewhere in this volume.

In some cases, governments attempted to suppress minority interests, for example, by mandating that instruction be provided only in the country's dominant or official language. Such was the case in Scotland several centuries ago, and more recently in Myanmar. Other countries expressed more tolerance of cultural difference, and in many countries tolerance of such differences has been increasing. The organization of education within countries also affects recognition of the difference. In some countries, education is managed at a national level and curricula are standardized throughout these countries as is the case in France. In others, local educators have more leeway to adjust their curricula and to consider differences between their students and students elsewhere.

Even within cultures, many differences among students can be observed. Such differences include not only language and religion but also differences in gender, sexual orientation, and learning styles among students. Gender is an important component of culture. Even well into the twentieth century, curricula for boys and girls differed considerably even in developed countries. Girls were taught skills to prepare them for motherhood and domestic life. Many were discouraged or forbidden to take courses in advanced science and mathematics and other subjects that boys were encouraged to study.

Above and beyond gender, many students have disabilities that affect them throughout their educations and later over the course of their lives as discussed in the chapter titled "Special Education." These include students who are blind, deaf, or have physical or cognitive disabilities. Historically, in many countries students with such disabilities had little or no opportunity to obtain any meaningful education. Partly because of their lack of education, many such children became isolated or institutionalized as adults. In general, however, educational systems have taken these considerations into account. Special education for students with disabilities has become the norm in the United States and many other countries, especially in developed countries that have more resources to be used in providing education.

The essays in this chapter, along with their references, examine various types of difference as it affects formal education. Indonesia, which is the fourth largest country in the world by population, is inhabited by a very large number of cultural groups that speak hundreds of distinct languages. The Indonesian government's efforts to promote national unity and the development of a distinct national culture via education have run into considerable resistance among cultures in various parts of the country. The United Kingdom lacks Indonesia's high degree of diversity, but people living in each of its four major components—England, Scotland, Wales, and Northern Ireland—have distinctly different views about how education should be conducted. In Scotland and Wales, in particular, there remains a long-standing concern that the traditional cultures of these areas, including their Celtic languages, are in danger of being wiped out entirely.

South Africa is characterized also by great cultural diversity. Its inhabitants include descendants of Indigenous Africans, descendants of immigrants from Europe and Asia, and many people of mixed-race ancestry. Here, educational authorities are grappling with effects of the country's apartheid policy that mandated racial segregation and privileged people of unmixed European heritage over those who had African ancestry. Kazakhstan has been dealing with the impacts of demographic changes that took place during its 70 years as part of the Soviet Union. The Soviets encouraged many ethnic Russians to move to Kazakhstan, and even today well over a third of Kazakhstan's citizens are of Russian ancestry although some returned to Russia after Kazakhstan became independent.

As compared to most other large countries, France is a highly centralized state. Yet present-day France's population includes millions of people who are from non-European parts of the world, or who are descended from such people. Thus, an ongoing dilemma in France today is how to balance centralization, and by implication the country's goal of creating French cultural identity, with the interests of these growing minority populations. One issue has been the role of religion in education, given that France is officially a secular state. Myanmar has a very diverse population that, as is the case with Indonesia, contains very different cultural, linguistic, and religious groups. However, Burmese people make up nearly two-thirds of the population and control the government, and government officials have attempted to impose Burmese culture on the entire country in part by requiring that all formal education be conducted in the Burmese language. Such policies continue to be resisted fiercely by non-Burmese speakers, some of whom belong to organizations that advocate more autonomy or outright independence.

Colombia's diversity is associated with its history of colonialism. More than half of Colombians are of full or partial European ancestry. However, more than 10 percent of Colombia's people are Afro-Colombians who are descended from slaves who had been imported from Africa prior to the nineteenth century. Afro-Colombians have been victimized by a long history of discrimination and poverty. Meanwhile, around 4 percent of Colombians are Indigenous people. Both groups are not only marginalized, but also illiteracy rates are much higher among these minority populations as compared to Colombia as a whole. The United States is also a highly diverse society. The history of public education in the United States is associated with the common school movement of the nineteenth century.

However, the white Protestant worldview associated with common schooling has been challenged by the needs of the country's diverse population.

COLOMBIA

The Republic of Colombia is located in northwestern South America, and it is the only South American country with coastlines on both the Pacific Ocean and the Caribbean Sea. Its land area is approximately 440,000 square miles, with a population estimated at 51.3 million in 2021. It is the third largest country in Latin America by population, following Brazil and Mexico. Colombia contains three distinct regions—the coastal regions to the west and north, the central cordillera including the northernmost section of the Andes Mountains in the center, and part of the lowland Amazon rainforest basin to the east and south. More than half of Colombia's people live in the central cordillera, while the Amazon basin region is sparsely populated. The demographics of each of these regions are distinct, helping to create the levels of difference that characterize Colombia today.

Colombia is named for Christopher Columbus, who visited the Caribbean coast of present-day Colombia in 1502. After Spanish colonization, the region became part of the viceroyalty of Peru. In 1717, it became part of the newly established viceroyalty of New Grenada, which also included present-day Venezuela, Ecuador, and Panama. The viceroyalty declared its independence in 1819 and was named Gran Colombia. However, Gran Colombia was dissolved in 1830, by which time Venezuela and Ecuador had become independent countries. The remaining territory, including present-day Colombia and Panama, adopted the name of Colombia in 1856. In 1903, Panama separated from Colombia and achieved its independence.

Colombia has had a long history of political instability, including guerilla warfare. Riots in the 1950s are believed to have resulted in the loss of nearly 200,000 lives. The Revolution Armed Forces of Colombia (FARC) movement, a Marxist-Leninist organization, became active in the late 1960s and early 1970s in an effort to take control of the government. FARC's activities were funded by illegal mining and drug trafficking, along with kidnapping of prominent Colombians and their family members for ransom. FARC was believed to be in control of more than a quarter of Colombia's land area by 2000 and was especially strong in southern Colombia near its borders with Peru and Ecuador. By that time, more than 200,000 Colombians had left the country as refugees. After nearly 50 years of civil war, a peace agreement between FARC leaders and the Colombian government was signed by both parties in 2016.

Education in Colombia

As was the case throughout South America, education in present-day Colombia was dominated by the Roman Catholic Church during the colonial period. For the most part, formal education was limited to children of the elite, and the curriculum emphasized religious instruction. After independence, the government of Colombia began to take a more active role in the educational process. Rates of literacy began to increase. However, formal education was limited largely to urban areas and was often lacking in the countryside. Moreover, parents were charged tuition and fees, with the result that children from poor families were often unable to attend school. Even as late as the 1960s, parents were required to pay tuition and to pay for textbooks, school supplies, and uniforms. Thus, Colombian education was the means by which class differences within Colombian society were reinforced.

Today, the Ministry of Education is responsible for education at all levels. Each of Colombia's 32 states is responsible for implementing the ministry's policies at the local level. Students attend primary school for five years, followed by four years of lower secondary school and two years of upper secondary school. Education is free and compulsory between the ages of 5 and 15, or till the completion of lower secondary school. At the upper secondary level, several tracks are available. Some are oriented to higher education, and others emphasize workforce preparation. Spanish is the language of instruction, although bilingual education is provided in areas where Spanish is not spoken as a first language.

Diversity, Cultural Differences, and Education in Colombia

Colombia's geography and demographics have created numerous challenges for the government as it works to deliver education to its highly diverse population. The three major regions of Colombia have distinctly different demographics. Well over 80 percent of Colombia's population consists of people of European ancestry or are mestizos who have both European and Indigenous ancestry. However, there are also substantial numbers of people of African ancestry and of Indigenous people. Ethnic diversity was recognized officially through an amendment added to the constitution of Colombia in 1991. This amendment implied that children had the right to free public education at the primary and secondary levels. In practice, however, disparities remain in the availability and quality of education available to people who are not of European ancestry.

More than 10 percent of Colombia's people are of African ancestry, although according to some estimates, over 20 percent of the population consists of Afro-Colombians. Many of these Afro-Colombians are descended from slaves who were imported from Africa by the Spanish colonizers prior to Colombian independence, although slavery was not eliminated legally in Colombia until 1851. Many Afro-Colombians live in coastal areas, and more than half of the people who live in several states along the Pacific coast are Afro-Colombian. However, hundreds of thousands of Afro-Colombians have migrated to the capital city of Bogota in the central cordillera, and many are also victims of discrimination, poverty, and a lack of education. Many of these Afro-Colombians live in segregated communities with substandard housing and an absence of public services.

Discrimination against Afro-Colombians dates back prior to independence, when most were slaves. Although official government policy guarantees education

These young girls in a school in Colombia are practicing writing. Although the majority of Colombia's people are of full or partial European ancestry, the country contains substantial minorities of Afro-Colombians whose ancestors were brought from Africa as slaves and of Indigenous people. Children of these minority populations often lack the opportunity to attain formal education. (Dtiberio | Dreamstime.com)

to all Colombians, in practice educational opportunities for Afro-Colombians are limited. Schools may not be available and, if they are available, may be dilapidated or substandard. Many Afro-Colombians parents cannot afford to pay school fees or to pay for school supplies and uniforms for their children. During the civil war, moreover, some Afro-Colombian children were recruited as child soldiers, thus keeping them away from school. In light of these issues, it is not surprising that levels of educational achievement among Afro-Colombian students are lower than the country average. According to recent estimates, as many as one-third of the Afro-Colombian population is illiterate. Lack of educational opportunity is, of course, reinforcing the already strong class differences that exist within Colombian society.

Meanwhile, about 1.5–2 million Indigenous people, or about 3–4 percent of the overall population, live in Colombia. Many live in the Amazon basin region of the country, which is much more sparsely populated than the central cordillera and the areas to the west and north. However, some Indigenous tribes live in the central cordillera. Throughout the country, the government recognizes more than 80 distinct Indigenous groups. Today, some Indigenous people in Colombian continue to practice traditional lifestyles. However, many of these Indigenous tribes are facing land pressure. Lands occupied by these Indigenous peoples are in demand by outside mining and agricultural parties, including the cultivation of plants used to produce illegal drugs. Tropical rainforests are being cut down, with land converted to the cultivation of commercial crops for export.

As with Afro-Colombians, children of Indigenous tribes often lack educational opportunities. Government funding is lacking, and there remains a shortage of facilities and qualified teachers. Moreover, many Indigenous tribes live in relatively isolated and sparsely populated areas that may be difficult to access from outside. An important additional issue, moreover, is the concern that education as provided by the Colombian government and administered at the national level may have the effect of destroying Indigenous cultures. Some tribal leaders have expressed their fear that Colombian education is forcing their children to "become Spanish," overlooking tribal heritage. The role of language in education is a special concern, and Indigenous community leaders are pushing hard for bilingual education along with inclusion of local cultural heritage and traditions in the curriculum.

Further Reading

Minority Rights Group International, "Afro-Colombians," *World Directory of Minorities and Indigenous Peoples*, 2008, https://minorityrights.org/minorities/afro-colombians/. Retrieved on January 21, 2020.

New Internationalist, "This is cultural genocide," July 1, 2017, https://newint.org/features/web-exclusive/2017/07/01/colombia-indigenous-education-project. Retrieved on January 22, 2020.

Lori S. Robinson, "Fighting for black lives in Colombia: The people do not give up," *The Root*, July 1, 2017, https://www.theroot.com/fighting-for-black-lives-in-colombia-the-people-do-no-1796521757. Retrieved on January 22, 2020.

Jonathan Watts, "Battle for the mother land: indigenous people of Colombia fighting for their lands," *The Guardian*, October 28, 2017, https://www.theguardian.com/environment/2017/oct/28/nasa-colombia-cauca-valley-battle-mother-land. Retrieved on January 22, 2020.

FRANCE

France, formally known as the French Republic or Republique Francaise, has a land area of about 213,000 square miles, including the land areas of several small overseas colonies such as French Guiana that are regarded as part of the republic. Mainland France occupies most of the territory between the Mediterranean Sea, the Pyrenees Mountains, the Atlantic Ocean, and the Rhine River. France's population as of 2021 was about 67 million. Thus, France is the largest country in the European Union by land area and the second largest by population, second only to Germany.

Most of present-day France was known as Gaul during ancient times. Gaul was occupied by various Celtic tribes until it was conquered by Julius Caesar (100 BCE–44 BCE) and became part of the Roman Empire in the first century BCE. After the collapse of the Roman Empire, various tribes and petty kingdoms controlled what is now France until the late ninth century, when it was united by King Charles the Great (742 AD–814 AD), who was known also as Charlemagne. Charlemagne was crowned as the first Holy Roman Emperor by Pope St. Leo III (750 AD?–816 AD) in 800 AD. Charlemagne's empire included much of central Europe, but it was divided into thirds in 843. The western third included most of France. The region controlled by French kings coincided largely with the territory under the sovereignty of the French Republic today.

By the Middle Ages, France had become one of Europe's most powerful kingdoms. Once the Age of Exploration began in the late fifteenth century, France established numerous overseas colonies although its defeat by the United Kingdom during the Seven Years' War in 1763 forced the French to give up most of its American colonies. The French monarchy was deposed during the French Revolution in the late eighteenth century. Napoleon Bonaparte (1769–1821) took control of France in 1799. In the early nineteenth century, Napoleon attempted to expand the French Empire throughout Europe until his armies were defeated at the Battle of Waterloo in 1815. After Waterloo, France's boundaries were delineated at the Congress of Vienna. Except for some of the boundaries between northeastern France and neighboring Germany, its boundaries have been stable ever since.

France became part of the Allied coalition that won both World War I and World War II. It became a founding member of what is now the European Union in 1951, and it played an instrumental role in promoting European unification. It continues to play a highly important role in the global economy, with a diversified economy including agricultural, manufacturing, services, and tourism.

Education in France

The rudiments of education of young people in present-day France date back to the Roman Empire. During his reign, Charlemagne was responsible for promoting the establishment of schools across his empire. Education was directed primarily at training people for the Roman Catholic clergy, although Charlemagne directed bishops to provide schools for the laity as well. The Church remained responsible for education until after the French Revolution. In the early nineteenth century, the state took over responsibility for education. Education became compulsory for both boys and girls between the ages of 6 and 12 in 1841, although in practice schools were not always available especially in rural areas until into the twentieth century.

Today, education in France is highly centralized and is administered by the government's Ministry of National Education. The ministry sets educational standards and administers the curriculum that is used throughout the country. Historically, identical curricula were used throughout the country. In 2015, however, the ministry allowed individual schools to determine up to 20 percent of their curricula independently of the national curriculum. Education is free and compulsory for children between the ages of 6 and 16, although many children begin preschool at the age of three or four years. Most students attend public schools although some attend private schools or are homeschooled; however, the curriculum is prescribed by the ministry regardless of which type of schooling is provided. Teachers and administrators in French public schools are state employees and are regarded as civil servants.

In keeping with the French philosophy of standardized education, the French school system emphasizes performance relative to national standards. Students are graded based on the quality of their test results as compared to national expectations and are ranked relative to their peers. Students attend primary school or ecole elementaire for five years. This is followed by four years of middle school, known as "college."

After completing college, the large majority of students continue on to high school or lycee, which lasts for three years. At this level, students can choose among several college preparatory tracks or vocational and technical tracks. In these tracks, students are expected to choose programs that prepare them for specific careers. Educational authorities tend to steer students into tracks based on previous performance, although critics have pointed out that children of immigrants and of non-French ethnic origins tend to be steered into vocational as opposed to college preparatory tracks. Special education programs are available for children with hearing or vision impairments, physical disabilities, and cognitive learning disorders.

Diversity, Cultural Differences, and Education in France

In contrast to the United States, Germany, India, and Canada, France is a unitary state. In unitary states, all formal power is held by the national government, and the purpose of the local governance is to implement national government policy. Moreover, French citizenship law prioritizes the state as opposed to ethnicity. In some countries, a person wishing to become a citizen of that country must prove their descent from a citizen of that country or a member of its national group. Someone who wishes to become a citizen of Estonia who has not descended from a person who was an Estonian citizen during that country's period of independence between 1918 and 1940 must pass a test of knowledge of Estonian history, governance, and culture given in the Estonian language. In France, as in the United States, nationality is not a consideration with respect to eligibility for French citizenship. Even today, French government officials are not allowed to collect statistics concerning national origin and ethnicity among residents of France.

The French colonial empire was one of the largest in the world during the late nineteenth and early twentieth centuries. After World War II, however, most of France's colonies became independent countries. Those few colonies that remain under French colonial administration are known as Overseas France or Overseas Collectivities. Residents of these colonies, including Guadalupe, Martinique, French Guiana, Saint Martin, and French Polynesia, are regarded as French citizens and have the right to vote in French elections and migrate to France. However, during the decolonization period many more persons from much larger and less distant French colonies moved to France, particularly from nearby Algeria, Morocco, and Tunisia. More recently, large numbers of people from North Africa, sub-Saharan Africa, and the Middle East have also moved to France.

These considerations have affected the relationships between differences and citizenship in France in recent years. Levels of difference, especially with regard to ethnicity and religion, have increased within France for several decades. These demographic changes have led French authorities to reconsider the historic degree of centralization, conformity, and competition associated with French public education. As in many countries, children of immigrants tend to perform less well in school than do children of native-born French citizens. Differences in performance have been observed also among children whose parents arrived in France from different places. In attempting to explain these observed outcomes, however, French authorities have downplayed ethnicity as a key factor. Rather, their focus has been on "social origin," or the economic status of parents as a major explanatory factor.

In keeping with the French philosophy of basing citizenship on the state as opposed to national origin, national policy encourages assimilation of all French residents, including immigrants, into French culture. In practice, however, many immigrants live in effectively segregated communities where public services and opportunities are seen as lacking. French law is seen by some immigrant communities as discriminatory. For example, French law prohibits women from wearing full-face veils in public, although this policy has been opposed by some conservative Muslim immigrant groups.

In response, members of some immigrant communities have advocated the establishment of schools intended specifically for their own children. For example, Turkish officials have pushed for the establishment of Turkish language schools in areas where substantial numbers of people of Turkish origin live. An estimated 600,000 people of Turkish origin live in France. Levels of educational achievement among students of Turkish origin are low, and many continue to speak Turkish at home. In response, the Turkish government is pressing for the establishment of government-funded schools for children of Turkish nationals. In such schools, Turkish would be the language of instruction, and the curriculum would be linked to the Turkish educational curriculum. The French government opposes this plan. An important reason is that such schools as advocated by Turkish authorities would include instruction in Islam, and religious instruction is inconsistent with France's official status as a secular state.

Further Reading

Hugh Fitzgerald, "Erdogan's grand plan for Turkish schools in France," *New English Review*, May 21, 2019, https://www.newenglishreview.org/blog_direct_link.cfm?blog_id=68383&Erdogans%2DGrand%2DPlan%2DFor%2DTurkish%2DSchools%2DIn%2DFrance. Retrieved on January 18, 2020.

Mathieu Ichou, "The educational fortunes of children of immigrants in France," *metropolitics.org*, July 6, 2018, https://www.metropolitiques.eu/The-Educational-Fortunes-of-Children-of-Immigrants-in-France.html. Retrieved on January 18, 2020.

Kutlay Yagmur and Fons J. R. van de Vijver, "Acculturation and language orientations of Turkish immigrants in Australia, France, Germany, and the Netherlands," *Journal of Cross-Cultural Psychology*, 43 (2012), pp. 1110–1130, https://www.researchgate

.net/publication/254906195_Acculturation_and_Language_Orientations_of_Turkish _Immigrants_in_Australia_France_Germany_and_the_Netherlands. Retrieved on January 18, 2020.

INDONESIA

The Republic of Indonesia consists of more than 17,000 islands, of which 922 are inhabited, located off the coast of mainland Southeast Asia. The four largest islands—Sumatra, Java, Borneo, and Sulawesi—are known as the Greater Sunda Islands. Borneo is shared among Indonesia, Malaysia, and Brunei. The Indonesian portion of the island, which contains about two-thirds of Borneo's land area and is located south of the Malaysian portion of the island and of Brunei, is known as Kalimantan. To the east, Indonesia includes the western half of the island of New Guinea, which it shares with Papua New Guinea. Indonesia's overall land area is about 735,000 square miles. The overall population as of 2021 was about 271 million, making Indonesia the fourth largest country in the world by population following China, India, and the United States. Indonesia is one of the most culturally diverse countries in the world, with several hundred distinct languages spoken locally throughout the country.

Anthropologists believe that humans reached present-day Indonesia nearly 50,000 years ago. Migrants from Taiwan and mainland Southeast Asia moved to the islands about 4,000 years ago, and their descendants became the dominant population. More than 2000 years ago, present-day Indonesia's location along the main ocean route between China and India enabled the creation of local kingdoms that profited from control of oceanic trade. During the early sixteenth century, Europeans from Portugal, the Netherlands, and Britain established settlements on the Greater Sunda Islands. The European colonial powers were anxious to tap into the lucrative oceanic trade throughout Southeast Asia. The Dutch became the predominant colonial power in the region, although they did not achieve full control of the archipelago until the early twentieth century. The Japanese seized control of Indonesia during World War II, and after the Dutch regained power following the war, Indonesia declared its independence. After intermittent warfare, the Netherlands recognized Indonesian independence in 1949, but they retained control of western New Guinea. The Indonesian portion of New Guinea, then known as Irian Jaya, was added to the country formally in 1961.

In its efforts to promote cultural unity after independence, the government considered the question of what should be the newly independent country's official language. The government rejected Javanese, which was spoken by more than half of the country's population, and also rejected Dutch as the language of the country's colonial power. Instead, the government decreed that the Malay language would become the country's official language. The language became known as Bahasa Indonesia, or Indonesian, and the idea was to promote national unity and national identity although the majority of Indonesians speak other languages at home. Today Indonesian is taught in schools throughout the country. It is the language of instruction in Indonesian schools, although Javanese and local languages are used also for instruction in primary grades.

Indonesia is characterized also by religious diversity. Islam was first brought to Indonesia by Arab traders in the twelfth and thirteen centuries AD. Today, more than 85 percent of Indonesians are Muslims, although people of other faiths form majorities on some islands. For example, most residents of Bali are Hindus, and there are substantial Christian communities on Sulawesi.

About 60 percent of Indonesia's people live on the crowded and densely populated island of Java. Over several decades, the Indonesian government has initiated efforts to reduce crowding on Java by encouraging people to move elsewhere. Under terms of the transmigration program, which peaked during the 1970s, residents of Java were encouraged to move from Java to Sumatra, Kalimantan, and other less densely populated islands. Transmigrants were offered free farmland and other incentives to move. However, unoccupied land on these outer islands was generally unproductive compared to the rich, volcanic soil of Java, making it more difficult for these farmers to support themselves. Conflicts also arose between transmigrants and local residents who felt that the interests of the transmigrants were given priority over their own interests. Transmigrants were often given priority in obtaining farmland and getting jobs. The transmigration program was also seen as an effort to privilege Javanese culture and to impose that culture on people living on outlying islands. Thus, the transmigration policy was seen as a means of reducing the difference within Indonesia's large and diverse population. Recently, the Indonesian government announced that it is considering a plan to move the country's capital from Jakarta on Java to a new site on Kalimantan, in part to further reduce overcrowding on Java. In 2022, the government announced that the new capital will be named Nusantara, which means "archipelago" in Indonesian.

Education in Indonesia

Formal education was first brought to present-day Indonesia by the Dutch. At first, education was provided primarily to children of Dutch residents, but in the late nineteenth century, schools established by the Dutch began to be opened to native Indonesians. However, entrance into these schools required students to be fluent in Dutch. In some rural areas, the Dutch established "Desa" or local village schools. Children attended these schools for two or three years and were taught the basics of reading, writing, and arithmetic.

Although the Dutch had introduced Desa schools in many areas, it has been estimated that in the 1930s only about 7 percent of native-born Indonesians were literate. After independence, the Indonesian constitution specified that education is a fundamental right for every Indonesian citizen. The Indonesian government created a new system that emphasized the elimination of illiteracy. As of 2011, an estimated 92 percent of Indonesians were literate. However, it has also been esti-mated that about half of Indonesians today are functionally illiterate.

Today, education in Indonesian is managed by the Ministry of Education and Culture. Schooling is compulsory for 12 years, including 6 years of primary school, 3 years of lower secondary school, and 3 years of upper secondary school. In practice, however, as of 2011 less than 60 percent of teenagers of high school age were actually enrolled in school. Public schools are officially secular and focused on Indonesian nationalism and unity. However, some parents object to this sec-ular emphasis and prefer a more religious emphasis on education. Many of their children attend Islamic schools, which are administered under the auspices of the Ministry of Religious Affairs. It has been estimated that about 16 percent of school-age Indonesian children attend Islamic schools.

Diversity, Cultural Differences, and Education in Indonesia

With nearly 1,000 inhabited islands and with great cultural diversity, Indonesia has been forced to struggle with how to provide education to each of its citizens regardless of their cultural, ethnic, and religious backgrounds. On the one hand, Indonesia has worked to create an Indonesian national identity including the pro-motion of Indonesian as the country's official language. On the other hand, many of Indonesia's cultural groups have resisted these efforts and have demanded rec-ognition of their uniqueness and diversity.

This tension is illustrated by three examples from central, far western, and far eastern Indonesia. About 3.5 million Dayak people live in Kalimantan in central Indonesia. Many of the Dayaks who live near the coast are Muslims, but most of those living further inland are Christians or practice the traditional, Indigenous Dayak religion. The Dayaks were affected heavily by the transmigration program, resulting in conflicts with the Indonesian government in part because of concern among Dayak people that the government was making an active effort to wipe out the Dayak culture. Hundreds of transmigrants were killed by Dayak guerillas between 1996 and 2003 before the Indonesian army stepped in to restore order. Although violence between Dayaks and transmigrants is no longer commonplace, many of Kalimantan's schools attended by Dayak children are underfunded, with inadequate facilities and poorly trained teachers. Above and beyond these struc-tural issues, Dayak leaders have expressed concern that the Indonesian educational system is imposing non-Dayak values on the local population. This concern has intensified since the government announced its plans to move the country's capital to Kalimantan.

Aceh is an Indonesian province located in far northwestern Sumatra. Prior to the arrival of Dutch colonists, Aceh was the center of a sultanate that controlled coastal areas both on Sumatra and on the mainland of present-day Malaysia, along with the Strait of Malacca in between. Aceh resisted Dutch efforts to control its ter-ritory for hundreds of years, and it submitted to Dutch rule only in 1904 following

30 years of intermittent warfare. Separatist movements have been active in Aceh since Indonesian independence. Currently, about 5.3 million people live in Aceh.

During the Middle Ages, Aceh was the first area of present-day Indonesia to be converted to Islam. Leaders in Aceh resisted Dutch incursions strongly, and Aceh was not incorporated fully into Indonesia until 1904. Even today, Aceh is the most conservative area of Indonesia, and it is the only province in Indonesia where Sharia law is practiced. Aceh is the land area closest to the epicenter of the major earthquake that caused the devastating tsunami of December 26, 2004. An estimated 150,000 residents of Aceh lost their lives in this disaster. During the following year, a peace agreement between separatists and the Indonesian government was signed by both sides, giving Aceh more autonomy with respect to religion. Especially since the 2004 earthquake, the Aceh government has intensified its efforts to force conformity to its conservative interpretation of Muslim.

Conflict over education in Aceh has centered on the role of Islam in the educational process. Indonesia is officially a secular society, but many in Aceh reject this secular orientation, and today more than half of Aceh's children attend Islamic schools. Some in Aceh have advocated eliminating public education in Aceh, with the provision of education there to be turned over to Muslim authorities. Although about 99 percent of Aceh's people are Muslims, this has become a concern to Aceh's small non-Muslim minority.

Far to the east, Indonesia occupies the western half of the island of New Guinea, which it shares with the independent country of Papua New Guinea. This area includes two of Indonesia's provinces, Papua and West Papua. Nearly five million people inhabit these two provinces combined. Papua and West Papua have a distinctive history compared to the rest of Indonesia. Papuans speak Papuan languages that are unrelated to Indonesian or most of the other Austronesian languages spoken throughout the country. Unlike the rest of the country, the Dutch retained control of present-day Papua and West Papua until it was transferred to Indonesia in 1961 via the New York Agreement. Under terms of the agreement, the transfer was to be temporary and Papuans would be given the opportunity to vote whether to become an independent country. However, most Papuans were not permitted to vote, and those who did were believed to have been handpicked by the Indonesian government. Thus, most international observers regarded this election as fraudulent. Independence-supporting guerillas have been active in Papua and West Papua ever since.

The provision of education in Papua and West Papua has been affected by a variety of factors, including ongoing ethnic and cultural conflict. Many Papuans live in isolated rural areas characterized by rugged and poorly accessible terrain, as is the case in the independent country of Papua New Guinea. This inaccessibility, along with the activities of those agitating for independence for the two provinces, has made it difficult for Indonesian officials to attract teachers who are willing to live and work there. And in part because of cultural and linguistic differences, some parents and local officials question the value of formal education for children who are likely to become perceived and treated as second-class citizens within Indonesia as adults.

Further Reading

Dhimaswij, "The challenges of education in West Papua, New Guinea," *Edupapua*, February 21, 2017, https://edupapua.wordpress.com/2017/02/21/the-challenges-of-education-in-west-papua-indonesia/. Retrieved on January 14, 2020.

Drigana Borenovic Dilas, Christopher Mackie, Ying Huang, and Stefan Trines, "Education in Indonesia," *World Education News and Reviews*, March 21, 2019, https://wenr.wes.org/2019/03/education-in-indonesia-2. Retrieved on January 6, 2020.

Clarry Sada, Yabit Alas, and Muhammad Anshari, "Indigenous people of Borneo (Dayak): Development, social cultural perspective and its challenges," *Cogent Arts and Humanities*, 6 (2019), https://www.tandfonline.com/doi/full/10.1080/23311983.2019.1665936. Retrieved on January 6, 2020.

Ritash Shah and Mieke Lopes Cardozo, "Education and social change in post-conflict and post-disaster Aceh," *International Journal of Educational Development*, 38 (2014), pp. 2–12.

Kiki Siregar, "New Indonesia capital: Indigenous tribes fear further marginalization," *Channel News Asia*, September 20, 2019, https://www.channelnewsasia.com/news/asia/indonesia-new-capital-east-kalimantan-indigenous-tribes-11920292. Retrieved on January 6, 2020.

KAZAKHSTAN

The Republic of Kazakhstan, a landlocked country in Central Asia east of the Caspian Sea, is the ninth largest country in the world by land area. With a land area of over one million square miles, Kazakhstan has a larger land area than all of Western Europe combined. However, most of the country is sparsely populated. Kazakhstan's population as of 2021 was only about 19 million.

Much of Kazakhstan's terrain consists of semiarid, relatively dry steppes. Anthropologists believe that the steppes of Kazakhstan were inhabited several thousand years ago. Beginning approximately 2,000 years ago, various tribes from present-day Turkey, present-day Mongolia, and other parts of Asia and Eastern Europe moved into the area. Given the area's dry climate, many of these inhabitants of present-day Kazakhstan were pastoral nomads. The area became part of the Mongol empire in the thirteenth and fourteenth centuries.

Beginning in the seventeenth century, Russians began to move into present-day northern Kazakhstan from the north. By the 1860s, what is now the northern half of Kazakhstan had been incorporated into the Russian Empire. After taking control of the former Russian Empire following World War I, the Soviets forcibly incorporated Kazakhstan and four neighboring Central Asian republics into the Soviet Union. Present-day Kazakhstan became known as the Kazakh Soviet Socialist Republic (KSSR).

In the middle of the twentieth century, the Soviet government promoted policies known as "Russification." The intent of the Russification program was to induce non-Russian people living in the Soviet Union to give up their languages,

Uighur Students Attend Boarding School in Turkey

About 11 million Uighurs, who speak a language related to Turkish and most of who practice Islam, live in Xinjiang Province in northwestern China. The Chinese government has long been accused of trying to wipe out Uighur culture. Meanwhile, many Uighurs want the Uighur-dominated areas of Xinjiang Province to become an independent country. Today, hundreds of thousands of Uighurs have been interned in "re-education camps" and have been separated from their children. Several hundred Uighur children, separated from their parents, now live in Turkey. Many attend boarding schools, while others live at home and take classes in Uighur language and culture.

Source: Durrie Bouscaren, "In Turkey, a boarding school cares for Uighur children separated from their families," *The World*, November 20, 2019, https://www.pri.org /stories/2019-11-20/turkey-boarding-school-cares-uighur-children-separated -their-parents. Retrieved on March 20, 2020.

Teaching Sakha and Preserving Yakut Culture in Siberia

The Sakha Republic, also known as Yakutia, comprises nearly 1.2 million square miles in eastern Siberia in Russia with a population of approximately one million. About half of the Republic's population consists of ethnic Yakuts, who speak a Turkish language unrelated to Russian. During Soviet times, education was conducted in Russia. Since the collapse of the Soviet Union, the Russian government has made efforts to recognize the Yakut language and other non-Russian languages as "state languages." Courses in the Yakut language are now included in the Sakha Republic's educational curricula. The curricula also include both Yakut and Russian culture and history.

Source: Stepan Konstantinovich Kolodeznikov and Lyubov Dmitrievna Kolodeznikova, "Specificity of teaching Sakha as an official language in the Russian-language schools of Yakutia," *IEJME—Mathematics Education*, 11 (2016), pp. 3477–3485, https://www .iejme.com/download/specificity-of-teaching-sakha-as-an-official-language-in-the -russian-language-schools-of-yakutia.pdf. Retrieved on March 20, 2020.

customs, and cultures, replacing them with the Russian language, Russian culture, and Soviet ideology. The Russian language was seen as a key component of Soviet culture. In promoting Russification, the Soviets also encouraged people of Russian ancestry to move to other parts of the Soviet Union, including to the KSSR. During the 1950s, Russians were recruited to move to the KSSR and begin farming after the Soviets diverted the Amu Darya and Syr Darya rivers with the intent of irrigating and promoting agriculture in an area where summer temperatures are hot enough to permit the cultivation of cotton and various fruits that require warm weather in order to grow. However, the diversion program resulted eventually in the near depletion of the Aral Sea into which these rivers had flowed. Although agriculture remains prominent in Kazakhstan today, mineral production including the production and export of oil and uranium represents about three-quarters of Kazakhstan's gross national product.

Kazakhstan became independent in 1991. Today, about two-thirds of Kazakhstan's people are of Kazakh ancestry, and about 20 percent are of Russian ancestry. The majority of Kazakhstan's Russians live in the northern portion of the country closest to the Russian boundary. Religious tensions have affected relationships between the two groups as well, in that most Kazakhs are Muslims and most Russians are Orthodox Christians.

In 1997, the government moved the capital from Almaty in the extreme south to Astana, which is located in what had been a predominantly Russian-speaking area to the north. Although less than 20 percent of Astana's residents were of Kazakh ancestry at the time the capital was moved, today nearly two-thirds of the residents of the city (whose name was changed to Nur-Sultan in honor of independent Kazakhstan's first president Nursultan Nazarbayev [1940–], in 2019) are of Kazakh origin largely because of the movement of government workers from Almaty. Cultural, religions, and ethnic differences between the Russian population and the Kazakhs themselves have affected education in Kazakhstan considerably.

Education in Kazakhstan

Prior to the nineteenth century, there was little formal education in present-day Kazakhstan in part because so many Kazakhs were nomads. Some education, primarily in Arabic, was provided to boys as part of the study of Islam. Girls had virtually no opportunities for education. It has been estimated that as late as 1900, only about 10 percent of children in the area were enrolled in school. However, Russians who lived in settled communities established schools to promote literacy and to train people of Russian ancestry for government and administrative positions.

Formal schooling was introduced throughout the KSSR by the Soviets. These schools were secular in orientation, in keeping with the Soviet Union's official policy of atheism. The curriculum emphasized Soviet Communist ideology, including the removal of ethnic identity. Hence, there was very little recognition of diversity within KSSR schools. Schooling was conducted in Russian, and emphasis was placed on mathematics and science. However, the elimination of illiteracy was an important goal of the Soviet regime. Compulsory education was implemented in the KSSR during the period of Soviet rule, and as a result, more than 99 percent of Kazakhstan's citizens are literate. Because education during the period of Soviet rule was conducted in Russian, Russian is understood by more than 90 percent of the population today.

After independence, Kazakhstan faced many obstacles in restructuring its post-Communist educational system. Economic ties between Kazakhstan and Russia were reduced, and the transition from the Soviet planned economy to a market economy was sometimes difficult. As a result, independent Kazakhstan faced a

On this university campus, high school students in Kazakhstan are participating in a historical reconstruction game. Such activities provide students with hands-on experience outside of the classroom. This gives students practical experience to complement academic studies in classroom settings. (Yorgy67 | Dreamstime.com)

significant shortage of income to be used in public services. This meant that public financing for education declined substantially during the first few years of independence, although such funding has been increasing more recently as the country's economy has expanded. Per capita gross domestic product has been increasing at rates greater than the worldwide average since 2010. However, Kazakhstan continues to face a shortage of school buildings and teachers, impeding the educational process for the country's children. This is an issue particularly in rural areas, where nomadism continues to be practiced and populations are dispersed. Even today, the average test scores of students living in cities are significantly higher than those of students in rural areas.

Today, education in Kazakhstan is managed by the Ministry of Education and Science. The educational system begins with four years of primary school. Parents have the right to send their children to kindergarten prior to primary school, but in practice, opportunities for kindergarten are limited especially outside cities. Primary school is followed by five years of basic general education and two to three years of secondary education. Schooling is free and education is compulsory through secondary education, which includes both vocational and college preparatory tracks. Education was very highly centralized during Soviet rule, and it remains centralized today although there is more recognition of diversity and difference than had been the case prior to independence. For example, the ministry determines what textbooks are to be used, and individual teachers have little or no choice over what educational materials are provided.

Diversity, Cultural Differences, and Education in Kazakhstan

Cultural and linguistic differences between the Kazakh majority and Russian minority have had ongoing impacts on education in Kazakhstan. The genesis of these impacts is linked to Kazakhstan's history.

The present constitution of Kazakhstan came into effect in 1995. Article 7 of the constitution specifies that Kazakh would be the country's official language. However, Section 2 of Article 7 states, translated from Kazakh, "In state institutions and local self-administrative bodies the Russian language shall be officially used on equal grounds along with the Kazakh language." Section 3 states, also translated from Kazakh, "The state shall promote conditions for the study and development of the languages of the people of Kazakhstan." These principles underlie education in Kazakhstan today, and Section 3 lays the groundwork for how education was to be developed in order to promote Kazakh identity.

In Kazakhstan today, students can be educated in Kazakh, Russian, or other languages spoken as first languages. In 2012, Kazakh was the language of instruction in 3,819 schools. Russian was the language of instruction in 1,394 schools, and other languages were used in 76 schools. In 2,113 schools, both Kazakh and Russian were used as languages of instruction. Fluency in both Russian and Kazakh, as well as in English, is a goal of the Kazakhstan educational system. In 2017, a new alphabet for Kazakh was introduced, with this Latin alphabet replacing the traditional Cyrillic alphabet. Although fluency in Russian ensures familiarity with the Cyrillic alphabet, it has been suggested that the introduction of the Latin alphabet signals more cultural independence from Russian influence.

In 2007, Kazakhstan's government implemented its Law on Education. The Law of Education initiated efforts to put the provisions of Section 2 of Article 7 into practice. The goal of the law has been to transition education in Kazakhstan to "inclusive" schooling that recognizes and promotes diversity. Such diversity includes linguistic diversity, with classes taught in Kazakh, Russian, and English. It also includes accommodating the needs of special-needs children, although according to one study some teachers were skeptical about the value of mainstreaming special-needs children. Others expressed concern that teachers were not given sufficient training in how to teach special-needs children from diverse backgrounds, especially in more than one language. However, by 2017 more than half of Kazakhstan's schools had been equipped with facilities that could accommodate special-needs children.

Further Reading

William Fierman, "Language and education in post-Soviet Kazakhstan: Kazakh-Medium instruction in urban schools," *Russian Review*, 65 (2005), pp. 98–116.

Human Rights Watch, "Kazakhstan: Education barriers for children with disabilities," March 14, 2019, https://today.ku.edu/2018/01/25/kazakhstan-seeks-use-language -tool-establishing-independence-scholar-says. Retrieved on December 15, 2019.

Tsediso Michael Makoelle, "Schools' transition toward inclusive education in post-Soviet countries: Selected cases in Kazakhstan," SAGE Open, May 29, 2020, https://journals .sagepub.com/doi/10.1177/2158244020926586#. Retrieved on January 24, 2022.

Organisation for Economic Co-Operation and Development, "Education Policy Outlook: Kazakhstan," December 2018, https://www.oecd.org/education/Education-Policy -Outlook-Country-Profile-Kazakhstan-2018.pdf. Retrieved on January 24, 2022.

Anna Pons, Jeremie Amoroso, Jan Herczynski, Igor Kheyfets, Marlaine Lockheed, and Paulo Santiago, "OECD Reviews of School Resources—Kazakhstan," 2015, http://www .oecd.org/education/school/OECD%20School%20Resources%20Review_Kazakhstan _FINAL_CRC_with%20cover.pdf. Retrieved on December 14, 2019.

University of Kansas, "Kazakhstan seeks to use language as tool for establishing inde- pendence," January 29, 2018, https://today.ku.edu/2018/01/25/kazakhstan-seeks-use -language-tool-establishing-independence-scholar-says. Retrieved on December 15, 2019.

MYANMAR

Myanmar is the westernmost country on the Southeast Asian mainland, and it is the only Southeast Asian country that shares boundaries with both India and China. It is the largest Southeast Asian country by land area with a territory of about 250,000 square miles. The population was estimated at 55 million in 2021. The country is known also as Burma, after the Burmese people who make up more than half of the country's population.

The Kingdom of Myanmar ruled much of modern-day Myanmar for nearly 1,000 years beginning in the ninth century AD. The kingdom was ruled by the Konbaung Dynasty beginning in 1752. During the nineteenth century, the British initiated efforts to incorporate Myanmar into the British Empire. Three Anglo-Burmese Wars were fought between 1824 and 1885. After the third Anglo-Burmese War, the Konbaung regime was overthrown, and the area became part of British India along with present-day India, Bangladesh, and Pakistan. In 1937, the British sep- arated what is now Myanmar from the rest of British India. This area included Ministerial Burma, which included the central part of the country, along with the Frontier Areas to the north, east, and west of Ministerial Burma. Most residents of Ministerial Burma were ethnic Burmese, in contrast to residents of the Frontier Areas where most people belonged to other cultural groups.

Ministerial Burma and the Frontier Areas were united in 1948 as the indepen- dent country of Burma, which became known as Myanmar beginning in 1989. Given the newly independent country's relatively large population and abundance of natural resources, many expected that Burma would become one of the wealth- iest and most developed countries in Southeast Asia. This prediction proved inac- curate after a military junta took control of the country in 1962. Subsequently, Myanmar became more and more isolated from the global community. Beginning in 2008, however, the autocratic government relaxed its control over Myanmar. Democratic elections have been held since 2010, and interaction between Myanmar and the international community has increased.

Since independence, Myanmar has experienced ongoing conflict between the Burmese, who make up about two-thirds of the population, and other ethnic groups. The largest of these ethnic groups are the Shan people, who live in eastern Myanmar near the boundaries with China to the northeast and Thailand to the east, and the Karen people who live further south along the Thai border. Activists representing both populations have agitated for political independence or greater autonomy. This agitation has taken place in part in response to the Burmese-controlled government's efforts to impose Burmese culture on the country's non-Burmese populations. Independence movements and guerilla activities are funded in part by income derived from illegal drug cultivation, illegal trade in wildlife, and smuggling of gemstones and other valuable commodities across Myanmar's porous boundaries in this region's rugged and somewhat inaccessible terrain. Today, portions of Shan-dominated and Karen-dominated territory have achieved semiautonomous status.

To the south, the predominantly Muslim Rohingya people are also involved in conflict with the predominantly Buddhist Burmese. Unlike the Shan and the Karen, the Rohingya live near the coast and are not able to take advantage of their location to support their separatist activities. It is believed that more than 25,000 Rohingya have lost their lives in this conflict, while hundreds of thousands of others have fled the country as refugees. Some of these refugees have moved across the international boundary into Bangladesh. However, Bangladesh has made it clear that these refugees are only temporary residents, and the government does not provide any formal education to Rohingya refugee children on the grounds that these children will eventually return to Myanmar.

Education in Myanmar

Before the arrival of the British, education in present-day Myanmar was provided primarily by Buddhist teachers associated with monasteries. Schooling was generally limited to males, and it emphasized religious training. The British introduced secular, Western-oriented education to Myanmar including the provision of schooling to girls as well as boys. English was the language of instruction during the colonial period.

After independence, Myanmar's government emphasized education, including literacy, throughout the country. After the government was taken over by the military in 1962, however, Burmese, which is a language related closely to Chinese and Tibetan, replaced English as the primary language of instruction throughout the country. As a result, the number of Myanmar's people who were proficient in English declined quickly. In addition, the government's insistence on the use of Burmese as the language of instruction was resisted strongly by non-Burmese speakers such as the Shan and Karen who lived outside of what was once Ministerial Burma. History curricula also emphasized the history of the Burmese majority, downplaying the histories of the various ethnic groups that inhabit the former Frontier Areas.

Today, education in Myanmar is managed by the government's Ministry of Education. The ministry's administration includes the Department of Education, which operates primary and secondary schools. Primary school, which is compulsory, lasts for five years. Primary school is followed by secondary school, which lasts for six years and is not compulsory. In order to enroll in secondary school, students must pass a national examination covering subjects taught in primary school. Burmese remains the primary language of instruction, although English is now taught throughout the country as a second language beginning in primary school. The literacy rate in Myanmar has been estimated at approximately 90 percent. About 90 percent of Myanmar's people practice Buddhism, and all students in the country are required to recite Buddhist prayers in school each day. Such is a concern among the Rohingya, most of whom are Muslims.

Education in Myanmar today remains beset by many problems. Secondary education in particular is oriented very strongly to rote memorization. In particular, because competitive national examinations are based on memorization, little attention is paid to critical and creative thinking or to problem-solving skills. The Ministry of Education remains poorly funded, and as a result, Myanmar faces problems similar to those experienced in other less developed countries including shortages of teachers, low salaries for teachers, a lack of facilities and educational materials, and overcrowded classrooms. These problems are intensified outside of the Burmese core area of the country, in part because both geographical inaccessibility and ongoing ethnic conflict make recruitment of teachers willing to work in these areas difficult.

Diversity, Cultural Differences, and Education in Myanmar

As with many other countries with a history of autocratic governance, education in Myanmar has paid little attention to various types of differences among students. The most significant differences with respect to education in Myanmar involve language and culture, although the country also faces difficulties in providing education to special-needs children.

As indicated earlier, Myanmar is characterized by considerable cultural and linguistic diversity. However, members of many of the non-Burmese ethnic groups speak languages that are unrelated to Burmese. For example, the approximately five million Shan people who reside in eastern and northeastern Myanmar speak the Shan language that is related closely to Thai and Laotian. The Shan and other national groups have been marginalized with respect to education by the national government, which in 1962 mandated that all education throughout the country be conducted only in Burmese.

Shan State occupies the northeastern quarter of Myanmar. Many of the region's inhabitants are ethnic Shan people, whose language and culture are distinct from those of Myanmar's Burmese majority. As is the case with other non-Burmese areas of Myanmar, literacy rates are lower, and local children have less opportunity to obtain formal education beyond primary school. Even though primary schooling is required, schools are not available to some children who live in isolated areas where transportation is poor or nonexistent. Some of the teachers, who are paid by the national government, speak only Burmese and are not fluent in Shan or other local languages. Local school officials in Shan State must apply to the national government for funds to pay teachers who can teach in Shan.

Schooling in Shan State is affected also by the region's history of violence and the illegal trade that helps to keep its resistance and independence movements afloat. The "Golden Triangle," which includes Shan State along with the neighboring areas in Thailand and Laos, is one of the world's leading opium poppy producing areas. The Burmese government working with the United Nations has attempted to curtail and eliminate opium poppy production. However, members of groups advocating Shan State independence or greater autonomy have used their knowledge of the region's rugged terrain in order to cultivate opium poppies and smuggle them across the border into China, where they are processed into heroin that is trafficked worldwide. Illegal trade in wild animals is also commonplace. These illegal commodities are sometimes stored in school buildings, and local teachers have often expressed concern about their personal safety and that of their students. As the national government and local rebel groups continue to contest for control of areas with Shan State, control of some places within the state has shifted frequency to and from government and rebel forces. According to surveys, many local leaders and residents do not want government-controlled schools where teachers from other parts of Myanmar are unable to speak Shan. Buddhist monks have attempted to fill in these gaps by implementing literacy programs in monasteries.

Further Reading

Ewan Cameron, "Myanmar education is failing disabled children," *Myanmar Times*, March 2, 2015, https://www.mmtimes.com/opinion/13283-myanmar-education -system-is-failing-disabled-children.html. Retrieved on October 21, 2019.

Human Rights Watch, "Are we not human? Denial of education for Rohingya refugee children in Bangladesh," December 3, 2019, https://www.hrw.org/report/2019/12/03/are -we-not-human/denial-education-rohingya-refugee-children-bangladesh. Retrieved on January 14, 2020.

Kim Jolliffe and Emily Speers Means, "Strength in diversity: Towards universal education in Myanmar's ethnic areas," Asia Foundation, October 2016, https://asiafoundation.org /wp-content/uploads/2016/10/Strength-in-Diversity-Toward-Universal-Education -Myanmar-Ethnic-Area.pdf. Retrieved on January 24, 2022.

Mwe Khur, "Challenges in teaching ethnic language in Burma," BNI Multimedia Group, January 10, 2017, https://www.bnionline.net/en/opinion/op-ed/item/2612-challenges -in-teaching-ethnic-language-in-burma.html. Retrieved on January 14, 2020.

Myat Moe Thu, "Teachers in Shan conflict zones beg for protection," *Myanmar Times*, October 8, 2019, https://www.mmtimes.com/news/teachers-shan-conflict-zones-beg -protection.html. Retrieved on January 14, 2020.

SOUTH AFRICA

The Republic of South Africa occupies the southernmost portion of the African continent, with coasts on the Atlantic Ocean to the west and the Indian Ocean to the east. Its land area is about 470,000 square miles. Its population as of 2021 was about 59 million.

Anthropologists have estimated that parts of present-day South Africa have been occupied by humans for more than 150,000 years. It is believed that the first human inhabitants of the region were ancestors of today's San people. The San are sometimes known by the exonym "Bushmen," which is now regarded as derogatory. About 1,500 years ago, Bantu-speaking people from central Africa moved into the area.

Although the Cape of Good Hope on the southwestern coast was sighted by the Portuguese sailor Bartolomeu Dias in 1488, the area was not occupied by the Europeans until the seventeenth century. The Dutch established the settlement now known as Cape Town as a refreshment station for ships sailing between the Netherlands and Dutch colonies in present-day Indonesia. Cape Town became the center of the Cape Colony where Dutch farmers, who became known as Boers, grew crops used to supply food for Dutch mariners stopping at Cape Town. Slaves were imported from Asia and from Madagascar. The Boers spoke Afrikaans, which is derived from the Dutch language.

The British took over Cape Town and the Cape Colony in 1795, and they abolished slavery throughout the British Empire in 1834. In response, thousands of slave-holding Boers moved northward and eastward in what came to be known as the Great Trek. The Boers, who spoke a variant of Dutch known as Afrikaans, established the Boer republics of Transvaal and the Orange Free State. Beginning in 1867, diamonds and gold were discovered in these Boer republics. These mineral resources attracted large numbers of British miners and other settlers, encouraging Britain to attempt to take over the Boer republics. British efforts to annex the Boer republics resulted eventually in the Boer War, which took place between 1899 and 1902. In 1910, Britain united Transvaal and the Orange Free State were united with the Cape Colony and British colony of Natal along the Indian Ocean, creating the Union of South Africa. The Union of South Africa was made a dominion of the British Empire. The Union became an independent country within the British Commonwealth in 1931.

Throughout the country's history, the majority of South Africans were of African ancestry. However, people of European descent controlled most of South Africa's land, resources, and wealth. In 1948, the National Party won nationwide elections in which Africans were not permitted to participate. The National Party spearheaded the development and implementation of apartheid. Under apartheid, all South Africans were grouped into four categories on the basis of their race, including whites, Blacks, "colored" or mixed-race people, and Asians. Integration was prohibited by strict legal codes, and non-whites were still not permitted to vote. In 1961, South Africa became an independent republic.

Protests against South Africa's apartheid regime intensified over time. Many opponents of the regime were affiliated with the African National Congress (ANC). The ANC's leader, Nelson Mandela (1918–2013), was imprisoned in 1962 and remained in prison until 1990, when the government released him and lifted its long-standing ban on the ANC's activities. Apartheid was removed in the early 1990s. In 1994, South Africa held its first multiracial elections, and Mandela was elected President.

South Africa remains a diverse, multiethnic society. About 80 percent of South Africans today are of African ancestry, representing several different cultural groups. About 9 percent are colored, 8 percent are of European ancestry, and 2.5 percent are Asian. South Africa has 11 official languages, including English, Afrikaans, and 9 African languages. Language differences have been a point of contention in South African education throughout the country's history.

Education in South Africa

South Africa is recognized as having one of the most developed economies of sub-Saharan Africa, although it remains plagued by poverty and income inequality. This inequality is a legacy of South African's apartheid history. Even today, the average median income of Black South Africans is less than 10 percent of the average median income of white South Africans.

The history of education in South Africa reflects its history of responses to differences characterizing South African society. During the eighteenth century, schools were established by Dutch Reformed Church officials in the Cape Colony. The curricula included basic literacy skills, basic mathematics, and religious instruction. After the British took over the Cape Colony, they established English language schools. However, many Boers objected to the use of English as the language of instruction as well as what they perceived to be a lack of respect for Boer culture. Many did not enroll their children in schools until the government permitted instruction in Afrikaans in the early twentieth century. It has been estimated that only about 10 percent of children in the Transvaal and the Orange Free State were enrolled in school at the end of the Boer War.

After the National Party took power in 1948, the government applied its apartheid policy to public education. Students were segregated by race, as institutionalized by the Bantu Education Act of 1953. Schools attended by African children were funded very poorly, and curricula were intended to prepare graduates for low-paying and menial employment. Schooling was compulsory for white children for nine years, as opposed to only seven years for African children. These restrictions were phased out after the collapse of apartheid in the 1990s. English became the language of instruction following the early years of primary school, although some children attend Afrikaans language schools where that language is the language of instruction.

Until 2009, all education in South Africa was managed by the government's Department of Education. In 2009, the department was split. Today, primary and

These students are gathered near a school bus in South Africa, whose population is very diverse culturally. For many years, the South African government used its apartheid policy to privilege the white minority population. Postapartheid South Africa is working to provide effective education to all of its citizens regardless of their cultural and ethnic status. (Peter Titmuss | Dreamstime.com)

secondary education in South Africa are managed by the Department of Basic Education while higher education is the responsibility of the Department of Higher Education and Training. Each of South Africa's nine provinces is responsible for managing education within themselves. About 95 percent of South African children attend public schools, with about 5 percent enrolled in private schools. However, the percentage of pupils in private schools is believed to be increasing because of perceived inadequacies of public schools.

Primary and secondary education in South Africa includes four components. Students begin with the General Education and Training band (GET). The GET includes the foundation phase, the intermediate phase, and the senior phase. Each of these phases consists of three years of schooling. These three phases are followed by the Further Education and Training band (FET). Some children attend one to three years of preprimary school prior to beginning the foundation phase. In practice, however, the first seven years of GET are referred to as primary school, and the remaining five years of schooling including the FET are referred to as secondary school. After completing the FET, students must pass a national examination in order to graduate from secondary school.

Public schooling is free and compulsory throughout these three phases. However, parents are responsible for some school fees and for purchasing uniforms, which are required in most South African schools. Historically, children from poor families could not attend school because their parents could not afford these fees and uniforms. Beginning in the late 1990s, however, impoverished parents were granted full or partial reductions in these fees so that their children could attend school. In 2015, it was estimated that about 95 percent of South Africans were considered literate. However, many South African students are regarded as functionally illiterate after completing the first two phases of formal education in that some are not able to read above a very basic level or solve simple problems in arithmetic. Dropout rates are high in part because of violence and gang activity in secondary schools along with the desire of some parents for their teenaged children to work in order to supplement their impoverished families' incomes.

Diversity, Cultural Differences, and Education in South Africa

The diverse nature of South Africa's population, including both Indigenous groups and descendants of immigrants from Europe and Asia, has affected and continues to affect South African education. The legacy of apartheid has contributed also to the development of the educational process and practice. During the apartheid period, the law mandated segregation of students by race along with separate curricula for the different races. Even today, South Africa is grappling with the legacy of these policies more than two decades after the end of apartheid.

In 1996, the first postapartheid government of South Africa enacted the South African Schools Act 84. The preamble contains the words: "This country requires a new national system for schools which will redress past injustices in educational provision, provide an education of progressively high quality for all learners and in so doing lay a strong foundation for the development of all our people's talents and capabilities, advance the democratic transformation of society, combat racism and sexism and all other forms of unfair discrimination and intolerance, contribute to the eradication of poverty and the economic well-being of society, protect and advance our diverse cultures and languages . . ." This preamble can be interpreted as a framework by which diversity could be brought into the educational process throughout South Africa.

According to the Act, "It is necessary to set uniform norms and standards for the education of learners at schools and the organisation, governance and funding of schools throughout the Republic of South Africa." In practice, however, educational outcomes continue to be affected by the legacy of apartheid. Today, less than 75 percent of students pass their high school graduation examinations, with Black students failing at higher rates. And many who do pass do so at the lowest level, which precludes them from entrance into higher education. Moreover, these figures do not take into account that many Black students drop out of secondary school and that these students would be unlikely to have passed the exams if they had taken them.

Moreover, the goal of "uniform norms and standards" itself can be a culture-bound concept. For example, educating students in English and/or Afrikaans, the languages of the white minority, can be interpreted as privileging European cultural norms and values over African cultural values in a country where more than three-quarters of the people are of African ancestry. English and Afrikaans remain the languages of instruction throughout South Africa, although in 2005, Western Cape Province, which includes Cape Town, mandated that the Xhosa language be a compulsory subject. Thus, South African education is also trying to deal with questions involving the nature of diversity and its impacts on South African society. How should diversity be taught and to what extent should this question be affected by the racial composition of various schools? How do these questions affect the teaching of South African history, especially the history of the apartheid period?

Further Reading

Alex Gluckman, "Realities of South Africa's post-*apartheid* educational system," *Odyssey*, June 7, 2016, https://www.theodysseyonline.com/realities-south-africas-post-apartheid-education-system. Retrieved on January 5, 2020.

Government of South African, "South African Schools Act 84 of 1996," https://www.gov.za/documents/south-african-schools-act. Retrieved on January 25, 2022.

Wilson Macha and Aditi Kadakia, "Education in South Africa," *World Education News and Reviews*, May 2, 2017, https://wenr.wes.org/2017/05/education-south-africa. Retrieved on January 5, 2020.

Finn Reygan and Melissa Steyn, "Diversity in basic education in South Africa: Intersectionality and critical diversity literacy," *Africa Education Review*, 14 (2017), pp. 68–81.

The Conversation, "South African education still fails many 20 years after *apartheid*," 2014, http://theconversation.com/south-african-education-still-fails-many-20-years-after-apartheid-22069. Retrieved on January 5, 2020.

UNITED KINGDOM

The United Kingdom of Great Britain and Northern Ireland (UK) includes the island of Great Britain along with Northern Ireland, which occupies the northeastern portion of Ireland. In addition to Northern Ireland, the United Kingdom includes England, Scotland, and Wales on Great Britain. The overall land area of the United Kingdom is about 94,500 square miles. Its population as of 2018 was about 66 million. England contains slightly more than half of the United Kingdom's land area and about 84 percent of its population.

The original inhabitants of the present-day UK were of Celtic origin and spoke Celtic languages. Beginning in the fifth century AD, however, Anglos and Saxons moved into Great Britain from present-day Germany. The Anglo-Saxons brought their Germanic language with them, which evolved eventually into the modern-day English language. Most of present-day England was unified beginning in the tenth century AD. In 1284, England took control of Wales, and England took control of Ireland in 1603. All of Ireland remained under UK control until 1921, when the island was partitioned and divided between the independent Republic of Ireland and Northern Ireland, which remained part of the United Kingdom.

Scotland became part of the United Kingdom following the unification of the English and Scottish monarchies via the Act of Union in 1707. Beginning in the sixteenth and seventeenth centuries, the United Kingdom established the world's largest colonial empire. It was also the birthplace of the Industrial Revolution. Its industrial dominance and its colonial empire helped the United Kingdom to become the strongest and most powerful country in the world during most of the eighteenth and nineteenth centuries.

As England expanded throughout Great Britain and Ireland, the traditional Celtic languages were replaced in many areas by English. This process accelerated throughout the nineteenth and twentieth centuries. The two remaining Celtic languages in the United Kingdom today, Scots Gaelic and Welsh, are now spoken primarily as first languages in isolated rural areas, notably in the Scottish islands off the coast of the Scottish mainland. However, in recent years there has been a revival of interest in these languages, with impacts on education in the areas where these languages continue to be spoken.

After World War II, the United Kingdom's global power was eclipsed by that of the United States. Most of the United Kingdom's colonies in Asia, Africa, and otherwise became independent countries between the 1950s and the 1970s. More recently, the UK granted expanded powers to locally elected governments in Scotland, Wales, and Northern Ireland. Separatist sentiment continues, particularly in Scotland where many persons support full independence. In 2014, Scottish voters turned down independence in a referendum by a slight majority. Two years later, a slight majority of voters throughout the United Kingdom voted to leave the European Union, which the United Kingdom had joined in 1973, in what became known as "Brexit." The UK left the European Union officially on January 31, 2020. However, Scottish voters opposed Brexit by a substantial majority. The prospect of the United Kingdom's departure from the European Union has induced some Scots to reconsider the prospect of independence. Such sentiment intensified after the 2019 general election, in which members of the pro-independence Scottish National Party won 48 of Scotland's 59 seats in the UK's House of Commons.

Education in the United Kingdom

During the Middle Ages, education in England was conducted by the Roman Catholic Church. Only a small minority of children, primarily boys, obtained formal education, and most of this education was intended to prepare boys for the priesthood or the law. Much of this education emphasized training in Latin. The large majority of the United Kingdom's residents were illiterate.

Beginning in 1529, England under the rule of King Henry VIII (1491–1547) broke away from the Roman Catholic Church, and the Church of England (also known as the Anglican Church and which is known as the Episcopalian Church in the United States) was established. Meanwhile, Protestantism also took hold in Scotland. In 1560, the Scottish government also rejected Catholicism, and the Presbyterian Church of Scotland became the state church. The Protestant Reformation had a profound effect on education throughout the United Kingdom. Protestant theology emphasized a direct relationship between the individual and God so that it became important that people be able to read the Bible in the English language. Thus, much more emphasis was placed on teaching children to read and write in English.

In England, the Church of England was primarily responsible for education into the nineteenth century. The government became involved in education in 1833, when Parliament voted for the first time to provide funds for public schooling in England and Wales. Education became compulsory between the ages of 5 and 10 years in 1880. Education became compulsory through the age of 14 in 1900 and through the age of 16 in 1973. In 2015, the age of compulsory education was raised to 18 for children born in or after 1997.

Today, each of the four constituent parts of the United Kingdom (England, Scotland, Wales, and Northern Ireland) is responsible for education within their own jurisdictions. However, the general structure of education in each of these areas is similar.

Once compulsory schooling begins, children pass through four "key stages." The first two stages, which together last for six years, constitute primary school. The third stage, which lasts for three years, is known as lower secondary school. Lower secondary school is followed by two years of upper secondary school. After completing upper secondary school, students take the General Certificate of Secondary Education (GCSE) examination. This examination replaced England's traditional General Certificate of Education or O-level examinations in 1988. Those who complete these examinations successfully can attend two additional years of secondary school, after which they take the advanced subsidiary level or A-level examination.

The system in Scotland is similar, but with some distinctions. Students in Scotland attend primary school for seven years and secondary school for four years. Two additional years of secondary school are optional. Scottish students take examinations for the Scottish Qualifications Certificate, which is analogous to but distinct from the GCSE examinations. However, those Scottish students who wish to attend universities in England or Wales take the GCSE examinations as well.

Diversity, Cultural Differences, and Education in the United Kingdom

Support for increased autonomy, or outright independence as advocated by many Scots, has affected the provision of education throughout the United Kingdom. In 1872, the Education (Scotland) Act was enacted by the UK Parliament. Under provisions of the act, all schooling was to be conducted in English, and children were forbidden to speak Scots Gaelic in school. The Scottish Parliament enacted the Education (Scotland) Act in 2016. The 2016 Act included provisions for the maintenance of Scots Gaelic schools as part of its Gaelic Medium Education policy. In these schools, Gaelic is the language of instruction with English taught as a second language. Thus, the 2016 Act overturned the anti-Gaelic provisions of the 1872

Act. Implementing this policy, however, has sometimes become difficult because some, but not all, of the children attending these schools speak Gaelic as a first language whereas others enter these Gaelic-medium schools speaking no Gaelic at all.

Gaelic-medium instruction highlights a dilemma that is found in many other parts of the world. On the one hand, Gaelic is seen as a means of preserving and celebrating Scottish culture, which could be wiped out entirely if Gaelic is no longer spoken. On the other hand, English is the primary language of the United Kingdom and of the global economy in general, and hence, people who do not speak English may be at a significant disadvantage compared to English speakers. In response, advocates of Gaelic-medium instruction point out that both goals can be met simultaneously. Graduates of such schools become bilingual, and although more and more Scots are fluent in Gaelic, most still speak English at home.

In contrast to Scotland, there is relatively little support for outright independence in Wales. Many Welsh people support greater degrees of autonomy, for preservation of Welsh culture rather than complete separation from the United Kingdom. Perhaps as a result, Welsh-medium instruction is much more commonplace in Wales compared to Gaelic-medium instruction in Scotland. In 2017, it was estimated that about 16 percent of Welsh students were attending Welsh-medium schools. As in Scotland, Welsh is the primary language of instruction in Welsh-medium schools, and English is taught as a second language. In those schools where English is the primary language of instruction, some advocates of Welsh-medium schooling have pushed to have Welsh included in the teaching of every subject, as opposed to the study of Welsh as a specific foreign language.

Further Reading

BBC, "Scottish independence: Sturgeon requests powers for referendum," December 19, 2019, https://www.bbc.com/news/uk-scotland-scotland-politics-50843024. Retrieved on January 18, 2020.

The Conversation, "Wales wants to make the Welsh language part of every lesson under new curriculum," July 30, 2019, http://theconversation.com/wales-wants-to-make -the-welsh-language-part-of-every-lesson-under-new-curriculum-120312. Retrieved on January 18, 2020.

Jenni Davidson, "Gaelic education: Is it effective?" Holyrood.com, December 6, 2018, https://www.holyrood.com/inside-politics/view,gaelic-education-is-it-effective_9611 .htm. Retrieved on January 18, 2020.

UNITED STATES

The United States has a long history of cultural diversity, as symbolized by the motto "E pluribus unum" or "Out of many, one." Cultural diversity is recognized increasingly in American primary and secondary education. Over several decades, the degree of cultural diversity within the U.S. population is increasing. By 2020, the number of non-white children enrolled in American public schools had exceeded the number of white children. However, bringing cultural diversity into the educational system in the United States has been a gradual process. Incorporating diversity into American schools, as elsewhere, includes two components—recognizing and understanding the diversity of student populations and bringing diversity into the educational process. Such diversity takes many forms, including not only race, religion, culture, and language but also disability, sexual orientation, and economic status.

The common school movement that shaped the development of public education in the United States was developed under the premise that all children, regardless of origin or social class, would receive a common education. As is detailed elsewhere in this volume, free and compulsory public schools had been established in every state by the late nineteenth century. However, this philosophy did not consider the diversity of the population. The curricula developed in many American public schools in the nineteenth century were geared toward the education of white Protestant boys. For example, children in many public schools were required to read from the King James version of the Bible. Not surprisingly, Roman Catholic and Jewish parents objected to this practice. History textbooks and lessons have often emphasized the achievements of white men, downplaying the roles of women and Blacks and other people of color in American history.

Especially in the South, Black children did not have the educational opportunities of their white peers. This segregation was legitimized by the Supreme Court in *Plessy v. Ferguson* (163 U.S. 357) in 1896. Under *Plessy*, segregation in public education was allowed if education provided to children of different races was "separate but equal." In practice, the quality of education provided to children of different races was far from equal. Far less money per pupil was spent to educate minority children as opposed to white children. African American children often attended schools in old and dilapidated buildings, with poorly trained and poorly paid teachers and without adequate textbooks or other school supplies. The "separate but equal" doctrine was overturned by the Supreme Court in *Brown v. Board of Education* (347 U.S. 483) in 1954, although disparities in the quality of education provided to white and non-white children remain significant today.

By the latter half of the twentieth century, cultural diversity within the U.S. population had become more recognized and appreciated. During the nineteenth and early twentieth centuries, public schooling was conducted almost exclusively in English. During World War I, in fact, some states made it illegal to teach foreign languages and, in some cases, made it illegal to use foreign languages in public, although such laws were declared unconstitutional by the Supreme Court in *Meyer v. Nebraska* (262 U.S. 390) in 1921. More recently, children who did not speak English at home were subjected to punishment if they spoke their first languages in school, even to one another on the playground.

Teaching cultural diversity involves helping students to both appreciate and value their own cultures and develop an understanding of other cultures. The white Protestant worldview characteristic of nineteenth-century American public education meant that non-whites, Roman Catholics, Jews, and immigrants were marginalized. Immigrant children were expected to become "American," giving up their traditional cultures of the "old country." Many Native American children

Native American Students Struggle

Many Native American students have felt neglected by American public school systems. For example, students and their families living who live on the Fort Peck Indian Reservation near Wolf Point, Montana, have felt that they are being ostracized by the school system. Most residents of the reservation deal with abject poverty, and some have had to deal with physical and emotional abuse at home. Although most Native American students in Montana attend racially integrated schools, Native American students are more likely to be suspended or disciplined and have been bullied or denigrated by fellow students and teachers. Such discouragement reinforces these differences.

Source: Erica L. Green and Annie Waldman, "'I feel invisible: Native students languish in public schools," *New York Times*, December 28, 2018, https://www.nytimes.com/2018/12/28/us/native-american-education.html. Retrieved on March 20, 2020.

were sent to government-sponsored boarding schools, where they were coerced into giving up the traditional cultures of their ancestors and adopt American customs, including personal names. The implication of this procedure was that Anglo-American culture was superior to Native American culture. Textbooks in common use at the time tended to portray Native Americans as "savages," "primitive," and/or "ignorant." Similarly, Blacks were portrayed as lazy, stupid, and incapable of mastering complex subjects.

Overcoming such negative stereotypes required students, teachers, and the general public to become more aware of diversity, including increased understanding of minority cultures. This goal was addressed in part by including lessons on cultural diversity and cultural appreciation in school curricula. Implementing such lessons successfully can depend on the degree to which teachers recognize how their own cultural values affect their own ideas about other cultures. For example, it is recognized now that it is inappropriate for a teacher to ask a Black student a question such as: "How do Black people feel about this issue?" as if that particular student is in a position to speak for all Blacks. Teaching about other cultures has also been shown to be important in teaching students to respect cultural diversity and to eliminate stereotyping. Learning activities have been developed to promote student understanding of diversity, including the use of virtual field trips, and exposing students to art, music, and literature of other cultures.

Further Reading

Becky Little, "How boarding schools tried to 'kill the Indian' through assimilation," history.com, November 1, 2018, https://www.history.com/news/how-boarding-schools-tried-to-kill-the-indian-through-assimilation. Retrieved on January 26, 2022.

J. A. O'Day and M. S. Smith, *Equality and quality in U.S. education: Systemic problems, systemic solutions.* Education Policy Center at American Institutes for Research. Policy Brief, 2016.

Denise-Marie Ordway, "Multicultural education: How schools teach it and where educators say it fall short," *The Journalist's Resource*, January 25, 2021, https://journalistsresource.org/education/multicultural-education-schools/. Retrieved on January 26, 2022.

Kate Rabinowitz, Armand Emamdjomeh, and Laura Meckler, "How the nation's growing racial diversity is changing our schools," *Washington Post*, September 12, 2019, https://oaarchive.arctic-council.org/handle/11374/2380. Retrieved on January 25, 2022.

United States Department of Justice, "Types of Educational Opportunities Discrimination," July 28, 2017, https://www.justice.gov/crt/types-educational-opportunities-discrimination. Retrieved on January 25, 2022.

Chapter 6: Special Education

OVERVIEW

As we have seen throughout this volume, the history of education around the world is one of increasing access to schooling. The goal of universal education has been achieved in developed countries, and most less developed countries are well on their way to achieving this objective. As a result, literacy has become universal in the developed world while a large majority of people elsewhere is able to read and write.

In addition, barriers to the availability of education on the basis of gender, ethnicity, religion, and other characteristics continue to be lifted. As recently as two centuries ago, very few girls were taught to read and write. Although literacy rates among females continue to lag behind literacy rates among males in many places, in most countries girls and boys now have equal access to education. Moreover, in the past education was sometimes denied to members of minority groups. For example, in the U.S. South prior to the Civil War, it was illegal to teach slaves to read and write. Likewise, Roma children in Eastern Europe were not given access to schooling in some countries. Legally, such barriers have largely been eliminated, although discrimination continues in practice, for example, because of inadequate funding, bullying, resources, staffing, and infrastructure.

As the goal of universal free education continues to be approached throughout the world, more and more attention has begun to be paid to the education of children with various special needs. Many children with disabilities were unable to succeed in ordinary public school settings. Hence, the term "special education" was coined in order to describe modifications to the educational process used to provide schooling for children with disability. The need to provide special education is recognized implicitly in the United Nations Declaration of Human Rights as adopted in 1948. Article 26, section 2, states, "Education shall be directed to the full development of the human personality and to the strengthening of respect for human rights and fundamental freedoms." This principle was expanded upon in the 2006 United Nations Convention on Rights of Persons with Disabilities. The convention states that in U.N. member countries, "persons with disabilities are not excluded from the general education system on the basis of disability, and that children with disabilities are not excluded from free and compulsory primary education, or from secondary education, on the basis of disability" and "persons with disabilities can access an inclusive, quality and free primary education and secondary education on an equal basis with others in the communities in which they live."

Children with Disabilities Remain Excluded in India

As is the case in many other countries, children with disabilities in India tend to be excluded from schooling. Many schools lack qualified special education teachers, and school authorities cite cost as a reason to exclude children with disabilities from their classrooms. Special schools are provided in some places, but in some such schools children are not only isolated but are also left unattended or placed in substandard and potentially dangerous environments. Although many Indian educational experts believe that improving education of children with disabilities should be a high priority, achieving this goal remains an uphill battle.

Source: Lachmi Deb Roy, "India still doesn't have a proper system to ensure education to children with disabilities," outlookindia.com, February 18, 2019, https://www.outlookindia.com/magazine/story/society-news-the-school-of-hard-knocks/301150. Retrieved on March 14, 2020.

Many different types of disabilities affect children and their opportunities to obtain educations. Some are physical disabilities including blindness and vision impairments, deafness and hearing impairments, and various disabilities that result in a loss of mobility. Others are mental and/or emotional disabilities. Some children have learning disabilities such as those associated sometimes with Down's syndrome. Other children are located on the autistic spectrum, which remains very poorly understood. And other children face depression and various phobias that affect learning. Many children have multiple disabilities. Regardless of disability, children with disabilities may be unaccepted by their peers, and some are bullied or ostracized. Under such circumstances, such children are often reluctant or afraid to attend school, making it more difficult for them to succeed and lead meaningful lives as adults.

Over the course of history, societies have dealt with disability in various and changing ways. Into the nineteenth century, children with disabilities were often isolated from society and received little or no formal education whatsoever. In the nineteenth century, some U.S. states and some other countries established schools for blind or deaf children. Braille and sign language were developed to facilitate communication. However, many of these schools were boarding schools whose students were separated from their families and therefore lacked family support systems. Some of these schools remain operational today.

Even within schools, many students with disabilities remained separated from their peers. Some were placed in special classrooms and were largely isolated from their fellow students. Over the years, however, this isolation began to give way to mainstreaming, by which students with disabilities were placed in regular classes with nondisabled peers to the extent that their specific disabilities permitted. Mainstreaming began to be regarded as advantageous to both disabled and nondisabled students, who by being exposed to disabled fellow students could learn to be tolerant and accepting of disability. In this context, the term "inclusion" is often used to incorporate the idea of mainstreaming special-needs children. Today, debate over the degree to which students with disabilities should be mainstreamed continues.

In some countries, efforts to educate children with disabilities have been compromised by a lack of resources. Most countries, in keeping with the United Nations Convention on the Rights of Children with Disabilities, are making efforts to provide education to such children. However, in practice it has been difficult to implement education for children with disabilities, especially in less developed countries. Many lack the resources to provide specialized training for teachers, and many do not have the resources to provide classroom facilities, equipment, and technology that would facilitate the education of special-needs children.

Difficulties in providing special education have been affected also by the need for improved awareness of types of disability. Physical disabilities such as blindness and deafness have been recognized since ancient times. However, such conditions as autism, bipolar disorder, and clinical depression also affect individual children in their efforts to obtain education. The causes and effective management of these and other conditions remain poorly understood, and hence not much is yet known about how they can affect learning and the educational process.

The entries in this chapter describe education of special-needs children and how these considerations affect such education. Iceland, as well as other Scandinavian countries, is recognized as having one of the best educational systems in the world. However, Iceland's small population has affected its ability to provide effective education to special-needs children, especially those who live in isolated coastal communities away from the capital city of Reykjavik. A similar situation prevails in St. Kitts and Nevis, which is one of the world's smallest functioning democracies with a population of less than 55,000. St. Kitts and Nevis is regarded as only a partially developed country, and so its government is finding it difficult to provide for the education of its small number of special-needs children. However, schools are being established on both islands to facilitate the education of students on the autistic spectrum.

A lack of sufficient resources has also affected the provision of education to special-needs children in two less developed African countries, Botswana and Togo. In Togo, the problem of providing education to children with disabilities is compounded by a long-standing cultural bias against disability. In many parts of West Africa, including Togo, disability is regarded as a curse or punishment against the family of a disabled child. Such families can face shaming or ostracism, and as a result, their children with disabilities are often hidden from others and receive little or no formal education. Thus, efforts to provide special education in Togo have been hindered by the need to overcome such biases against the disabled.

Canada (whose educational system is profiled in detail in the chapter titled "Multicultural and Multilingual Education") typifies larger developed countries in that its governments at both the federal and provincial levels have a sustained commitment to the education of special-needs children. However, it has been estimated that as many as half of special-needs children in the province of Ontario are not integrated fully into the educational process. Many face bullying, experience safety concerns, and suffer from a lack of resources to provide for their needs. And in fact, some principals recommend and encourage parents of special-needs children to keep these children at home for at least part of each school day for these reasons. In northern Canada, with its sparse population, it is often difficult to provide special education given the relatively small number of children affected over vast areas.

Special education in Ecuador is hindered by that country's high degree of cultural diversity, including ongoing discrimination against Ecuadorians of African descent and against Indigenous people who live in the Amazon River basin east of the Andes Mountains. Lack of supplies and other educational resources for special-needs children is an ongoing issue in Ecuador, especially in these minority communities. And, as in other countries, many school buildings and other facilities are old and antiquated. For example, some lack ramps or elevators, and as a result, some children with physical disabilities are unable to use these facilities. Likewise, Lithuania continues to address issues with transition between the centrally planned, Russian-oriented educational system that had been used in the Soviet Union prior to Lithuanian independence. In each of these seven countries, however, various innovative programs to provide special education are being developed and implemented at least on a trial basis.

The United States has been a leader in the development of special education programs and facilities. As we have seen elsewhere, the U.S. educational system has evolved from the common school model of the nineteenth century to more recognition of the educational needs of individual students. Today, more and more efforts are being made to recognize the importance of differences in learning styles as they affect opportunities to provide all children with educational opportunities consistent with their specific needs. In turn, such recognition can inform efforts to provide and use specialized educational materials suited best to these special needs.

BOTSWANA

The Republic of Botswana is a landlocked country located in southern Africa, north of South Africa. It has a land area of about 225,000 square miles, and its population as of 2022 was about 2.4 million. Thus, Botswana is one of the most sparsely populated countries in Africa. The Kalahari Desert takes up about two-thirds of the country's land surface, and the country has been plagued by drought throughout its history.

Anthropologists believe that present-day Botswana has been inhabited for as many as 400,000 years. The original inhabitants of the area were probably the San people, who are called sometimes by the derogatory exonym "Bushmen." Bantu tribes moving southward from present-day Zambia, Zimbabwe, and Angola settled in the region that now includes Botswana, beginning approximately 1,500 years ago. The newcomers pushed the San people into the western deserts, where some continue to live although the San population of Botswana has been estimated at only about 10,000 today. In contrast to the Bantu, who were farmers or pastoralists, most of the San continue to survive as hunters and gatherers.

During the nineteenth century, conflict among the descendants of the early Bantu settlers and other tribes who had moved into the area more recently arose. Conflict also arose between the Indigenous Africans in the area and slave-owning Boers who were moving northward and eastward from what is now the Cape Colony of South Africa. Indigenous leaders requested protection from the British, who formally placed the area under its protection in 1885. Present-day Botswana became known as the Bechuanaland Protectorate.

South Africa became independent in 1910, and the British considered transferring the Protectorate to South Africa. However, after South Africa established its apartheid policy following World War II, the British abandoned this idea. Instead, they retained control of the Protectorate until 1966, when it became a fully independent country under its present name. The name Botswana was derived from the Tswana ethnic group, and the name means "of the Tswana people." Nearly 80 percent of Botswanans are members of the Tswana tribe, although seven other tribes are represented formally in the government. Since independence, Botswana has been a parliamentary democracy, and it has become one of sub-Saharan Africa's wealthiest countries in part because of the presence of diamonds and other mineral resources. However, the country has been affected in recent years by the worldwide pandemic of HIV/AIDS.

Education in Botswana

Prior to the arrival of Europeans, the training of children was conducted locally at a tribal level, focusing on the development of life skills needed for adulthood as tribal members. As was the case in many former European colonies in Africa, formal education in present-day Botswana was provided initially by religious organization. The first schools were established by the London Missionary Society in the nineteenth century. Government involvement in education began in 1904, but secondary education was not provided until 1944. Students who wished to attend secondary school received this education in neighboring South Africa, although the South African government eliminated this practice in 1953. In fact, no secondary schools were built in Botswana until after independence.

Thus, the government of newly independent Botswana faced a severe lack of educated people upon independence. Since that time, education has been a priority within the constraints of available resources. Shortly after independence, the Education Act of 1966 was enacted. The act specified procedures for educational administration and included the establishment of the Ministry of Education, which has remained in charge of education ever since.

Today, each student is guaranteed at least 10 years of education. Education is compulsory beginning from the age of 6 to 16, although in practice many students leave school after completion of the primary grades. Preschool is available in some areas but is not compulsory. Compulsory education begins with seven years of primary school and is followed by three years of lower secondary school and two years of non-compulsory upper secondary school. Most students attend public school, although some are enrolled in private schools and a few are homeschooled. The languages of instruction are both English and Setswana, which is the language of the Tswana people.

Special Education in Botswana

At first, formal education of special-needs children as it developed in Botswana was not prioritized as the country developed an educational system that had been only rudimentary at the time of independence. At that time, whatever special education was available was provided primarily by religious bodies and other nongovernmental organizations. For example, a school for blind children was established by the Dutch Reformed Church in 1969.

In 1984, the government established the Special Education Unit under the auspices of the Ministry of Education. The Revised National Policy on Education, which updated the initial Education Act, was implemented beginning in 1994. The policy stated specifically that the government was responsible for the education of all Botswanan children, including those with special needs. As in other countries, however, the implementation of the policy has proven to be difficult. According to a survey, a majority of early childhood educators participating in the study expressed doubts about the effectiveness of inclusion of special-needs children in their classrooms. As elsewhere, many of these teachers were concerned about a lack of resources and specialized training for providing education to special-needs children. Some also expressed concern about lack of support from parents, principals, and school administrators.

The Ministry of Education's policy regarding special education was updated in 2011. According to this updated policy, "An inclusive education system addresses 'the needs of all,' including those with special educational needs, regardless of their gender, life circumstances, health, disability, stage of development, capacity to learn, level of achievement, financial or any other circumstances. Informed by the principles of non-exclusion, an inclusive education system ensures that children, young people and adults can learn effectively as long as their special education needs are met, 'wherever possible' in regular preschools, primary and secondary schools, vocational training programmes, colleges and universities."

Implementation of this policy has been more difficult in practice because of limited resources and personnel as well as the relatively small number of special-needs children, especially in sparsely populated rural areas. However, in 2019, the Camphill Community Trust schools in the village of Otse was awarded the UNESCO-Japan Prize on Education for Sustainable Development. The prize was awarded for its "community-based 'Integrated Learning for Living and Work Programme (ILLWP)' which helps youth with intellectual and developmental disabilities to develop and excel through an integrated learning experience that blends environment, society and economy—the three pillars of sustainable development." Many of the students in ILLWP have autism, Down's syndrome, or cerebral palsy. As part of the Programme, students develop and maintain a community organic garden.

Further Reading

Simmi Chhabra, Kabita Bose, and Neerja Chadha, "Botswana early childhood educators' perceptions on factors associated with the inclusion of children with disabilities," *International Journal of Learning, Teaching, and Educational Research*, 15 (2016), pp. 1–19.

Obonye Jonas, "The right to inclusive education in Botswana: Present challenges and future prospects," African Disability Rights Yearbook, 2014, http://www.saflii.org/za/journals/ADRY/2014/1.html. Retrieved on January 21, 2020.

Sourav Mukhopadhyay, Boitumelo Mangope, and Fazlur Moorad, "Voices of the voiceless: Inclusion of learners with special education needs in Botswana primary schools," *Journal of Exceptionality: A Special Education Journal*, 27 (2018), pp. 232–246, https://www.tandfonline.com/doi/full/10.1080/09362835.2018.1470446. Retrieved on January 21, 2020.

UNESCO, "A Botswana special needs programme wins UNESCO sustainability education prize," November 14, 2019, https://en.unesco.org/news/botswana-special-needs-programme-wins-unesco-sustainability-education-prize. Retrieved on January 16, 2022.

UNESCO, "Education profile: Botswana," revised September 5, 2021, https://education-profiles.org/sub-saharan-africa/botswana/~inclusion. Retrieved on January 16, 2022.

CANADA

As discussed in detail in chapter 4, Canada's educational system is decentralized. Each of Canada's 10 provinces and 3 territories is primarily responsible for providing and managing education. However, Canada's federal government guarantees children throughout the country the right to special education. Section 15 of the Canadian Charter of Rights and Freedoms, which is an integral component of Canada's constitution, states, "Every individual is equal before and under the law and has the right to the equal protection and equal benefit of the law without discrimination and, in particular, without discrimination based on race, national or ethnic origin, colour, religion, sex, age or mental or physical disability." Section 15 means that all children with disabilities or special needs have the right to education. However, the actual provision of special education is the formal responsibility of each province, independently of the others. Eligibility for special education within these general guidelines varies among the provinces. For example, students in Newfoundland and Labrador are eligible for special education only if they been diagnosed with an "exceptionality" by a qualified health-care professional. Specific exceptionalities are also defined by the provincial government.

Although educational and social inclusion of special-needs children is regarded in general as a cornerstone of Canadian education, in practice some children with special needs are being excluded from schools. In Canada's largest province of

Ontario, the majority of special-needs students are mainstreamed into classes when possible and are provided with individualized curricula when necessary. In a study reported in 2018, however, it was found that more than half of school principals surveyed in Ontario had recommended that students with special needs stay home for at least part of each school day. Safety of special-needs pupils, including bullying, was cited as a major reason for these recommendations. Other principals indicated that their schools lacked resources required to meet the special-education students' needs. More generally, while inclusion remains an objective, this objective has sometimes been difficult to realize in practice.

The parents or guardians of many Canadian special-needs students can face significant financial hardships, which are often associated with the care of their children. In response, some of the provinces provide financial assistance to these families. For example, during the 2017–2018 school year the government of Saskatchewan allocated $4,000 in Canadian dollars to each family with children under the age of six who are autistic. However, budgetary issues forced the provincial government to close some programs for such children.

Providing special education in accordance with the charter is especially problematic in Canada's three sparsely populated territories—Yukon, Northwest Territories, and Nunavut. Many of these territories' residents are First Nations people (Canada's official name for Indigenous people), and nearly 85 percent of Nunavut's residents are Inuit. As with Canada's other provinces and territories, Nunavut law stresses commitment to equality, including services for the disabled and including special education. However, in practice, opportunities to provide meaningful education to children with special needs have been limited. This failure is due in part to Nunavut's small population of only around 40,000, many of whom live in scattered and isolated settlements. Many teachers have not been trained in the delivery of special education services. In addition, Nunavut faces a shortage of psychologists and diagnostic services specialists who are qualified to assess special needs. Cultural factors may play a role as well, in that the majority of Nunavut's teachers are non-Inuit and may not be fully appreciative of Inuit culture and worldviews.

Further Reading

Sherri Brown, "Inclusive education in Canada: Steps taken and the long road ahead," Worlds of Education, December 3, 2018, https://worldsofeducation.org/en/woe_homepage /woe_detail/16078/inclusive-education-in-canada-steps-taken-and-the-long-road -ahead-by-dr-sherri-brown. Retrieved on February 8, 2020.

Michelle McQuigge, "Ontario students with special needs asked to stay home: Report," The Globe and Mail, June 26, 2018, https://www.theglobeandmail.com/canada/article -ontario-students-with-special-needs-increasingly-asked-to-stay-home/. Retrieved on February 8, 2020.

Laurie Pelly, "Inclusive education in Nunavut—A rights perspective," Northern Public Affairs, 6 (2018), http://www.northernpublicaffairs.ca/index/volume-6-issue-3-the -fight-for-our-lives-preventing-suicide/inclusive-education-in-nunavut/. Retrieved on February 8, 2020.

Katelyn Wilson, "Saskatchewan to provide individualized funding for children with autism," *Global News Canada*, April 13, 2018, https://globalnews.ca/news/4141581 /saskatchewan-to-provide-individualized-funding-for-children-with-autism/.

ECUADOR

The Republic of Ecuador is located in northwestern South America along the coast of the Pacific Ocean. The country is crossed by the equator, giving the country its name. Its land area is about 110,000 square miles with a population of roughly 18.2 million as of 2022. Its territory includes three distinct regions—the arid area along the Pacific Ocean coast to the west, the Andes Mountains in the center of the country, and a portion of the hot, humid, and sparsely populated Amazon River basin to the east, which are known as La Costa, La Sierra, and La Amazonia or El Oriente, respectively. Many inhabitants of La Amazonia are Indigenous people.

The western and central portions of present-day Ecuador were part of the Inca Empire prior to the arrival of Spanish explorers. The Spanish overthrew the Incas in the early sixteenth century, after which this territory became part of the Spanish Viceroyalty of Peru. In 1717, present-day Ecuador was transferred from the vice-royalty of Peru to the viceroyalty of New Grenada, which also included present-day Venezuela, Colombia, and Panama. The viceroyalty declared independence from Spain in 1822 as the country of Gran Colombia. In 1830, Ecuador withdrew from Gran Colombia and became a fully independent country.

As was the case with many Latin American countries, Ecuador oscillated between democracy and dictatorship for its first century and a half of independence. Ecuador was governed by a military regime between 1960 and 1979, when it returned to civilian rule. The country has remained a democracy ever since, despite an ongoing history of political turmoil, protest, and occasional violence. Ecuador's economy remains oriented to the extraction and export of agricultural products and natural resources. The economy remains vulnerable to changes in global markets for these commodities along with natural disasters that can affect resource extraction and production. For example, a major earthquake of 7.8 magnitude struck near the coast of Ecuador on April 16, 2016. Several hundred persons were killed, and as many as 20,000 were injured. As a result, the government was forced to divert substantial amounts of financial resources in order to address recovery efforts.

Education in Ecuador

Prior to independence, the Roman Catholic Church was primarily responsible for education in present-day Ecuador. Government involvement in education, including the establishment of public schools, began after independence. The first government agency responsible for education was established in 1836. However, at that time curricula included "religious and moral education" associated with principles of Roman Catholicism. The law prohibited the teaching of any subjects that were not consistent with Church principles.

These children are attending school in Quito, the capital city of Ecuador. It has been difficult for Ecuador to provide effective education to its special-needs children, in light of its highly diverse population and lack of resources. According to estimates, nearly half of Ecuador's children with disabilities receive no formal education at all. (Pablo Hidalgo | Dreamstime.com)

The current Constitution of Ecuador, which came into effect in 1945, specifies that children are required to attend school until they have achieved "a basic level of education." Over the next several decades, efforts were made to implement this provision. However, at first there were no school facilities available for many rural children. These were built gradually, although a shortage of school facilities continues to be an issue today. As a result, many rural students attend schools with very large classes and a shortage of qualified teachers. Government efforts to implement the constitutional requirement of basic education have been handicapped by a lack of government resources.

Today, education in Ecuador is compulsory for nine years. The system, which is administered by the Ministry of Education, begins with six years of primary education. Primary schooling is followed by three years of lower secondary school and three years of upper secondary school or high school. Although lower secondary school is compulsory, more than 25 percent of children dropped out by the end of primary school.

Public education at the primary and secondary levels is free, but parents are responsible for school fees and transportation. This means that it is difficult for children from poor families and those who live in isolated areas to go to school, especially at the secondary level. School facilities are lacking in some of these isolated and rural areas. As a result, rates of secondary school attendance vary widely throughout the country. Most children in urban areas attend secondary school, but it has been estimated that in rural areas and/or poor communities less than 20 percent of children of secondary school age are enrolled. This discrepancy is especially evident among Indigenous people. It has been estimated that the average Indigenous adult in Ecuador has completed only 4.5 years of formal schooling, as compared to 8 years for non-Indigenous adults.

Special Education in Ecuador

Lack of educational resources has affected opportunities to provide education for Ecuadorian children with special needs. As in many other countries, Ecuador's efforts to improve schooling have been focused on universal public education, with fewer opportunities to provide for special education. However, it has been estimated that as many as 500,000 Ecuadorians have disabilities. Of these, about half are physical disabilities.

Ecuador continues to face difficulties in providing educational opportunities to disabled children. In some cases, these difficulties involve problems with infrastructure. For example, many schools lack ramps or elevators that would allow children with disabilities to enter classrooms. Learning materials geared to special-needs children are lacking in some schools. Although many teachers recognize the importance of special education, some experts have concluded that programs to train teachers in special education methods and techniques are inadequate.

And as elsewhere, Ecuadorian children with disabilities face bullying, ostracism, and other social concerns that discourage them from attending school. According to one recent estimate, less than 12 percent of children of high school age with disabilities attend upper secondary school, as compared with nearly 25 percent of nondisabled children of high school age. As recently as 2004, it was estimated that nearly 40 percent of children with disabilities had received no formal education at all. All of these factors have made it difficult for Ecuadorians with disabilities to support themselves as adults and to find meaningful inclusion in the larger society.

Some progress in improving the education of special-needs children has been made in recent years, however. The article by Humphries and Guaipatin, cited below, describes a project sponsored jointly by the Inter-American Development Bank and a Jesuit nongovernmental organization Fe y Alegria. The project was developed and implemented in an impoverished neighborhood in the city of Santo Domingo, which is the third largest city in Ecuador and is located in the western foothills of the Andes. Two separate schools were constructed, one for children who are deaf or hard of hearing and the other for children with intellectual disabilities. In both schools, the project emphasized the importance of social inclusion in order to prepare students for participation in mainstream society as adults. Technologies that promote inclusion as opposed to isolation of people with disabilities have been emphasized. Projects of this sort have been regarded as models for further improvements in special-needs education in Ecuador.

Further Reading

Maria Olivia Humphries and Carlos Guaipatin, "Social innovation in practice: The case of the Fe y Alegria Project for educational inclusion of children with disabilities in Ecuador," 2014, https://publications.iadb.org/en/social-innovation-practice-case-fe-y-alegria-project-educational-inclusion-children-disabilities. Retrieved on February 6, 2020.

Inter-American Development Bank, "Ecuador's bet on inclusion," 2020, https://www.iadb.org/en/improvinglives/ecuadors-bet-inclusion. Retrieved on February 6, 2020.

Ricardo Moreno-Rodriguez, Jose Luis Lopez, Jose David Carnicero, Immaculada Garrote, and Sergio Sanchez, "Teachers' perception on the inclusion of students with disabilities in the regular education classroom in Ecuador," *Journal of Education and Training Studies*, 5 (2017), pp. 45–53, https://files.eric.ed.gov/fulltext/EJ1150517.pdf. Retrieved on February 6, 2020.

ICELAND

Iceland occupies an island located in the North Atlantic Ocean, slightly south of the Arctic Circle. It is located about 600 miles west of the mainland of Norway and about 200 miles east of Greenland. The country is located on the Mid-Atlantic Ridge and is home to several active volcanoes. The overall land area of Iceland is about 40,000 square miles. Its population as of 2022 was about 345,000, about two-thirds of whom live in or near the capital city of Reykjavik on the southwestern coast of the country. Most other Icelanders live in other coastal communities, while much of the interior of the country is uninhabited.

Historians believe that Iceland was visited and perhaps inhabited by Irish monks and hermits beginning in the seventh and eighth centuries AD. Archaeologists have uncovered ruins that have been carbon-dated back to that period. In 874 AD, the first permanent settlements in Iceland were established by Vikings from present-day Norway. Over the next 60 years, almost all of Iceland's arable land was settled.

Iceland was a self-governing commonwealth for nearly 400 years until 1262, when Icelander leaders agreed to become part of Norway in what became known as the Old Covenant or Gamli Sattmali. In the fifteenth century, Norway became united with Denmark and Sweden as part of the Kalmar Union. The Kalmar Union was dissolved in 1814, and Norway and Denmark were separated. Iceland then became a Danish colony. During the periods of Norwegian and later Danish rule, Iceland experienced very hard times and was affected on various occasions by volcanic eruptions and plagues including epidemics of the bubonic plague or Black Death. Iceland's geographical isolation and its economic dependence on fishing and agriculture further impoverished its population. Iceland was given limited home rule by Denmark in 1874, and in 1944, it became fully independent. Although fishing remains Iceland's leading economic activity, its economy has diversified since home rule and independence, and today Iceland is one of the wealthiest countries in the world.

Education in Iceland

Unlike most of the other countries covered in this chapter, Iceland is a very homogenous society. Most Icelanders are descended from the Vikings who first settled in Iceland more than a thousand years ago. And, as an island country, Iceland is not inhabited by tribes and national groups characterized by conflicting cultures and values. Almost all Icelanders speak Icelandic. However, Iceland has become an important leader in the development and implementation of policy regarding individual differences among students, particularly with respect to disability.

Formal education in Iceland was first provided to a few children during the eleventh century, when the first school was established in Reykjavik. During and after the Middle Ages, some children attended schools although efforts to provide education in a formal setting were impeded by Iceland's poverty, history of natural disasters and disease, and the geographic isolation of many communities. However, education was valued among most Icelanders. Most young children were taught to read and write at home, and it is believed that literacy in Iceland was nearly universal by the end of the eighteenth century.

In 1907, the first national education law was enacted in Iceland, which at that time remained under Danish control. Perhaps reflecting the history of home schooling of young children, the law mandated compulsory education from the ages of 10 through 14. The first national curriculum was developed and implemented beginning in 1926. Following independence, education was made compulsory for children between the ages of 6 and 15 in 1946.

Today, education in Iceland is managed by the Ministry of Education, Science, and Culture. The system is managed at the national level, although local authorities have some leeway to address local needs in providing schooling in their geographical areas. Prior to higher education at the university level, the system includes three components—preschool, compulsory, and upper secondary. Preschool, which is also known as "playschool," is intended for children beginning at three to four years of age. The intent of this program is to prepare children for mandatory education that begins at the age of six. Preschool is not compulsory, and parents must bear some of the costs associated with its provision.

The compulsory education component, known in Icelandic as *grunnskoli* or "basic school," lasts for 10 years. It includes 7 years of primary school followed by 3 years of lower secondary school. As its name implies, attendance at these schools is mandatory and free. Because of the geographic isolation of many Icelandic villages, some of these grunnskoli enroll as few as 10 pupils, whereas those in and near Reykjavik are much larger in capacity. After completing *grunnskoli*, many students move on to upper secondary education although this component is not compulsory. At this stage, students can elect to enroll in grammar or college preparatory schools or in various vocational and technical programs. This component is free also, although parents are required to pay nominal enrollment fees and for textbooks. Throughout the system, Icelandic is the language of instruction although English and Danish are also taught as second languages.

Special Education in Iceland

Educational equality, including recognition of special needs, is a stated policy of the Icelandic government. This policy is articulated in the mission statement of the Ministry of Education, Science, and Culture that reads, "A fundamental principle of the Icelandic educational system is that everyone should have equal opportunities to acquire an education, irrespective of sex, economic status, residential location, religion, possible handicap, and cultural or social background." Policies associated with this principle have been provided since independence, and an "inclusive education" policy directed specifically toward the education of special-needs children was implemented in 2008. The Icelandic educational system has been developed in order to provide effective education to children with "possible handicap[s]" or children with special needs. Children with special needs include those who are blind or vision-impaired, those who are deaf or hearing-impaired, those with intellectual disabilities, those with autism, and those with emotional issues.

Each school is required to provide educational services to all special-needs children. Many special-needs children are placed in mainstream schools that provide these services themselves. However, five schools in Reykjavik include classrooms specifically intended for children who are on the autistic spectrum. Another provides services specifically for deaf- and hearing-impaired students. As in other countries, both parents and educational authorities disagree regarding the relative merits of mainstreaming special-needs students and placing them in schools that are oriented to the specific special needs of these children.

In practical terms, providing educational services to special-needs children is difficult because of Iceland's small population, especially outside the Reykjavik metropolitan areas where rural populations are scattered and sometimes isolated. This issue is exacerbated by difficulties in recruiting teachers who are willing to live and work in these small and isolated communities. Concern has been raised also about the costs associated with special education, again outside Reykjavik especially, including providing training for teachers with skills to provide such special education. As Hildur Onnudottir has written, "The sentiment that is consistently repeated by parents and teachers, in studies, surveys and the media is that currently the [inclusive education] policy is nothing but an ideology, there is no true implementation leaving children with special needs without the assistance and adjustments they need." Nevertheless, Iceland continues to try and ensure the education of special-needs children.

Further Reading

Government of Iceland, "The Icelandic national curriculum guide for compulsory schools—With subjects areas," 2014, https://www.government.is/library/01-Ministries/Ministry

-of-Education/Curriculum/adalnrsk_greinask_ens_2014.pdf. Retrieved on January 6, 2020.

Edda Oskarsdottir, Hafdis Gudjonsdottir, and Karen Rut Gisladottir, "Policies for inclusion in Iceland: Possibilities and Challenges," in *Including the North: A Comparative Study of the Policies on Inclusion and Equity in the Circumpolar North,* Sustainable Development Working Group, 2019, pp. 57–69, https://oaarchive.arctic-council.org/handle/11374/2380. Retrieved on May 4, 2022.

Berglind Ros, "Is the system of education in Iceland among the best?" *I Am Reykjavik,* December 27, 2017, http://www.iamreykjavik.com/education-in-iceland. Retrieved on January 6, 2020.

LITHUANIA

Lithuania is an Eastern European country located on the Baltic Sea, west and north of Belarus, east of Poland, and south of Latvia. Along with Latvia and Estonia, Lithuania is considered one of the Baltic States. Its land area is about 25,000 square miles, with a population of about 2.65 million as of 2022.

Lithuania has long been a center of communication and trade among nearby maritime and continental countries and cultures, and control over the area has been contested for centuries among various foreign powers. Baltic peoples, who were the ancestors of many of today's Lithuanians, are believed to have begun occupying the region beginning at least 4,000 years ago. Beginning in the tenth century AD, Lithuanians were forced to pay tribute to Viking raiders from Scandinavia, and later to rulers of Russia. In the thirteenth century, the Grand Duchy of Lithuania was established, eventually expanding to include parts of present-day Russia, Belarus, Ukraine, and Poland. The Duchy became part of the Polish-Lithuanian Commonwealth in 1569. The Commonwealth was dissolved in 1791, and the territory was divided between Russia and Prussia.

Lithuania became independent following the Treaty of Versailles in 1918. However, it was occupied by the Soviet Union during World War II. After the war ended, the Soviets incorporated Lithuania as one of the constituent republics of the Soviet Union. Lithuania remained under Soviet control until the Soviet Union collapsed. It declared independence in 1990, and it joined the United Nations in 2004. Lithuania has been a stable democracy since independence, and its stability and location as a central point of northern Europe has made the country one of the wealthiest countries of the former Soviet Union.

Education in Lithuania

Formal education in Lithuania dates back to the late Middle Ages. Schools were first founded by the Roman Catholic Church, which remains the dominant religion of Lithuania, whereas the other two Baltic states, Latvia and Estonia, are predominantly Lutheran. Over the next several centuries, schooling in present-day Lithuania was dominated by successive foreign powers that controlled the country. Both Russia and Germany used education to try to impose their respective empires' values on the people of Lithuania.

Special Education and Tracking Systems in Germany

In some countries, standardized examination results and primary-school performance are used to determine whether students are placed in college preparatory secondary schools. Such is the case in Germany, where this separation takes place after 10 years of school. However, this system is seen as discriminatory against students who have disabilities. As a result, such children, including immigrant children who are classified as "special-needs" children because of poor command of the German language, may lack the opportunities available to children without disabilities. This discrimination can be reinforced when parents of nondisabled children oppose allowing these children to be placed in classrooms with peers who do have disabilities.

Source: Elizabeth Schumacher, "How Germany is failing disabled and special-needs students," dw.com, March 11, 2019, https://www.dw.com/en/how-germany-is-failing-disabled-and-special-needs-students/a-47825546. Retrieved on March 14, 2020.

During Lithuania's half-century of Soviet rule, the Soviet educational system was imposed upon Lithuania. The Soviet system was highly centralized throughout the country, emphasizing Russian history and culture and Marxist-Leninist ideology. All classes were conducted in Russian. The system was reformed after Lithuania became independent, and emphasis on Russian language and culture and Soviet ideology was replaced by increased emphasis on Lithuanian culture and history. The Lithuanian constitution of 1992 established that education would be free and compulsory for children between the ages of 7 and 16.

Preprimary and preschool programs are available to young children, but they are not compulsory. Compulsory education begins with four years of primary schooling. This is followed by four years of lower secondary education, known as "progymnasium." Foundation education is followed by two years of high school of "gymnasium." Students who wish to do so can then proceed to two further years of high school to prepare themselves for university or to schools emphasizing vocational and technical training. Lithuanian is the primary language of instruction, although schooling in Russian and Polish is provided to students who live in areas where these languages predominate. Literacy is universal at 99.8 percent.

Special Education in Lithuania

During the period of Soviet rule, government policy specified that children who were deemed to be "different," or who had special needs, were to be segregated from other children. Many were sent to boarding schools, which necessitated separating them from their families. Some special-needs students, especially those with vision or hearing impairments, continue to be educated in boarding schools today. For example, the Lithuanian Educational Center for the Deaf and Hard of Hearing, located in the capital city of Vilnius, maintains programs for students between the

These students live in Kaunas, which is the second largest city in the former Soviet republic of Lithuania. Under Soviet rule, children with special needs were separated from other students. Today, post-Soviet Lithuania is emphasizing mainstreaming its special-needs children. (Meunierd | Dreamstime.com)

ages of 3 and 18. Education is provided both orally and in sign language. And in contrast to Soviet-era boarding schools, teachers in the Center keep in close contact with parents, and students generally go home on weekends.

More generally, however, it is estimated that half or more of students with disabilities are educated in schools and programs where they are isolated from mainstream peers. Such isolation, which can occur because mainstream schools refuse to accept or provide adequate services for special-needs pupils, has been seen as making it more difficult for these students to gain admission to colleges and universities or to have the opportunity to obtain good and well-paying jobs as adults.

After the Constitution of 1992 was adopted, the Lithuanian legislature enacted the Act of Special Educational Provision for Children with Special Educational Needs in Mainstream Educational Institutions in 1993. The act identified several methods by which children with special needs could be educated. These included placing special-needs children into mainstream classes with or without special accommodations as necessary, placing them in special classes only, or dividing their school time between mainstream or special classes. Centers were established to provide resources and training for special education teachers. Some of these centers were converted from boarding schools that had once been used to educate special-needs children separately from other students prior to independence.

Inclusion remains a goal of Lithuanian special education, in keeping with the provisions of the Act of Special Educational Provision. However, this goal has been difficult to achieve consistently in practice. For example, some older school buildings lack ramps or elevators that would allow students with disabilities to enter the buildings. Some teachers are not trained in pedagogical techniques appropriate to special education. These problems are particularly evident in rural areas within Lithuania, which has a higher percentage of rural residents than do most other European countries. An additional concern that has been raised is lack of communication between parents and teachers about the progress of special-needs children.

Efforts to educate special-needs children and to integrate them into mainstream schools can be enhanced by emphasis on various types of play. Play opportunities can be limited for children with various types of disabilities. But play activities, geared to the specific needs and capabilities of individual children, have been recognized as important in efforts to provide effective education to special-needs children. Art and music as well as indoor and outdoor games are regarded as promoting these objectives in Lithuania and elsewhere.

Further Reading

Egle Celiesiene and Giedre Kvieskiene, "Play for children with disability: Case study from Lithuania," *Social Education*, 42 (2016), pp. 70–82, https://pdfs.semanticscholar .org/53da/cb9a63abc2dbcdb4085f59fbb2b0a6d3d7eb.pdf. Retrieved on February 9, 2020.

Deaf Planet, "Lithuanian Educational Center for the Deaf and Hard of Hearing," October 27, 2017, http://deaf-planet.ru/en/europe-en/lithuania/lithuanian-educational-center -for-the-deaf-and-hard-of-hearing/. Retrieved on February 9, 2020.

Human Rights Monitoring Institute, "Disabled Lithuanian children still isolated by the education system," March 8, 2016, https://www.liberties.eu/en/news/lithuania-lack-of -inclusive-education/7431. Retrieved on February 9, 2020.

ST. KITTS AND NEVIS

The Federation of St. Christopher and Nevis includes the islands of St. Christopher (which is generally known as St. Kitts) and Nevis in the Leeward Islands of the Caribbean Sea. The two islands are separated by about two miles at the shortest point. The total land area of the federation is slightly over 100 square miles. The population as of 2022 was about 54,000. Thus, St. Kitts and Nevis is the smallest independent country in the Western Hemisphere by both land area and population, as well as its smallest democracy. St. Kitts contains about 60 percent of the country's land area and nearly 80 percent of its population.

Like its neighbors, St. Kitts and Nevis were inhabited by Carib people at the time that they were first visited by Europeans in the late fifteenth and early sixteenth centuries. During the sixteenth and seventeenth centuries, the two islands were contested between Britain and France. Sovereignty over Nevis was granted to Britain via the Treaty of Utrecht in 1713, and sovereignty over St. Kitts was granted to Britain also via the Treaty of Paris in 1763. The economies of both islands were dominated by sugar production. Sugar plantations in St. Kitts and Nevis were worked by slaves until 1834, when slavery was abolished throughout the British Empire. Even today, more than 90 percent of the country's population consists of people with African ancestry.

St. Kitts and Nevis became a fully independent country in 1983. Since that time, tension between the two islands has been evident. Some residents of Nevis have claimed that the country's political system and its distribution of funds favor the larger St. Kitts. In 1998, a secession referendum was held on Nevis. Around 62 percent of Nevis's voters supported the referendum, but it failed to receive the necessary two-thirds majority. Historically, the country's economy was based on sugar production. However, the sugar industry in St. Kitts and Nevis has largely collapsed, and tourism is the most important economic activity today.

Education in St. Kitts and Nevis

After slavery was abolished in 1834, efforts to establish schools to educate freed slaves and their descendants were initiated in St. Kitts and Nevis. Most of these schools were operated by churches and religious organizations until 1914, when the British colonial government assumed this responsibility. The British influence on education in St. Kitts and Nevis remains very strong.

Today, education in St. Kitts and Nevis is the responsibility of the government's Ministry of Education. Schooling is compulsory between the ages of 5 and 16, and English is the language of instruction. Students begin formal schooling with 7 years of primary school. This is followed by 4 years of secondary school. After completing secondary school, students take the Caribbean Secondary Education Certificate (CSEC) examination, which is used in several other Caribbean countries as well. This examination is equivalent to O-level examinations as used in the United Kingdom. After completing the CSEC examination, students who wish to do so can attend school for an additional 2 years, either in preparation for college or in vocational training.

Special Education in St. Kitts and Nevis

The problems with providing effective education in St. Kitts and Nevis, as in many developing countries, are compounded by its very small size and population. The population of approximately 54,000 includes only about 8,000 children of school age. Hence, the number of school-age children with disabilities and/or special needs is also very small. However, the Ministry of Education has established a Special Needs Unit to address the educational needs of these students. Its efforts have been augmented by nongovernmental organizations such as the St. Kitts Association of Persons with Disabilities, whose mission is to "advocate for the rights of persons with disabilities, to ensure that we are not marginalized or in any way left out of the nation's development plans. In addition to advocacy the association was created to provide peer support plus much needed programs and services to persons with disabilities."

At the time of independence, the ministry founded two schools for special-needs children, one on St. Kitts and the other on Nevis. The school on St. Kitts is known as the Cotton Thomas Comprehensive School. Its mission is "to equip each student with skills that will enable them to lead as independent of a life as possible; thus creating a spirit of self-acceptance that would enhance their self- confidence and self-esteem." Its students include those diagnosed with disabilities and those who are referred to the school by teachers and administrators in regular classroom set-tings. Programs are also available for disabled adults, for parents of special-needs children, and for teachers who wish to improve their ability to work with students with special needs. A similar school known as the Cicele Brown School has been established on Nevis.

In 2018, another special unit providing educational services for children with autism was established on St. Kitts. This unit was facilitated by the Play and Learn-ing for Autistic Youngsters (PLAY) project, an American-based nongovernmen-tal organization whose mission is to provide services to children on the autistic spectrum throughout the world. (Note that the term "autistic children" is seen as inappropriate today; "children with autism" is regarded as more correct.) Upon its establishment, the PLAY project school on St. Kitts was the first such school to be founded in the Caribbean. Its services include diagnoses of children who may be on the autistic spectrum as well as schooling for such children outside the regular classroom environment.

Further Reading

Borgen Project, "10 facts about education in St. Kitts and Nevis," November 14, 2017, https://www.borgenmagazine.com/facts-about-education-in-st-kitts-and-nevis/. Retrieved on February 8, 2020.

PLAY Project, "The PLAY project meets the Caribbean," February 8, 2019, https://www.playproject.org/the-play-project-meets-the-caribbean/. Retrieved on February 9, 2020.

UNESCO, "Education profiles: St. Kitts and Nevis," 2021, https://education-profiles.org/latin-america-and-the-caribbean/saint-kitts-and-nevis/~inclusion. Retrieved on May 4, 2020.

TOGO

Togo, which is known officially as the Togolese Republic, is found in West Africa. It is directly east of Ghana, and it is separated from Nigeria by the country of Benin. The country's territory is long and narrow, extending northward from a short coastline on the Gulf of Guinea. Its land area is approximately 22,000 square miles, with a population as of 2022 estimated at about 8.7 million.

The coast of the Gulf of Guinea, including the coast of present-day Togo, was known as the "Slave Coast" during the sixteenth to eighteenth centuries because numerous West Africans were captured and sold into slavery. During the "Scramble for Africa" in the 1880s, present-day Togo and eastern Ghana were claimed by Germany as the Togoland Protectorate. During World War I, French and British forces invaded the protectorate and assumed control of the area. French forces occupied present-day Togo, and the League of Nations assigned it to France as a League of Nations mandate. Togo remained under French control until 1960, when it became independent. In 1967, Gnassingbe Eyadema (1935–2005) seized power and ruled Togo as a dictator for 38 years. After his death, his son Faure Gnassingbe (1966–) became president. The younger Gnassingbe has been reelected for five-year terms three times, although international observers have expressed serious doubt about the legitimacy of these elections. Togo's economy is based primarily on agriculture and mineral resource extraction. Its gross domestic product per capita is among the lowest in the world.

Education in Togo

Prior to independence, Western-style education in present-day Togo was conducted primarily by Christian missionaries and organizations. Both Roman Catholic and Protestant organizations participated in the process. However, some Indigenous Togolese rejected this formal education on the grounds that they regarded it as an affront to traditional cultural values. During the early twentieth century, the French made efforts to promote public education although in practice this education was directed largely to children of local elites living in cities and towns. The French structure of education was adopted, and it continues to be used in Togo today.

After Togo became independent in 1960, the government set universal education as a goal. At that time, it was estimated that about a quarter of Togolese children were enrolled in school. This percentage increased to about 44 percent by 1970, 63 percent by 1990, and nearly 90 percent in 2017. Today, education is free and compulsory for six years. Primary school fees, which had discouraged some parents from sending their children to school, were eliminated in 2008. After completing primary school, students may continue to junior secondary school for four years followed by three years of senior secondary school. However, according to a 2017 estimate only about 41 percent of eligible children were enrolled in secondary school. French is the language of instruction although the two most widely spoken Indigenous languages, Ewe and Kabiye, are also used.

As in other less developed countries, school enrollment rates in Togo are lower in rural areas compared to urban areas. Many parents, especially in rural areas, cannot afford to pay fees required for secondary schooling. Some areas lack schools entirely, and in some cases, access to school is limited by poor transportation. In addition, teachers in Togo are paid very poorly. Since 2013, Togolese teachers have gone on strike on several occasions seeking higher salaries.

Special Education in Togo

Given limited resources, education of Togolese children with special needs has been difficult to implement. Special education has been impeded in Togo especially because of traditional attitudes toward disability. In traditional Togolese cultures, as is the case in other West African countries, disability is sometimes regarded as the result of witchcraft or as evidence of punishment for the families of their children who have disabilities. In some cases, such disabilities are regarded as contagious. This view meant that people would avoid any contact with disabled children.

Because of these attitudes, many Togolese families who have children with disabilities can face shame and ostracism. Some of these children are hidden from public view, and some are neglected or abused by their parents. Many of these families keep their children at home rather than allow them to go to school. As adults, these people with disabilities continue to suffer from discrimination and many cannot find meaningful employment. Some are able to survive only by begging.

Until the 1970s, Togolese children with disabilities were generally forbidden from attending school. However, since then schools have been established in order to provide education with visual impairments, hearing impairments, or physical disabilities. The government has strengthened its commitment to addressing problems faced by people with disabilities, but traditional cultural attitudes have been difficult to overcome. Some children with mental illnesses or significant learning disabilities continue to be excluded. Mental illness, such as physical disability, is often associated with witchcraft or punishment. Children with such mental illnesses, along with adults, have been confined to "prayer camps" where some are shackled and chained to trees or concrete blocks and/or denied medication, counseling, or vocational training.

Further Reading

Samar Abi, "Something is happening," *Development and Cooperation*, July 26, 2014, https://www.dandc.eu/en/article/togo-sees-progress-struggle-rights-people-disabilities. Retrieved on February 7, 2020.

Benedict Carey, "Given medicine, the patients got better. They remained in shackles anyway," *New York Times*, January 17, 2018, https://www.nytimes.com/2018/01/17/health/mental-disorders-chains-west-africa.html. Retrieved on February 7, 2020.

Camryn Lemke, "8 facts about education in Togo," Borgen Project, July 16, 2019, https://borgenproject.org/8-facts-about-education-in-togo/. Retrieved on February 7, 2020.

Janet Njelesai, Goli Hashemi, Cathy Cameron, Deb Cameron, Danielle Richard, and Penny Parnes, "From the day they are born: A qualitative study exploring violence against children with disabilities in West Africa," *BMC Public Health*, 18 (2018), https://bmcpublichealth.biomedcentral.com/articles/10.1186/s12889-018-5057-x. Retrieved on February 7, 2020.

UNITED STATES

The history of American education is one in which the original concept of "common schooling" has evolved over time to consider large-scale differences in ethnicity, religion, and other characteristics. Yet within any population, some children have special needs that are often the result of various disabilities. Here, we focus on individual differences among children with respect to how their education has evolved over time and how it is practiced today. This process includes the identification of children with special needs and the stages through which these children are educated formally.

Historically, little or no provision was made to provide formal education for such special-needs children. It was thought that deafness was a form of mental illness, for example, and that deaf children were not capable of being educated. During the nineteenth century, some states began to initiate efforts to provide at least the rudiments of formal education for deaf and blind children. State schools for the blind and the deaf, some of which continue to exist, were established. Sign language was used to teach deaf children, and blind children were taught to read using Braille. However, children attending these schools had to live far from home, away from their families, and with little opportunity to interact with children or adults who lacked their disabilities.

Despite these efforts, it has been estimated that less than half of special-needs children, including deaf and blind children, were given any sort of education as late as the early twentieth century. In fact, laws in some states specifically excluded children with disabilities, including those who were deemed emotionally disturbed or "mentally retarded," from formal education. (Please note that the terms "mentally retarded" and "handicapped" are no longer considered appropriate to describe persons with special needs.)

This began to change after World War II, when the federal government began to allocate funds to support special education. Funds were disbursed to support the training of teachers of deaf children and those with other types of disabilities. Some courts upheld the responsibility of their states to provide education for special-needs children. For example, Pennsylvania had enacted a law that allowed school districts the authority to deny education to children who were deemed to be "mentally retarded." This law was struck down as unconstitutional in *Pennsylvania Association for Retarded Citizens (PARC) v. Commonwealth of Pennsylvania* (334 F. Supp. 1257) in 1972.

In 1975, Congress enacted the Education for All Handicapped Children Act, which was signed into law by President Gerald Ford. The act specified that all school districts that received federal funding were required to provide equal access to education for children with physical and/or mental disabilities. The act also included language that required that children with special needs were to be educated in the "least restrictive" possible environment. Thus, this provision meant that children with special needs were to be placed in regular classrooms to the extent that their disabilities permitted. The act was revised and extended in 1990 through the passage of the Individuals with Disabilities Education Act.

Recognizing individual differences to a greater degree, the 1990 act specified that each child with a disability was to be provided with an individualized education plan. This requirement was upheld by the Supreme Court in *Endrew F. v. Douglas County School District* (580 U.S. ___) in 2017.

The "least restrictive" provisions of the 1975 and 1990 laws called attention to an ongoing debate about the degree to which children with special needs should be placed in regular classrooms as opposed to being taught separately from other students. Experts have identified various advantages and disadvantages of mainstreaming these students. On the one hand, the practice provides special-needs children with more opportunities to socialize with their nondisabled peers. It also exposes nondisabled children to experience and help understand difference. However, it may also force teachers to devote more of their time to addressing the special needs of special-needs children. Special-needs children in regular classrooms may also be subjected to bullying and teasing by other children.

How special education is organized and provided varies, of course, by the types of special needs experienced by different children. Many special needs are much more difficult to categorize than is the case with blindness or deafness. Very little is known about how the human brain operates. For example, there are many different manifestations of the autistic spectrum, and diagnosing autism with any degree of precision is very difficult in part because the degree to which autism is associated with genetic or environmental factors is not known. Similarly, many children enter school with clinical depression, bipolar disorder, or other mental disorders. Not only are these disorders difficult to diagnose, but it is also very difficult to identify the most effective methods of educating each individual child. According to one study, effective bonding between individual students and their individual teachers is very important to the academic success of children

---

Many U.S. States Fall Short of Achieving Special Education Needs and Goals

In 2018, the United States Department of Education released the results of a study comparing the 50 states and the District of Colombia that were compared on the basis of success in special education during the 2016–2017 school year. The states were evaluated on the basis of two basic criteria, including the degree to which their educational systems were in compliance with special education laws and policies and the academic success of students with disabilities. The results showed that 22 states met the goals and requirements, whereas Michigan and the District of Colombia were seen as needing intervention. The four largest states—California, Texas, Florida, and New York—were all regarded as needing assistance.

Source: Christina Samuels, "Majority of states fall short on special education compliance, Ed. Dept. says," July 20, 2018, http://blogs.edweek.org/edweek/speced/2018/07/2018 _special_education_determinations.html. Retrieved on March 14, 2020.

This photograph shows children in a special-needs classroom in Thailand. Throughout the world, many children have various physical disabilities such as loss of vision or hearing or have mental or emotional disabilities such as autism. Historically, children with disabilities were often ostracized and/or given little or no formal education. Today, most countries devote resources to educating special-needs children to prepare them to become useful members of society. (Gaysorn Eamsumang | Dreamstime.com)

with autism. However, establishing these relationships can be very difficult and requires understanding of the personalities and specific needs of each child and each teacher.

Clearly, the progress of special education in the United States over the course of its history has gone far beyond the common school philosophy that governed American education in the nineteenth century. Much more attention is now paid to the identification of special needs and the processes by which children with special needs can be educated more effectively. However, challenges remain. For example, many teachers would benefit from more training and experience in learning to provide instruction to special-needs children as effectively as possible. As in other countries, it is also more difficult to provide special education to children who live in rural and sparsely populated places. Special education is associated also with differences in learning styles. For example, children with autism often learn in very different ways than the children who do not appear on the autistic spectrum. Moreover, the creation of effective individualized education plans depends on the effective determination of the nature of an individual student's special needs. How technology can be used in effective special education is also a challenge. Nevertheless, the United States' experiences with special education continue to inform other areas of the world in their efforts to provide education to each of their students.

Further Reading

Mark Alter, Marc Gottlieb, and Jay Gottlieb, "Four ways schools fail special education students," *Education Week*, February 23, 2018, https://www.edweek.org/ew/articles/2018/02/15/four-ways-schools-fail-special-education-students.html. Retrieved on January 19, 2020.

Tess Eyrich, "For children with autism, strong bonds with teachers are key to success," *UC Riverside News*, September 10, 2018, https://news.ucr.edu/articles/2018/09/10/children-autism-strong-bonds-teachers-are-key-success. Retrieved on January 19, 2020.

Allison Gilmour, "Has inclusion gone too far?" *Education Next*, September 26, 2018, https://www.educationnext.org/has-inclusion-gone-too-far-weighing-effects-students-with-disabilities-peers-teachers/. Retrieved on January 19, 2020.

Megan Gross and Ace Parsi, "A 21st century model of special education," June 24, 2018, https://www.gettingsmart.com/2018/06/a-21st-century-model-of-special-education/. Retrieved on January 19, 2020.

Mentalhelp.net, "The choice of educational settings: The pros and cons of mainstreaming children with intellectual disabilities," n.d., https://www.mentalhelp.net/intellectual-disabilities/educational-settings-the-pros-and-cons/. Retrieved on January 19, 2020.

Synapse, "Education and autism spectrum disorders," n.d., http://www.autism-help.org/autism-education-school-effects.htm. Retrieved on January 19, 2020.

Chapter 7: School Violence

OVERVIEW

Recent mass shootings of students attending schools in Colorado, Connecticut, Florida, and Michigan have attracted worldwide attention. Ninety-two school shootings occurred across the United States between 2018 and 2021. The horrific mass shooting at Sandy Hook Elementary School in Newtown, Connecticut, on December 14, 2012, was especially devastating because most of the victims were small children. Americans and people throughout the world have debated hotly about the best and most effective ways to prevent such violent incidents in the future.

By no means, however, is violence in schools confined to such mass shootings. Nor is it confined to the United States. According to recent estimates, some 150 million children between the ages of 13 and 15 worldwide have become victims of various types of violent actions. Violent attacks by teachers against individual students, by students against teachers, and by students against one another have marked the educational process in many different countries throughout the world. The educational process in many places has become characterized by violence. Throughout the world, students and teachers have been victimized by various types of violent acts, and numerous school buildings have been bombed, burned, or otherwise destroyed.

In some parts of the world, attacks on schools, teachers, and students have been linked to religious or civil conflict between countries or between factions fighting for control of governments within countries. For example, the radical Islamist group Boko Haram, which operates in northeastern Nigeria and nearby countries and is attempting to establish an Islamic caliphate there, has been linked to several violent actions in Nigerian schools. In 2013, Boko Haram soldiers opened fire on a secondary school in the town of Mamudo. At least 42 students and teachers were killed in this attack. In the following year, Boko Haram fighters attacked a government-operated secondary school in the town of Chibuk. There, 276 schoolgirls were abducted and kidnapped, and as of 2018, more than 100 of these girls were reported as still missing.

In Afghanistan, the radical Islamist Taliban regime seized control of that country's government in the mid-1990s. Among the goals of the Taliban was to eliminate education for girls. In order to enforce this goal and to keep girls and young women away from school, Taliban fighters resorted to violence. Following numerous such attacks, it was estimated that by 2000, only about 50,000 girls of school age were attending school. The Taliban was ousted from power in 2001 but continued to

Increased School Violence in West Africa

The militant Islamic group Boko Haram is responsible for numerous violent attacks on students, teachers, and administrators in Cameroon and Nigeria. But more recently, similar groups have been active in other West African countries. Between 2014 and 2019, the number of incidents involving school security in Mali, Niger, and Burkina Faso has increased substantially. Militant groups in these countries have exploited long-standing ethnic conflicts as they attempt to use school violence as a means to secure political control. At the end of 2019, it was estimated that more than eight million children in these three countries were unable to attend school because of the ongoing violence.

Source: David McKenzie and Brent Swails, "8 million children have been forced out of school by growing violence in west Africa," *CNN,* January 28, 2020, https://www.cnn .com/2020/01/28/africa/sahel-violence-unicef-burkina-faso-intl/index.html. Retrieved on March 8, 2020.

contest control over Afghanistan, regaining control of the government in 2021. In 2018, 192 attacks on schools in Afghanistan were recorded. In other countries, violence in schools has been associated with discrimination against religious and ethnic minorities such as the Roma people in southeastern Europe. Again, intimidation is often a goal of those who are responsible for such attacks.

These types of mass violence against schools and students have had several repercussions above and beyond immediate fatalities, injuries, and destruction of school property. The threat of violence, as well as violence itself, affects the educational process. Many schools that had been targeted and attacked remain closed, and many students refuse to attend school given the possibility of further violence. Also, it becomes more difficult for government officials to recruit teachers who are willing to move to regions and teach at schools where violence is a serious threat. As a result, in many countries thousands upon thousands of school-age students lack access to schooling.

Other types of violence affect students and teachers independently of civil war on a larger scale and armed political conflicts. Such actions often go unpublicized because many of the victims are individuals, rather than large numbers of people victimized simultaneously as was the case in Sandy Hook, Mamudo, and Chibuk. In some countries, teachers and school officials have been threatened and, in some cases, have been beaten, robbed, or even murdered by students. However, some teachers, school administrators, and other educational authorities have instigated violence on their own. Corporal punishment remains commonplace in some countries, sometimes reinforced by parents who regard corporal punishment as a form of discipline for their children. Students who fear being beaten by school authorities are more likely to drop out or stay away from school. In some countries, teachers have been accused of sexually assaulting or raping students. Most of the victims are teenage girls. As in other situations involving sexual assault, victims often find it difficult to report such attacks because of fear of reprisal or embarrassment or because the legal systems of many countries tend to be biased against female victims of sexual assaults. In addition, violent attacks on students by fellow students are not unusual.

The threat of violence can be almost as destructive to victims as the violence itself. Many students are victims of various types of harassment. For example, some teachers demand sexual favors from students in exchange for good grades or equitable treatment. Bullying is an ongoing issue in the United States and elsewhere. Sometimes, bullies harass their fellow students with the intention of robbing them or stealing their money or possessions. Cyberbullying, or the use of social media to harass or intimidate students, is happening more frequently given the increased use of social media throughout the world. Such bullying and harassment of students has had profound and destructive impacts on victims. Some drop out, and performance in school can be affected. In some cases, victims of such harassment have committed or attempted suicide.

What can be done to minimize or prevent violence associated with education? Recently, the United Nations International Children's Emergency Fund (UNICEF) issued a report on some strategies intended to address problems with school violence. The UNICEF recommendations included the following: implementing policies and legislation to protect students from violence in schools, strengthening prevention and response measures in schools, urging communities and individuals to join students as they speak up about violence and work to change the culture of classrooms and communities, making more effective and targeted investments in proven solutions that help students and schools stay safe, and collecting better, disaggregated data on violence against children in and around schools and sharing what works.

Of course, recommendations such as these are very broad and general guidelines that are focused on individual-level violence as opposed to the actions of mass shooters or the impacts of war and religious conflict. The recommendations do not consider any particular country's economy, culture, or political situation. As the entries in this section indicate, the nature of school violence varies throughout the world and is often related to a country's political situation. The African country of Cameroon, for example, shares a long boundary with Nigeria, where Boko Haram is based. Boko Haram's activities have spilled across the border into northern Cameroon. Because of the ongoing threats of violence and attacks upon schools, many Cameroonian children no longer attend school. Northern Cameroon faces a significant shortage of teachers, reducing local educational opportunities further.

Violence associated with terrorist activity has also had major impacts on education in Uganda. There, the terrorist organization known as the Lord's Resistance Army has been struggling for power with the country's government, although the Army is active also in several nearby countries. Sexual assaults upon female students are not unusual, and this tendency is exacerbated by the patriarchal nature of

Ugandan society. In addition, corporal punishment of students, including canings and beatings, is not unusual despite a law making these practices illegal.

In Honduras, school violence is associated with that country's long history of political turmoil. But the activities of drug cartels and criminal gangs are having even more immediate impacts on education in Honduras, which has the dubious distinction of the highest murder rate in any country in the world. Gangs have de facto control over impoverished neighborhoods in several Honduran cities. Students stay away from school because of the threat of abduction or kidnapping.

School violence is by no means confined to less developed countries. Also, it is an issue in several European countries. School violence has become a significant issue in Bulgaria. Here, the problem of school violence is associated with ongoing tension between Bulgarian nationals, who constitute the large majority of the population, and the country's Turkish and Roma minorities. Many observers have predicted that levels of violence in schools across Europe may increase in the years ahead as more and more non-European immigrants move to European countries. In Poland, school violence including bullying has been linked to the prevalence of aggressive behavior on the part of some students. This tendency, in turn, has been associated with the impacts of economic and social change over the course of Poland's recent history. The incidence of school violence has been associated with levels of social capital or the degree of interconnectedness and mutual trust within communities.

Substantial numbers of school children in other European countries also report having been victimized by school violence or having witnessed such behavior. Bullying in particular tends to be directed against children of immigrants or minorities at a time when Europe's population is becoming more and more diverse. Such is the case in Ireland, where 44 percent of teenagers have reported witnessing bullying or violent behavior in schools. The Irish government is in the process of initiating

---

School Violence in Norway Increases

The Scandinavian countries have long been recognized as peaceful places. Yet levels of school violence have been increasing even in Scandinavia. In Norway, even young children have been observed threatening fellow students and teachers with weapons. According to one survey, a third of Norwegian primary school teachers reported having been threatened. Norwegian authorities have expressed concern that most schools do not yet have plans in place to deal with such violence. Teachers and administrators are not given adequate training about how to deal with school violence incidents when they occur. Some have blamed a lack of discipline and respect for authority for intensifying the school violence problem.

Source: Nina Berglund, "Violence rising at primary schools," *Norwegian News in English*, March 20, 2019, https://www.newsinenglish.no/2019/03/20/violence-rising-at-primary-schools/. Retrieved on March 8, 2020.

a program intended to provide training and support for teachers and school officials to deal with these issues. In Switzerland, violent attacks on students and schools are very rare, despite the prevalence of gun ownership in the country. Bullying remains a problem, although levels of violent and disruptive behavior on the part of young primary school pupils have also increased.

BULGARIA

The Republic of Bulgaria is located in the Balkans region of southeastern Europe, north of Greece and south of Romania. Its land area is about 43,000 square miles, with a population of about 6.8 million as of 2022. More than 80 percent of its people are ethnic Bulgarians, who speak a Slavic language that is related closely to Russian and is written using the Cyrillic alphabet. However, Bulgaria's population also includes substantial numbers of Turks and Roma people.

Present-day Bulgaria was incorporated into the Roman Empire during the first century AD and became part of the Eastern Roman Empire or Byzantine Empire after the Roman Empire was divided in the late fourth century AD. Over the next three centuries, Slavic speakers moved into the area and displaced the Byzantines. Bulgarian dynasties, which were responsible for creating a Bulgarian identity, ruled various parts of the region until 1393, when it was incorporated into the Ottoman Empire that was based in present-day Turkey.

In 1878, war broke out between Russia and the Ottoman Empire. After winning the war, the Russians took control of what is now part of northern and eastern Bulgaria. The remainder of the country remained under Ottoman control, but it was granted autonomous status within the empire. In 1908, Bulgaria declared its full independence. Its boundaries fluctuated over the next several decades, in part because Bulgaria supported Germany in both World War I and World War II. The Soviet Red Army assumed control of Bulgaria near the end of World War II in 1944, establishing the People's Republic of Bulgaria. The country remained a Soviet satellite until after the Communist government of the People's Republic was overthrown in 1990. Democracy was established, and Bulgaria is now a member of the European Union.

Education in Bulgaria

Public education in Bulgaria dates back about 200 years. In the early nineteenth century, schools were established where children were taught the rudiments of reading, writing, and arithmetic. After the 1878 war, the Bulgarian government encouraged the construction of schools in rural villages as well as in cities. Primary schooling was made compulsory, although school attendance was not enforced until the twentieth century. During the period of Communist rule, as elsewhere in Eastern Europe, education was highly centralized and oriented to Communist ideology. With democratization came more decentralization along with eliminating stress on Communism as a guiding educational principle.

In this photograph, students in Bulgaria are on their way to visit the village of Koprivshtitsa, Bulgaria. In 1876, Bulgarian patriots began a fight for Bulgarian independence from the Ottoman Empire in what became known as the April Uprising. The architecture of the town at the time of the April Uprising has been preserved. Visits to sites of historical and cultural significance play a significant role in the educational process in many countries. (Louise Rivard | Dreamstime.com)

Today, education in Bulgaria is managed by the Ministry of Education and Science. Education is compulsory, beginning with 2 years of preschool education and continuing until the age of 16. Most children begin preschool education at around the age of 5. After completing preschool, students attend primary school for 4 years followed by 3 years of middle school.

Upon completion of middle school, students in Bulgaria take a series of examinations. Their performance on these examinations, along with their performance in middle school, is used to determine the next step of their education. Those who do well in the examinations are eligible to attend comprehensive high schools with an academic orientation, while others are steered into vocational high schools. Although more than 15 percent of the country's people do not speak Bulgarian as their first language, it is the language of instruction throughout preschool, primary, and secondary schools. Exit examinations following completion of high school are administered in Bulgarian. During Communist rule, education was conducted in Bulgarian exclusively. Today, students of non-Bulgarian ancestry can take courses in their local languages, although children who do not speak Bulgarian at home remain at a disadvantage.

School Violence in Bulgaria

School violence has been recognized as a significant issue in Bulgaria. According to a study undertaken by the United National International Children's Emergency Fund (UNICEF), more than a third of Bulgarian students were bullied, harassed, or victimized by violence during the 2016–2017 academic year. In 2018, at least one incident of violence was reported in 80 percent of Bulgaria's schools. Many of these incidents involved aggressive behavior by students victimizing fellow students. In one case in the capital city of Sofia, a group of students aged 14 and 15 beat a fellow student, filmed the incident, and posted the video on social media. Observers have noted that the incidence of violence in Bulgarian schools may be associated with Bulgaria's poverty and inequality compared to other European countries.

Some school violence in Bulgaria is related to ethnic conflict, particularly between ethnic Bulgarians and the country's Turkish and Roma minorities. People of Turkish ancestry comprise about 9 percent of Bulgaria's population, Many are descended from Turkish people who moved into present-day Bulgaria during the period of Ottoman rule. Many Bulgarian Turks speak Turkish as their first language.

There has been uneasy tension between the majority Bulgarians and Bulgarian Turks for many decades. This tension intensified during Communist rule. In 1956, the Communist government imposed a series of policies intended to force the Turks to assimilate into the majority culture. At various times, speaking Turkish in public was forbidden and mosques were closed. In 1987, the Bulgarian government implemented the Revival Process by which Bulgarians of Turkish ancestry were required to change their names to Slavic names. For example, members of the family of Naim Suleymanoglu (1967–2017) were required to change their surnames to Shalamanov. Known as "Pocket Hercules," Suleymanoglu defected eventually to Turkey, changed his surname back to the original Turkish, and while competing for Turkey won gold medals in weightlifting at the Olympic Games in 1988, 1992, and 1996. During this period, textbooks used in Bulgarian schools emphasized the history of Bulgaria's majority population and downplayed or ignored the role of people of non-Bulgarian ancestry.

These and other efforts to force assimilation met with fierce resistance among the Turkish community, including several bombings and acts of violence. After the Communist regime was overthrown, the Communist assimilation policies were relaxed. The new government allowed Turkish to be taught as an optional subject in schools. Nevertheless, Bulgarian Turks remain targets of discrimination and violence in schools.

The Roma population has experienced even greater levels of discrimination. Sometimes known by the derogatory exonym "Gypsies," the Roma are believed to be descended from people who migrated to southeastern Europe from present-day northwestern India beginning in the ninth and tenth centuries AD. The exact number of Roma people in Bulgaria is unknown, in part because some Roma avoid being counted by census takers and because some identify themselves as Turks. However, outside observers believe that as many as 10 percent of Bulgaria's residents are Roma and that Bulgaria has the largest Roma population by percentage of any country in the world.

In Bulgaria and many other countries, Roma people are regarded with suspicion and distrust. Many Roma move frequently from place to place, and assimilation into the majority Bulgarian culture is sometimes minimal. Many ethnic Bulgarians regard Roma people as dishonest, lazy, dirty, and prone to criminal activity. Bulgarian officials insist that Roma people in Bulgaria are not targets of discrimination.

However, Roma children are less likely to attend school compared to other Bulgarian students. According to one estimate, as of approximately 2007 only about 60–75 percent of Roma children of primary school age were enrolled in school in part because of the frequency with which Roma families move. This figure might be inflated because Roma children who are enrolled may not actually be attending school. Less than 10 percent of eligible Roma teenagers were enrolled in secondary schools, and literacy among the Roma has been estimated at less than 85 percent as compared to more than 99 percent among the Bulgarian population overall. Observers have noted that discrimination against the Roma in Bulgaria may be intensifying.

Further Reading

Hello, Bulgaria, "Students beat their classmates, filmed, and distributed a video," January 5, 2022, https://newsbeezer.com/bulgariaeng/students-beat-their-classmates-filmed-and-distributed-a-video-society-bulgaria-hello-bulgaria/. Retrieved on January 16, 2022.

Tomasz Kamusella, "Bulgaria's denial of its Ottoman past and Turkish identity," *New Eastern Europe*, March 24, 2019, http://neweasterneurope.eu/2019/03/24/bulgarias-denial-of-its-ottoman-past-and-turkish-identity/. Retrieved on June 29, 2019.

United Nations International Children's Emergency Fund, "The situation in Bulgaria," 2018, https://www.unicef.org/bulgaria/en/together-against-violence-schools. Retrieved on June 29, 2019.

Atanas Zahariev, "Welcome to Bulgaria! That is, if you are not Roma," European Roma Rights Centre, September 14, 2017, http://berberian11.tripod.com/atanasov_education.htm. Retrieved on June 29, 2019.

CAMEROON

The Republic of Cameroon is a west-central African country that borders Nigeria to the west and has a substantial coastline on the Gulf of Guinea. The name of the country is spelled Cameroun in French, which is the predominant colonial language of the country. Cameroon has a coastline on the Gulf of Guinea, which is part of the Atlantic Ocean. It has a land area of approximately 184,000 square miles. Cameroon's population as of early 2022 was approximately 28 million.

The territory comprising present-day Cameroon was contested by various Bantu kingdoms for hundreds of years prior to the arrival of the European colonial powers. In 1884, Cameroon was claimed by Germany. After Germany was stripped of its foreign colonies following World War II, the League of Nations gave a mandate over most of the present-day country to France, while mandates over two small areas along the present-day Nigerian border were assigned to Britain. The latter areas became known as British Cameroons.

The French portion of the mandate was granted independence in 1960 under its current name. During the following year, the British held referenda allowing residents of the two areas comprising the British Cameroons to decide whether to become part of independent Cameroon or part of Nigeria. A majority of residents of the northern portion of British Cameroons voted to become part of Nigeria, whereas a majority of the southern portion of the British mandate voted to become part of Cameroon. For most of its history as an independent country, Cameroon has been governed by autocratic rulers who have suppressed opposition and have been accused of maintaining political power by fraudulent means. However, relative stability coupled with the availability of natural resources and commercial crop production has made Cameroon one of sub-Saharan Africa's more prosperous countries.

Education in Cameroon

Public education in Cameroon is associated with both French and British antecedents, reflecting the country's colonial history. The country's constitution specifies that the country will guarantee a child's right to an education. Although most of Cameroon was under French control between World War I and independence, English has become the primary language of instruction. Education in Cameroon begins with six years of primary school, which is compulsory. This is followed by five years of lower secondary school or middle school and two years of upper secondary school or high school.

Although the government made education compulsory in 2000, as of 2013 the literacy rate among Cameroonians between the ages of 15 and 24 was estimated at about 80 percent. Thus, many children in Cameroon do not or have not attended school. Primary schooling is free, but parents must pay for uniforms and school supplies, and hence, some parents cannot afford to send their children to school. In addition, child labor remains a common practice in Cameroon, keeping working children away from school. Many primary school facilities are regarded as inadequate because of a lack of sufficient seats, toilet facilities, and running water.

Cameroon also experiences substantial geographical differences in school access, school attendance, and literacy. Southern Cameroon, including the areas surrounding the capital city of Yaounde and the major port city of Douala, is more prosperous than the north. In the south, literacy rates are higher, and schools are more likely to be staffed adequately. The northern areas suffer from a shortage of qualified teachers and are especially prone to lack adequate infrastructure and learning materials. The two northernmost provinces of Cameroon, North and Far North, which extend northward to the southern margins of the Sahara Desert to Lake Chad, are believed to have literacy rates of less than 50 percent. However, literacy rates are believed to exceed 90 percent in the south. This difference has been attributed not only to the greater prosperity of the south but also to terrorist activities.

School Violence in Cameroon

Rates of school attendance in Cameroon have been affected not only by poverty, lack of access, and lack of infrastructure but also directly and indirectly by violent actions. Sexual abuse has been commonplace. According to a 2011 study, more than 40 percent of Cameroon's children have been abused by parents, teachers, or other adults. Within schools, girls as young as 9 or 10 years of age have been sexually assaulted or raped by teachers and other school officials.

The actions of the radical militant Islamicist terrorist group Boko Haram (described in more detail in the entry on Nigeria) have also affected education in adjacent Cameroon. Boko Haram has claimed responsibility for various terrorist actions in northeastern Nigeria. These terrorist acts have included attacks on schools. The brutal actions of Boko Haram have displaced thousands of refugees, many of whom have moved across the international boundary into Cameroon.

In 2019, Boko Haram fighters attacked several villages in the Far North province of Cameroon. More than 80 Cameroonian soldiers, Boko Haram fighters, and civilians were killed following a Boko Haram attack in Cameroonian territory near Lake Chad. The ongoing possibility of continued attacks on the part of Boko Haram has meant that many children, especially girls, no longer attend school. Also, fear of Boko Haram has discouraged teachers from willingness to serve in northern Cameroon, exacerbating the ongoing shortage of teachers in this region.

Conflict between French-speaking and English-speaking Cameroonians has also impacted schooling. This conflict stems from Cameroon's colonial history. Most of Cameroon was under French colonial administration until independence, whereas the southern portion of what had been British Cameroons joined the newly independent country in the following year. Some residents of the former British Cameroons have agitated for independence. In early 2019, armed separatists attacked and abducted 170 schoolgirls from a boarding school in the town of Kumbo. It has been estimated that as many as 80 percent of schools in this region have been closed because of further threats of violence. More generally, all of these violent activities have depressed school attendance, making it difficult if not impossible for children to receive education and threatening their futures. Although the impacts of this violence have been especially prevalent in war-torn northern and western Cameroon, they have affected the process and practice of education throughout the country.

Further Reading

Hans de Marie Heungoup, "Boko Haram in Cameroon," International Crisis Group, April 6, 2016, https://www.crisisgroup.org/africa/central-africa/cameroon/q-boko-haram-cameroon. Retrieved on July 29, 2019.

Lewis Mudge, "Residents caught in outbreak of violence in Cameroon," *Human Rights Watch*, February 20, 2019, https://www.hrw.org/news/2019/02/20/residents-caught-outbreak-violence-cameroon. Retrieved on July 29, 2019.

Mbom Sixtus, "In Cameroon, education has become a victim of war," *The New Humanitarian*, July 24, 2019, https://www.voanews.com/africa/child-sexual-abuse-growing-cameroon-study-says. Retrieved on July 29, 2019.

Voice of America, "Child sexual abuse growing in Cameroon, study says," August 17, 2011, https://www.voanews.com/africa/child-sexual-abuse-growing-cameroon-study-says. Retrieved on July 29, 2019.

HONDURAS

The Republic of Honduras is a Central American country, located between Guatemala and El Salvador to the northwest and Nicaragua to the southeast. It has a land area of 43,278 square miles and a population of approximately 9.6 million, as of 2022.

What is now Honduras was occupied by Mayans and other Indigenous cultures until 1524, when Spanish forces moving southeastward from Mexico invaded the territory. Present-day Honduras was incorporated into the Spanish Empire in 1526. Along with Guatemala, El Salvador, Nicaragua, and Costa Rica, Honduras became part of the colony of Guatemala, which became independent in 1821. In 1823, these countries created the Federal Republic of Central America, but Honduras seceded from the Federal Republic and became a separate independent country in 1828. Agriculture is a mainstay of Honduras's economy. During the early twentieth century, Honduras came to be characterized as a "banana republic" whose economy was dominated by U.S.-based fruit companies. According to United Nations estimates, Honduras has the lowest human development index in Central America. Natural disasters including a major earthquake in 1972 and Hurricane Mitch in 1998 have also had widespread impacts on Honduras' economy.

Education in Honduras

Until after World War II, Honduras had no public schools. Education was confined largely to children of the wealthy, who could afford private schooling. Most children of the peasantry were illiterate. In 1957, however, Honduras initiated efforts to create a national system of public education, including the construction of thousands of school buildings. The system as it operates today includes six years of primary school followed by three years of lower secondary school and three years of upper secondary school or high school. The government made six years of education compulsory in the late 1950s, and the length of compulsory education was increased to nine years in 2012. Castilian Spanish, which is the official language of Honduras and is spoken by a large majority of Hondurans, is also the language of instruction.

Although primary education is compulsory in Honduras, in practice many Honduran children of primary school age do not attend school. Public education is free, but parents are responsible for school supplies, uniforms, and transportation costs, and many parents cannot afford these expenses for their children. Especially among low-income families, girls are more likely than boys to be withdrawn from school by their parents in order to assist their families through household tasks, caring for younger siblings, or employment for wages.

As in other less developed countries, progress in expanding educational opportunities has been hindered by a lack of resources and infrastructure, including a shortage of qualified teachers. In 1998, more than 3,000 school buildings were destroyed or damaged heavily by Hurricane Mitch, making the problem of

These children are attending school in a village in Santa Barbara Department in Honduras. Honduras has the highest murder rate in the world, and school violence is commonplace. Some children have to cross territories controlled by rival gangs and drug cartels on their way to school, putting them at risk of being shot or kidnapped. (Matyas Rehak | Dreamstime.com)

providing adequate infrastructure even more difficult. As of 2011, adult literacy in Honduras was estimated at about 83 percent. Also, violence or the threat of violence has had a significant impact on school attendance.

School Violence in Honduras

Compared to most other countries, Honduras experiences high rates of violence. As of 2014, according to statistics reported by the United Nations, Honduras had the highest murder rate in the world. Honduras's rate of homicide is roughly 10 times that of the global homicide rate. Rates of sexual assault and other types of violence are also very high compared to global standards. The violence associated with contemporary Honduras has had significant impacts on education. Violence of many sorts has been reported by journalists observing Honduran schools. Students who are on the autistic spectrum have been bullied. Other children are bullied on the basis of their sexual orientation or ethnic identity. Some teenage girls have been raped or sexually assaulted by teachers who have demanded sexual favors in exchange for good grades.

Very high rates of murder and other violent crimes have been attributed in part to the actions of organized criminal gangs. Many of these gangs are active in the international illegal drug trade. According to one estimate, violence in Honduras has cost as much as 10 percent of the country's overall gross domestic product. Concern about violence has been a factor encouraging many Hondurans from impoverished backgrounds to undertake the arduous journey northward to enter the United States, often illegally.

Criminal gang activity is particularly commonplace in Honduras's larger cities. Impoverished neighborhoods have been especially prone to being controlled by these gangs, and murders as well as rapes, sexual assaults, and kidnappings are common occurrences. Young teenagers are especially prone to being recruited by gangs or forced into joining them. Some secondary school students are gang members themselves. Parents may be forced to pay protection money, or what are called "war taxes," to gangs in order to prevent kidnappings or abductions of their children.

In some cases, children are abducted on their way to or from school. This prospect is particularly dangerous when the child's home and his or her school are located in areas controlled by rival gangs. Young girls are forced into prostitution in order to provide revenues to support the gangs' criminal activities. Those who do not bring in what gang leaders consider to be enough money can be subjected to brutal beatings or other forms of abuse. Because of these threats, many Honduran children living in gang-infested areas do not go to school or they drop out of school before completing lower secondary school. One survey revealed that 60 percent of Honduran students report that they do not feel safe in school. According to an estimate based on a survey conducted by the Norwegian Refugee Council, half of Honduras's children who live in these areas do not attend school.

In 2018, the government of Honduras launched a program intended to address the prevalence of school violence associated with the activities of drug cartels and criminal gangs. The goal of this program is to turn schools into safe spaces, including using the infrastructure for other uses in addition to the schooling process itself. Efforts include improved training of teachers and school administrators to cope with and address violence in their classrooms.

Further Reading

Global Partnership for Education, "Combating violence through education in Honduras," August 2, 2019, https://www.globalpartnership.org/blog/combating-violence-through -education-honduras. Retrieved on July 31, 2019.

Noe Leiva, "Gang wars mean school can be a battleground in Honduras," *Theirworld. org*, March 28, 2017, https://theirworld.org/news/gang-wars-hit-honduras-schools. Retrieved on July 31, 2019.

Norwegian Refugee Council, "Violence has pushed thousands of children in Honduras and El Salvador out of school," May 16, 2019, https://www.nrc.no/resources/reports/vio lence-has-pushed-thousands-of-children-in-honduras-and-el-salvador-out-of-school/. Retrieved on July 31, 2019.

Charles Parkinson, "Latin America is world's most violent region: UN," *InSight Crime*, April 21, 2014, https://www.insightcrime.org/news/analysis/latin-america-worlds-most-violent -region-un/. Retrieved on July 29, 2019.

Adriana Zehbrauska and Olga Chambers, "Teenagers in Honduras face violence, bullying in schools," UNICEF, September 14, 2018, https://www.unicef.org/stories/teenagers -honduras-face-violence-bullying-schools. Retrieved on January 16, 2022.

IRELAND

The Republic of Ireland is located on the island of Ireland. Its land area is about 27,000 square miles, with a population of 5 million as of 2022. The Republic of Ireland contains about 82 percent of the island's land area. The rest is Northern Ireland, which is a component of the United Kingdom.

For hundreds of years, Ireland's history has been linked to the history of England. At various times throughout the Middle Ages, Ireland was invaded by English forces. However, the English did not dominate Ireland until the sixteenth century, when the history of both Ireland and England was affected by the Protestant Reformation. During the 1530s, King Henry VIII (1491–1547) broke with the Roman Catholic Church. The Church of England was established in England, while Ireland remained Catholic. King Henry initiated efforts to incorporate Ireland into what would come to be known as the United Kingdom. He proclaimed himself to be King of Ireland in 1541. England assumed control of all of Ireland in 1603, and by 1653 it had, in effect, become a British colony. During the 1640s and 1650s, the British under the leadership of Oliver Cromwell (1599–1658) encouraged Protestants from Great Britain to migrate to Ireland. By the early eighteenth century, a majority of northeastern Ireland's residents were Protestants as remains the case today. After taking full control of Ireland, the United Kingdom enacted the Penal Laws. The Penal Laws were highly discriminatory against Roman Catholics in Ireland, who among other things were not permitted to vote.

In part because of these Penal Laws, many Irish leaders began to agitate for political independence in the eighteenth and nineteenth centuries. The Irish Potato Famine, which occurred between 1845 and 1850, caused the deaths of more than 500,000 Irish Catholics. The famine's devastation was made more severe by England's discriminatory laws and its tardy response to the crisis. Following the famine, independence efforts intensified. Several bills to grant home rule to Ireland were considered by the United Kingdom's parliament during the late nineteenth century, although these proposals were opposed bitterly by many Protestants, especially in Protestant-majority northeastern Ireland.

Ireland declared independence in 1919, following the end of World War I, despite Protestant opposition. Two years later, representatives of the United Kingdom and Ireland drafted the Anglo-Irish Treaty. The treaty specified that Ireland would become a self-governing state but would remain part of the British Empire, later the British Commonwealth. However, the counties of northeastern Ireland were given the right to vote as to whether to remain part of the United Kingdom. Six did so, and these counties remain Northern Ireland as part of the United Kingdom. The other 26 counties became the Irish Free State. The Irish Free State withdrew from the Commonwealth in 1949, becoming the fully independent Republic of Ireland.

Education in Ireland

The history of education in Ireland parallels the country's history, especially its relationship with the United Kingdom. During the eighteenth century, the United

Kingdom's government banned formal education for Catholic children in an effort to encourage Irish Catholics to convert to Anglicanism, since Anglican children were eligible for formal schooling, whereas Catholic children were not eligible. However, many Irish Catholics received the rudiments of education in what became known as "hedge schools" because they often operated outdoors. At these hedge schools, children were taught reading, writing, arithmetic, and other basic skills.

Operation of these hedge schools was illegal during most of the eighteenth century, although in practice these laws were seldom enforced. Hedge schools received no government funding, however, and there were no formal standards ensuring any sort of quality control. The laws making formal education illegal to Irish Catholics were repealed in 1791. In the nineteenth century, education became a formal responsibility of the state. At that time, the law required that schools be open to all children regardless of their religion, despite opposition by some Catholic leaders who pushed for more religious control of education. These laws remain in force today.

Education in the Republic of Ireland today is managed by the Department of Education and Skills. Public education is free and compulsory beginning at the age of six, although the majority of young Irish children attend Junior Infant and Senior Infant schools at the ages of four and five, respectively. Children complete six years of primary school and then move on to the Junior Cycle, which lasts for three years. Education remains compulsory until the child reaches the age of 16 or completes the Junior Cycle, after which students complete the government-administered Junior Certificate examination. After the Junior Cycle is completed, most students continue on to the Senior Cycle, which lasts for two to three years. English is the primary language of instruction, although some children attend gail-escoileanna or Irish-language schools where English is taught as a second language.

School Violence in Ireland

Violence in school, and especially in the Junior and Senior Cycles, is a significant problem in Ireland. A report by the United Nations International Children's Emergency Fund includes the statement that violence "is a pervasive part of young people's education in Ireland."

Much of this violence involves bullying, which is usually initiated by peers. According to one report, 44 percent of Irish secondary school students reported having experienced violence at school. Some 28 percent of students between the ages of 13 and 15 reported having been bullied at school "over the past couple of months," and 27 percent reported having been involved in at least one physical fight over the past year. As in some other countries, girls are more likely to have been targets of cyberbullying, whereas boys are more likely to have been targets of physical violence on the part of bullies.

Bullying behavior in Ireland, as in other countries, may be linked to levels of difference. Children who have been targeted by bullies are more likely to have been picked on because of their race, national origin, or appearance, including bullying of disabled pupils. This tendency is of particular concern to the contemporary Irish government because Ireland is experiencing higher levels of immigration and is becoming a more multiethnic, multicultural society.

In 2018, the government of Ireland initiated a program intended to reduce bullying behavior and to promote online safety among Irish students. The program, which is based on a program currently in use in Finland, includes assigning a staff member as an anti-bullying coordinator to each school and providing training for teachers as to how to address bullying issues. The program was introduced on a trial basis in elementary schools in two Irish counties near Ireland's capital city of Dublin. If this program is successful, the government's intention is to extend the program to secondary schools and on a nationwide basis.

Further Reading

Galen English, "Irish teen, 13, pens powerful anti-bullying song after seeing friends go through hell," *Evoke*, February 22, 2019, https://evoke.ie/2019/02/22/health/irish-girl -writes-anti-bullying-song. Retrieved on September 1, 2019.

Aine McMahon, "Report finds 44% of Irish teens subjected to violence at school," *Irish Times*, September 6, 2018, https://www.irishtimes.com/news/education/report-finds-44-of-irish -teens-subjected-to-violence-at-school-1.3618457. Retrieved on August 31, 2018.

Ellen O'Riordan, "Appearance and race top reasons for bullying of schoolchildren," *Irish Times*, June 4, 2019, https://www.irishtimes.com/news/social-affairs/appearance-and-race-top -reasons-for-bullying-of-schoolchildren-1.3914822. Retrieved on September 1, 2019.

Robert Slonje, "A new approach to deal with the scourge of bullying," *Raidio Teilifis Eireann*, May 30, 2019, https://www.rte.ie/brainstorm/2019/0528/1052139-a-new-approach-to -deal-with-the-scourge-of-bullying/. Retrieved on September 1, 2019.

POLAND

The Republic of Poland is located along the coast of the Baltic Sea in north-central Europe, east of Germany. With a land area of approximately 121,000 square miles, Poland has a population of approximately 38 million as of 2022.

Poland's location between the Baltic Sea to the north, Alpine ranges to the south, Germany to the west, and Russia to the east has made it a central point within Europe for hundreds of years. Control of present-day Poland has been contested between local rulers and foreign powers since the Middle Ages. The area was ruled by the Polish-Lithuanian Commonwealth, which was one of the largest kingdoms in Europe, beginning in 1386. However, the Commonwealth was dissolved in 1795, and its territory was divided among Austria, Prussia, and Russia. After World War I, Poland regained its status as an independent country in 1918. In 1939, however, representatives of Nazi Germany and the Soviet Union agreed to divide the Polish republic into German and Soviet spheres of influence. World War II began with Germany's invasion of Poland in 1939, and the Germans made concerted efforts to eliminate Polish culture.

After the war ended, Poland regained its independence. However, it became a satellite of the Soviet Union despite strong resistance by many Poles. Resistance intensified after Karol Wojtyla (1920–2005), the archbishop of the Polish city of Krakow, was elected as Pope John Paul II (now St. John Paul II) in 1978. The pope provided quiet encouragement to the resistance movement. In 1989, the Communist dictatorship was overthrown. Democratic elections were held, and anti-Communist candidates received majorities of the votes. Poland joined the European Union in 2004.

Education in Poland

During the seventeenth and eighteenth centuries, formal education in the Polish-Lithuanian Commonwealth was provided by the Society of Jesus, or the Jesuit order of the Roman Catholic Church. As elsewhere, such formal education was limited primarily to children of the nobility and to boys preparing for the Roman Catholic priesthood, while most Polish peasants remained illiterate. In the early 1770s, however, Pope Clement XIV (1705–1774) took steps to suppress the Jesuits and to close down the Jesuit order. Shutting down the Jesuits would have meant that education of ordinary Poles would have ceased. In response, the government of the Commonwealth established the Ministry of Education. The ministry is believed to have been the first such secular ministry in Europe. Because much Jesuit education had been conducted in Latin, the ministry authorized the publication of both religious and secular textbooks and learning materials in the Polish language.

After the partition of Poland, each of the Austrian, Prussian, and Russia portions of the country administered education separately. The three educational systems were unified under the government of independent Poland in 1932, when education was also made compulsory. During the World War II period, the Nazis suppressed and, in some cases, banned formal education. Schooling was conducted in underground institutions. Although teachers were threatened with execution or deportation to concentration camps, it has been estimated that more than a million Polish children participated in these clandestine school programs.

The Communists reestablished free and compulsory education, although their efforts were made more difficult because many Polish teachers at all levels had been executed or had left the country during the war. As in other Eastern European countries, education under the Communist regime was dominated by Marxist-Leninist principles to which all teachers and students were expected to conform. This system was dismantled after the Communists were ousted from power in 1989.

Today, compulsory education in Poland begins with primary school. Until 2016, primary school lasted for six years. This was followed by three years of middle school, after which the period of compulsory education ended. After middle school, most students continue to upper secondary school. Upper secondary schooling includes general upper secondary school, which prepares students for college and vocational and technical schooling. The 2016 educational reforms eliminated middle school. Instead, the length of primary schooling was increased from six to eight years.

School Violence in Poland

Although Poland's government is stable and its gross domestic product per capita is greater than that of the world as a whole, violence has become and remains an issue within Polish schools. Violent acts have been linked to an onset of "aggression," or a tendency toward aggressive and hostile behavior on the part of some Polish students. Observers are divided as to why such aggressive behavior takes place. Some have attributed this aggression toward Polish history, given the large-scale changes in Polish culture and society since before World War II.

According to Polish law, teachers are responsible for reporting incidents of violence to appropriate authorities. Those who fail to do so may be subject to fines or prison sentences. Parents of students who perform violent acts can also be fined. However, these policies apply to direct incidences of violence but not to bullying, which has come to be recognized as a significant problem in many Polish schools. According to a study by Joanna Mazur et al, nearly 13 percent of lower secondary school students reported having been victims of bullying. Eleven percent admitted being perpetrators of bullying and an additional 31 percent having observed bullying activity "frequently" at school.

The prevalence of bullying behavior was affected by the context in which such schooling took place. The authors found that bullying was more commonplace in urban schools compared to those located in rural and agricultural areas. On a related note, it was found that bullying behavior was more likely in large schools and in schools where the ratio of teachers to students was low. This was attributed to differences in what the authors called social capital, in that people in rural areas tend to have closer relationships with one another and their communities than in the case with city dwellers. Also, transitions within Polish society and its economy are felt more directly in the cities.

Levels and types of bullying varied by age and by gender. Studies have shown that girls and younger children are more likely to have been victimized by bullies, whereas boys and adolescents were more likely to be engaging in bullying behavior against other students. In addition, girls were more likely to have experienced cyberbullying, whereas boys were more likely to have been victimized by direct physical violence on the part of bullies.

Further Reading

Maria Januszewska-Warych, "Polish school looking for ways to counteract violence and aggression," *Art and Education Russia*, 2017, http://www.art-education.ru/electronic -journal/polish-school-looking-ways-counteract-violence-and-aggression. Retrieved on August 24, 2019.

Joanna Mazur, Izabela Tabak, and Dorota Zawadzka, "Determinants of bullying at school depending on the type of community: Ecological analysis of secondary schools in Poland," *School Mental Health*, 9 (2017), pp. 132–142.

Estera Twardowska-Staszek, Izabela Zych, and Rosario Ortega-Ruiz, "Bullying and cyber-bullying in Polish elementary and middle schools: Validation of questionnaires and nature of the phenomena," *Children and Youth Services Review*, 95 (2018), pp. 217–225.

Mirek Wojciechowski, "The Polish education system and issues of violence," *Journal of School Violence*, 4 (2005), pp. 119–130.

SWITZERLAND

Switzerland, known formally as the Swiss Confederation, is a landlocked country located in central Europe. Its land area is about 16,000 square miles, with a population of about 8.8 million as of 2022. Much of Switzerland's land surface is mountainous, and it contains many of the high peaks of the main range of the Alps.

Switzerland consists of 26 provinces or cantons that united to become a single country over several hundred years. In 1291, the present-day cantons of Uri, Schwyz, and Unterwalden signed an alliance to maintain trade routes across the Alps and promote common political and economic interests. This agreement, known as the Federal Charter, is regarded by the Swiss as the founding of Switzerland. By the sixteenth century, most of the remaining cantons had joined the Swiss Confederation. The confederation's independence and neutrality were guaranteed in accordance with the Peace of Westphalia, which ended the Thirty Years' War in 1648. Several additional cantons joined the confederation between 1803 and 1815, when Swiss independence was guaranteed once again during the Congress of Vienna, which ended the Napoleonic Wars in 1815.

Switzerland's location in central Europe at the central point of Europe's diverse cultures has contributed to its cultural, religious, and linguistic diversity. Historically, the population of Switzerland was divided roughly between Roman Catholics and Protestants. Four languages are spoken in Switzerland, and all four—German, French, Italian, and Romansch—are recognized as official in accordance with the Swiss constitution. As of 2000, more than 60 percent of Swiss citizens speak German as their first language or "mother tongue." However, each canton has the right to designate one or more of these four languages as its "public use language."

Education in Switzerland

Switzerland's governance is highly decentralized, and each canton has considerable autonomy with respect to the provision of various public services, including education. The constitution of Switzerland states that each canton is required to provide free and compulsory public schooling to all resident children. Today, nine years of compulsory education are required throughout the country.

At the federal level, the State Secretariat for Education, Research, and Innovation is responsible for overseeing education. However, each canton has responsibility for the specific process by which this education is delivered, and this delivery process varies from canton to canton. These differences can affect families who move from one canton to another while their children are in school. The language of instruction is generally the public use language of that canton. However, students are taught one or more of Switzerland's other official languages beginning in primary school. Many students also study English.

Details vary, but for most Swiss children formal education begins with one to two years of kindergarten, which in many cantons is required. With a few exceptions, children enter primary school at the age of six years. Primary school lasts for six years in most cantons. Primary schooling is followed by secondary education, during which students are generally separated between academic tracks, preparing them for college and vocational tracks.

At the end of primary school, the track in which each pupil is placed is determined on the basis of canton-sponsored examinations, teacher evaluations, and input by students and their parents or guardians. In some cantons, students in different tracks may attend the same classes. Students attend lower secondary school for three years in most cantons. This is followed by upper secondary schooling, in which curricula are geared to the individual tracks in which the students have been placed.

School Violence in Switzerland

Issues associated with school violence in Switzerland have been affected by Switzerland's unique history with respect to foreign relations and national defense. Since 1815, when its independence was guaranteed by the European powers, Switzerland has remained neutral in its relationships with other countries. This neutrality was recognized explicitly by the League of Nations in 1920. More recently, Switzerland did not join the United Nations until 2002, and it has never joined the European Union or the North Atlantic Treaty Organization (NATO).

Switzerland's policy of neutrality is regarded as one of "armed neutrality." Military service remains compulsory for young men, who remain part of the country's reserve forces until reaching their thirties. Rates of gun ownership are high, and target shooting is a popular recreational activity. Soldiers are allowed to take their firearms home, and reservists who are no longer on active duty must continue to keep the weapons that they had used during their periods of active duty. This policy has come into question because of problems associated with actual or threatened domestic violence, including fatal shootings of domestic partners. However, Switzerland's low rate of gun-related violence compared to that of the United States and some other countries has been attributed to its policy of compulsory military service, because recruits are given thorough and extensive psychological and physical testing as they begin their active service. Perhaps because of this testing despite the high rate of ownership of firearms, Switzerland has not experienced any mass school shootings during the twentieth or early twenty-first centuries.

Although mass shootings and gun-related violence are absent in Switzerland's schools, the country is not immune to other types of school violence. In particular, bullying (which is known as "mobbing" in Switzerland) has become a significant problem. In the canton of Valais, for example, one study indicated that as many as 10 percent of students reported having been bullied. Many victims of such bullying, including cyberbullying, are targeted because of sexual orientation, ethnicity, or physical appearance including being overweight. As elsewhere, bullying victims suffer from a loss of self-esteem, which can in turn lead to poor school performance, feelings of isolation, depression, and suicidal actions. The same study indicated that more than 85 percent of students in the canton had observed bullying behavior on the part of their peers. Meanwhile, bullies tend to have more trouble integrating into the school community, and these bullies are much more likely to become delinquents and/or compile criminal records as adults.

Violent behavior on the part of students has also been a problem in Swiss schools. In contrast to bullying, young children between the ages of four and eight are most prone to be violent and belligerent in school settings. Children engaging in such inappropriate behavior tend to come from broken homes or from immigrant families. Also, teachers may be reluctant to discipline these children because of concerns that parents will take legal action against them.

Further Reading

Matt Davis, "In Switzerland, gun ownership is high but mass shootings are low. Why?," *Big Think*, March 17, 2019, https://bigthink.com/politics-current-affairs/switzerland-high-gun-ownership. Retrieved on September 2, 2019.

Living Switzerland Education Consulting, "Bullying in Swiss schools," 2017, https://living switzerland.ch/bullying-in-swiss-schools/. Retrieved on September 2, 2019.

Soraya Sarhaddi Nelson, "What's worked, and what hasn't, in gun-loving Switzerland," *NPR*, March 19, 2013, https://www.npr.org/2013/03/19/174758723/facing-switzerland-gun-culture. Retrieved on September 2, 2019.

Katy Romy, "Bullying at school: Breaking the silence to prevent suffering," *swissinfo.ch*, March 30, 2016, https://www.swissinfo.ch/eng/school-a-living-hell_bullying-at-school-breaking-the-silence-to-prevent-suffering/42053064. Retrieved on September 2, 2019.

UGANDA

The Republic of Uganda is a landlocked country located in the highlands of east-central Africa, north of Lake Victoria. Uganda's land area is about 91,000 square miles. Its population as of 2022 was about 48.5 million.

During the eighteenth century, most of present-day Uganda was controlled by the Bunyoro and Buganda Kingdoms. European colonial powers began to take an interest in the kingdoms beginning in the middle of the nineteenth century and established trade linkages with local rulers. In 1892, the British Protectorate of Uganda was established.

Uganda became independent in 1962. Because of the considerable ethnic, linguistic, and religious diversity characterizing the newly independent country, establishing a concrete national identity became difficult. In particular, many residents of northern Uganda are Acholi people and members of other tribal groups whose economy emphasizes livestock herding and who speak Nilotic languages spoken in many parts of east-central Africa. To the south, the majority of Ugandans are Bugandans or members of other groups who are primarily farmers and who speak Bantu languages spoken commonly throughout west-central and southern Africa.

In 1971, Idi Amin (1925–2003) seized power. Amin was a Nilotic-speaking northerner who had been the supreme commander of Uganda's military prior to the coup d'état in which he took control of the country. It is believed that as many as half a million Ugandans were murdered during Amin's brutal dictatorship before he was deposed in 1979. Even after Amin's regime was toppled, it has been difficult for Uganda to establish a democratic government. Yoweri Museveni (1944–) has been the president of Uganda since 1986, but his presidency has been criticized for corruption and suppression of political opposition. By spearheading efforts to remove term limits and maximum age requirements for the chief executive, Museveni has in effect made himself the president for life.

Since Museveni became the president, Uganda has been involved in a civil war against guerilla forces associated with the Lord's Resistance Army (LRA). The LRA is a rebel organization that has been active in northern Uganda and neighboring countries including South Sudan. Its primary goal has been to topple Museveni's government. The United States and other countries have identified the LRA as a terrorist organization whose members are well known for murder, rape, child abduction, and various other atrocities. It has been estimated that as many as 100,000 Ugandan civilians have been murdered by LRA fighters since the 1990s. Although the war has subsided in recent years, it continues to have had a strong impact on school violence in Uganda.

Discussions are underway to unite Uganda with nearby Tanzania, Kenya, Rwanda, Burundi, and South Sudan to form an East African Federation. If this plan succeeds, the federation would become the second largest country in Africa (behind Nigeria) and the eighth largest country in the world by population.

Education in Uganda

Education as practiced in Uganda reflects its British colonial history. Uganda's educational system is managed by the Ministry of Education and Sports. The system includes seven years of primary education, beginning at the age of six. Primary schooling is followed by four years of lower secondary education and two years of upper secondary education. Education is compulsory through primary school although in practice less than half of Uganda's children complete primary school. Secondary education is not compulsory, and it has been estimated that only about 25 percent of students attend secondary school after completing primary school. English is the language of instruction, although a shortage of qualified English-speaking teachers outside urban areas has meant that, in practice, classes are taught in local languages.

The government of Uganda recognizes education as a basic human right. However, in practice it has been difficult to provide education to many children, especially those from impoverished and/or more isolated rural areas. Uganda remains one of the poorest countries in the world, with relatively little revenue available to spend on education. Rapid population growth has meant increased shortages of teachers, facilities, and learning materials. Because southern Uganda has been relatively peaceful over the past few decades, large numbers of refugees have moved into Uganda from neighboring countries. Providing education to refugee children as well as to native-born children and to children living in the war-torn northern portions of the country has also proven to be a challenge. Access to schools in rural areas is often difficult, especially given the absence of effective local transportation.

Gender disparities in Uganda education have been evident. Throughout Uganda, female school attendance rates have continued to lag behind male attendance rates. These differences have been attributed to the prevalence of early marriage and childbearing among girls under 18 years of age, to cultural pressures in a patriarchal society, and to a perceived need for girls to stay home and provide for their families rather than to attend school. Some parents prioritize the education of their sons over the education of their daughters in the belief that their sons' educations will benefit their families, whereas their daughters will marry into other families and their labor will benefit their husband's families rather than benefit their birth families.

The threat of sexual assault and violence, including violent attacks on the part of members of the Lord's Resistance Army, has discouraged many girls of secondary

These children are attending a primary school in Kibale, Uganda. Like other less developed countries, Uganda has been experiencing considerable levels of school-related violence. This includes assaults by students on one another, assaults on teachers, and sexual harassment of female students. The threat of violence deters some parents from sending their children to school. (Turfantastik | Dreamstime.com)

school age from attending school. Since the 1990s, LRA fighters have committed many atrocities against Ugandan children. Children as young as 10 years of age have been abducted and forced into military service, and young girls were forced into prostitution and to become sexual slaves to service the guerillas. Trauma associated with these atrocities has impacted these victims for years after these acts were committed. According to research, most children who were victimized by the LRA stopped attending school in part because of fears of further violence.

School Violence in Uganda

Violence in Uganda's schools includes corporal punishment of students by teachers, violent acts against students on the part of fellow students, teachers, and school officials, and violence associated with Uganda's civil war against the Lord's Resistance Army.

Corporal punishment has been an issue in Uganda's schools. In 1997, the government first banned the use of corporal punishment including caning. However, in part because of loopholes in the law imposing this ban, it continued to be practiced widely. In 2015, according to one study, 90 percent of primary school pupils reported having been beaten by teachers on at least one occasion. The prevalence of caning and other forms of corporal punishment has discouraged some children from attending school, and the practice of caning students is believed widely to have reduced the levels of educational achievement. The government enacted a stronger law against corporal punishment in 2016, but how well this law will work in practice remained unclear as of 2019. Some have questioned the effectiveness of such a law in a society where corporal punishment at home remains a common practice.

Above and beyond corporal punishment, many Ugandan students have been victims of violence associated with schooling. Sexual assaults, rapes, and various forms of sexual harassment have been reported in secondary schools as well as in colleges and universities. The problem of sexual assault is especially acute in Uganda because of the country's high prevalence of HIV/AIDS infections. In 2018, the Ugandan parliament authorized the formation of a select committee to investigate these issues. Bullying remains a significant issue in Ugandan schools. In one case, a child who had been bullied was hit over the head with a chair by a fellow pupil, and the victim died while being treated at a local hospital. Some parents and teachers have attributed bullying to observations by children of violent behavior. As one headmaster quoted in the article by Monitor below said, "If a child comes from a family where the father bullies the mother or elder siblings misuse power, they learn to behave the same way when they meet children they find inferior."

In 2015, the Ugandan government implemented the National Strategic Plan on the Elimination of Violence against Children in order to further reduce the incidence of bullying and other forms of school violence.

Further Reading

Borgen Project, "10 important facts to know about education in Uganda," July 10, 2017, https://borgenproject.org/10-facts-about-education-in-uganda/. Retrieved on July 27, 2019.

Karen M. Devries, Jennifer Christine Child, Elizabeth J. Van Allen, Eddy Joshua Walakira, Jenny Parks, and Dipak Naker, "School violence, mental health, and educational performance in Uganda," *Pediatrics*, 133 (2014), pp. 129–137, https://www.ncbi.nlm.nih .gov/pubmed/24298004. Retrieved on July 27, 2019.

Monitor, "Bullying, a vice that must be kicked out of schools," revised January 10, 2021, https://www.monitor.co.ug/uganda/news/education/bullying-a-vice-that-must-be -kicked-out-of-schools-1857236?view=htmlamp. Retrieved on January 16, 2022.

Natalie Ojewska, "Can Ugandans overcome trauma of LRA's violent crimes?," *Aljazeera. com*, September 25, 2017, https://www.aljazeera.com/indepth/features/2017/08/ugan dans-overcome-trauma-lra-violent-crimes-170829071931893.html. Retrieved on July 28, 2019.

Nakisanze Segawa, "Two years after ban, corporal punishment still used, debated, in Ugandan schools," *Global Press Journal*, August 27, 2018, https://www.ncbi.nlm.nih.gov /pubmed/24298004. Retrieved on July 27, 2019.

Godfrey Ssali, "Uganda Parliament to probe sexual abuse in schools," *The Independent*, April 14, 2018, https://www.independent.co.ug/uganda-parliament-to-probe-sexual-abuse -in-schools/. Retrieved on July 28, 2019.

UNITED STATES

School violence, and especially mass shootings of students, has become a major issue in the United States. In recent years, dozens of students have been shot and killed while attending school in Newtown, Connecticut; Parkland, Florida; Littleton, Colorado; and other communities across the country. These and other tragedies were given worldwide media attention, but many other incidents of violence also occur in American schools. The Newtown shooting was seen as especially tragic because most of the victims were elementary school students, some as young as six years of age. During the 2017–2018 school year, according to one report there were 279 violent incidents in U.S. schools. Many of these incidents involved discovery of guns, knives, or other weapons on campus, but others involved successful or thwarted attacks. During the first half of 2019, 22 school shootings in which at least one student was killed or wounded were reported.

In countries such as Cameroon, Nigeria, Afghanistan, and Uganda, school violence is a by-product of ongoing civil war or religious conflict and confrontation. In some European countries, school violence has been linked to discrimination against minorities or immigrant populations. Although prejudice against minorities and immigrants remains an issue in the contemporary United States, such prejudice has not been linked closely to school violence, including mass shootings. Nor is the United States involved in civil war. Given these circumstances, why is school violence so prevalent in the United States, especially compared to other developed countries? This question, along with the issue of how to address problems associated with school violence most effectively, has become a major issue of debate and discussion among Americans.

Especially compared to other developed countries, ownership and use of guns, knives, and other weapons is commonplace in the United States. This tendency is reflected in the prevalence of weapons in schools. Many students have reported or admitted taking weapons to school. In 2017, about 15.7 percent of surveyed students reported having carried a gun, knife, club, or other weapon at school at least once within the previous month. Boys are much more likely than girls to carry weapons, although little difference was reported among students from different ethnic groups. Students in urban schools are more likely to carry weapons than in schools outside of cities, although violent behavior has also been observed in suburbs and rural areas as well.

The percentage of students with weapons at school has declined, however, since the early 1990s. This declining percentage has been associated with increased security at schools, including metal detectors and screening devices and the prevalence of armed security guards. Nevertheless, during 2017–2018 more than 5 percent of high school students reported having been threatened with a weapon within the previous year. Such school violence includes not just actions that take place in school buildings on school days. For example, in 2019 10 teenagers attending a high school football game in Alabama were shot during a shooting incident, although fortunately none were killed or injured seriously.

Of course, not all incidents of violence in American schools involve the use of weapons. According to a survey conducted under the auspices of the Center for Disease Control, nearly 10 percent of high school students reported having been in a fight or physical confrontation on school property within the previous 12 months. Seven percent of students reported having missed or skipped school because of fear or the threat of violence directed against themselves.

Gang activity is also associated with school violence in the United States, especially when such violence involves weapons. Many teenagers are induced or coerced into joining gangs, which confront one another for control over "turf" and for control of local illegal drug trade and other illegal activities. Psychologists have recognized that some teenagers join gangs in order to achieve identity, recognition, or acceptance. In many cases, these confrontations have resulted in violence between members of rival gangs. Such gang activity tends to be concentrated in urban schools, although such activity within suburban and rural schools is not unknown. Gang members have sometimes assaulted or raped young girls or forced them into prostitution.

What can be done to prevent such shootings or at least minimize their impacts has been an ongoing issue of debate and discussion throughout the United States. Proposals to eliminate violence are linked to perceptions of the causes of such violence. Some have proposed arming teachers and administrators, and some states have enacted legislation that would allow teachers to be armed with training in the use of firearms provided. In Florida, for example, investigators looking into the 2018 mass shooting at Marjorie Stoneman Douglas High School in Parkland concluded that the impacts of the shooting could have been minimized had teachers been armed and authorized to use firearms, if necessary, to prevent mass violence.

In many cases, those who have attempted mass shootings have been afflicted with significant problems involving their mental health and stability. Some are former students who hold grudges against the school and its students, teachers, and administrators. Many are loners who have felt that they do not fit into the culture of the schools. In some cases, teachers have been targeted and threatened with being shot, stabbed, or otherwise attacked by disruptive current or former students. In response, some experts have called for expanding mental health services and screening with the idea of keeping guns, and especially machine guns that can be fired rapidly and repeatedly, out of the hands of such potential shooters.

A related issue involves access to guns. The question of gun access is a continuing matter of debate. Compared to most other countries, Americans have easy access to guns, which can be sold at various stores or at gun shows in some cases with few or no background checks. This situation provides an important contrast with Switzerland, in that military service is compulsory among young Swiss men and is coupled with extensive investigation of their physical and mental health. That mass shootings are highly unusual in Switzerland and much more commonplace in the United States has been attributed to this difference in policy.

Of course, violence in American schools is by no means limited to shootings and stabbings. As in other countries, bullying is a significant problem in the United States. According to the nonprofit National Voices for Equality Education and Enlightenment (NVEEE), 30 percent of American high school students have been bullied at some point during their school careers, and 70 percent have observed bullying behavior on the part of peers. As elsewhere, such bullying can result in reduced academic performance, feelings of sadness, and depression. NVEEE has reported that about 160,000 students miss school each day because of bullying. In response, every state has enacted laws or promoted policies against bullying, and a majority of the states have done both.

It is recognized that to prevent school violence parents and families should be involved, as well as school officials and teachers. Nonprofit organizations have made suggestions as to how parents can help eliminate the problem of violence in schools. Many of these suggestions involve maintaining communication among parents, teachers, and students, including identifying warning signs suggesting that students are dealing with problems related to mental health and stability. Such

---

Preventing Bullying in the United States

Bullying remains a major problem in the United States and many other countries. As bullying continues, educators have worked to develop resources intended to prevent it. The United States Department of Health and Human Services now maintains a website devoted to information about ways to stop bullying. According to this site, the most important thing that parents and adults can do is to keep lines of communication open. Parents should also be aware of and pay close attention to remain up to date about what is going on with their children in school, including contact with teachers and counselors. Adults can also play a role in teaching children how to treat others with kindness and respect.

Source: www.stopbullying.gov.

warning signs include isolating behaviors such as withdrawing from friendships and school organizations.

Further Reading

Childhelp, "States ranked by biggest bullying problems," n.d., https://wallethub.com/edu/e/best-worst-states-at-controlling-bullying/9920. Retrieved on July 18, 2020.

Chip Grabow and Lisa Rose, "The US has had 57 as many school shootings as the other major industrialized nations combined," CNN, May 21, 2018, https://www.cnn.com/2018/05/21/us/school-shooting-us-versus-world-trnd/index.html. Retrieved on July 29, 2018.

Patricia Mazzei, "Florida moves toward arming teachers, despite opposition from Parkland students," *New York Times*, April 23, 2019, https://www.nytimes.com/2019/04/23/us/florida-teacher-armed.html. Retrieved on September 3, 2019.

National Parent-Teacher Association, "Checklist to help prevent violence in schools," n.d., https://www.pta.org/home/family-resources/safety/School-Safety/Checklist-to-Help-Prevent-Violence-in-Schools. Retrieved on September 3, 2019.

Marina Pitofsky, "There were nearly 1,300 more threats made at U.S. schools this past year, report says," *USA Today*, August 14, 2018, https://www.usatoday.com/story/news/2018/08/14/school-violence-us-schools/987901002/. Retrieved on September 2, 2019.

Christina Walker, "10 years. 180 school shootings. 356 victims," CNN, July 2019, https://www.cnn.com/interactive/2019/07/us/ten-years-of-school-shootings-trnd/#storystart. Retrieved on July 29, 2018.

Chapter 8: STEM Education

OVERVIEW

Technology and its applications are playing a more and more central and significant role in the contemporary world. As a global society, we are gaining scientific knowledge at an increasing rate and applying this knowledge to the development of new technologies. Such everyday items as tablets, laptop computers, cellular telephones, and microwave ovens were unknown as recently as 50 years ago.

The economies of many countries are dependent increasingly on the use of technology and the production of items whose operations are based on such technology, for example, optics, robotics, and artificial intelligence. Given that science and technology are playing such an important role in the development of society today, it is not surprising that more and more attention is being paid to teaching these subjects and how they are taught. The term "STEM," which is an acronym for science, technology, engineering, and mathematics, was first used by officials at the United States National Science Foundation in 2001. It has now come into everyday use. The topics in this chapter consider the teaching of STEM subjects in the United States and other countries.

Historically, science has played little role in education. In most societies, education emphasized on two points: teaching young people to read, write, and do basic arithmetic and providing instruction about religious principles underlying the societies in which these people were to live as adults. The development of science education would await two important changes—the development of the scientific method and the transition from the provision of education by religious institutions to its provision by the state.

The scientific method is based on linkages between inductive and deductive reasoning. Scientists use direct observation as well as observations from secondary sources to develop hypotheses, and these hypotheses are tested rigorously based on empirical observations and the analysis of data drawn from these observations. The scientific method as we know it today developed in Europe during the Renaissance, although aspects of what we recognize today as scientific method can be found in the history of many non-Western societies.

In England, Roger Bacon (c. 1220–c. 1292) was among the first scholars to set forth the basic principles of scientific inquiry, including observation, hypothesis formulation, experimentation, and independent verification through repeated experiments. However, the scientific method was not accepted universally among scholars and political leaders for several centuries. For example, Galileo Galilei (1564–1642) was among the first scientists to use technology in scientific observation when he developed and used a telescope powerful enough to allow him to undertake systematic astronomical observations. On the basis of these observations, Galileo concluded that the earth revolves around the sun. Because this observation was contrary to the accepted teachings of the Roman Catholic Church at that time, Church officials subjected Galileo to house arrest for the remainder of his life.

Today, of course, it is universally accepted that the earth does revolve around the sun, and scientific method is a standard practice. Nevertheless, teaching scientific principles to large numbers of children did not become commonplace until the nineteenth century, by which time education was managed by secular as opposed to religious authorities in many societies. In 1867, the British Academy for the Advancement of Science argued for the teaching of science and scientific method in public schools throughout the United Kingdom. In the United States, a framework for the teaching of science was prepared in the 1890s. (This framework is discussed in greater detail in the entry about STEM education in the United States.) By the early twentieth century, teaching of science had become commonplace. Usually, at the secondary level such teaching was divided into three branches—biology, chemistry, and physics. Relatively little attention was paid to the integration of these branches or to the relationships between them and mathematics.

In the United States and other countries, science and mathematics education in the early twentieth century often involved rote memorization. For example, students were expected to memorize multiplication tables and various chemical formulas. Memorization was often privileged at the expense of teaching and applying scientific method. Gradually, principles of scientific inquiry became a more important component of teaching science although relatively few initiatives to teach science in a more holistic manner were developed. As the twenty-first century approached, however, critics of scientific education argued for greater emphasis on observation and experimentation, integrating the traditionally separated scientific disciplines and the development of problem-solving skills that often required the use of technology.

Another key development in the teaching of STEM thinking has been the idea that everyone is able to grasp, understand, and use scientific concepts and methods. Historically, scientific knowledge was limited generally to the highly educated. Most people throughout the world prior to the nineteenth and twentieth centuries were illiterate. However, even those who were able to read and write and who had obtained some formal education were largely ignorant of the scientific process and its importance in the development and use of technology.

In recent years, this point can be illustrated by examining the history of computers. Of course, the first computers that were built and used after World War II were very large, sometimes taking up an entire room. But at that time, movies, comic strips, and television programs depicting these computers usually showed a man (invariably) next to them. This man was shown wearing a white lab coat with a slide rule in his pocket, and he usually spoke with a German accent. The message was that computers could be understood and used only by brilliant and highly trained scientists and that ordinary people could not hope to understand and operate them. Today, of course, even preschool children can use computers far more complicated and powerful than the primitive computers of the 1940s and 1950s. This example illustrates the importance of STEM in education of all people at all levels.

The need to integrate scientific disciplines with one another and with other components of education is recognized increasingly. Integration of traditional science with other aspects of teaching and learning was also advocated. In that context, the word "arts" has sometimes been added to the traditional acronym, turning the acronym into "STEAM." The concept of integrated and cross-disciplinary education has become especially significant as applied to the teaching of science and technology, particularly in light of the role that such technology now plays in the economic development of societies throughout the world. It is also important in developing problem-solving skills that will become necessary to address twenty-first century challenges such as climate change, environmental degradation, and other problems whose understanding requires a combination of scientific knowledge along with social studies and the humanities.

As the essays in this chapter indicate, approaches to STEM learning vary among countries and are related closely to a country's geographical position, demographics, and level of economic development. In some countries, STEM teaching has developed in a somewhat reactive manner. Such has been the case in the United States. For example, during the Cold War period in the 1950s many American educators and political leaders became concerned that the United States was falling behind the Soviet Union in the development of technology and in military capability. Hence, the U.S. government invested heavily in what we know today as STEM education. This included what was then known as the "new math," and in general a shift away from rote memorization toward a greater understanding of basic scientific principles.

STEM education has been critical to the economy of highly developed Singapore. Here, leading-edge technology has been very important to economic development given Singapore's small size and lack of natural resources. A similar situation characterizes Taiwan. The United Arab Emirates is one of the wealthiest countries in the world today. However, the UAE's economy is almost completely dependent on petroleum products. STEM education is regarded as essential to the UAE's efforts to diversify the country's economy in the long run.

Brazil is the fifth largest country in the world by both population and land area, and it has abundant natural resources and a young population. However, Brazil lags behind other countries in STEM education, in part because of corruption and bureaucracy and also because of a lack of coordinated planning. Once these issues have been resolved, it is expected that the technology sector will play a larger role in Brazil's economy, and STEM education is recognized as key to these developments. Slovenia has become the wealthiest and most developed country that was once part of Yugoslavia during the Cold War. High-technology activities have helped to augment Slovenia's traditional dependence on manufacturing. Observers of STEM education have noted that the country has done well in implementing STEM into its curricula, but that it has done less well in promoting science and technology among especially qualified and gifted students.

In less developed countries such as Guatemala and Jamaica, high-technology activities are regarded as important to economic development in that they are seen as means to reduce dependence on exports of agricultural products, minerals, and low-skill manufactured goods to developed countries such as the United States. Guatemala has been recognized as a typical "banana republic," while exports of sugar and bauxite along with tourism have dominated Jamaica's economy for many years. STEM education in these and other less developed countries has been developed, not only in order to develop their economies but also to reduce out-migration among young and more highly educated persons from these countries.

BRAZIL

The Federative Republic of Brazil is located in eastern South America and is by far the largest country in South America by both land area and population. It is the fifth largest country in the world by land area (following Russia, Canada, the United States, and China), with a land area of 3,287,597 square miles. Its population was estimated at more than 215 million as of 2022, making Brazil the fifth largest country in the world by population following China, India, the United States, and Indonesia.

Numerous Indigenous cultures lived in present-day Brazil for thousands of years prior to the arrival of European settlers in the late fifteenth and early sixteenth centuries. As European mariners began to explore and lay claim to non-European portions of the world, under the supervision of Pope Alexander VI (1432–1503) Spain and Portugal signed the Treaty of Tordesillas in 1494. Under terms of this treaty, a Line of Demarcation was to be drawn approximately 1100 miles west of the Cape Verde Islands off the coast of Africa. Areas west of the Line of Demarcation were to become part of the Spanish sphere of influence while areas to the east of the line were to become part of the Portuguese sphere of influence.

Because the Line of Demarcation cuts across the eastern portion of what is now Brazil, Portugal claimed sovereignty over areas along Brazil's Atlantic Coast. Portugal began to establish settlements along the coast in the 1530s and founded the city of Rio de Janeiro in 1565. The Portuguese expanded along the coast and eventually into the interior, establishing plantations upon which tropical crops were produced for export. In order to provide labor, the Portuguese imported millions of slaves from Africa. Today, Brazil's population remains highly diverse and contains large numbers of persons of mixed African, European, and Indigenous ancestry.

Brazil remained under Portuguese control until it became independent in 1822. The country was governed by a monarchy during most of the nineteenth century, but the monarchy was overthrown in 1889 and the country became a republic. For most of the next century, however, Brazil was governed by various dictators. Since 1985, Brazil has been a multiparty democracy. Its large land area and population

How Can STEM Education Help to Transition a Developing Country's Economy?

The economies of many less developed countries are dependent on agriculture, mining, and/or manufacturing, placing them at the mercy of global economic and environmental conditions. Education in the STEM fields is seen as an important aspect of helping to position a country's economy in today's information-based economy. Government education ministries and agencies such as the Ministry of Education in Guyana are working to develop STEM education by implementing technology and providing effective teacher training. Here, a fifth-grade student in Guyana interviewed the government's Minister of Education about how Guyana is developing its STEM education programs.

Source: Guyana Chronicle, "Transitioning Guyana through STEM education," April 7, 2019, http://guyanachronicle.com/2019/04/07/transitioning-guyana-through-stem-education. Retrieved on March 15, 2020.

along with a wide variety of natural resources have helped Brazil's economy to grow rapidly. It is now recognized as an emerging power, as part of the BRIC (Brazil, Russia, India, and China) group of quickly developing countries.

Education in Brazil

After Brazil was first settled by the Portuguese, Jesuit priests of the Roman Catholic Church were sent to Brazil beginning in 1549. The Jesuits established schools in the colony, although the majority of the people remained illiterate. However, the Jesuits operated largely outside the control of the Portuguese government, and they were accused of enriching themselves at the expense of Portugal. In 1759, the Portuguese crown expelled the Jesuits from the Portuguese empire, including Brazil. This expulsion was reinforced by Pope Clement XIV (1705–1774), who formally suppressed the Order in 1773.

After the expulsion and suppression of the Jesuits, the Portuguese government took over the administration of education. This function was transferred to the government of newly independent Brazil in 1822. However, at this time educational opportunities remained limited. In a census conducted in 1872, it was found that less than 20 percent of free Brazilian citizens could read and write. At that time, about 15 percent of Brazil's people were slaves, most of whom were also illiterate. Literacy rates began to increase in the twentieth century as successive governments began to invest more seriously in education. In 2017, it was estimated that about 92 percent of Brazilians over the age of 15 were literate.

Education is compulsory for Brazilian children between the ages of 6 and 14. Public education, which is administered by the Brazilian Ministry of Education, is free although many students attend private schools. Compulsory education consists of nine years, which corresponds roughly to kindergarten followed by grades 1 through 8 in American schools. Students may then continue on to secondary school, which lasts for three years. At that point, students may elect to pursue curricula intended to prepare them for college, or to pursue technical curricula to prepare them directly for the workplace. Portuguese is the language of instruction in public schools, although other languages may be used as languages of instruction in private schools. Students in upper elementary school are also taught one or two foreign languages, usually including English. However, critics are concerned that Brazil's education lags behind that in other large countries in that standardized test scores for Brazilian students are lower than those of comparable countries.

STEM Education in Brazil

Natural resources and agriculture have long been the core of Brazil's economy, along with tourism associated with Brazil's culture and diverse natural environments. Experts in Brazil have called attention to the presence of Brazil's large, relatively young, and well-educated population as evidence of the country's potential for the development of technology as a means of promoting economic development. Since the 1980s, however, the percentage of Brazil's gross domestic product devoted to high-technology industries has declined compared to other sectors of its economy.

Why has this happened? The decline has been attributed to expansion of the agricultural and service sectors, along with corruption and bureaucracy that have stymied high-technology start-up efforts. Also, Brazil's governments have tended to prioritize more traditional economic activities. However, economists suggest that Brazil would do well to develop high-technology operations associated with the country's traditional economic strengths. These could include agricultural technology and high-technology mining operations, including deep-sea drilling for oil and natural gas. Government investment in research and development increased during the first decade of the twenty-first century, although the rate of increase declined after 2012 as Brazil's economy went into a slowdown.

Historically, Brazil's educational system paid little attention to science. This began to change, however, during the 1960s. At that time, a program to modernize the teaching of physics was implemented, and science education centers were established. Despite the activities of Brazil's science education centers, efforts to promote STEM education in Brazil have been slowed down by a shortage of qualified teachers in STEM subjects. Also, many Brazilian teachers are paid poorly, and some have to work at second jobs in order to make ends meet. This shortage has been caused, in part, by Brazil's young and growing population that has increased the number of students. In response, various nongovernmental organizations and private corporations have initiated efforts to train STEM teachers. Thousands of trained teachers are now active in teaching these subjects.

These students are participating in a robotics "olympic" competition at their school in Salvador, Brazil. Brazil has invested considerable resources into the development of STEM education, as the government regards the development of high-technology industries and activities as critical to its further economic development. (Joa Souza | Dreamstime.com)

Further Reading

Lael Brainard and Leonardo Martinez-Dias (eds.), *Brazil as an economic superpower? Understanding Brazil's changing role in the global economy.* Washington, DC: Brookings Institution Press, 2009.

Patrick Greeley, "South America: Science education in Brazil striving for success," *Borgen Magazine*, August 10, 2017, https://www.borgenmagazine.com/science-education-in-brazil/. Retrieved on September 28, 2019.

Martin Raiser, "Brazil can improve education by copying its own successes," Brookings Institute, March 6, 2018, https://www.brookings.edu/blog/future-development/2018/03/06/brazil-can-improve-education-by-copying-its-own-successes/. Retrieved on September 28, 2019.

Julia E. Sweig, "A new global player: Brazil's far-flung agenda," *Foreign Affairs*, November/December 2010.

GUATEMALA

Guatemala is the northernmost and largest country by population in Central America, bordering Mexico to the north and west. Guatemala has a land area of about 42,000 square miles and a population of approximately 19 million as of 2022.

Much of present-day Guatemala was part of the Mayan Empire during the first millennium AD. Even today, Guatemala's population consists of a substantial number of people who are descended from persons living in the Mayan Empire and who speak Mayan as their first language. Present-day Guatemala was conquered by Spain in the early sixteenth century. It became part of the Spanish colonial empire for the next three centuries.

In 1821, Guatemala became independent as part of Mexico. Two years later, Guatemala seceded from Mexico and joined the United Provinces of Central America, which also included Honduras, El Salvador, Nicaragua, and Costa Rica. The United Provinces dissolved in 1840, and each of the provinces including Guatemala itself became an independent country. Guatemala has claimed sovereignty over present-day Belize, which was once a British colony known as British Honduras, since the nineteenth century. Today, Guatemala recognizes Belize's independence but continues to claim some of Belize's territory.

Beginning in 1960, Guatemala experienced a protracted civil war pitting the government against rebels drawn from the peasantry, including Indigenous Mayans. For much of this period, Guatemala was governed by dictators. It has been estimated that as many as 200,000 Guatemalans lost their lives during the civil war. Peace accords terminating the war officially were signed in 1996, and although accusations and evidence of corruption continue, the government has been led by popularly elected civilian presidents since then. However, the impacts of the protracted civil war and its aftermath continue. Today, Guatemala is the poorest country in Central America with a very large wealth disparity between the rich and the poor. Many Guatemalans leave the country temporarily or permanently in search of employment in the United States, Mexico, or other wealthier countries. Remittances from these expatriate workers have become a significant contributor to Guatemala's economy. Especially when such migration is illegal, however, the flow of Guatemalans to the United States and elsewhere has become a significant political issue in these countries.

Education in Guatemala

Guatemala has the least productive educational system in Central America, with very little government revenue devoted to schooling. Public education is managed by the Ministry of Education. However, education did not become compulsory until 1985. Many children attend private schools, many of which are run by Jesuits or other Roman Catholic organizations.

Guatemala's educational system, and the degree to which the Guatemalan population has been educated, has long been affected by Guatemala's poverty. Guatemala's literacy rate, which as of 2018 was only about 75 percent of the population, is the lowest in Central America. Schooling is free and compulsory for six years, although in practice the average Guatemalan child attends school for only four years.

Because of the Guatemalan Civil War, little progress in improvement in education was made during the 1960s, 1970s, and 1980s. The situation began to improve after the 1996 peace accords were signed. It has been estimated that the percentage of Guatemalan students who completed primary school increased from less than 40 percent in the early 1990s to more than 70 percent by 2006. However, education in Guatemala faces challenges associated with its history of civil unrest and government instability and its poverty. These problems include a lack of infrastructure along with a shortage of well-trained teachers. Many school buildings lack adequate space, teaching materials, and furniture, and some lack running water and sanitation facilities. Even today, less than half of girls and young women of Indigenous ancestry who live in rural areas are able to read and write.

Disparities in the quality of education remain substantial within Guatemala, where children of the poor continue to be at a disadvantage compared to children of the elite. Although public education in Guatemala is free, parents and legal guardians are responsible for uniforms, books, school supplies, and transportation, and many parents cannot afford these expenditures. Gender disparities are also evident, as boys have higher rates of literacy and higher rates of school attendance and completion than do girls. These differences have been attributed to Guatemala's patriarchal culture, in which girls are expected to devote their time and energy to taking care of the household and are not paid for such labor.

In 1965, the government mandated that Spanish would be the language of instruction throughout Guatemala, although it has been estimated that 40 percent of Guatemalans do not speak Spanish as a first language. As part of the 1996 peace accords, plans to promote bilingual education along with recognition of Indigenous peoples and their contributions to Guatemalan culture were implemented. Also, students in Guatemalan schools are now taught English as a second language.

Guatemala is one of the poorest countries in the Western Hemisphere. Many Guatemalans including these students are of Indigenous Mayan ancestry. Historically, Guatemala was a "banana republic" whose economy was dependent heavily on agriculture. With the help of international organizations, Guatemala is developing STEM education in an effort to diversify its economy. (Meunierd | Dreamstime.com)

The teaching of English has been beneficial to Guatemala's efforts to reorient its economy toward higher levels of technology.

Lack of access to educational opportunities is a particular problem among Mayans and other Indigenous Guatemalans. Many students not only lack access to educational opportunities but also many do not attend school at all or drop out early in order to work to support their families. Others, especially boys, regard school as useless because they intend to migrate to other countries in search of work when they become old enough to do so.

STEM Education in Guatemala

Historically, Guatemala's economy was based primarily on agriculture and the export of tropical crops of which sugar, coffee, and bananas have long been the most important. Guatemala's history of economic dependence on bananas and other crops, along with its history of government instability, has meant that it has been seen as a typical Central American "banana republic." In recent years, however, Guatemala's dependence on agriculture as a component of its economy has been declining. In 2013, it was estimated that only about 12 percent of Guatemala's gross domestic product was derived from the export of agricultural products. Manufacturing and tourism have been contributing increasingly to Guatemala's income from outside the country, although manufacturing has tended to emphasize low-value products such as apparel whose production generates low wages and poor working conditions.

Guatemala's poverty and history of economic dependency have meant that the degree to which its economy has been linked to higher levels of technology remains minimal. As late as 1996, it was estimated that only about 0.2 percent of Guatemala's gross domestic product was derived from technology. However, the Guatemalan government has begun to initiate efforts to promote the development and use of such technology. In particular, the government has developed programs that can provide entrepreneurs with venture capital and other resources to promote technology-oriented businesses.

These efforts must overcome many significant challenges. In 2017, for example, the Ministry of Education estimated that only 32 percent of Guatemalan high school graduates were proficient in math, including less than 10 percent of girls of Indigenous ancestry. STEM education has also been improving, in part because of investments and contributions from technology-oriented firms from outside Guatemala. For example, one firm has provided tablets to each teacher and administrator at an elementary school located in an impoverished part of the country's capital of Guatemala City. Training on how to use these tablets, including their use in the classroom, was also provided. Computer labs are also being set up. Although programs of this sort are still in the rudimentary and experimental stages, they are setting the stage for improving STEM education in Guatemala. It is anticipated that these improvements can eventually carry over into the country's economy as a whole, perhaps reducing the number of young Guatemalans who leave the country because of a perceived lack of opportunity at home.

Further Reading

Avivara, "Education in Guatemala," 2014, https://prezi.com/4xsd7cevlhbi/education-in -guatamala/. Retrieved on June 6, 2022.

Lakeala Frink, "Technology to empower students in Guatemala," Point of Rental Software, June 3, 2016, https://www.point-of-rental.com/technology-education-empower/. Retrieved on September 11, 2019.

MAIA, "Education and empowerment for girls in Guatemala," globalgiving.org, n.d., https://www.globalgiving.org/projects/education-empowerment-for-girls-in-guate mala/reports/?subid=146684. Retrieved on January 19, 2022.

Manuel Orozco and Marcela Valdivia, "Educational challenges in Guatemala and conse- quences for human capital and development," *Thedialogue.org*, February 2, 2017, https://www.thedialogue.org/analysis/educational-challenges-in-guatemala-and-con sequences-for-human-capital-and-development/. Retrieved on August 1, 2019.

JAMAICA

Jamaica is located in the Caribbean Sea, south of Cuba. The main island is one of the Greater Antilles along with Cuba, Hispaniola, and Puerto Rico. The country of Jamaica itself includes the main island of Jamaica and several small nearby islands. The overall land area of the country is 4,244 square miles. In 2022, Jamaica's pop- ulation was estimated at about 3 million.

Jamaica was first settled by Arawak and Taino people whose ancestors had moved northward from the Orinoco River basin in mainland South America. Christopher Columbus sighted Jamaica in 1494 and claimed it for Spain. However, Britain cap- tured Jamaica in 1655 and remained in de facto control of the island for the next two centuries until Spain formally ceded Jamaica to the British in 1870. The British developed Jamaica as a center for sugar production, and many African slaves were brought to Jamaica to provide labor. The economy was controlled by white planta- tion owners. Slavery was abolished throughout the British Empire in 1834, but even today about 90 percent of Jamaica's population consists of people of African ancestry.

In 1958, the British created and granted independence to Jamaica as part of the Federation of the West Indies, which also included Barbados and Trinidad along with several smaller islands. However, the Federation was unsuccessful, in part because Jamaica was far larger by both population and land area than the other islands and was also located well to the northwest of the Federation's other members. The Federation was dissolved in 1962, and Jamaica became fully inde- pendent. Since that time, Jamaica's economy has diversified, and it has come to be dominated by manufacturing, tourism, and the production of bauxite. Jamaica is well known throughout the world for its cultural and musical traditions, but it remains a relatively poor country characterized by high levels of violence. Devas- tating hurricanes have also hindered Jamaica's development.

Education in Jamaica

During the colonial period, most of Jamaica's people were slaves who received no education and were illiterate. Children of the wealthy were educated by private tutors and/or were sent to England for their schooling. After slaves were emancipated in 1834, the British began to provide basic education throughout Jamaican society. At first schooling was conducted by missionary societies, but beginning in the 1860s, it came to be managed by the colonial government. Although most former slaves and their descendants were now literate, during that time education was focused on training in agriculture and other occupations to prepare for their status as members of the lower class in Jamaican society as adults.

Following independence, the government of newly independent Jamaica made concerted efforts to provide universal public education and to eliminate the class distinctions associated with education during the colonial era. It has been estimated that while about 75 percent of Jamaican children of primary school age were enrolled in school in 1953, nearly 100 percent were enrolled by the late 1960s. Six years of schooling became compulsory.

In general, public schooling in Jamaica is based on the British model. Managed by the Ministry of Education, the Jamaican educational system includes six years of primary school, although many children also attend preschool. Pupils take national examinations after completing the fourth year and the sixth year of primary school. These examinations are highly competitive in that the results are used in placing students in secondary schools. Many students take extra classes on weekends and during vacation periods in order to prepare for these examinations.

Secondary school includes three years of "lower school" followed by two years of "upper school." After completing upper school, students take examinations administered by the Caribbean Examination Council. These examinations are seen as equivalent to O-level examinations in the United Kingdom. Students may then continue for another year and prepare for Caribbean Advanced Proficiency (CAPE) examinations. CAPE examinations, which are administered to students in former British colonies throughout the Caribbean region, are regarded to be equivalent to A-level examinations under the British system. English is the language of instruction throughout the entire period of schooling.

STEM Education in Jamaica

As is the case with many other less developed countries, Jamaica's economy is dependent on the economies of wealthier countries in North America and Europe. Historically, Jamaica was dependent on agriculture, notably the production and export of sugar and bananas. Bauxite, which is a form of sedimentary rock that contains substantial amounts of aluminum, was discovered in Jamaica in the 1940s. Bauxite production and exports of aluminum became a major contributor to Jamaica's economy. More recently, low-wage manufacturing and tourism have augmented these traditional extractive industries.

All of these activities, however, have kept Jamaica's economy dependent on those of more developed countries. In order to reduce such dependency, Jamaican officials have begun to place more emphasis on high-technology industry and other activities that can make Jamaica more competitive. Although Jamaica has attempted to become more competitive in the global economy, critics have argued that the country has not done enough to promote technology. It was pointed out that Jamaica's high technology remains overly dependent on foreign investment and that coordinated planning to implement technology is lacking. In order to address this issue, it is argued that Jamaica needs to develop a coordinated plan integrating efforts of the government, the private sector, and academia.

Such coordination has been seen as an important component of the development of education in the STEM disciplines. Recently, the Ministry of Education's policy included the words: "Emphasis will be placed on project-based and problem-solving learning, with science, technology, engineering and mathematics/ science, technology, engineering, arts and mathematics integrated at all levels." Perhaps significantly, the ministry's approach to the teaching of STEM includes the role of the arts and humanities in the conceptualization of problems and the development of solutions to such problems.

In order to implement this emphasis, the ministry has initiated efforts to develop a national STEM education policy including an integrative, multidisciplinary approach to the teaching and learning of science, technology, education, and mathematics. This program, which was first implemented on an experimental basis in 2014, includes efforts to improve the preparation of teachers to provide instruction in these subjects using this integrative approach at the primary and secondary levels. The program will also focus on research applications of the STEM disciplines, particularly as they may apply to the ongoing development of Jamaica's economy.

Further Reading

Jodi-Ann Gilpin, "Growth and jobs—Technology potential still untapped," *The Jamaica Gleaner*, December 18, 2018, http://jamaica-gleaner.com/article/news/20181218 /growth-jobs-technology-potential-still-untapped-thorpe. Retrieved on September 16, 2019.

Aldin Sweeney, "Promoting STEM education and literacy in Jamaica," *The Jamaica Gleaner*, April 7, 2019, http://jamaica-gleaner.com/article/art-leisure/20190407/promoting-stem -education-and-literacy-jamaica. Retrieved on September 16, 2019.

Miguel A. Thomas, "STEM has gathered steam . . . increased ministry funding; the arts now included," *Jamaica Observer*, September 24, 2017, http://www.jamaicaobserver.com /career-education/stem-has-gathered-steam_111822. Retrieved on September 16, 2019.

SINGAPORE

The Republic of Singapore is a small island country located off the coast of the Malay Peninsula, with Indonesia to the south and Malaysia to the north. The country contains the main island, also known as Singapore, and 62 smaller islands nearby. The Republic has a land area of 274 square miles, with 98 percent of this land on the main island. Singapore's population has been estimated at about 6 million in 2022.

Located along the Strait of Singapore connecting the Indian and Pacific Oceans, present-day Singapore has been an important trading and commercial and cultural center for more than 2,000 years. In the early nineteenth century, the British East India Company signed a treaty with the Shah of Johor in present-day Malaysia allowing the company to establish a trading port on the island. In 1824, the company obtained ownership of the entire island, and Singapore became a formal British colony in 1826.

Singapore remained a British colony until 1963, when it became part of the Federation of Malaysia. Singapore left the federation in 1965 and became independent. With a small land area and lacking natural resources, some doubted whether Singapore could succeed as an independent country. However, the government under the leadership of President Lee Kuan Yew (1923–2015) moved quickly to develop Singapore's economy. A key to Singapore's rapid economic development was the Port of Singapore, which by the early twenty-first century had become the largest port in the world. Singapore also embarked on a program of export-led industrialization analogous to that developed in Japan, by which goods for export were produced, and the profits from these exports used to strengthen and modernize industries. Singapore is a multicultural society. As of 2015, about 75 percent of Singapore's people were ethnic Chinese. Thirteen percent were of Malay ancestry and nine percent were of Indian descent.

Education in Singapore

Trade and industrial production have propelled Singapore from a less developed country to one of the strongest economies in the world. In 2017, Singapore's gross domestic product was estimated at more than $93,000 per capita, with the result that Singapore had the third highest per capita gross domestic product in the world.

Development and use of sophisticated technology has been an important key to Singapore's rapid economic development. Early in its history, Singapore's factories produced relatively inexpensive consumer goods for export. As its economy grew, Singapore began to use the profits associated with the export of these goods to invest in technology, especially in telecommunications, electronics, and biotechnology. Singapore expanded its impact on international trade by becoming a financial and banking center, and it remains a leading oil-refining center.

Singapore's emphasis on technology, banking, and trade as drivers of ongoing economic development, along with its diversity, has had an important impact on education in Singapore. Education has been an ongoing high priority, with about 20 percent of the national budget devoted to education as compared to about 14 percent worldwide. The educational system is geared to Singapore's position in the global economy. For example, although Chinese, Malay, Tamil, and English are all official languages in Singapore, English became and remains the language of instruction. English was chosen as the primary language for education because of the importance of English in the global economy, although pupils also study at least one of Singapore's other official languages.

Within these contexts, the educational system in Singapore is based on the British model reflecting Singapore's history as a British colony. Beginning at the age of three, students in Singapore complete three years of preschool followed by six years of primary school and five years of secondary school. Attendance is compulsory, and parents who do not comply with compulsory education laws are subject to criminal punishment. Primary school students study English along with their "mother tongue," and they also study science, mathematics, and social studies. After four years of primary school, students are given examinations in these subjects. Those who score very well on these examinations are streamed into the Special or Express track. Those with lower scores are placed in the Normal track, which is subdivided between Normal (Academic) and Normal (Vocational) curricula. Students completing secondary school take O-level or A-level examinations, similar to the procedure used in the United Kingdom. However, those regarded as "academically gifted" can skip the O-level examinations and proceed directly to the A-levels and to universities.

Given that education is highly prioritized, the streaming process has resulted historically in social stigma against those students who are placed in what are considered the "lower" tracks. In particular, many believed that placement in the vocational track was associated with low academic achievement and lack of intellectual ability. Parents were concerned also that their children placed in this track would get lower-quality educations and would have difficult times obtaining good jobs upon graduation.

At the secondary level, Singapore's educational system has also emphasized meritocracy, with levels of merit associated with high levels of performance in competitive examinations. Public education is free, except parents are charged nominal fees for "miscellaneous expenses." However, competitive pressure has encouraged many students to send their children to private schools and/or to programs providing additional instruction outside of normal classroom hours. These programs are expensive and lower-income families often cannot afford them. However, according to one estimate, about 70 percent of Singaporean parents of secondary school pupils send their children to these private schools.

According to some measures including international comparison of standardized test scores, the educational system of Singapore has been identified as one of the best educational systems in the world. However, critics have argued that Singapore's educational system is elitist and rigid and that it stifles creative thinking. Moreover, the highly competitive nature of the system has resulted in significant psychological pressure on many students, even at the beginning of secondary school.

STEM Education in Singapore

Throughout the educational system, the government of Singapore has emphasized using its resources to link education to expected workforce demands. In particular, since Singapore has emerged as a highly developed country, training in technology and its use in schooling have been regarded as essential to Singapore's competitiveness in the world economy. Government officials have stressed encouraging

Singapore is a small island country lacking natural resources, but it is one of the wealthiest countries in the world. Telecommunications, biotechnology, electronics, and other technology-oriented industries have been very important to Singapore's development. Singapore pays careful attention to teaching STEM subjects to its students to prepare them for careers in high-technology sectors. (Valerie Lee | Dreamstime.com)

high-achieving students to focus on science, technology, engineering, and mathematics although many such students are focusing on finance, medicine, or law. Technology has played an important role in the educational process as well. For example, Singapore is regarded as one of the world's leaders in the use of digital technology in the classroom.

These considerations have also affected vocational and technical training. In the 1990s, the government established the Institute of Technical Education (ITE), which provides training and apprenticeships in a variety of technical fields. Strong efforts were made to persuade students and parents that enrollment in ITE should not be regarded as a fallback program for students lacking academic ability. Curricula in ITE and similar schools have been oriented to the projected needs of Singapore's increasingly service-oriented economy. Overall, Singapore's educational system and its emphasis on technology, despite its shortcomings, have been regarded as highly successful and crucial to Singapore's ongoing development.

Further Reading

Pearl Lee, "Science, technology, engineering, math skills crucial to Singapore for the next 50 years," *The Straits Times*, May 8, 2015, http://www.straitstimes.com/singapore/education/science-technology-engineering-math-skills-crucial-to-singapore-for-next-50. Retrieved on February 2, 2018.

Hetty Musfirah and Abdul Khamid, "Pursuing a vocational track—An alternative pathway to success?" channelnewsasia.com, November 8, 2015, https://www.channelnewsasia.com/news/singapore/pursuing-a-vocational-track-an-alternative-pathway-to-success-8250196. Retrieved on February 2, 2018.

Shivali Nayak, "Singapore schools: 'The best educational system in the world' putting significant stress on young children," ABC News Australia, January 5, 2016, http://www.abc.net.au/news/2016-01-06/best-education-system-putting-stress-on-singaporean-children/6831964. Retrieved on February 2, 2018.

Vivien Stewart, "Singapore: Innovation in technical education," 2016, https://asiasociety.org/global-cities-education-network/singapore-innovation-technical-education. Retrieved on February 2, 2018.

SLOVENIA

The Republic of Slovenia is located in central Europe between Italy, Austria, Hungary, and Croatia. It has a short coastline on the Adriatic Sea to the south. A former constituent republic within Yugoslavia, Slovenia has a land area of about 7,800 square miles and a population of about 2.1 million, as of 2022.

Given its location, it is not surprising that present-day Slovenia has been contested by various neighboring powers for more than 2000 years. The region became part of the Roman Empire during the first century BC. In the late fourth century, Germanic and Slavic peoples invaded the territory, which was abandoned by the Romans in about 400 AD. The Slavic invaders, most of whom moved to the region in the ensuing two centuries, became the ancestors of today's Slovenians. During the fifteenth century, present-day Slovenia became part of the Habsburg Empire. It remained part of the Habsburg Empire, which later became the Austrian Empire, until the empire was dissolved and dismembered after World War I.

After the war, Slovenia joined with nearby Croatia and Serbia to form the Kingdom of the Slovenes, Croats, and Serbs. In 1929, the kingdom became known as the Kingdom of Yugoslavia. Before and during World War II, present-day Slovenia was invaded by the Axis Powers, and control of the area was divided between Nazi Germany and fascist Italy. After the war, Slovenia became part of reconstituted Yugoslavia, which was ruled by a Communist government that nevertheless operated independently of the Soviet Union.

The Yugoslav federation split apart in 1990. At that time, a large majority of Slovenes voted to make the country an independent state. Independence was declared in 1991, and Slovenia joined the European Union in 2004. Both before and after World War II, Slovenia had been industrialized substantially by the Yugoslav government. This industrial activity, along with Slovenia's location adjacent to Italy and Austria, has made Slovenia the most developed and wealthiest country in the former Yugoslavia and has facilitated its transition to a post-Communist economy and society. Most residents of Slovenia speak the Slovenian language, which is known as Slovene and is the official language of the country. However, some Slovenians speak Hungarian or Italian as their first language. Many of these people live near Slovenia's borders with Hungary to the northeast and Italy to the west.

In these regions, Hungarian and Italian are recognized as having coequal official status with Slovene.

Education in Slovenia

In 1869, the Austrian Empire enacted the Law on Primary School Education, via which state-supported schools were established throughout the empire. The law made eight years of schooling compulsory in many parts of the empire, but only six years of schooling were compulsory in Slovenia and other poorer, less developed parts of the empire. Rates of illiteracy dropped rapidly, although for most children formal schooling ended after six to eight years. Although both boys and girls attended primary schools, secondary education beyond the age of compulsory schooling was generally limited to boys.

The Kingdom of the Slovenes, Croats, and Serbs mandated equal access to education for both boys and girls and made secondary education more accessible to the general population. After World War II, school attendance became universal. By 1971, the percentage of Slovenian children attending primary school was nearly 100 percent, while the percentage of eligible students attending secondary school doubled from 20 percent to more than 40 percent between 1953 and 1971. As the most industrialized and wealthiest republic comprising the former Yugoslavia, Slovenia led that country in educational attainment before Yugoslavia's breakup and continues to do today compared to the other countries that comprised Yugoslavia.

Today, education in Slovenia is managed by the National Education Institute of the Republic of Slovenia. Education is compulsory between the ages of 6 and 15. Primary school takes place within this age range. The system includes two periods. The first five years comprise the first period, and the next four years comprise the second period. During the first period, students are taught in their first language (Slovenian, Hungarian, or Italian). Science and foreign languages are taught formally beginning during this second period. After completing the second period, most Slovenian students move on to secondary school. Students may select between general grammar schools, which are intended to prepare them for college, and vocational and technical schools.

STEM Education in Slovenia

Before World War I, present-day Slovenia's economy was oriented to agriculture, forestry, and fishing. After that war, however, Yugoslavia's government emphasized the development of manufacturing, including heavy machinery. Slovenia's manufacturing sector has contributed significantly to the country's prosperity relative to the prosperity of the other former Yugoslav republics. Today, Slovenia is encouraging the development of high-technology economic activity. Such activities include information technology, cyber-security, and software development. However, some economists express concern that such activity is oriented excessively to export, as opposed to the development of local high-technology activities whose profits would remain within the country. Critics have also suggested that Slovenia would benefit with a more aggressive and concerted program of promoting high-technology start-ups.

Achieving the goal of expanding high-technology industry has resulted in renewed and expanded interest in STEM education in Slovenia. However, such improvements remain in the rudimentary stage. In particular, Slovenia has been seen as lagging behind other countries with comparable economic status in the identification and nurturing of children who have demonstrated talent in science and mathematics. The country is seen as having been slow in adapting its science curricula to the needs of such students. In addition, teachers generally have little input in the development of STEM curricula, including promotion of problem-solving, integrative, and collaborative approaches to learning.

On the positive side, Slovenia has done well in providing education in digital technology at schools throughout the country. Computers are used universally at the second-stage primary and the secondary levels, allowing students to access, process, and display information digitally. This is seen as an improvement upon traditional methods of learning involving pencil and paper. Also, efforts to introduce girls and young women to technology have succeeded. In 2017, the European Union reported that the percentage of STEM college graduates who were female was the highest among all European Union member countries.

Further Reading

Borgen Project, "Education in Slovenia," 2017, https://borgenproject.org/education-in-slovenia/. Retrieved on September 30, 2019.

Claudia Patricolo, "Slovenia: An optimistic, export-led economy with first-world problems," Emerging Europe, January 18, 2018, https://emerging-europe.com/intelligence/slovenia-an-optimistic-export-led-economy-with-first-world-problems/. Retrieved on September 30, 2019.

Gregor Torkar, Stanislav Avsec, Mojca Čepič, Vesna Ferk Savec, and Mojca Juriševič, "Science and technology education in Slovenian compulsory basic school: Possibilities for gifted education," *Roeper Review*, 40 (2018), pp. 139–150.

TAIWAN

The Republic of China claims to be the legitimate government of all of China. However, the republic actually controls only the island of Taiwan along with several small offshore islands. Taiwan is located in the western Pacific Ocean about 100 miles southeast of mainland China, about 150 miles southwest of Japan's Ryukyu Islands, and about 250 miles north of the Philippines. The overall land area of Taiwan, including the nearby islands, is about 14,000 square miles. In 2022, the population was estimated at 24 million.

Humans are believed to have first settled in Taiwan as many as 25,000 years ago. Descendants of these Indigenous people continue to live in Taiwan today. However, about 84 percent of Taiwan's people are ethnic Taiwanese, whose ancestors first moved to Taiwan about 5000 or 6000 years ago. Portuguese mariners first visited Taiwan in 1544 and named the island Formosa. Over the next several centuries, other European powers attempted to establish colonies on Taiwan, but China remained in control. Japan took over Taiwan in 1895 and retained control of the island until after World War II, when sovereignty was returned to China. The Chinese civil war between the Nationalist government and Communist rebels was in full swing when China resumed control of Taiwan. In 1949, the Communists took control of mainland China, renaming the country the People's Republic of China. Nationalist leaders, including President Chiang Kai-Shek (1887–1975), moved to Taiwan and continued to claim sovereignty over the mainland. Today about 15 percent of the population of Taiwan are descended from these immigrants from mainland China. However, the People's Republic of China continues to claim sovereignty over Taiwan.

Taiwan's economy boomed beginning in the 1960s and 1970s. Chiang Kai-Shek maintained authoritarian rule over Taiwan until he died in 1975. After Chiang's death, Taiwan began to transition toward multiparty democracy while its economy grew rapidly. The first fully democratic election was held in 1996. Taiwan's economic boom has been associated with government-sponsored efforts to promote science, engineering, and technology. Semiconductors, information technology, nanotechnology, artificial intelligence, and optronics, or the development and use of instruments designed to detect and control light and forms of invisible radiation such as gamma rays and X-rays, are particularly important to the contemporary Taiwanese economy. As in Japan and other Asian countries, high-technology firms in Taiwan operate in close association with governmental agencies. Government efforts include the maintenance of three high-technology science and industrial parks.

Education in Taiwan

European colonists, Christian missionaries, and Chinese government officials first established formal schools in Taiwan during the seventeenth century. However, only a very small minority of children in Taiwan actually attended school. During the early twentieth century, the Japanese established an island-wide system of primary schools, and it has been estimated that by 1945, the literacy rate in Taiwan exceeded 70 percent. Under the Japanese, six years of primary education became compulsory. The length of compulsory education was increased to nine years in 1968.

Today, the government's Ministry of Education is in charge of education in Taiwan. The system includes six years of primary school followed by three years of junior high school. Formal education beyond junior high school is not compulsory. However, it is estimated that about 95 percent of Taiwanese teenagers continue to high school, which lasts for three years. Mandarin Chinese is the language of instruction, although students also study English beginning in the third year of primary school. The overall literacy rate in Taiwan exceeds 98 percent.

As is the case in other East Asian countries, students must pass a stringent set of national examinations before entering high school and before graduating from high school. In 2014, the government announced a plan to extend the number of years of compulsory education from 9 years to 12 years. This plan also meant that students would no longer be required to pass an examination before entering high school. However, high school curricula in Taiwan include an academic track and a vocational track. Those students wishing to pursue an academic track must still pass a rigorous national examination, and results on this examination are used in determining placement within academic high school programs.

At the junior high school and senior high school levels, Taiwanese students achieve some of the highest proficiency scores in mathematics and science in the world. However, critics have argued that the Taiwanese educational system overemphasizes rote memorization at the expense of creativity and critical thinking. Critics have also claimed that the system places undue stress on students. In addition to formal instruction in schools themselves, many Taiwanese junior high school and high school students take additional instruction outside of formal schooling, known as "cram schooling," in order to prepare themselves for the national examinations. Such a system is seen as not only placing additional pressure on students, but it also takes time away from socializing, sports, the arts, and other activities. It has been argued also that cram schools, along with emphasis on standardized testing and memorization, have reduced students' motivation to learn and succeed in school.

STEM Education in Taiwan

Science and technology are emphasized in junior high school and for many students in high school. Junior high school students take courses in technology for all three years as well as one year each of biology, chemistry, physics, and earth science. The academic high school curriculum contains two tracks, including a science track and a liberal arts track. The science track is focused on preparing students for careers in science and engineering and includes advanced mathematics and science courses. The intent of such courses is to enhance preparation of Taiwanese students for careers in advanced technologies, with the underlying goal of promoting ongoing economic development.

Despite Taiwan's tradition of learning via rote memorization in keeping with China's Confucian traditions, in recent years the Ministry of Education has begun to take steps to move away from this traditional model. During the 1990s, the ministry developed and implemented a revised mathematics curriculum that places more emphasis on solving problems and applying them to real-world situations, as opposed to the traditional practice of teaching mathematics through the memorization of formulas. In 2017, the ministry began to implement additional changes, reinforcing problem-solving and focusing on the development of group projects and understanding the reasons underlying solving problems. Less emphasis is being placed on simply attaining correct answers in order to score highly in competitive examinations. Similar goals are being implemented with respect to other aspects of STEM instruction.

These shifts in STEM teaching have been accompanied by ongoing shifts in educational technologies, including the use of online resources and smart boards.

In one private school, the library was replaced by an open space known as the Information Commons. However, STEM education in Taiwan, as in other countries, has been affected by gender bias. In response, the government's Department of Gender Equality has promoted efforts to reach out to girls and young women in order to promote the STEM disciplines. Concerns have also been raised about relationships between STEM participation and wealth disparities. Children of the wealthy are more likely to be educated in the STEM disciplines, and children from relatively poor families are likely to be disadvantaged in that regard. This has been a particular issue with respect to Taiwan's Indigenous population, whose members have been disadvantaged traditionally. New educational plans involving more understanding of Indigenous cultures are being developed, with the intent of integrating these populations further into the Taiwanese economy.

Further Reading

Timothy Ferry, "Bringing technology into the classroom," *Taiwan Business Topics*, November 23, 2015, https://topics.amcham.com.tw/2015/11/bringing-technology-into-the-class room/. Retrieved on September 9, 2019.

Andrew Paulsen, "The shifting landscape of math education in Taiwan," andrewpaulsen. org, April 29, 2018, https://andrewpaulsen.org/2018/04/29/the-shifting-landscapes-of -math-education-in-taiwan/. Retrieved on September 9, 2019.

Anna Shen, "At Taiwan's APEC workshop, a call to promote women in STEM," *Huffington Post*, November 19, 2017, https://www.huffpost.com/entry/at-taipeis-apec-workshop-a-call-to -promote-women_b_59f0092fe4b057084e532cc9. Retrieved on September 9, 2019.

Jessie Yang, "Taiwan's educational system is failing its youth," *TheNewsLens*, November 8, 2016, https://international.thenewslens.com/article/46431. Retrieved on September 9, 2019.

UNITED ARAB EMIRATES

The United Arab Emirates (UAE) is a federation of seven emirates located in the southeastern portion of the Arabian Peninsula. The seven emirates that comprise the UAE include Abu Dhabi, Ajman, Dubai, Fujairah, Ras al-Khaimah, Sharjah, and Umm al-Quwain. Each of these seven emirates is ruled by a hereditary monarch, and the seven rulers jointly form the country's governing Federal Supreme Council. The overall land area of the UAE is about 32,000 square miles, although most of this land surface consists of uninhabited desert.

As of 2022, the population of the UAE was approximately 10.2 million. About half live in either Abu Dhabi or Dubai, which are the two largest emirates and which dominate the UAE both economically and politically. The UAE contains vast proven oil reserves whose exploitation has made the federation one of the wealthiest countries in the world.

Located along trade routes connecting the Persian Gulf and the Indian Ocean, the present-day UAE has been an important center for trade for more than 2000 years. In the nineteenth century, the British became the dominant naval power in the region. In 1892, Britain and the local emirates signed a treaty that would guarantee British protection from attacks by foreign powers in exchange for grant-ing the British control of shipping lanes in the Persian Gulf. The present-day Emir-ates became known as the Trucial States.

In 1929, Dubai became a duty-free port. It enlarged its port facilities to accom-modate deepwater oceangoing ships. In the late 1960s, leaders of the emirates began negotiations to unite. Dubai agreed to federate with Abu Dhabi under the condition that Dubai would be allowed to retain its status as a duty-free port. The other five emirates soon joined the federation, which became fully independent in 1971. Oil was discovered in the region in the 1960s and soon became the mainstay of the UAE's economy, although the economy has subsequently diversified con-siderably. Since then, the population of the UAE has grown very rapidly. Because of the availability of jobs associated with petroleum production, it is believed that more than 75 percent of the UAE's population consists of expatriates, especially from South Asia.

Education in the United Arab Emirates

Prior to the establishment of the UAE as an independent federation in 1971, most formal education in the emirates was conducted locally by Muslim imams, who were known as Mutawas. Mutawas were religious leaders of their communities, and they taught students the Qur'an along with principles of the Islamic faith, reading, writing, and basic mathematics. Many of the Mutawas taught these les-sons in mosques.

More secular education was introduced in the mid-twentieth century. The fed-eral government of the UAE assumed responsibility for education following inde-pendence. At that time, the government mandated the establishment of free public schools in communities throughout the country. Its aim was to promote literacy and education as important components of economic development. Since then, levels of literacy have increased dramatically. In 1975, it is believed that less than 45 percent of UAE's citizens could read and write, including less than a third of women. Today, by contrast, the literacy rate in the UAE is over 95 percent for both genders.

Education in the contemporary UAE is administered by the government's Min-istry of Education. The ministry is responsible for adherence to the basic structure, although each of the seven emirates has specific responsibility for schooling within its jurisdiction, and the specific educational process varies among them. Formal schooling is compulsory for nine years, beginning at the age of six. Children must complete six years of primary school, followed by three years of lower secondary or "preparatory" school. After completing this schooling, students may go on to upper secondary school for three additional years. In 2016, about 96 percent of eligible students graduated from upper secondary schools.

Arabic, which is spoken throughout the country and is the first language for most native-born UAE citizens, is the language of instruction in public schools. English is also taught at the secondary level and is the language of instruction at most colleges and universities in the UAE. However, because of the large expatriate population a majority of children of native-born parents residing in the UAE attend private schools. Each emirate oversees and audits its private schools, with the stipulation that each private school must provide classes in Islamic principles and in the Arabic language.

STEM Education in the United Arab Emirates

Prior to independence, what formal education existed in the present-day United Arab Emirates emphasized religion and was based on principles of rote memorization. Since independence, however, the UAE government has placed substantial emphasis on the teaching of science and technology. Education in the STEM disciplines is seen as crucial to continued integration of the UAE into the global economy. Despite recognition of the importance and value of STEM, most UAE schools do not begin formal instruction in these areas until completion of primary school.

Critics of STEM education in the UAE have argued that the system is antiquated. They have claimed that the UAE's educational procedures continue to emphasize a teacher-centric, lecture-oriented, and memorization-based method of instruction. This approach to teaching, which some regard as archaic, may be a carryover from the UAE's history of educating students based on rote memorization as opposed to a focus on problem-solving and applications to real-world issues and problems. The four components of STEM are generally taught separately, rather than in an integrated fashion, further reducing the effectiveness of STEM education. Many STEM teachers in the Emirates are recruited from overseas, making integration of STEM education into the educational process more problematic.

Critics have claimed also that the system is more reactive than proactive and that technologies likely to become important in the future such as artificial intelligence and robotics have been downplayed or overlooked. Overlooking such

---

Robotics in South Sudan

South Sudan, which became independent in 2011, is one of the world's poorest countries. Its poverty and its history of civil war since independence have made the provision of even basic education very difficult. However, in 2017, a STEM educational center was established at the University of Juba in South Sudan's capital city. Students associated with this center designed and built robots that can be used to remove plastics and other polluting wastes from bodies of water with the idea of helping to address ongoing problems with ocean pollution. The South Sudanese students entered an international robotics competition where the team finished in the top third of teams from 189 countries.

Source: Xinhua.net, "Young tech enthusiasts emerge in conflict-torn South Sudan," February 17, 2020, http://www.xinhuanet.com/english/2020-02/17/c_138792476.htm. Retrieved on March 15, 2020.

technologies has been regarded as reducing the degree to which graduates of UAE's schools will be less prepared for careers in engineering and technology in the globalized world of the twenty-first century. However, in 2015, two schools in which programming and robotics were taught at the primary-school level were opened in Dubai. The release of the World Economic Forum's report on economic changes associated with rapid technological development has also spurred government efforts to improve STEM education. For example, teachers are not only focusing in more detail on problem-solving approaches to instruction in STEM disciplines, but they are also incorporating technologies such as smart boards and tablets as opposed to traditional blackboards, pencils, and paper in delivering this knowledge to UAE students.

Further Reading

Ali Alhebsi, Lincoln D. Pettaway, and Lee Waller, "A history of education in the United Arab Emirates and trucial sheikdoms," *The Global eLearning Journal*, 4 (2015), pp. 1–6, https://aurak.ac.ae/publications/A-History-of-Education-in-the-United-Arab-Emirates-and-Trucial-Sheikdoms.pdf. Retrieved on September 9, 2019.

Edarabia, "Two UAE public schools to introduce STEM classrooms," 2015, https://www.edarabia.com/104763/two-uae-public-schools-to-introduce-stem-classrooms/. Retrieved on September 9, 2019

Dhanusha Gokulan, "Pricey STEM education not good enough," *Khaleej Times*, January 19, 2019, https://www.khaleejtimes.com/news/education/pricey-stem-education-not-good-enough. Retrieved on September 9, 2019.

Caline Malek, "UAE embraces emerging technologies in education," *The Arab Weekly*, April 29, 2018, https://thearabweekly.com/uae-embraces-emerging-technologies-education. Retrieved on September 9, 2019.

UNITED STATES

STEM education in the United States has undergone several fundamental transitions over the course of American history. In many cases, these transitions have occurred in response to important changes in the American economy and geopolitical situation.

Prior to the late nineteenth century, little attention was paid to the teaching of science in public schools. Common schooling as introduced during the nineteenth century emphasized reading, writing, and arithmetic. This pattern began to change especially after 1890, however, in part because the percentage of American youths attending high school was increasing quickly. At that time, the Committee of Ten on Secondary School Studies, under the auspices of the National Education Association, issued a report with recommendations concerning the structure of high school education. The report contained recommendations concerning science teaching, including advocacy of laboratory work as well as memorization. However, over the next half century education came to emphasize standardization, with science being seen as a set of facts to be memorized.

Concerns about the status of science and mathematics education in the United States resurfaced during and after World War II, and especially during the 1950s at the height of the Cold War. On October 4, 1957, the Soviet Union launched Sputnik I, which was the world's first artificial satellite. The successful launch of Sputnik I led to what became known as the Sputnik crisis, as many American political and business leaders, journalists, and scientists became alarmed that the Soviets were outpacing the United States in technology.

A year later, President Dwight D. Eisenhower (1890–1969) gave a televised address in which he articulated his view that the Sputnik launch meant that Americans needed to recognize the possibility that the Soviets were ahead of the United States in the development of space technology and that if this lead continued then the Soviets could become a more direct military threat to the United States. In response, the National Aeronautics and Space Administration (NASA) was established in 1958, when the first American artificial satellite was launched. This achievement led to what became known as the "space race," in which the Soviets and Americans competed for success in the exploration of outer space. American leaders were also concerned about the Soviets' perceived superiority in the numbers and quality of long-range missiles that could conceivably have been used in a war, a perception leading to what was called the "missile gap."

Education played a prominent role in American response to Sputnik, the space race, and the missile gap. During and after the Sputnik crisis, considerable attention began to be paid to the structure and process of American public education. Critics argued that American education was poorly organized and had become antiquated in light of changes associated with the Cold War. For example, many school districts in rural areas provided service to only small numbers of students, some of whom were still educated in one-room schoolhouses. Thus, it was argued that education could be provided more effectively and efficiently once these small districts were consolidated into larger districts.

In 1958, Congress passed the National Defense Education Act (NDEA). Proponents of the NDEA argued that the United States was suffering from a shortage of highly trained scientists, engineers, and mathematicians. The development of computers also created a need for qualified programmers. Moreover, many of the leading American scientists and mathematicians at that time were refugees who had been born, raised, and trained in Europe but moved to the United States before, during, and after World War II. Among the best known of these refugee scientists and mathematicians were Albert Einstein (1879–1955), Enrico Fermi (1901–1954), and Hans Bethe (1906–2005). Thus, it was argued that there was a strong need for the training of American-born scientists and engineers.

The NDEA provided federal funding for mathematics and science education. By 1960, federal funding to support STEM education was nearly six times more than it had been in the early 1950s. Many of these funds were directed toward college and postgraduate education, although the NDEA had a significant impact on K-12 education as well. New curricula for the teaching of high school biology, chemistry, and physics were developed. These curricula emphasized scientific method and the process of scientific inquiry. A physics curriculum was developed by a committee of prominent physicists known as the Physical Science Study Committee (PSSC).

In describing the work of the committee, Nathan Belcher wrote, "Physics was not to be presented as a body of unchanging facts that students must memorize; rather, physics is best understood as living discipline with which students engage. Although one goal of the PSSC course was that students would learn physics content, the other goal of the PSSC course emphasized the process of reasoning from empirical evidence." This meant that students were to find evidence, often from laboratory work, and use this evidence to evaluate hypotheses and theories. This knowledge, in turn, would be used in teaching students to solve problems and to apply these solutions to real-world situations. The biology curriculum developed under NDEA auspices was based on an analogous approach. However, it became controversial because it included the teaching of evolution as a scientific theory—a perspective that continued to be rejected by some religious fundamentalists even today.

Another development associated with the implementation of the NDEA was what became known as the New Mathematics, or "New Math." As was the case with science education prior to the Sputnik crisis, critics of mathematical education at the time of the Sputnik crisis argued that such teaching emphasized memorization and repetition at the expense of developing understanding of underlying concepts and principles. In response, memorization of multiplication tables was de-emphasized, while more emphasis was placed on understanding the meaning of multiplication as successive addition. Concepts of algebra, set theory, and other mathematical principles were introduced into elementary as well as secondary curricula, again with the idea of teaching the understanding of underlying concepts.

Beginning in the 1990s, educational experts began to recognize a need for renewed improvement in the teaching of STEM subjects. As before, this recognition was driven in part by global events. The collapse of the Soviet Union paved the way for rapid increases in economic and political globalization as Russia and other formerly Communist countries began, with varying degrees of success, to implement market economies and democratic governments. Also, concern about the state of the global environment intensified. Awareness of and concern for the state of the natural environment and its quality had increased during the 1960s, culminating in the first Earth Day on April 22, 1970. However, by the beginning of the twenty-first century the impacts of human activity on the environment had become much better understood. By this time, most scientists and many members of the general public had become aware of global warming and its potential effects on society.

At around the same time, the levels of student achievement in science and mathematics were compared across different countries. Average achievement scores for American students lagged behind those of other countries. For example, in a 2015 study scores on tests administered to 15-year-old students via the Program for International Student Achievement were compared among countries throughout the world. The average American score ranked the United States in the 24th place, with Singapore, Japan, Estonia, Taiwan, and Finland ranking in the top five. In mathematics, the United States ranked 38th, with Singapore, Taiwan, Japan, South

---

A STEM-Focused High School Provides Opportunities for Students with Autism

The STEM3 Academy in Los Angeles is one of many high schools throughout the country whose curricula are focused on STEM disciplines. But STEM3 is unique in that its enrollment is composed of students who are on the autistic spectrum or have other learning disabilities such as attention-deficit disorder. The school provides a low-stress environment for its students with learning disabilities. Lesson plans are personalized to fit the needs of each student, and teachers link instruction in social and life skills to the teaching of scientific concepts. The curriculum also emphasizes preparation for employment in STEM-related fields beyond high school.

Source: Samantha Cowan, "Kids with autism find paths to success at STEM-focused school," takepart.com, October 31, 2016, http://www.takepart.com/feature/2016/10/31/los-angeles -stem-school. Retrieved on March 15, 2020.

Korea, and Switzerland in the top five. Examination of data such as these generated concern that American students were falling behind their peers in other countries in learning science and mathematics, especially in comparison with students from East Asia.

These considerations encouraged American educational experts to rethink once again the process of teaching STEM subjects to K-12 students. In particular, experts advocated a more integrative approach to STEM teaching. Historically, mathematics, biology, chemistry, and physics each had been taught as independent subjects. However, during the early twenty-first century it came to be recognized that teaching them in an integrative, collaborative manner could be more effective. For example, as indicated in the chapter on sustainability in this volume, educators became aware that more meaningful teaching of environmental issues could be achieved best by integrating not only the STEM disciplines but also economics and the social sciences. The integration of arts and the humanities was also advocated, leading to adding arts to the traditional acronym and changing it to "STEAM."

STEM teaching has also become linked more and more to developing technology. Online resources, including virtual laboratories, are being used increasingly. With a virtual laboratory, for example, a student can repeat an experiment hundreds or thousands of times without relying on the actual laboratory equipment. These considerations have also focused attention on the role of computer programming, including teaching these skills at the K-12 level, even at the elementary school level.

Another issue of concern is that of gender. Boys and men continue to study STEM subjects at advanced levels more than girls and women do. For example, more than twice as many boys as girls take advanced placement tests in computer science each year. This gap is especially noteworthy among Black and Latina girls compared to boys. In particular, given that a large number of jobs in the foreseeable future involve STEM disciplines and their applications, it is important that more girls, and particularly girls from non-white and poor families, be encouraged to participate in STEM education.

Further Reading

Nathan Belcher, "A brief history of U.S. science education—Leading to modeling instruction," medium.com, February 28, 2018, https://medium.com/@ntbelcher/a-brief-history-of-u-s-science-education-leading-to-modeling-instruction-3a9bdbd801f2. Retrieved on April 26, 2020.

Drew Desilver, "U.S. students' academic achievement still lags that of their peers in many other countries," *Pew Research Center*, February 15, 2017, https://www.pewresearch.org/fact-tank/2017/02/15/u-s-students-internationally-math-science/. Retrieved on April 27, 2020.

Todd R. Kelley and J. Geoff Knowles, "A conceptual framework for integrated STEM education," *International Journal of STEM Education*, 3 (2016), https://stemeducationjournal.springeropen.com/articles/10.1186/s40594-016-0046-z. Retrieved on April 26, 2020.

MandLabs, "Current state of STEM education in the US: What needs to be done?," 2018, https://mandlabs.com/blog/current-state-of-stem-education-in-us-what-needs-to-be-done/. Retrieved on April 26, 2020.

National Academies Press, "A descriptive framework for integrated STEM education," 2014, https://www.nap.edu/read/18612/chapter/4#34. Retrieved on April 26, 2020.

UCLA Psychology Information Resource, "Schools and closing the gender gap related to STEM," 2015, http://smhp.psych.ucla.edu/pdfdocs/gengap.pdf. Retrieved on April 27, 2020.

Chapter 9: Arts and Humanities Education

OVERVIEW

Throughout history, education has been imparted in order to prepare children and youths for productive lives within their societies. Thus, education has always focused upon the teaching of skills seen as necessary for survival. Before the invention of agriculture thousands of years ago, such skills included training in hunting and gathering techniques. After agriculture was developed, children were taught to farm. Children were also taught fundamental values associated with their cultural traditions. Training in survival techniques and cultural transmission was often undertaken outside of what we today would recognize as formal education. Rather, such skills were taught to children directly by their parents or other adults, with children also learning on the basis of experience.

Today, of course, society is far more complex than was the case in ancient and medieval times. Basic literacy and numeracy skills are regarded as necessary survival skills. Most countries throughout the world now require children to complete several years of formal schooling. The curricula in these schools include not only basic literacy and numeracy skills but also many other subjects including mathematics, science, foreign languages, history, and geography. Knowledge about each of these subjects is regarded as highly important for young people entering the complexity of contemporary life. As is seen in the chapter on science, technology, engineering, and mathematics (STEM) education has been given more and more emphasis in light of the speed of technological change that can be observed today. However, most experts recognize that the arts and the humanities are also an essential component of modern education.

The arts and humanities are especially important because of their role in the maintenance and development of cultures as they exist in different societies throughout the world. Culture includes the set of social norms, behaviors, and beliefs associated with individual societies. Components of culture include material culture, nonmaterial culture, and cultural symbols. Material culture consists of tangible artifacts such as food, clothing, tools, and architecture. Nonmaterial culture consists of underlying values such as religious beliefs, attitudes toward relationships between people and the natural world, and views about how people are expected to act toward one another. Symbols are items of cultural significance that are not material objects in and of themselves, but often appear as important components of material culture. Such symbols often appear on flags, currency, and other material objects. For example, many American coins contain the mottoes "E pluribus unum" and "In God we trust," both of which symbolize the United States as a country. In examining culture, it must be recognized that culture is learned and that culture is shared. For example, an infant born in China who is adopted by an English-speaking American couple will grow up speaking English, not Chinese, as his or her first language.

The arts and humanities represent expressions of cultures. These expressions include the visual arts including paintings, drawings, and sculptures. They also include music, dance, and drama. The humanities include nonmaterial expressions of cultural values including works of literature and texts of cultural or religious significance. These include languages via which culture is transmitted, especially between generations. Cultural symbols appear in the visual arts, and they are often contained within drama and music. For example, most countries have national anthems that are seen as representing the countries' basic values. Animals and birds such as the bear in Russia, the kiwi in New Zealand, and the bald eagle in the United States are well recognized as symbols of these countries.

Flags in particular have symbolic meanings to people who associate themselves with various cultures. The flags of many countries contain images of cultural significance including images of animals and birds that represent their countries' cultures. Colors themselves have symbolic meanings. For example, the majority of flags used in sub-Saharan African countries include at least some of the colors such as red, green, yellow, and black. These colors in combination are seen to represent Africa. To the north, the flags of many Middle Eastern countries contain the star and crescent symbol of Islam, along with the colors red and/or green that are regarded also as symbolizing Islam.

Flags play an important role in helping to express nationalist aspirations of people who belong to cultures that lack political sovereignty. For example, many Uighurs who live in northwestern China would like to see this territory become an independent country. The Uighur nationalist flag is light blue and white and contains a star and crescent. Blue and white symbolize Uighur culture, and most Uighurs practice Islam in contrast to the historically Buddhist culture of China and the officially atheistic policies of the current Chinese government.

Of course, many cultures transcend international boundaries. Scholars often refer to "Western culture" or "East Asian culture" in referring to those parts of the world, for example. Thus, the study of Western culture, or the cultures of Europe and North America, includes study of art, music, and literature from many different countries such as the writings of Shakespeare and Hemingway, the music of Mozart and Beethoven, and the paintings of van Gogh and Picasso. Nor is culture static; it evolves constantly as new cultural forms supplant older ones. These changes often reflect changes in technology. Thus, the illuminated calligraphy of the Middle Ages became obsolete, except for its historical value, following the invention of the printing press during the Renaissance.

Cultures borrow from one another very frequently. Languages as they evolve contain words that were originally part of other and sometimes unrelated languages.

English in particular is a highly flexible language and contains thousands of words that are derived from other languages. For example, the English words "canoe," "toboggan," "chipmunk," "hurricane," "coyote," and "barbecue" are derived from various Native American languages that were spoken in the Western Hemisphere long before the arrival of European settlers. Similarly, the words "sushi," "tycoon," and "tsunami" come from Japanese and the words "banana," "gumbo," and "jazz" are believed to have sub-Saharan African origins.

The process of colonialism in particular has had important impacts on culture. As European colonial powers established colonies outside of Europe, millions of people were killed outright, died following exposure to European diseases, were enslaved, or were displaced and forced to move elsewhere. Even when Indigenous people escaped such displacements, colonial powers sometimes made efforts to stamp out their cultures and languages. Non-Western cultures and their values were regarded as "savage," "uncivilized," or "primitive." Efforts were made to stamp out Indigenous cultures and force these Indigenous people to adopt Western cultural values and practices.

Often, these efforts were linked to religious motivations. For some representatives of the European colonial powers, conversion of Indigenous people to Christianity was associated with efforts to promote or in some cases require Indigenous people to adopt Western culture and to abandon their traditional cultures. As discussed in detail in the chapter on language in this volume, pressure to abandon traditional culture is often associated with forcing Indigenous people to learn and use the languages of the Western colonial powers. The European languages became the languages of instruction in many schools, and children who spoke Indigenous languages to one another, even outside of class or on playgrounds, would be punished.

All these factors concerning the arts and humanities are considered in the vignettes included in this chapter. How should artistic and cultural traditions be taught? The teaching of these traditions involves two components, including educating the general public about artistic expression and the training of professional artists. Both of these components have evolved in conjunction with the evolution of education more generally. For example, during the Middle Ages, visual artists were usually trained after having been apprenticed to an experienced master artist. Although such private instruction continues today, many professional artists are trained in formal educational institutions. Debate over what aspects of the arts and humanities should be taught in schools has continued since public schooling first became commonplace during the nineteenth century. What types of art should be privileged, and what types should be ignored or subject to criticism and derision?

Concern over arts and humanities in education remains a lively and important issue throughout the world. Arts education has a long history in both Denmark and Hungary. Both countries have long and vibrant traditions in the arts, especially in music. In Denmark, education in music and the visual arts has long been recognized as a key to which Danish educational officials call "cultural citizenship." Hungary's musical traditions differ from those of other European countries because of its Magyar history, including its distinctive, non-Indo-European language. The Kodaly method of teaching music, which is used today throughout the world, was developed in Hungary. However, recent political changes in Hungary have resulted in a de-emphasis on musical and artistic education. The long-run implications of this changing philosophy are yet to be known. In the Netherlands, arts education emphasizes the long-standing traditions of the visual arts as epitomized by Rembrandt, van Gogh, and many other well-known painters of the past.

In many less developed countries, an important component of arts and humanities education is to preserve and maintain Indigenous cultures that were affected strongly by colonialism. Such is the case in Zimbabwe, whose traditional sub-Saharan culture was overrun by the British beginning in the late nineteenth century. Moreover, Britain and other European colonial powers drew the boundaries between their colonies for their own purposes. Indigenous cultures were divided between colonies, while individual colonies contained numerous and often conflicting ethnic groups within their boundaries. Thus, arts and humanities education is regarded as an important component of the creation of a national identity in light of such colonial history.

National identity is important to arts and humanities education in many other countries as well. Nepal's artistic traditions date back for at least 2000 years. During the nineteenth and twentieth centuries, Nepal was able to maintain political independence given its location as a buffer state between India and China. Here artistic expression was able to develop without being suppressed by outside influences. Today, Nepal's economy has become more and more tied to tourism. International tourists visit Nepal not only to view its dramatic and breathtaking landscapes but also to experience its unique culture as symbolized in the country's art. Arts and humanities education helps the Nepalese to preserve these cultural values and symbols for both intrinsic and economic reasons.

Barbados has a culture associated with many different origins. The Carib Indians, who inhabited Barbados prior to the arrival of Europeans in the late fifteenth and early sixteenth centuries, soon died out as a result of exposure to European diseases, deportation, and enslavement. Yet their cultural values influence Barbados's contemporary culture. Most of Barbados's citizens today are descended from slaves who were imported from Africa to work on sugar plantations. However, Barbados's culture has also been influenced by European, South Asian, and other antecedents. The government of Barbados recognizes this cultural diversity and regards the arts as "an essential component of the education offered in schools."

As a less developed island in the western Pacific Ocean, Solomon Islands is a country that is threatened particularly with the potential effects of global environmental and climate change. Here, education in the arts and humanities is seen not only as a means of promoting national identity and preserving Indigenous culture, but it is also seen as a key component in development of environmental sustainability as a cultural value. Education in the arts and humanities combines instruction in local cultural values, traditions, and histories with preparation for sustainable living in a world threatened by large-scale environmental change and degradation.

BARBADOS

Barbados is an island country in the western Atlantic Ocean. It is located about 65 miles east of the Windward Islands that separate the Atlantic from the Caribbean Sea and about 250 miles northeast of the coast of mainland South America. Barbados's population as of 2022 was about 288,000. The island's land area is about 179 square miles.

The British settled Barbados beginning in 1627, and British planters began to cultivate sugarcane for export in the 1640s. Thousands of slaves were imported from Africa over the next two centuries and forced to work on labor-intensive sugar plantations. Even today, more than 90 percent of Barbados's citizens are of African ancestry, and many are descended from these slaves. Even after slavery was abolished throughout the British Empire in 1834, the island's economy was dominated by British plantation owners.

Barbados became a fully independent country in 1966. Since then, tourism has become the most important component of Barbados's economy. An estimated 40 percent of Barbados's tourists come from the United Kingdom, with another 40 percent coming from North America. Tourism revenues have contributed significantly to Barbados's recent economic success, and today Barbados is the third wealthiest country in the Western Hemisphere by per capita income, trailing only the United States and Canada. Barbados has no standing army, and the wearing of camouflage clothing by local residents or by tourists is illegal.

Education in Barbados

Reflecting its heritage as a British colony, education in Barbados is modeled after the British educational system. Public education is free and compulsory between the ages of 5 and 16. The literacy rate in Barbados is nearly 100 percent.

Children in Barbados begin primary school at the age of five. Pupils complete six years of primary school, followed by five years of secondary school. After completing secondary school, students take the Caribbean Secondary Education Certificate (CSEC) examination. Barbados is one of 15 independent countries and territories in the Caribbean, along with mainland Guyana, where the CSEC examination is required. Completing the CSEC examination is regarded as equivalent to completing the O-level examinations in the United Kingdom. In general, passing of the CSEC examination is seen as a necessary condition for employment. Students who wish to go ahead for university education attend secondary school for an additional year and then take the Caribbean Advanced Placement Examination, equivalent to A-level examination in the United Kingdom. The government of Barbados maintains national standards and educational targets to which education at all levels is directed.

Arts and Humanities Education in Barbados

Barbados's culture combines African, British, and West Indian influences. English is the official language and the language of instruction although most residents of Barbados speak a local dialect known as Bajan. Barbados's contributions to the visual and musical arts have been recognized both within the Caribbean region and in other parts of the world.

Recognizing the need for promoting the arts, humanities, and culture of Barbados, the government established the National Cultural Foundation of Barbados (NCF) in 1983. The goals of the NCF are to promote understanding of Barbados's cultural heritage among its citizens. It also helps to provide opportunities for Barbadian visual artists and musicians to develop and showcase their work for national and international audiences and for tourists. These efforts include training in art-related technologies. The NCF also promotes festivals held throughout the year in Barbados where local art is displayed and exhibited.

The NCF's influence extends also to public education. In 2018, Barbados's Ministry of Education and Human Resource Development issued its Primary Visual Arts Curriculum Guide. The guide's recommendations were based on recognition of the value of education in the arts. The guide's rationale states

> The arts are not merely a desirable but an essential component of the education offered in schools. The arts provide the critical balance in what could otherwise be described as a purely academic curriculum and can make a significant contribution to the way children develop their feelings and understand their emotions. The Visual Arts may be described as *the results of graphic and visual expressions of thoughts, feelings, emotions and interpretations of an individual or group which reveal truthfully and sensitively some aspects of existence common to particular societies and eras* [emphasis original]. Visual arts make a significant contribution to education through the development of the imagination, critical and creative thinking, discipline, emotions, and expression while encouraging experimentation and inventiveness.

In keeping with Barbados's emphasis on national standards, the curriculum articulated in the guide "has been developed in recognition of the significant contribution of the arts to education and the need to have clear guidelines which would help teachers in the planning and presentation of their art lessons. The Curriculum is therefore designed to provide firm and clear guidelines for art teachers and serve as a reference for them in guiding students to use their initiative to explore, think critically and intuitively, discover and experiment."

The curriculum, which was developed for students between 7 and 11 years of age, articulated in the guide is based on the achievement of several objectives. Some of these objectives are related directly to appreciation of the visual arts and the development of artistic expression. For example, children are taught to "develop sensitivity to the elements and principles of art," "develop self-expression, imaginative and conceptual abilities to visualize, recognize and improvise in creating works of art," and to develop association of "manipulative skills" with creating visual artwork. However, other objectives were related less directly to the creation and appreciation of visual art. These objectives included developing children's skills at working collaboratively, appreciating art as a manifestation of the culture of Barbados, creative and critical thinking, and to "occupy one's leisure-time in beneficial pursuits."

From STEM to STEAM

Many educational experts agree that emphasis on STEM education should not mean that the arts and humanities should be ignored or neglected. Some have argued that the arts should be included in the acronym, changing STEM to STEAM. It has been argued that increased integration of the arts into STEM education has a variety of benefits to students. In particular, incorporation of the arts is seen as enhancing creativity, helping students to think outside of the box, and improving students' decision-making and problem-solving skills. It can also improve visual learning and improve the design and implementation of science and engineering-related activities and projects.

Source: Sprout School Supplies, "STEAM—The importance of art in STEM education," May 28, 2019, https://sproutsupplies.com/blog/steam-the-importance-of-art-in-stem-education/. Retrieved on March 14, 2020.

Thus, the government of Barbados has paid explicit attention to the role of artistic expression and appreciation as a fundamental component of K-12 education. In 2018, the Ministry of Education indicated the importance of the arts in education by adding the letter "A" to the traditional STEM acronym. The ministry announced that a new approach to learning would be described using the acronym STEAM, or Science, Technology, Engineering, Arts, and Mathematics. In 2019, efforts to promote music, as well as the visual arts, in the curriculum were also initiated. Critics have also suggested that more efforts should be made to develop vocationally oriented education for those students who have no interest in postsecondary education. It is unclear, however, how education in the arts and humanities would fit into such a program.

Further Reading

Barbados *Advocate*, "Education ministry going full 'steam' ahead," October 17, 2018, https://www.barbadosadvocate.com/news/education-ministry-going-full-%E2%80%98steam%E2%80%99-ahead. Retrieved on May 5, 2019.

Barbados Today, "Barbados education system: The need for change," May 15, 2019, https://barbadostoday.bb/2019/05/15/barbados-education-system-the-need-for-change/. Retrieved on May 5, 2022.

Lucille Phillips, "Towards a policy in arts education (Drama) in Barbados," *Caribbean Quarterly*, 45 (1999), pp. 121–145.

Melissa Pollock, "Schools' music festivals to develop young musicians," Barbados Government Information Service, February 14, 2019, https://gisbarbados.gov.bb/blog/schools-music-festival-to-develop-young-musicians/. Retrieved on May 5, 2019.

DENMARK

Located in north-central Europe, the Kingdom of Denmark includes the Jutland Peninsula that extends northward from Germany into the North Sea to the west and the Baltic Sea to the east. Denmark also includes more than 400 islands in the

Baltic Sea itself. These islands include Zealand and Amager, upon which the capital city of Copenhagen is located. Denmark's land area is approximately 16,640 square miles, and its population was estimated at 5.8 million in 2022.

Although Denmark is not located on the Scandinavian peninsula, it is considered part of Scandinavia. Copenhagen is separated from the Swedish mainland by a narrow strait that connects the Baltic with the North Sea. In 2000, the Oresund Bridge crossing this strait and connecting Copenhagen with Sweden was opened to vehicular traffic. Moreover, Denmark's history is intertwined closely with those of Norway and Sweden, and the Danish language is related closely to Norwegian and Swedish.

Given its location along the waterways connecting the Baltic Sea with the North Sea and the North Atlantic Ocean, present-day Denmark has been a center for trade throughout the Baltic Sea region and across northern Europe throughout recorded history. Beginning in the late eighth century AD, Vikings based in Denmark and on the Scandinavian peninsula conducted raids throughout much of Europe. In 1396, Denmark joined the Kalmar Union, which also included present-day Sweden and Norway. Sweden withdrew from the Kalmar Union in 1523, but Denmark and Norway remained united politically until 1814 when Norway became part of Sweden in accordance with the Treaty of Kiel. Following the signing of the treaty, Denmark continued as an independent country with approximately its current boundaries. Denmark joined the European Union in 1973. Denmark remains a highly developed and prosperous country, ranking 16th among countries throughout the world in per capita income in 2017.

Education in Denmark

Education in Denmark is compulsory for 10 years, from ages 5 or 6 through 15 or 16. Public education is free, although many children attend private schools. In 2017, about 15 percent of Danish children of school age were enrolled in private schools that receive some subsidies from the government. As is the case throughout Europe, Denmark's literacy rate is nearly 100 percent.

Formal education in Denmark, as with other European countries, began during the Middle Ages and was sponsored by the Roman Catholic Church. In 1536, the Danish crown converted from Roman Catholicism to Lutheranism during the Protestant Reformation. After Lutheranism became Denmark's official religion, the state took over responsibility for education. However, the provision of education was haphazard until the eighteenth century, and many schools existed primarily to train future members of the Lutheran clergy. At that time, Danish Lutheranism became influenced strongly by the Pietist movement, which emphasized individual piety and devotion as components of spiritual awakening. Literacy was regarded as essential to individual religious belief and action, and the Danish government established schools throughout the country where children were taught the basics of reading, writing, and arithmetic as well as religious principles. Government-funded public education was established formally in 1894.

Education in Denmark is managed by the government's Ministry of Education. The structure of public primary and secondary education in Denmark is encapsulated in the *folkeskole* procedure as administered by the government. Folkeskole includes both primary and lower secondary schooling, and an important underlying concept is that teaching should emphasize individual differences among students to the extent that this goal can be achieved in practice. After completing folkeskole, education is no longer compulsory. However, students have several options with respect to upper secondary education. These include "general" upper secondary school, which includes preparation for entry into university-level education. Alternatives include technical and commercial upper secondary school and formal vocational training. Private schools, which are subsidized by the state, must conform to national curricular and assessment standards.

Arts and Humanities Education in Denmark

The musical and visual arts, and music in particular, have a long history in Denmark. Prior to the Industrial Revolution, amateur "town musicians" performed at dances, weddings, festivals, and other celebrations in their towns and in the nearby countryside. The roles of these town musicians changed, however, as Danish society came to be influenced by the Industrial Revolution and by the arrival of classical music and other musical genres from outside of Denmark.

Over several centuries, the Danish monarchy played an important role in patronizing music and supporting professional musicians. The first opera house in Denmark was opened by King Frederick IV (1671–1730) in 1703. Operas and both religious and secular compositions were written and performed by Danish musicians and composers. More recently, Danish musicians have contributed substantially to jazz, rock, and other genres of contemporary music. Because jazz had a negative connotation and was regarded historically as a "low" form of music with little or no cultural value, Danish musical educators coined the term "rytmisk music" or "rhythmic music" to describe jazz and underscore its importance to Danish artistic education. The idea was to promote jazz and other forms of music as a means of promoting music appreciation among adult residents of Denmark. In practice, it also is used to promote participatory activities in that children are encouraged to sing, draw, and learn to play musical instruments. The visual arts have also been a long-standing and important aspect of Danish culture. The visual arts, the dramatic arts, and musical production throughout Denmark are all subsidized in part by the Danish government.

Denmark's emphasis on the arts and humanities extends to the educational sphere. The folkeskole curriculum includes artistic expression and various aspects of the humanities. At the primary school level, the curriculum includes six years of instruction in music, five years of instruction in the visual arts, and instruction in "design, wood, and metalwork." The Danish government also subsidizes schools where music is taught to children and young adults up to the age of 25 outside of the formal, standard folkeskole curriculum. Each of Denmark's 98 municipalities is

This photograph shows the Tietgen Kollegiet or Tietgen Dorm in Copenhagen, Denmark. The building, which was constructed in 2005, contains apartments that are rented to university students in the city. In designing and constructing the Tietgen Kollegiet, the architects paid careful attention to aesthetics in such a way as to reinforce the value of formal education in Danish society. (Imagestef | Dreamstime.com)

required to maintain a formal music school. Private schools where the visual arts, dance, and drama are taught are also found throughout the country.

In Denmark, arts and humanities education is seen as an important means of reinforcing Danish history and culture and in particular its current status as a liberal social democracy. Art and musical education, including attending musical performances and visiting museums and art exhibitions, contribute to the development of what some Ministry of Education leaders regard as "cultural citizenship." Denmark's educational system promotes this "cultural citizenship" by promoting learning about artistic forms and traditions, and in many cases, such learning is participatory. Such learning, in turn, promotes "character formation," including broader awareness of the outside world, Danish culture, and cultures of other parts of the world.

Further Reading

Danish Agency for Culture, "Art and culture give children a life that works," 2015, https://slks.dk/fileadmin/user_upload/0.../BKK_engelsk_web_72dpi_27_03_15.pdf. Retrieved on June 1, 2019.

Sven-Erik Holgersen, "Music education for young children in Scandinavia: Policy, philosophy, or wishful thinking?" *Arts Education Policy Review*, 109 (2008), https://www.tandfonline.com/doi/abs/10.3200/AEPR.109.3.47-54?journalCode=vaep20. Retrieved on June 1, 2019.

Peder Kaj Pedersen, "Danish music education and the 'rhythmic music' concept: Some aspects," Aalborg University, Interdisciplinary Research Group in Culture, 2014, https://vbn.aau.dk/en/publications/aspekter-af-dansk-musikundervisning-og-ideen-om-rytmisk-musik-som. Retrieved on June 1, 2019.

HUNGARY

The Republic of Hungary is located in east-central Europe, and much of its territory includes the relatively flat Hungarian basin that is bordered on the east by the Carpathian Mountains. Hungary has a land area of nearly 36,000 square miles and a population of about 9.6 million as of 2022. More than 95 percent of Hungary's people are ethnic Hungarians who speak the Hungarian language, which is not an Indo-European language and is instead related more closely to Finnish and Estonian. The population also consists of minorities who speak German or various eastern or southeastern European languages. Between 300,000 and 500,000 Romani people, many of whom are impoverished and regarded as social outcasts, also live in Hungary.

Many historians believe that the ancestors of today's Hungarians were Magyars who moved into the Hungarian Plain from the east, crossing the Carpathians, beginning in the ninth century AD. Much of present-day Hungary was united by St. Stephen I (c. 975 AD–1038 AD), who became King of Hungary in 1000 AD. Stephen's successors ruled Hungary until 1526, when Hungary was taken over by the Ottoman Empire. Thereafter, Hungary was successively part of the Ottoman Empire, the Habsburg Empire, and the Austro-Hungarian Empire until after World War I, when it became independent. Although Hungary remained an independent country, after World War II it was taken over by a Communist regime that remained in control of the country until 1989. Hungary joined the European Union in 2004.

Education in Hungary

Education in Hungary is managed by the Ministry of Human Resources. Compulsory school attendance begins at the age of 3 and continues until the age of 16. Children attend 8 years of primary school beginning at the age of 6. After primary school is completed, pupils are divided into three categories. Those who are considered highly talented academically attend gymnasium, which prepares them for college. Others attend vocationally oriented high schools that emphasize technical training, and the third group attends vocational schools that prepare them directly for the workforce in less technologically oriented jobs. Literacy is virtually universal, although some Romani children do not attend school. As in many other countries, contemporary Hungarian education emphasizes science and technology. However, within this context Hungary has a long history and tradition of education in the arts and humanities.

Arts and Humanities Education in Hungary

Artistic traditions in Hungary include the visual arts, architecture, and music. The tradition of visual arts dates back at least to the unification of Hungary under St. Stephen. Much of Hungary's medieval artwork and architecture was associated with the Roman Catholic Church. Although the Ottomans ransacked or destroyed

---

Making Music Education Culturally Responsive

For generations, music teachers have been trained in various aspects of musical theory and history and have been trained to conduct bands, orchestras, and choruses. Yet these components of training persons to teach music may be lacking in cultural relevance for students. Cultural relevance means that it is important for teachers to be "culturally responsive," which means "teaching music where kids are, and with what interests them." Teaching students to play traditional instruments such as violins, or to sing traditional songs, may have little meaning or value to students whose lives are more oriented to more contemporary forms of musical expression. Advocates of more cultural responsiveness have proposed encouraging students to write, perform, and record their own music.

Source: Lee Whitmore, "What's missing in musical education? Cultural and social relevance," The Hechinger Report, July 15, 2019, https://hechingerreport.org/opinion-whats-missing-in-music-education-cultural-and-social-relevance/. Retrieved on March 14, 2020.

---

some of these traditional Hungarian paintings, buildings, and sculptures, many were preserved and can still be seen today.

Hungarian music is distinctive within the Western musical tradition in that it has been influenced considerably by Hungarian folk music. Hungarian folk music is distinctive in particular because of Hungary's history in that many of the ancestors of today's Hungarians are descended from the Magyars who originated east of central and western Europe. Historians of music have recognized that Hungarian folk music has been influenced by the musical traditions of western and central Asia including the Mongols, Uighurs, and Tatars.

Perhaps Hungary's best-known classical composers were Bela Bartok (1881–1945) and Zoltan Kodaly (1882–1967). As young composers, both collected folk songs from throughout rural Hungary and incorporated these songs into their classical compositions. In doing so, Kodaly in particular became concerned about what he considered poor quality of music education in Hungary's schools.

At that time, music was taught only in secondary schools, but Kodaly and his associates developed music curricula and teaching methods for use by younger pupils. These curricula and methods of instruction came to be known as the Kodaly method.

The Kodaly method links musical education to the physical and intellectual development of children more generally. The method is highly sequential, and it emphasizes active participation on the part of children, who sing various syllables and participate in other musical activities. Both traditional folk music and classical compositions by Hungarian as well as foreign composers are used. Rhythmic movement is also emphasized, and children walk, march, clap, or engage in other physical activities while singing or listening to music. These rhythmic movements are intended to reinforce the learning of various notes and musical sequences. Hand signs are also used to reinforce these concepts. After having mastered these concepts, children are then taught musical notation. Today, primary and secondary students are required to have two lessons in music per week and one lesson in drawing and the visual arts weekly. Proponents of the Kodaly method have argued that its use not only promotes musical literacy but also helps children develop motor skills and improves their ability to learn mathematics, science, and reading.

Despite these requirements, in recent years, the role of humanities in Hungarian education has been diminished. In 2010, the nationalistic, conservative Fidesz party under the leadership of Victor Orban (1963—) won a majority in Hungary's parliamentary elections, and Orban became prime minister. Since then, Orban's government has become increasingly authoritarian and oriented to national self-sufficiency, with opposition to unrestricted immigration into Hungary and the European Union as the cornerstone of his government's policies.

These changes have affected Hungarian education, in that arts and humanities education has been de-emphasized under the Orban government. Some of Orban's critics have argued that reducing the role of humanities in education also restricts the teaching of critical thinking, which could promote opposition to the regime. Higher education has been affected in that government officials have regarded it as luxury that is not critical to Hungary's efforts to boost its economy and make it more competitive with the economies of other countries within Western Europe. Humanities in particular are regarded as luxuries because they are not seen as having direct impacts on economic growth within the country.

Orban's government has also influenced education at the primary and secondary levels. Since Orban's government took power, the Ministry of Human Resources has taken a more active role in the development and implementation of educational curricula. For example, many textbooks are now prepared and distributed by the ministry, and these textbooks emphasize the nationalist policies of Orban's regime. The government has invested heavily in opera and other elements of classical culture, but in doing so, it also emphasizes Hungarian nationalism, self-sufficiency, and what opponents of the regime refer to as xenophobia. These concepts have extended into artistic education, particularly in the realm of music, in that Hungarian music is seen as the means of reinforcing these ideas. However, critics are pointing out that this emphasis is downplaying appreciation for other cultures and artistic traditions.

Further Reading

Alasdair Coates, "Music education in Hungary," *Compare: A Journal of Comparative and International Education*, 5 (1975), pp. 17–21, https://doi.org/10.1080/0305792750 9408826. Retrieved on January 23, 2018.

Michael Houlahan and Philip Tacka, *Kodály Today: A cognitive approach to elementary music education inspired by the Kodály Concept.* New York: Oxford University Press 2015.

Sheena McKenzie, "Why Hungary's state-sponsored schoolbooks have teachers worried," *CNN*, February 6, 2019, https://www.cnn.com/2019/02/01/europe/hungary-education -orban-textbooks-intl/index.html. Retrieved on May 26, 2019.

Luca Tiszai, "Kodaly approach in the crossroad of education and therapy," *Voices: A World Forum for Music Therapy* 15 (2015), https://voices.no/index.php/voices/article/view /2274. Retrieved on May 5, 2022.

NEPAL

The Federal Democratic Republic of Nepal is located in South Asia between India and China. Nepal shares Mount Everest, the world's highest mountain with an elevation of over 29,000 feet above sea level, with the Chinese province of Tibet that borders Nepal to the north. The land area of Nepal is 56,827 square miles with an estimated population of 30 million in 2022.

Nepal is divided into three distinct geographic regions. The southern part of the country contains the Terai Plains along the border with India to the south. The majority of Nepal's people live in this region. To the north of the Terai Plains is the Hill Region, which includes the capital city of Kathmandu. The Himalayas region, which is very sparsely populated, is located north of the Hill Region and south of Tibet.

Present-day Nepal was first united by King Prithvi Narayan Shah (1723–1775) in 1768. However, the British East India Company claimed Nepal in the early nineteenth century. War broke out after British forces attacked the Kingdom of Nepal in 1814. The war ended when both sides agreed to the Siguali Treaty in 1816. Under terms of the Siguali Treaty, Nepal agreed to cede about a third of its territory to the British. In exchange, Britain recognized Nepal's independence.

Nepal's role as a buffer state between India and China has become increasingly important after World War II. Although Nepal has been an absolute monarchy throughout most of its history, in 2006 the Nepalese royal family agreed to establish democracy and reduce its role to ceremonial status. Thus, today the King of Nepal is the head of state but is no longer the head of government. In 2015, a devastating earthquake centered north of Kathmandu caused nearly 9,000 fatalities and resulted in more than $10 billion in damaged property—nearly 50 percent of Nepal's gross domestic product.

Education in Nepal

Historically, formal education in Nepal was limited largely to children of the nobility and the elite. As recently as 1951, it has been estimated that only 5 percent of Nepalese people were literate. Only about 300 schools, enrolling only about 10,000 pupils, were operating in the country. In that year, Nepal initiated efforts to provide publicly supported education to the general population. A formal education plan known as the National Education System Plan went into effect in 1971. By 2015, more than 35,000 schools were operating and the country's literacy rate had increased to 63.9 percent. It is estimated currently that more than 97 percent of Nepalese children of elementary school age are enrolled in school. The structure of education in Nepal is based on the educational system of neighboring India, which in turn is based on the traditional British educational system. The system is managed by the government's Ministry of Education, which is headed by the Secretary of Education who is appointed by the government. Public education is free. Primary school attendance, which is compulsory, lasts for eight years.

Primary education is followed by two years of lower secondary school and two years of upper secondary school, after which students take national examinations. However, secondary education is not compulsory. Many students leave school after completing primary education. This is particularly true among children from impoverished rural farming families in that the labor of a primary school graduate is seen as necessary to support the family. Girls are more likely to drop out of secondary school than boys, or not attend secondary school at all, in part because many girls marry and have children while still teenagers.

Despite the success of Nepalese education in improving literacy and providing basic education to most Nepalese citizens, problems remain. The curriculum is standard for the entire country, failing to consider the substantial cultural and geographical differences within Nepal. Emphasis on preparing students for uniform national examinations has been criticized on the grounds that such curricula emphasize memorization as opposed to critical thinking, both in the STEM disciplines and in the arts.

Political instability, lack of resources, and rugged terrain in many parts of the country have made it difficult for the ministry to provide adequate infrastructure to support public education throughout the country. The 2015 earthquake compounded this problem in that many school buildings were destroyed or heavily damaged, and as of 2019, many of these facilities had yet to be rebuilt or restored. The system has also been criticized for its focus on academics as opposed to more practical or vocational training. In 2016, an optional vocational and technical track was added to the curriculum, although this program is still in the inaugural phase.

Arts and Humanities Education in Nepal

Nepal's culture is highly diverse. As of 2011, about 81 percent of Nepalese citizens were Hindus. About 9 percent were Buddhists, with the remainder practicing other religions. Siddartha Gautama (563 BC–483 BC), known as the Buddha, is believed to have been born in the town of Lumbini in present-day southern Nepal near the Indian border.

Officially, Nepal is a secular state, but before 2007, Hinduism was recognized as the state religion. However, Hinduism and Buddhism within Nepal are intertwined closely, with Hindus worshipping at Buddhist temples and vice versa. Nepal's Hindu tradition, including the caste system, has affected access to education. Even today, only about a quarter of Nepal's Dalits or "untouchables" at the bottom of Nepal's caste structure are believed to be able to read and write.

Nepal has even more diversity with respect to languages. Nepali, which is an Indo-European language that is somewhat related to Hindi and other languages of northern India, is the country's official language. However, according to census estimates, less than half of Nepalese citizens speak Nepali as their first language. More than 120 other languages are spoken as first languages throughout the country. Public education is conducted primarily in Nepali and in English,

Nepal's government is actively pursuing teaching its students in traditional Nepalese artistic forms. Such training is seen as very valuable to the preservation of Nepalese cultures as well as a means of promoting tourism. These students are learning Thangka painting, in which images of Buddhist deities are painted on cotton or silk applique. (Whiteisthecolor | Dreamstime.com)

and educational authorities have been criticized for ignoring other languages that are spoken in Nepal although government policy specifies that primary schooling shall be conducted in the predominant language of the area where the schools are located.

Hinduism and Buddhism have had important influences on the culture of Nepal throughout its history, dating back to the establishment of these religious traditions more than 2,500 years ago. Music and the visual arts have old traditions in Nepal. Traditionally, Nepalese art and music were focused on religious themes although secular themes such as paintings of landscapes, flowers and trees, people, and animals have become more prevalent. Following the arrival of the British, Nepalese art came to be more influenced by Western artistic patterns and traditions.

Art and music have become incorporated increasingly into Nepalese education. Historically, Nepalese education focused on basic literacy and numeracy skills. As education became more widespread, however, and as the number of years of compulsory schooling was increased from five years to eight years in 2016, the arts have played an increasingly important role in Nepalese education. Some parents in Nepal regard education in the arts as a luxury and believe that Nepalese education should be more focused on practical skills. However, in 2007, the Nepalese Ministry of Education stated that one of the basic goals of Nepalese schooling was to "help prepare citizens committed to conserve and promote Nepali art, aesthetic values, ideals, and other specialties."

Education in the arts is also seen to be essential to the efforts made to preserve Nepal's rich cultural heritage in an increasingly globalized and secular world. The preservation of Nepalese cultural traditions, including its visual art, music, drama, dance, and architecture, is also regarded as important to government efforts to promote international tourism, in that many tourists want to observe Nepalese culture along with observing the country's dramatic and unique physical environment. In 2018, the Ministry of Education released a proposed 5-year program for educational reform in Nepal. The proposed reform included increasing the number of years of compulsory education from 8 to 12 years. It also promoted the development of arts programs "to address the varying interests of students." Reducing emphasis on memorization and on preparing students for national examinations has also been seen as providing more opportunities for artistic and humanities education by providing students with more opportunities for creative expression within the context of Nepalese culture.

Further Reading

Dragana Borenovic Dilas, Jean Cui, and Stefan Trines, "Education in Nepal," *World Education News and Reviews*, 2018, https://wenr.wes.org/2018/04/education-in-nepal. Retrieved on May 16, 2019.

Deepak Raj Parajuli and Tapash Das, "Performance of community schools in Nepal: A macro-level analysis," *International Journal of Scientific and Technical Research*, 2 (2013), pp. 148–154. Retrieved on May 16, 2019.

Rastriya Samachar Samiti, "Education Minister unveils five-year roadmap for education sector reform," *The Himalayan Times*, April 11, 2018, https://thehimalayantimes.com/nepal/education-minister-unveils-five-year-roadmap-for-education-sector-reform/. Retrieved on May 16, 2019.

THE NETHERLANDS

The Netherlands, which is located on the North Sea coast of northwestern Europe, is the most densely populated country in that continent. Its land area is 16,158 square miles and its population was estimated to be 17.6 million in 2022. Most residents of the Netherlands are of Dutch ancestry and speak Dutch as a first language, although in recent years numerous immigrants have settled in the Netherlands. These include immigrants from former Dutch colonies such as Suriname as well as people moving into the Netherlands from the Middle East, Africa, and elsewhere. The increasing diversity of the Netherlands' population has impacted and continues to impact Dutch education.

Collectively, the Netherlands along with neighboring Belgium and Luxembourg have long been known as the "Low Countries," reflecting the low-lying, flat landscape. Indeed, a substantial portion of the Netherlands' land area consists of land that has been reclaimed from the North Sea over several centuries. Given its location and maritime orientation, the region that now includes the Low Countries has been contested among various European powers since the days of the Roman Empire. During the sixteenth and seventeenth centuries, the Netherlands emerged as an important commercial center. The Dutch were major players in the colonization of non-European parts of the world, claiming present-day South Africa, Indonesia, and various areas within the Western Hemisphere. However, Dutch influence in Europe began to decline in the eighteenth century in association with competition from larger and more powerful Britain and France.

Following the Napoleonic Wars, the European Powers agreed to establish the United Kingdom of the Netherlands in 1815. One motivation underlying the establishment of the United Kingdom of the Netherlands was to create a buffer state between the major powers of France, Central Europe (which became the modern-day country of Germany), and Britain.

A Dutch-speaking, Protestant royal family was installed upon the throne of the United Kingdom. However, Dutch rule was resented by leaders in present-day Belgium and Luxembourg, in that many people living in southern Belgium and Luxembourg were Roman Catholics who spoke French or German. Belgium and Luxembourg declared their independence in 1830, and the Netherlands recognized their independence in 1839. The Netherlands has remained independent, with only minor adjustments to its 1839 boundaries, ever since. It remains one of the most prosperous countries in the world.

Education in the Netherlands

As has been the case with other European countries, education in the Netherlands during and after the Renaissance was the responsibility of private religious institutions. Young men achieved vocational training after being apprenticed to experienced members of guilds associated with particular professions. Prior to the creation of the United Kingdom of the Netherlands, the enactment of the Elementary Education Act in 1801 established the principle that education would become the responsibility of the state. This responsibility was formalized after the United Kingdom was established, and its constitution specified that all citizens had the right to free elementary education.

In the United Kingdom, and later in the Netherlands itself after the United Kingdom was dissolved, many children were educated in these free public schools. However, both Protestant and Roman Catholic churches provided such education in private, religion-oriented schools. Controversy over whether the government should pay to support such schools continued for many years. In 1917, the new constitution of the Netherlands specified that state-sponsored and private schools would receive equal government funding. It has been estimated that about two-thirds of Dutch children of elementary school age now attend private schools—some (called "special" schools) sponsored by religious institutions and others with more secular orientations.

Today, education in the Netherlands is compulsory between the ages of 5 and 16. The educational system is administered by the government's Ministry of Education,

Culture, and Science. Schooling begins with eight years of primary school or *basis-school*. The first year of basisschool is intended for four-year-olds. Formal education for children below the age of five is not compulsory, but the large majority of four-year-olds are enrolled in this first-year program. Five-year-olds who do not begin school at four are placed in the second grade upon initial enrollment. After completing all eight grades, most Dutch students take government-sponsored academic aptitude examinations.

After completing eight grades of basisschool, students move on to secondary school. There are three secondary school streams, including a college preparatory stream, a more general stream emphasizing polytechnic instruction, and a prevocational stream known as Voorbereidend middelbaar beroepsonderwijs (VMBO) or "prevocational secondary education." Results of the aptitude examinations are used by students, their parents, and their teachers to determine which of these three tracks is most appropriate for each student. More than half of Dutch secondary school students participate in VMBO programs, which last for four years, and about 20 percent participate in each of the other two tracks.

The college preparatory stream lasts for six years, after which many of its participants go on to college or university-level education. Within this stream, there are four tracks or "profiles." These include two profiles that emphasize the natural sciences, a profile emphasizing history and economics and Cultuur en Maatschappij or "culture and society." The latter track emphasizes the arts, literature, and foreign languages.

Arts and Humanities Education in the Netherlands

The arts, and the visual arts in particular, have a long history in the Netherlands. During the seventeenth century, Dutch painting was regarded as the best in the world at a time known still as the "Golden Age" of Dutch art. Painters such as Rembrandt van Rijn (1606–1669) and Johannes Vermeer (1632–1675) were highly esteemed during their lifetimes, and they have been regarded to be among history's most outstanding visual artists ever since. Vincent van Gogh (1853–1890) is also regarded as one of history's greatest painters. Although the Netherlands is not regarded as highly in the realm of music, Dutch composers flourished in particular during the Golden Age that coincided with the development of the baroque musical tradition throughout Europe. In the twentieth and early twenty-first centuries, Dutch musicians have made significant contributions to rock, jazz, and other musical genres.

These traditions have influenced arts and humanities education in the Netherlands. Art, emphasizing the visual arts and music, is a compulsory subject throughout basisschool although more time is spent on the arts in the lower grades compared to the upper grades of primary school. Art is a compulsory subject also during the first two years of secondary school. The Ministry of Education, Culture, and Science regards art and artistic education as of great importance to citizenship and involvement in local communities. Artistic education is seen also as promoting and stimulating creativity and promoting self-expression.

Digital Art in Twenty-First Century Education

Although education in the visual arts continues to emphasize and recognize the importance of teaching skills in drawing, painting, and sculpture, contemporary technology is playing a larger and larger role in visual arts instruction. Many arts curricula in the United States and elsewhere now include the use of digital technology in their instructional programs. Digital art, including computer graphics and animation, has a wide variety of applications including architecture, video game design, cartography, and interior design. Technology plays a larger and larger role in the teaching of the sciences, but experts recognize increasingly that it can also contribute to increased interest in and appreciation of the visual arts among students as well.

Source: Study International Staff, "Digital art classes prepare students for the future," August 7, 2019, https://www.studyinternational.com/news/digital-art-prepare-students-future/. Retrieved on March 14, 2020.

Art education in the Netherlands faces several other challenges in addition to pressures associated with reduced emphasis on arts and humanities compared to other subjects. Linkages between art education at the primary and the secondary levels are regarded by some observers as tenuous, and there are no formal policies linking art and the humanities to other aspects of the curriculum. Tensions also remain between the goal of art as cultural experience and the goal of training visual artists, musicians, actors, and other participants in the performance side of the arts. Also, critics have pointed out that more emphasis should be placed on the use of contemporary technology such as digital arts in the teaching process.

Further Reading

Education, Audiovisual and Culture Executive Agency, "Arts and cultural education at school in Europe: Netherlands," 2008, http://mediatheque.cite-musique.fr/media composite/cim/_Pdf/10_40_Netherlands_EN.pdf. Retrieved on June 16, 2019.

Yvonne Leeman, "Education and diversity in the Netherlands," *European Educational Research General*, 7 (2008), pp. 50–59, https://journals.sagepub.com/doi/pdf/10.2304 /eerj.2008.7.1.50. Retrieved on June 16, 2019.

Kirsten Reininga, "Arts education in the Netherlands," Dutch-Scandinavian Exchange on Cultural Education, 2016, https://www.lkca.nl/~/media/downloads/bijeenkomsten /dutch-scandinavian%20exchange/netherlands.pdf. Retrieved on June 16, 2019.

SOLOMON ISLANDS

Solomon Islands is located in the southwestern Pacific Ocean. The country includes 922 islands, of which 347 are inhabited. The archipelago includes the island of Bougainville, which is politically part of Papua New Guinea. The overall land area of the country is 10,965 square miles, with a population of about 720,000 as of early 2022. The country is located about 700 miles east of the mainland of the island of New Guinea and about 1,200 miles northeast of Australia.

Like New Guinea, Fiji, and other countries of the western Pacific Ocean south of the equator, Solomon Islands is regarded as part of Melanesia.

Anthropologists believe that the Solomon Islands archipelago has been inhabited by people of Melanesian origin for at least 30,000 years. In 1885, Germany claimed a protectorate over the northern Solomon Islands archipelago, including Bougainville. The British established a protectorate over the southern part of the archipelago in 1893. Germany transferred sovereignty over its protectorate, except for Bougainville, to the United Kingdom in 1900.

The British retained sovereignty over Solomon Islands until it became independent in 1978. Since independence, it has been a parliamentary democracy, but it has suffered from governmental instability and frequent changes in leadership. Solomon Islands remains a predominantly rural society, and many Solomon Islanders continue to practice subsistence agriculture combined with fishing as their ancestors had done for thousands of years.

Education in the Solomon Islands

The formal educational system in Solomon Islands includes six years of primary school followed by seven years of secondary school. Children generally begin primary school at the age of six. In contrast to most other countries throughout the world, however, formal education in Solomon Islands is not compulsory. As of 2012, it was estimated that less than 80 percent of children aged between 6 and 12 were enrolled in primary school. Only about 30 percent of teenagers were enrolled in secondary school.

The secondary school curriculum in Solomon Islands emphasizes STEM disciplines along with training in agriculture and other vocational and work-related skills. However, Solomon Islands is a poor country and as such has limited resources to devote to education. Many classrooms are overcrowded and lack adequate numbers of up-to-date textbooks and learning materials. Moreover, many villagers regard school as a waste of their children's time, especially above the primary level. Rather, older children are expected to spend their time helping the family and are taught farming, fishing, handicrafts, and other skills by their parents. Some children live on isolated islands without direct access to schools. As with other less developed countries, Solomon Islands suffers from a lack of qualified teachers, especially in more remote areas.

Despite these issues, the government's Ministry of Education and Human Resource Development is initiating efforts to increase the percentages of children who attend school. The ministry's goal, as articulated in its recent Education Strategic Framework, is to ensure that all children have access to free primary and secondary schools and to eliminate illiteracy entirely among young Solomon Islanders. As is the case with many less developed countries, however, rates of school attendance and completion are somewhat lower among girls than among boys.

About 70 distinct Indigenous languages are spoken in Solomon Islands. English is the official language of the country, although it has been estimated that less than

5 percent of the people are fluent in spoken or written English. However, an artificial pidgin language known as Pijin has emerged as a lingua franca, promoting communication among Solomon Islands' language communities. It is spoken by about 300,000 people, or nearly half the population, particularly in urban areas to which many Solomon Islands residents are moving and where interethnic marriages and relationships are becoming more commonplace.

Pijin is similar to Tok Pisin in Papua New Guinea, and some linguists regard Pijin as a dialect of Tok Pisin. In Papua New Guinea, Tok Pisin has become a written language with official status in that country. Books, newspapers, magazines, and websites are published in Tok Pisin. In Solomon Islands, however, Pijin has only recently become a more standardized written language. The Bible was translated fully into Pijin and published in Pijin in 2008, and both religious and secular authorities are hopeful that this effort will encourage the development of Pijin as a national language. English is officially the language of instruction in Solomon Islands, but in practice, many students are taught in Pijin.

Arts and Humanities Education in the Solomon Islands

Solomon Islands' leaders recognize the value of national unity while also recognizing the importance of cultural diversity and the need to preserve the country's many languages and cultures. Also, officials have become aware of the potential impacts of global change, especially rising sea levels, on the country's future. Hence, educational efforts are becoming linked increasingly to the objective of sustainable development. It is in this context that the arts and humanities are integrated into education in Solomon Islands, and they are linked to the concepts of sustainable development and cultural diversity.

This integration involves two components: the teaching of Indigenous cultural values in light of globalization and the development of appreciation for and understanding of cultural forms such as Indigenous music, dance, and visual arts. Cultural values include the basic principles associated with day-to-day life within particular communities. These day-to-day principles are referred to in Pijin as *kastom* (meaning "custom" in English).

One study of how kastom can be integrated into education has been undertaken among Solomon Islanders who speak Kahua. People who speak Kahua live on the island of Makira, which is the southeasternmost large island in the country. About 40,000 people live in Makira-Ulawa Province, which includes Makira itself and several smaller islands. The Kahuan community is small and relatively isolated, and it includes only about 5,000 people who live in the easternmost portion of Makira. Kahuan culture emphasizes the principles of *ramatenia*, or behavioral expectations. The principles include sharing, asking for permission, respect for others and their property, and discussion as opposed to imposing upon others.

Some residents of the Kahua region see their culture as being threatened by outside values. People who attend school outside of the region may be perceived to be influenced by Western values to the extent that they become dismissive of the ideas associated with ramatenia. In response, educators in the Kahua region have begun to use and emphasize traditional Kahuan songs and folklore in teaching, with the idea of combining appreciation for Kahuan culture with preparation for life in the larger world. As much as possible, local languages are being used in primary education; local materials are used to prepare learning resources; and lessons in the principles of ramatenia are coupled with instruction in reading, mathematics, and other skills. Thus, local artistic forms have become critical to efforts for preserving cultural diversity while preparing young people for the contemporary world.

Further Reading

Australian Government, Division of Foreign Affairs and Trade, "Solomon Islands Country Brief," 2017, http://dfat.gov.au/geo/solomon-islands/Pages/solomon-islands-country-brief.aspx. Retrieved on June 23, 2018.

Lindsay J. Burton, "Building on living traditions: Early childhood education and culture in Solomon Islands," *Current Issues in Comparative Education*, 15 (2012), pp. 157–175, https://files.eric.ed.gov/fulltext/EJ1000221.pdf. Retrieved on June 23, 2018.

Solomon Islands Government Ministry of Education and Human Resource Development, "Education Strategic Framework, 2016–2030," 2015, http://www.mehrd.gov.sb/images/PDF_Files/PAR/Education_Strategic_Framework_2016-2030.pdf. Retrieved on June 20, 2018.

UNITED STATES

In keeping with its history, the United States has developed a unique and highly diverse culture. American culture is derived primarily from the cultures of western Europe, but it is also influenced strongly by the cultures of Indigenous Native Americans as well as by the cultures of Africa, Latin America, Asia, and elsewhere. Given the American dominance of the contemporary global economy, the culture of the United States has influenced most other parts of the world. People throughout the world wear American clothing, eat American food, listen to American music, and watch American movies and television shows. Global communications and social media have expedited this rapid spread of American culture.

American culture was oriented primarily to England during the colonial period and into the early years of American independence. American painters, sculptors, and musical composers looked to England and elsewhere in Europe for inspiration. Many were trained in England and elsewhere in Europe as they launched their own careers. Especially since World War II, however, many American professional visual artists and musicians have been educated in the United States, either in schools and colleges specializing in artistic education or as part of curricula in more comprehensive institutions.

Over the course of the nineteenth century, Indigenous and other non-European cultural traditions began to influence American art. This was particularly true with respect to the musical arts. As early as the middle of the nineteenth century, songwriters such as Stephen Foster (1826–1864) drew inspiration from African

American musical traditions. After the Civil War, music associated with African influences, including the experience of slavery, began to affect American music more profoundly. Blues and jazz are heavily influenced by African American music, which in turn has been developed in part from the cultures of Africa. These influences entered the realm of more traditional classical art forms, such as the opera "Porgy and Bess" by George Gershwin (1898–1937). The Appalachian folk music tradition, which was associated originally with Scotch-Irish and northern British settlers of this region, developed into contemporary country music.

After World War II, these various influences were synthesized into a more distinctly American musical culture and tradition. Rock and roll developed in the 1950s as an amalgamation of blues, jazz, and country music. Yet various musical traditions within the overall genre of rock and roll also developed in and remain associated with particular areas of the country. Examples include the doo-wop music of the urban Northeast; the rockabilly music of the upper South; surf music of southern California; soul music of Detroit, Memphis, and Philadelphia; and the grunge tradition of Seattle and the Pacific Northwest. The development of these traditions parallels similar regional variation in other aspects of American culture, for example, the literary traditions of the South associated with writers such as William Faulkner (1897–1962) in contrast to writing associated with novelists such as Willa Cather (1873–1947) and Ole Rolvaag (1876–1931) in the Great Plains and the Upper Midwest.

Arts and Humanities Education in the United States

The diversity of American culture and its influences derived from many cultures throughout the world have had considerable impact on education in the arts and humanities in the United States over the course of its history. Arts education has tended to emphasize the values and traditions of dominant elements in American culture while bypassing or overlooking more marginalized segments of American society.

As described in more detail elsewhere in this volume, universal public education spread throughout the United States during the nineteenth century. The common school movement that was associated with universal public education was intended to provide an instructional framework via which all children would be taught reading, writing, arithmetic, history, and geography. The curricula also included instruction in moral and ethical principles. However, curricula were oriented to the values associated with Anglo-Saxon Protestant Christianity, which at that time dominated most aspects of American culture.

Within the realm of literature and the arts, curricula associated with common schooling also emphasized this Christian worldview. Literature and art outside of these traditions, or which originated in Indigenous or non-Western cultures, were ignored or downplayed. Even in the twentieth century, many educators dismissed jazz, rock and roll, and other American musical genres as unworthy of serious attention as compared to European-based classical music.

The degree to which art and humanities education should be prioritized has also been a subject of debate. Some have argued that the teaching of art, literature, and music is unnecessary compared to more "practical" aspects of formal education that would help children be successful in obtaining and holding productive jobs as adults. However, many educators recognized linkages between education in the arts and humanities and other goals associated with schooling as preparation for adulthood. For example, Carol D. Ryff wrote that "educational experiences in the arts and humanities are critical in cultivation of the sensibilities that attune individuals to appreciate, and even need, what the arts and humanism, more broadly, have to offer in the pursuit of a full, meaningful life as well as in building good and just societies."

The place of art and the humanities in educational curricula in the twenty-first-century United States continues to be debated. Some regard education in the arts as frivolous and/or less important than the teaching of other subjects. When funding to support education in general is cut, art education is often the first to bear the brunt of such cuts. On the other hand, many educators have pointed out that education in music and in the visual arts is important in that it promotes critical thinking and creativity—skills that translate into other aspects of the educational process. Learning to play a musical instrument requires self-discipline and hard work, and becoming a member of a band, orchestra, or choir also promotes skills associated with teamwork. Public opinion surveys have indicated that a large majority of American adults believe that arts should be an important component of the educational process.

American public education today remains influenced strongly by the Elementary and Secondary Education Act of 1965. Within the context of the act, most of the states have adopted standards for art education. However, many schools do not offer specific instruction in art or music. One survey indicated that only 3 percent of American elementary schools offer specific instruction in dance and only 4 percent offer specific instruction in the theater arts. Surveys have shown also that the amount of time devoted to instruction in the arts and humanities in American schools has decreased over the past few decades. These declines might be related to increased emphasis on standardized testing. These declines have been especially pronounced in schools located in poor regions and neighborhoods. Despite such evidence of the value of arts and humanities education, the extent to which American education will increase emphasis on these aspects of schooling remains to be seen.

Further Reading

Marc Joseph, "Has America given up on arts education?," *Huffington Post*, August 3, 2015, https://www.huffpost.com/entry/has-america-given-up-on-a_b_7860710. Retrieved on June 15, 2019.

Brian Kisida and Daniel H. Bowen, "New evidence of the benefits of arts education," Brookings Institute, February 12, 2019, https://www.brookings.edu/blog/brown-center-chalkboard/2019/02/12/new-evidence-of-the-benefits-of-arts-education/. Retrieved on June 16, 2019.

Jesse Raber, "The arts in the public schools: An intellectual history," *Process: A Blog for American History*, March 28, 2017, http://www.processhistory.org/raber-arts-public-schools/. Retrieved on June 15, 2019.

Carol D. Ryff, "Linking education in the arts and humanities to life-long well-being and health," Mellon Foundation Research Reports, January 2019, https://mellon.org /resources/news/articles/linking-education-arts-and-humanities-life-long-well-being -and-health/. Retrieved on June 16, 2019.

ZIMBABWE

The Republic of Zimbabwe is located in south-central Africa. The landlocked country has a land area of 150,871 square miles with a population estimated at about 15 million in 2022.

For about 200 years beginning in the twelfth century, much of the country's present-day territory was ruled by the Kingdom of Zimbabwe, which had been established by Bantu tribes that had migrated into the area from the north about 1,000 years ago. The country's present name is derived from the name of the original Kingdom of Zimbabwe.

The Kingdom of Zimbabwe was overthrown in the fifteenth century by the Kingdom of Mutapa, which ruled the region until the arrival of the British South Africa Company in the late nineteenth century. The company, led by Cecil Rhodes (1853–1902), overthrew the local rulers and took control of the territory. Present-day Zimbabwe was named Southern Rhodesia after Rhodes himself and was ruled by the British South Africa Company, which governed Southern Rhodesia until 1924. In contrast to most other European colonies in Africa, substantial numbers of European settlers moved to Southern Rhodesia.

The British established and administered the Federation of Rhodesia and Nyasaland in 1953. The federation included Southern Rhodesia along with Northern Rhodesia (present-day Zambia) and Nyasaland (present-day Malawi). Zambia and Malawi left the federation and became independent in 1964, but Southern Rhodesia remained a British colony. During the following year, leaders of Southern Rhodesia announced the Unilateral Declaration of Independence with the intention of keeping the colony's white-minority government in power. During the 1970s, civil war broke out between the white-dominated government and rebel forces associated with the Zimbabwe African National Union (ZANU).

In 1980, Southern Rhodesia became fully independent under the name of Zimbabwe. After independence, the large majority of white residents left the country. Today more than 99 percent of Zimbabweans are of African ancestry. Robert Mugabe, who had been one of the leaders of ZANU, became the independent country's first prime minister. By the end of the 1980s, Mugabe had become in effect a dictator, and his regime was accused of numerous human rights violations. In 2009, however, Mugabe agreed to share power with political rivals, and the county began to transition to a multiparty democracy.

Zimbabwe has been affected by numerous health-related crises including the AIDS epidemic along with major outbreaks of cholera and other infectious diseases. As a result, in the first decade of the twenty-first century Zimbabwe's life expectancy was less than 40 years, among the lowest in the world. However, with governmental stability and investments in health and medicine, life expectancy has increased to more than 50 years today.

Education in Zimbabwe

After the British South Africa Company began to administer Southern Rhodesia, the government promoted the establishment of Christian missionary schools. However, many Indigenous Africans lacked access to these schools. Moreover, the missionary school curriculum for African natives emphasized agricultural and vocational training as opposed to academic subjects. Critics have argued that the missionary school system reinforced the economic and political dominance of the white minority within Southern Rhodesia. After World War II, the government began to invest in public education. However, schools were segregated by race. Moreover, nearly 90 percent of government funding for education went to schools for white children although Africans formed a majority of the country's population.

After independence in 1980, the new government declared education to be a fundamental basic right. The constitution states that education is to be free and compulsory. Today, education in Zimbabwe is administered by the Ministry of Primary and Secondary Education. Students in Zimbabwe attend primary school for seven years. These seven years of primary schooling are compulsory. Primary school is followed by six years of secondary school. As is the case with other former British colonies, upon finishing secondary school students take standardized national examinations.

As of 2014, Zimbabwe's adult literacy rate was estimated at 88 percent. However, the government's goal of providing free public education to all Zimbabwean children has been difficult to reach for several reasons, including political turmoil, economic problems, and outbreaks of epidemic diseases including AIDS and cholera. Many schools were closed in 2008 and 2009 because of the cholera epidemic and because of political conflict prior to the development of multiparty democracy. Since then, however, most schools have reopened. It is estimated today that more than 90 percent of Zimbabweans between the ages of 15 and 24 are able to read and write.

Despite these successes, public education continues to be plagued by inadequate infrastructure and teacher shortages. In some places, a shortage of school facilities has forced local authorities to split students into two groups, with some attending school in the morning and others attending school in the afternoon. As in other less developed countries, girls are less likely than boys to attend or graduate from secondary school because of early marriage, the need for their labor, and gender-based sexual harassment and assault on the part of male students and teachers. It has also been difficult for the educational sector to provide education for children of refugees. Thousands of Zimbabweans fled the country during the period of Mugabe's dictatorship, but as the government and economy have stabilized recently, refugees have begun to move into Zimbabwe from other countries.

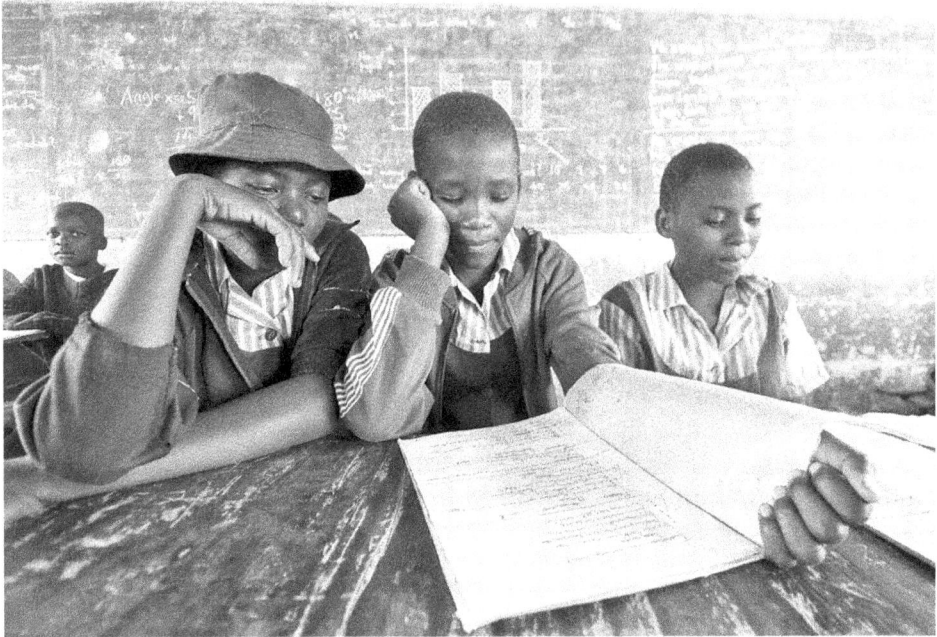

These children attend a primary school in Zimbabwe, which was a British colony for many years before independence. Zimbabwe has a highly diverse population and experiences ongoing conflict among its many ethnic groups. Education in the arts is seen as important to the development of a Zimbabwean national identity. (David Snyder | Dreamstime.com)

Arts and Humanities Education in Zimbabwe

As with many former European colonies in sub-Saharan Africa, Zimbabwe is characterized by substantial linguistic diversity. Many Zimbabweans speak Bantu languages as first languages. The most frequently spoken Bantu language is Shona, which is spoken by more than half of the population. However, English is used in government and in most commercial activity. English is also the language of instruction in Zimbabwe's secondary schools. Generally, primary schooling is conducted in the local language until the fourth year, at which time English becomes the language of instruction. The government of Zimbabwe recognizes Shona, English, and 14 other languages as official languages.

The culture of Zimbabwe is equally diverse. Artistic forms and traditions within Zimbabwe include textiles, ceramics, sculptures, and various carved objects. Musical instruments that were used in the performance of Zimbabwean music were also produced. Historically, Zimbabwean art carried substantial religious significance. However, the direct religious significance and meaning of art produced in Zimbabwe has declined since the arrival of Europeans in the nineteenth century. At that time, many Zimbabweans converted to Christianity, and about 80 percent of Zimbabwe's people today are Christians. Prior to independence, most Zimbabwean artists who were recognized outside their local communities were members of the white minority. Today, however, art produced by Zimbabweans of African ancestry is gaining international recognition, with sculpture in particular noted throughout the world for its high quality.

Despite these artistic traditions, art has for most of Zimbabwe's history been given little attention as a subject for formal study. Historically, art was seen as frivolous and as an unnecessary component of formal education. Girls, who were not expected to pursue careers outside of the home, tended to be steered into art whereas boys were more likely to study science and other STEM subjects. Artistic education, like art itself, was presented from a highly Eurocentric point of view. What art education did exist was confined primarily to schools enrolling white children, while little or no artistic education was available to the African majority of the population.

This traditional situation has been undergoing change in recent years, especially since 2000. Zimbabwe signed on to the UNESCO Universal Declaration on Cultural Diversity in 2002. Its representatives participated in several UNESCO-sponsored conferences concerning arts education. In 2015, the Ministry of Primary and Secondary Education drafted a Junior School Visual and Performing Arts Syllabus. The syllabus is intended for grades 3 through 7 in upper primary school—in other words, for children approximately 8–12 years of age. The syllabus is intended also to place education in the visual and performing arts within the larger context of Zimbabwean culture. As stated in an article about the syllabus that appeared in *Music and Africa*, "This syllabus is likely to place visual and performance arts in its socio-economic, political and cultural context in order to help learners understand and appreciate their culture and society." A nationwide educational plan presented in 2016 specified that education in the visual and performing arts was to become a compulsory subject in upper primary school. Visual and performing arts, or what Ministry officials termed "expressive arts," was also placed in the lower primary school curriculum. At each level, officials emphasized relationships between artistic forms, the humanities in general, and Zimbabwean culture.

Further Reading

Music in Africa, "Zimbabwe drafts new policy for performing arts education," July 27, 2015, https://www.musicinafrica.net/magazine/zimbabwe-drafts-new-policy-performing-arts-education. Retrieved on May 23, 2019.

The New Humanitarian, "Is Zimbabwe's education sector on the road to recovery?" January 24, 2013, http://www.thenewhumanitarian.org/news/2013/01/24/zimbabwe-s-education-sector-road-recovery. Retrieved on May 18, 2019.

Pindula, "New Education Plan Zimbabwe," 2016, https://www.pindula.co.zw/New_Education_Curriculum_Zimbabwe. Retrieved on May 23, 2019.

Chapter 10: Sustainability and Education

OVERVIEW

The environment of the earth is undergoing changes that are unprecedented in recorded history. The world's population has increased from about 1 billion in 1800 to 3 billion in 1960 to more than 6 billion in 2000 and more than 7.9 billion in 2021. Demographers predict that between 9 and 10 billion people will be living on the planet by 2050.

Population increases have been linked to, and in many cases have caused, large-scale environmental change. Average surface temperatures worldwide have increased in recent years, and most experts on climate attribute these increases to human activity. Air pollution, water pollution, habitat fragmentation, and other destructive changes have been occurring at more and more rapid rates. Once pristine forests are being cut down to make way for agriculture and mining. Numerous species of animals and plants have become extinct or are highly vulnerable to extinction. All of these and other deleterious impacts of human activity have called into question how long our contemporary, technology-oriented global society can survive as it currently exists.

Questions about ongoing impacts of human activity and behavior on the natural world has led to considerations of environmental sustainability. The concept of sustainability refers to the ability of a system to operate in a desired manner over a long period of time. As applied to the relationships between humans and the environment, sustainability implies the opportunity to maintain human-environment relationships over the foreseeable future, without dramatic impacts or crashes to these relationships.

Herman Daly (1938–) is a pioneer in the field of environmental sustainability. In 1990, Daly proposed three underlying principles of environmental sustainability. He argued that the rate of use of renewable natural resources should not exceed the rate of regeneration of these resources. This is known as the rate of sustainable yield. For example, at least as many trees should be planted as are cut down. Daly also proposed that rates of waste generation should not exceed the capacity of the environment to absorb these wastes, and he suggested that the depletion of nonrenewable resources such as fossil fuels should be associated with the development of renewable substitutes, for example, replacing energy derived from fossil fuels with energy derived from solar or wind power. Daly and others also articulated what they referred to as the "three pillars" of sustainability, including social sustainability, economic sustainability, and ecological sustainability. It is well recognized that these three pillars cannot be separated from one another and must be studied and taught interactively if they are to have any meaningful impact on creating a sustainable world.

Human activity has had impacts on local environments since the dawn of civilization. Many anthropologists recognize that the extinction of megafauna such as the woolly mammoth (Mammathus primigenius) and the giant ground sloth (Megatherium americanum) in North America was caused by overhunting by ancestors of today's Native Americans and Canadian First Nations people. Forests were cut down and streams were diverted in order to grow and irrigate crops. Overpopulation, which led to soil depletion, may have contributed to the collapse of the Mayan civilization in present-day Mexico and Central America over a thousand years ago. These impacts of human activity were primarily local, however, and the degree to which environmental problems are global was not recognized until after all of the habitable portions of the earth's surface had been identified and mapped.

It is recognized today that human impacts on the global environment accelerated beginning in the eighteenth and nineteenth centuries. In many cases, science and technology were responsible for these impacts. For example, the world's population skyrocketed beginning about 1800 largely because cures for infectious diseases were found, along with the development of vaccines and public health measures that reduced rates of infection. The Industrial Revolution allowed mass production of many different types of goods. Transportation technology has permitted the rapid transfer of food and medicine that allow control of hunger and disease associated with famine. Indeed, it has been estimated from written records that although on average 1 famine has occurred in Britain every 10 years over the past two thousand years, the last great famine in the Western world was the Irish Potato Famine of 1845–1850. And to this day, many historians blame the British government's slow and ineffective response to the famine as a partial explanation for the deaths of hundreds of thousands of Irish residents who died during this period.

There is no doubt that standards of living including longer life expectancies and improved health have risen throughout the world. For example, life expectancy in the United States was about 52 years in 1900 as compared to about 78 years today. However, these improvements in standards of living and the quality of life have come with a cost. The world's land surfaces, rivers, oceans, and atmosphere have become increasingly polluted. Hundreds of species of animals and birds have become extinct, and others have become highly vulnerable to extinction because of habitat fragmentation and loss. Average surface temperatures have been increasing steadily, and most climate experts have attributed these increases to human activity, most notably to increased carbon dioxide emissions associated with industrial production. All of these factors have led scientists, economists, journalists, government leaders, and educators throughout the world to question whether societies as we know them today will be able to survive in the future. Can we maintain our current standard of living if the world's population increases to 10 billion or more by the middle of the twentieth century? In order to answer these questions, it has become increasingly important to consider whether the relationships between humans and the planet are sustainable. Is it possible to implement Daly's principles of sustainability?

Education is recognized as very important to the implementation and practice of sustainability. In 1975, the International Environmental Education Workshop led by the United Nations Educational Scientific, and Cultural Organization (UNESCO) and the United Nations Environment Programme began to articulate visions for education about environmental sustainability. In the report's words, "The goal of environmental education is to develop a world population that is aware of, and concerned about, the environment and its associated problems, and which has the knowledge, skills, attitudes, motivations and commitment to work individually and collectively toward solutions of current problems and the prevention of new ones." Thus, education has come to be seen as an important means of making people aware of environmental problems that imperil the planet.

Environmental and sustainability education have been introduced into the formal curricula of educational systems in many different countries. In many cases, environmental education efforts have been linked to increased public awareness of sustainability. In the United States, for example, environmental education became increasingly important in response to the environmental movement of the 1960s and 1970s. At that time, the U.S. government established the Environmental Protection Agency and implemented laws such as the Clean Air Act, the Endangered Species Act, and the Clean Water Act in order to address increasingly evident environmental issues. As has been the case in many other countries, such environmental and sustainability education has integrated natural science with the social sciences.

On a global level, Sweden and New Zealand are recognized as two highly sustainable countries. According to a 2015 survey by the United Nations, Sweden was rated as the most sustainable country in the world. The Swedish government is committed to eliminating the use of fossil fuels by 2030. As in other countries, sustainable education in Sweden has emphasized participatory learning, as opposed to learning primarily from textbooks and other classroom materials. In particular, relationships between sustainability, environmental protection, and environmental justice are stressed upon.

A similar approach has been taken in New Zealand. Here, sustainability is regarded as especially important because New Zealand has been isolated geologically from the rest of the world for millions of years. Hence, New Zealand contains many endemic species of plants and animals found nowhere else in the world. Preservation of its unique environment is seen as essential to sustainability in New Zealand, intensifying the value of sustainability education in that country. As is the case with many other countries, New Zealand has a substantial Indigenous population. Maoris, whose ancestors settled in New Zealand hundreds of years before the arrival of the British, retain a store of Indigenous environmental knowledge that also influences environmental education and sustainability policy.

Argentina and Kenya face ongoing internal conflicts between two disparate goals: economic development and environmental preservation. Like India and Brazil, Argentina is regarded as a semideveloped country. Some of Argentina's wealth has been generated from polluting mining and manufacturing operations, but it contains a diversity of relatively pristine and little-known natural environments. Kenya is also pushing economic development and dealing with a rapidly increasing population. However, Kenya contains several large national parks where visitors can observe large wild animals in their native habitats. Thus, the national parks can be considered as a resource to promote economic development. However, attracting too many tourists, even though they contribute money needed for its economy, can imperil the sustainability of the environments that the parks have been intended to protect.

Kiribati, which consists of 33 islands scattered over more than a million square miles of the Pacific Ocean, is in a unique position because most of the land surface on all but one of its islands lies at less than 10 feet above sea level. Thus, Kiribati is highly vulnerable to potential sea-level rise associated with global warming. It is possible that most of its land will be under water by 2100. Environmental issues are a very important component of education in Kiribati, although many recognize that Kiribati has no control over the global environment that could cause its destruction.

Costa Rica and Dominica are semideveloped countries that are both recognized worldwide as leaders in the promotion of sustainability and the implementation of sustainability education. In contrast to Argentina and Kenya, both Costa Rica and Dominica have made sustainability cornerstone of their economies. About a quarter of Costa Rica's land surface is being preserved in its national park system and is off limits to development. Environmental education in Costa Rica emphasizes not only knowledge of ecological and sustainability principles but also preparation for employment in ecotourism and other economic activities associated with sustainability. Dominica is known in the Caribbean as the "Nature Isle" and, in contrast to other Caribbean countries, has discouraged mass tourism that could lead to destruction of its natural environment. Rather, environmentally friendly tourism and other activities that reduce impacts on the natural environment have been emphasized. Here too, sustainability is a very significant component of education as Dominica seeks to maintain a sustainable environment in the face of global environmental change.

ARGENTINA

Argentina, which is known formally as the Argentine Republic, is the second largest country in South America both by land area and by population. Located in southeastern South America south of Brazil, Argentina has a population of about 46 million as of 2022 and a land area of about 1,068,000 square miles.

Numerous Indigenous tribes inhabited present-day Argentina for thousands of years before Spanish explorers first viewed the coast of what is now Argentina in 1502. The Spanish settled in present-day Buenos Aires at the mouth of the Rio de la Plata in 1536. This settlement was abandoned five years later because of repeated attacks by local Indigenous inhabitants, but a permanent settlement was established at that site in 1580. The region was part of the Viceroyalty of Lima until 1776, when the Spanish established the viceroyalty of the Rio de la Plata. Buenos Aires became the capital of the viceroyalty of the Rio de la Plata, which included the northern two-thirds of present-day Argentina along with all of present-day Paraguay and Uruguay and portions of present-day Chile and Bolivia.

The viceroyalty declared its independence from Spain in 1816. In 1829, the provinces of what is now northern Argentina became united as the Argentine Confederation. During the late nineteenth century, the confederation expanded southward to incorporate Patagonia along with territories southward to the Straits of Magellan and the island of Tierra del Fuego. More than 90 percent of Argentines have full or partial European ancestry, and many are descended from immigrants from Italy, Spain, Germany, and other European countries. Only about 2 percent of Argentines are Indigenous peoples. As is the case of the United States, Argentina is a federal state. Power is shared formally between the federal government and the governments of its 23 provinces along with the autonomous city of Buenos Aires. Argentina has experienced a long history of political instability, including periods of military rule and rule by dictators as well as elected civilian governments.

Education in Argentina

Historically, the Roman Catholic Church has played an important role in Argentina's education. Systematic public education in Argentina was first established in the 1870s. In 1884, the government enacted its first law that mandated free, compulsory, and secular education throughout the country. The requirement that education be secular was opposed by some leaders of the Church who wanted religion to remain a central component of public education. Tension over the degree to which education should be secular, without religious influences, has continued into the twenty-first century.

Today, responsibility for public education is shared between the federal government and the governments of the provinces. Although the basic structure of education in Argentina has been established at the federal level, each of the provinces (including the autonomous city of Buenos Aires) is responsible for funding and managing education within its jurisdiction. Throughout the country, education is free and is compulsory for 13 years. Children can begin kindergarten at as young as 2 years old. The final year of kindergarten, at the age of 5, is compulsory.

After kindergarten, students move on to primary school followed by secondary school. In some areas, students attend primary school for six years and secondary school for six years, whereas other students attend primary school for seven years and secondary school for five years. At the secondary school level, students specialize in either academic or vocational tracks. The language of instruction throughout the country is Spanish, although government educational policy gives Indigenous peoples the right to schooling that is intended to preserve their cultures and languages. Argentina's literacy rate has been estimated at 99 percent, one of the highest literacy rates in Latin America.

Sustainability and Education in Argentina

Argentina is one of the wealthiest countries in Latin America, as measured by per capita income. However, at a global level Argentina is a middle-income country. In 2018, its per capita gross domestic product was estimated at about US$20,000. This figure was comparable to Mexico and Bulgaria, but only slightly more than a third as those of the United States, the Netherlands, and Germany. Given this status, and as is the case with many other countries around the world, many Argentine officials see a conflict between economic growth and sustainability.

The structure of Argentina's economy reinforces this perception of conflict. As of 2015, about 17 percent of Argentina's jobs were in the industrial sector. However, many of these jobs were in relatively unsustainable and/or polluting activities including oil and natural gas refining and chemicals. Environmental degradation affects the agricultural sector, which is a mainstay of Argentina's economy as well. Deforestation, soil erosion, and water pollution associated with discharge of agricultural pollutants into streams and rivers continue to impact Argentina. Discharge of toxic chemicals from chemical-production plants has also contributed to these pollution problems. Also, Argentina's economy has long been beset by poverty, income inequality, inflation, and international debt. These considerations have put more pressure to create jobs and stimulate the economy in the short run, perhaps at the expense of long-run environmental sustainability.

Nevertheless, concern over the environment underlies official policy. According to Article 41 of the constitution of Argentina, "The authorities will provide for the protection of this right [to a healthy environment], the rational use of natural resources, the preservation of natural and cultural heritage and biological diversity, and environmental information and education." Innovative efforts to promote a sustainable economy in Argentina have been initiated. For example, Asociacion de Cooperativas Argentinas, which is an organization dedicated to improving Argentine agriculture, has implemented programs intended to use geospatial data analysis and other digital technologies to promote sustainable farming practices. Greenbelts and effective access to clean drinking water are being implemented in low-income neighborhoods in Buenos Aires and other Argentine cities. However, it is recognized in accordance with Article 41 that efforts to expand upon such initiatives in agriculture and other economic sectors in Argentina will depend on effective education.

The curricula used in Argentina's schools include units involving environmental knowledge in social science and natural science courses. However, environmental education as a stand-alone subject is not part of these curricula. Experts on environmental education have called for inclusion of environmental issues as a specific subject within the curriculum. In the autonomous city of Buenos Aires, the Buenos Aires Ministry of Education has been active in developing and implementing programs to give environmental issues a more prominent place in the curriculum. Here, the ministry has established a Green Schools Program, or Escuelas Verdes.

The Green Schools Program includes instruction in four systematic areas including waste management, environmental health, climate change, and renewable energy. Each of these emphases cuts across the traditional curricular differences between the natural sciences and the social sciences. In each case, curricula include various hands-on projects and initiatives. For example, students are encouraged to ride bicycles to school and to grow vegetables in gardens on school property.

Both Argentine authorities and international observers recognize that the continued implementation of sustainability education in Argentina presents significant challenges. These include the need for efforts to reduce poverty and to combat the high degrees of income inequality within the country. A shortage of qualified teachers and the relative lack of effective teacher training programs is also a concern. Perhaps most significantly, however, it could be the development of awareness that economic growth and a sustainable environment are not mutually exclusive objectives.

Further Reading

Earth Charter, "Publication about Green Schools in Argentina," June 6, 2019, https://earth charter.org/publication-about-green-schools-in-argentina/. Retrieved on May 5, 2022.

Carly Graf, "How can Argentina achieve sustainable economic growth?" *Buenos Aires Times*, October 18, 2019, https://www.batimes.com.ar/news/economy/how-can-argentina -achieve-sustainable-economic-growth.phtml. Retrieved on January 24, 2020.

Robin Meyerhoff, "Argentina gets smarter about sustainable agriculture," *Forbes*, October 22, 2019, https://www.forbes.com/sites/sap/2019/10/22/argentina-grows-a-more -sustainable-and-efficient-agricultural-sector-with-machine-learning-and-geospatial -technology/#1dc21363bc5f. Retrieved on January 24, 2020.

Organisation for Economic Co-operation and Development, "Argentina: Further reforms are needed to boost sustainable and inclusive growth," July 27, 2017, https://www.oecd .org/newsroom/argentina-further-reforms-are-needed-to-boost-sustainable-and -inclusive-growth.htm. Retrieved on January 24, 2020.

UN Environment, "Chemicals and waste: Bringing about change in Argentina," February 7, 2019, https://www.unenvironment.org/news-and-stories/story/chemicals-and-waste -bringing-about-change-argentina. Retrieved on January 24, 2020.

COSTA RICA

The Republic of Costa Rica is located on the isthmus of Central America, southeast of Nicaragua and east of Panama and between the Caribbean Sea to the east and the Pacific Ocean to the west. Costa Rica's land area is nearly 20,000 square miles, with a population estimated 5.2 million in 2022.

Christopher Columbus sighted the east coast of present-day Costa Rica in 1502 and gave the area its name, which means "Rich Coast." The Spanish established the region's first permanent European settlement in 1524. Costa Rica was incorporated into the Spanish Viceroyalty of New Spain, which included territory northward from the Costa Rica itself to present-day California and Texas. It remained part of the viceroyalty for the next three centuries until the Spanish possessions in Central America declared their independence in 1821. Along with Guatemala, El Salvador,

Honduras, and Nicaragua, Costa Rica became part of the United Provinces of Central America. Costa Rica declared its independence in 1838, shortly before the United Provinces dissolved two years later.

During Spanish rule and throughout the nineteenth century, present-day Costa Rica was the poorest and most isolated area within Central America. Today, however, Costa Rica is the wealthiest country in Central America with a per capita gross domestic product of about $14,000 per year. Historically, the economy of Costa Rica was based largely on agriculture, and especially the production of coffee, bananas, and other tropical crops. However, more recently other sectors of the economy have grown rapidly. The government has promoted tourism within the framework of environmental sustainability, emphasizing ecotourism. Today, tourism is the largest sector of Costa Rica's economy. Education is a very important component of Costa Rica's commitment to sustainability.

Education in Costa Rica

During the colonial period, relatively few Costa Ricans were educated. What education did exist was provided by the Roman Catholic Church and was restricted generally to children of the landed elite. After independence, the government took a more active role in education. In 1844, education was declared a right of all Costa Rican citizens. Education was made free and compulsory for the first time in 1869.

Today, Costa Rica's educational system is managed by the Ministry of Public Education. Schooling begins with basic general education, which lasts for nine years and is compulsory. Basic general education includes six years of primary school and three years of secondary school. Although basic general education is required, in practice several barriers prevent all Costa Rican students from attending or completing secondary school, especially in remote rural areas where facilities may not be accessible. Poverty has also impacted school attendance. However, in 2011 it was estimated that about 80 percent of Costa Rican children of secondary school age were enrolled in secondary schools.

Following the completion of basic general education, two or three additional years of free public secondary school follow, although these years are not required. This stage is known as Diversified Education, and students can pursue academic or technical tracks. Spanish is the language of instruction, although secondary school students also study English. With a literacy rate of 95 percent, Costa Rica has one of the highest literacy rates in all of Latin America.

Sustainability and Education in Costa Rica

Costa Rica's environment is highly diverse and often fragile. Its environment includes its coasts on the Caribbean Sea and the Pacific Ocean, as well as mountains and highlands in the interior. The climate of much of the country is wet, and hence much of the land was forested originally. Large tracts of forest land can still be found in Costa Rica today. Costa Rica is also home to a wide variety of animals including jaguars, tapirs, sloths, and monkeys. It has been estimated that as much as 5 percent of the world's overall biodiversity can be found in Costa Rica.

Costa Rica has become a global leader in sustainability efforts and initiatives. The country's leaders have recognized that environmental sustainability has been of great importance to Costa Rica's economy and development. In order to preserve and protect its diverse environment, about 25 percent of Costa Rica's land area is protected within the country's national park system, which is known as the National System of Conservation Areas. The country is strongly committed to the use of renewable energy, with over 99 percent of its energy supplies coming from renewable sources as of 2017.

Ecotourism has become a very important component of Costa Rica's economic development. Tourism in general is the largest sector of the economy, with nearly three million foreign tourists visiting the country in 2016. However, Costa Rican policy emphasizes ecotourism in order to promote sustainability and preserve the country's diverse natural environment. Large-scale and environmentally destructive tourism is discouraged. For example, Costa Rica has banned sport hunting, whereas in the past hunting trips had been organized so that participants could shoot and kill wild animals. The prevalence of ecotourism has encouraged nature conservation even outside of Costa Rica's large national park system. However, some have expressed concern that the increasing numbers of tourists, even ecotourists, may contribute to damage and the potential destruction of the very environments that the country has worked hard to protect.

Costa Rica's leaders recognize the value and importance of education in promoting its environmental sustainability. The government's commitment to environmental education is codified by law, which gives the Ministry of Public Education the authority and the responsibility to develop environmental education programs. The Environmental Education Act articulates this responsibility specifically, stating that "education for the protection of the environment is of public interest." Ecotourism has also been seen as an important source of employment for local residents, further enhancing the value of sustainability education in Costa Rica. Recognizing the importance of ecotourism to Costa Rica's economy, schools have initiated efforts to prepare students for jobs in ecotourism.

Environmental education is an integral component of the curriculum at all levels of education, beginning with the early years of primary school. However, experts advocate a more complete integration of the natural sciences and the social sciences in environmental education curricula. Educators can and sometimes do take advantage of local environmental conditions in teaching sustainability. For example, teaching of sustainability in coastal areas has been focused on maintaining and preserving marine ecosystems.

Further Reading

Nathanael Johnson, "Costa Rica modernized without wrecking the environment. Here's how," *Grist*, December 15, 2016, https://grist.org/food/costa-rica-modernized-without-wrecking-the-environment-heres-how/. Retrieved on February 2, 2020.

Claire Menke and Martin Carnoy, "Education for a sustainable future: Analysis of the educational system of Osa and Golfito," 2013, https://inogo.stanford.edu/sites/default/files/INOGO%20-%20Education%20Sustainable%20Future%20FINAL.pdf. Retrieved on February 2, 2020.

Jenn Parker, "Ecotourism in Costa Rica: Sustainable tourism," *Howler Magazine*, July 1, 2018, https://howlermag.com/ecotourism-in-costa-rica-sustainable-tourism. Retrieved on January 28, 2020.

Rebecca Parsons, "How Costa Rica is paving the way for sustainable tourism," *Men's Journal*, 2018, https://www.mensjournal.comadventure/costa-rica-paving-way-sustainable-tourism/. Retrieved on January 28, 2020.

DOMINICA

The Commonwealth of Dominica (whose name is pronounced with the accent on the third syllable) is an island country in the Caribbean Sea, located south of the French colony of Guadeloupe and north of the French colony of Martinique. It has a land area of 290 square miles and a population estimated at 72,000 in 2022. It is the most mountainous country in the Caribbean. As a result, Dominica has the highest annual rainfall in the region, and its rugged interior is covered with tropical rainforest. Dominica's rugged topography has played an important role in its history.

Carib Indians whose ancestors had moved northward from mainland South America inhabited Dominica before Christopher Columbus first sighted it in 1493, giving the island its current name because he sighted it on a Sunday. The French claimed the island in 1715. In 1763, however, Dominica became a British colony under the terms of the Treaty of Paris that ended the Seven Years' War. The French occupied the island again beginning in 1778, but British sovereignty over the island was reinforced by the 1783 Treaty of Paris that also ended the Revolutionary War for American independence.

As elsewhere in the Caribbean, the British imported thousands of slaves into Dominica to work on plantations. However, some of these slaves escaped and moved into the interior of the island, where they were protected from recapture by the area's tropical rainforest vegetation and rugged topography. These escaped slaves were known as "Maroons," and some of their descendants continue to live in inland Dominica today. For similar reasons, significant numbers of Caribs were also able to survive the European takeover of Dominica. Today, about 5,000 Caribs continue to live in Dominica, where they comprise the only significant population of Caribs remaining on the Caribbean islands. Dominica remained under British control until it became independent in 1978.

Agriculture continues to be a mainstay of Dominica's economy, but the island is highly vulnerable to hurricanes that affect agricultural production as well as housing and infrastructure. In 2017, Dominica was devastated by category 5 Hurricane Maria, which damaged or destroyed more than two-thirds of the buildings in the country and resulted in 65 fatalities. Maria also affected education directly, in that an estimated 83 percent of the country's schools were destroyed or damaged. Many students could not attend school for several months, while other schools were set up temporarily in tents, community centers, or other buildings. Student performance was also affected by the trauma that many experienced during the storm.

Education in Dominica

Reflecting its history as a British colony, Dominica's educational system is based on the British model. Education is managed by the government's Ministry of Education and Human Resources, whose mission statement is "to educate and prepare all students to live productive lives in a complex and changing society."

Children in Dominica begin their formal education with seven years of primary school. This is followed by five years of secondary school. Primary school and the first three years of secondary school are free and compulsory. The last two years of secondary school are necessary for those who wish to go on to university education. However, these last two years are not free, and students who attend these last two years must rely on their families' resources or on scholarships. As a result, significant numbers of students from poor families leave school after three years of secondary education. This is particularly true among children whose labor is seen to be needed on family farms, and also among the Carib population. Nevertheless, the literacy rate in Dominica is virtually 100 percent. Those students who do complete all five years of secondary school then take the Caribbean Secondary Education Certificate Examination, and those who wish to go on to higher education also take the Caribbean Advanced Proficiency Examination (CAPE). CAPE, which is used in 15 other Caribbean countries, are equivalent to O-level and A-level examinations in the United Kingdom.

Sustainability and Education in Dominica

Environmental sustainability is a matter of concern throughout the Caribbean for several reasons. The rise in sea level associated with global warming threatens coastal areas of islands throughout the Caribbean and around the world. Given the islands' vulnerability to hurricanes, flooding associated with intense and heavy rainfall from these tropical systems is a major issue. Also, tourism is a major source of income in many Caribbean countries, and the maintenance of tourist facilities is an important economic consideration.

Concerns about environmental sustainability are especially evident in Dominica, which has been referred to as the "Nature Isle." Compared to other Caribbean islands, Dominica's landscape is relatively undeveloped. This is especially the case in the rugged and mountainous interior, areas of which receive an average of more than 200 inches of rain annually. Several species of birds and animals that have been extirpated elsewhere in the Caribbean can still be found in Dominica's rainforests. Although agriculture has been the mainstay of Dominica's economy historically, tourism has become increasingly important. Officials in Dominica are concerned about how to balance generating income from foreign tourists with preserving the island's relatively unspoiled and pristine natural environment, and in doing so, they are promoting ecotourism as opposed to mass tourism.

Dominica has been recognized internationally as being at the forefront globally of adopting and implementing sustainability initiatives, such as the Climate Resilient National Plan that was adopted in 2018. Education is being recognized as very important to the implementation of initiatives such as the National Plan. The country's Forestry, Wildlife, and Parks Division has established an Environmental Education Unit, whose mission is "to spread awareness of the conservation, protection and management of Dominica's National Parks, forests, flora, and fauna." The unit's website is https://www.govserv.org/DM/Roseau/574968226039832/Dominica%27s-Forestry%2C-Wildlife-%26-Parks-Division%3AEnvironmental-Education-Unit. Its initiatives have included several projects involving schoolchildren. For example, students throughout the country have studied and participated in efforts to recognize World Migratory Bird Day—an issue of particular importance in Dominica because the island is home to many birds that migrate to the island from North America each winter. Students were involved also in nationwide efforts to plant trees at all primary and secondary schools throughout the country.

Further Reading

Anichi Development, "From survival to sustainability—A resilient Dominica," August 9, 2018, https://www.anichidevelopment.com/from-survival-to-sustainability-a-resilient -dominica/. Retrieved on January 26, 2020.

Josh Lew, "Dominica is still recovering from Hurricane Maria—But you can help," Mother Nature Network, August 2, 2018, https://www.mnn.com/lifestyle/eco-tourism/stories /Dominica-still-recovering-hurricane-maria-you-can-help. Retrieved on January 26, 2020.

Elliot Preece, "How Dominica is leading the way in sustainable development," *Repeatingislands .com*, December 21, 2017, https://repeatingislands.com/2017/12/21/how-dominica -is-leading-the-way-in-sustainable-development/. Retrieved on June 21, 2019.

KENYA

The Republic of Kenya is located in East Africa along the coast of the Indian Ocean. Its land area is about 224,000 square miles, with a population estimated at about 56 million in 2022. Politically and economically, Kenya is one of the most stable countries in sub-Saharan Africa.

Various tribes moved into present-day Kenya from other parts of Africa beginning more than 5,000 years ago. Trade relationships with distant cultures, notably in the Middle East, were established at least 2000 years ago. The largest Kenyan port on the Indian Ocean, Mombasa, was founded more than 1,000 years ago. Mombasa served as a center for trade between the interior of East Africa and the Middle East, South Asia, and Southeast Asia through the Indian Ocean. Here Kiswahili (Swahili), which is one of the official languages of Kenya and neighboring Tanzania and whose vocabulary includes a substantial number of words borrowed from Arabic, was first developed and spoken.

The Portuguese mariner Vasco de Gama visited Mombasa in 1498, reinforcing the coastal region's status as a center for long-distance maritime trade. However, Europeans showed relatively little interest in the interior of present-day Kenya until the late nineteenth century. The British established the East African Protectorate, which included most of what is Kenya today, in 1895. In 1920, the protectorate was incorporated into the British Empire as the colony of Kenya. British settlers controlled the colony's economy and its government, and in response, several African nationalist movements arose after World War II. Kenya became independent in 1963 and has remained a democracy for most of its history since that time, although recent democratic elections have been characterized by charges of fraud and corruption and by outbreaks of violence. Kenya's stability and relative prosperity have resulted in the arrival of several hundred thousand refugees from neighboring countries. In the long run, Kenya's government regards its economic and political stability as an important key to Kenya's development and prosperity. Increasingly, this economic and political stability has been linked to environmental sustainability.

Education in Kenya

Many historians believe that inhabitants of present-day Kenya were taught to read and write in Kiswahili hundreds of years ago. After European contact and as was the case elsewhere in sub-Saharan Africa, Christian missionaries began to establish schools. The British government gradually assumed control of education in colonial Kenya, and Kenyan education today remains influenced by the British educational system. Today, education throughout Kenya is administered by the Ministry of Education, Science, and Technology.

Free education was guaranteed by the Kenyan government upon independence. At first, the system included seven years of primary education followed

---

A Sustainability-Oriented School in the Democratic Republic of the Congo

The Democratic Republic of the Congo (DRC) is the largest country in sub-Saharan Africa by land area, with a population approaching 90 million. With a per capita income of less than US$1,000 per year and a rapidly growing population, relatively little attention is being paid to questions of environmental sustainability in the DRC. However, a school in the village of Kalebuka has been established with specific emphasis on sustainability. The school maintains a farm on which crops that provide two meals per day for each student are grown. In addition to teaching sustainable farming practices, the school emphasizes providing opportunities for girls in the DRC's patriarchal society.

Source: Study International, "In the DRC, a school that advances education, women's rights, and sustainability," January 17, 2020, https://www.studyinternational.com/news/sustainable-school-congo/. Retrieved on March 20, 2020.

by four years of secondary education. The number of years of primary school was increased from seven to eight years in 1985.

Primary education is compulsory, but in practice, it is believed that only about 85 percent of Kenyan children of primary school age actually attend school. Of these, about 75 percent proceed to secondary school, which is free but not compulsory. After completing four years of secondary school, students take an examination for the Kenya Certificate of Secondary Education. Primary and secondary education rates are lowest in impoverished, isolated, and rural areas that also face a shortage of supplies and qualified teachers. Also, many parents in these areas cannot afford to pay mandatory school fees. Others expect children, especially at the secondary level, to contribute farm or wage labor to help support their families. Both Kiswahili and English are used as languages of instruction, although Indigenous languages are also languages of instruction in some areas where neither of these official languages are used.

Sustainability and Education in Kenya

Although Kenya is one of sub-Saharan Africa's more prosperous and stable countries, it remains less developed compared to the rest of the world. In 2019, Kenya's per capita gross domestic product was estimated at only about $2,000—more than most of its neighbors, but far less than the worldwide average.

Kenya's efforts to develop its economy at faster rates are being hindered, moreover, by significant environmental issues. About a third of Kenya's workforce is employed in agriculture. Many Kenyan farmers are subsistence farmers, but many others grow coffee, tea, and various fruits and vegetables for export. However, much of Kenya's land surface is arid or semiarid. Annual rainfall varies significantly from year to year, and these areas are subject to periodic droughts. These droughts have become especially prevalent since the first decade of the twenty-first century, and thousands of people have died from starvation in drought-stricken areas. In 2019, northern Kenya experienced its most severe drought in nearly 40 years, and it has been estimated that more than 500,000 infants and small children are in danger of malnutrition because of food shortages associated with this drought.

Above and beyond the short-term impacts of drought, soil in semiarid agricultural areas is subject to erosion, and dust storms and swarms of voracious locusts affect Kenya's agricultural land as well. The locusts eat not only crops but also grasses that are eaten by livestock. Rainfall that does occur in these areas often comes in short bursts, resulting in sometimes catastrophic flooding. The capital city of Nairobi, with its rapidly increasing population, is also facing potentially severe shortages of clean water.

Tourism contributes significantly to Kenya's economy. More than a million tourists, primarily from Europe, visit Kenya each year. Many of these tourists visit Kenya's national parks where they can see lions, leopards, giraffes, elephants, and other large animals in the wild. However, influxes of tourists result in pollution and deforestation, as well as destruction of land cover in order to build roads,

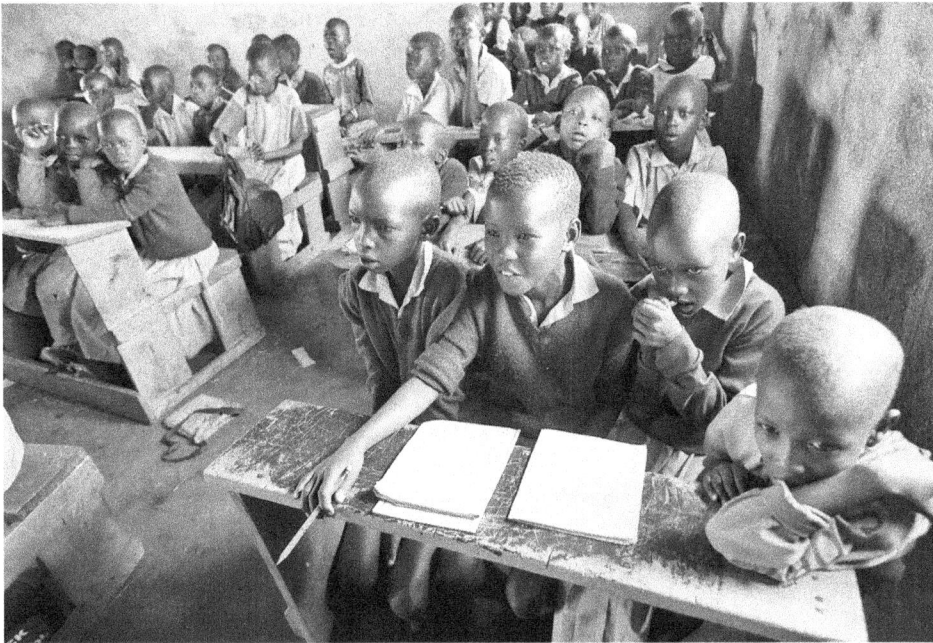

These children are in a classroom in a school located near Tsavo National Park, which is one of the oldest and largest national parks in Kenya. Tsavo is well known for its biodiversity, and careful management of the park is critical to maintaining a sustainable society in Kenya. Some of these students may be preparing for careers in wildlife management, ecotourism, or conservation. (Joe Sohm | Dreamstime.com)

hotels, and other facilities for tourists. These considerations, as well as the impacts of population growth, have reduced populations of wild animals that are already being threatened by poaching. Ecotourism, which is less destructive to the environment, is being promoted in order to minimize the effects of these pressures on Kenya's environment.

All of these considerations illustrate the fragility of Kenya's natural environment and the importance of sustainability in maintaining the environment and promoting economic growth and development in the long run. Drought and other environmental problems are affecting Kenyan education more directly in that many children are not attending school because of their impacts. For example, many families have been forced to move in order to survive in areas where food supplies are exhausted.

Kenyan officials have recognized the importance of education as a means of promoting environmental sustainability. Often with the assistance of more developed countries and international and nongovernmental agencies, they have worked to restructure education in order to help achieve this goal. In 2014, the Ministry of Education, Science, and Technology began to prepare policies for sustainable education. The result of these efforts was the Education for Sustainable Development Policy, which was launched in 2017. Under this policy, multidisciplinary approaches to education have been emphasized. Attention is also being paid to agricultural education, which remains a mainstay of Kenya's economy although according to one estimate the average age of a Kenyan farmer is more than 60 years. Many young Kenyans are reluctant to farm, recognizing that agriculture is less lucrative than the prospect of jobs in other economic sectors in the cities or overseas.

In 2019, the government adopted a new approach to education known as Curriculum-Based Competency (CBC). The CBC arose in response to concerns that students were not given sufficient training in practical problem-solving skills. "Environmental activities" is now being included as part of the primary school curriculum. Within this curriculum, students plant gardens, water trees, and participate in other practical projects associated with sustainability. A long-running goal of CBC is to promote greater awareness of the threats of climate change and environmental degradation throughout Kenyan society.

Further Reading

Global Partnership for Education, "Prolonged drought in East Africa forces millions of children out of school," April 3, 2018, https://www.globalpartnership.org/blog/prolonged-drought-east-africa-forces-millions-children-out-school. Retrieved on January 25, 2020.

Evance Jowi, "Encourage study of agriculture in schools in Kenya," Standard Digital, September 5, 2016, https://www.standardmedia.co.ke/article/2000214658/encourage-study-of-agriculture-in-schools-in-kenya. Retrieved on January 25, 2020.

James Macharia, "Sustainable development in Kenya," Center for International Relations and Sustainable Development, 2019, https://www.cirsd.org/en/horizons/horizons-winter-2019-issue-no-13/sustainable-development-in-kenya. Retrieved on January 25, 2020.

Edward Mungai, "Embrace environmental sustainability for growth," *Business Daily*, August 26, 2019, https://www.businessdailyafrica.com/lifestyle/pfinance/Embrace-environmental-sustainability-for-growth/4258410-5249994-rn2teqz/index.html. Retrieved on January 25, 2020.

Janet Murikira, "Can Kenya's new educational system address climate change?" One Earth, October 25, 2021, https://www.oneearth.org/can-kenyas-new-education-system-address-climate-change/. Retrieved on January 20, 2022.

KIRIBATI

The Republic of Kiribati is an island country in the central Pacific Ocean and straddles both the equator and the International Date Line. Kiribati (pronounced KEER-i-bass) contains 33 islands, which are scattered over nearly a million square miles of ocean. However, the total land area of Kiribati is only about 313 square miles. The islands are divided into three main groups, each separated from the others by hundreds of miles of ocean. These groups include the Gilbert Islands to the west, the Phoenix Islands in the center, and the Line Islands, which are directly south of the U.S. state of Hawaii, to the east. As of 2022, the total population of Kiribati was about 123,000. About half of Kiribati's people live on Tawara Atoll, which includes the capital city of South Tawara, in the Gilbert Islands.

Anthropologists believe that the islands of present-day Kiribati were first set-tled by Micronesians as long as 5,000 years ago. Later, people of Melanesian and Polynesian ancestry arrived and intermarried with the Micronesians. More than 95 percent of Kiribati's people today are of mixed Micronesian, Polynesian, and Mel-anesian ancestry and speak the Indigenous language, I-Kiribati. The westernmost islands of present-day Kiribati were named for a British explorer, Thomas Gilbert, in 1820. In 1892, the islands became part of the British protectorate of the Gilbert and Ellice Islands. The two groups of islands were given separate administrative status by the British in 1975, and the Ellice Islands became later the independent country of Tuvalu. The Gilbert Islands were granted independence in 1979 under the country's present name, which is a pronunciation of "Gilbert" in the Indigenous language. Many of the Phoenix and Line Islands are located some 2,000 miles east and southeast of the Gilbert Islands and had been under U.S. administration prior to 1983, when they were ceded to Kiribati.

Most of the islands that comprise Kiribati are atolls that rise only a few feet above sea level. The only exception is the island of Banaba, whose highest point is 266 feet above sea level but has only about 300 inhabitants and whose environ-ment has been devastated because of the mining of phosphates that at one time had been Kiribati's major export. Today, the leading exports of Kiribati include copra, breadfruit, and other tropical crops along with fish and other ocean prod-ucts. However, these economic activities and the very survival of Kiribati itself are threatened by the impacts of global warming. Because of sea-level rise, which is associated with global warming and environmental change, much of Kiribati could become submerged by the end of the twenty-first century.

The government of Kiribati has initiated efforts to address these issues associ-ated with the potential impacts of sea-level rise on the country. These efforts have included initiatives to resettle Kiribati's people on other "high islands," or volcanic islands that, like the islands of Hawaii, contain mountains that rise much higher above sea level. In 2008, the Kiribati government approached Australia and New Zealand, asking them to consider admitting "climate refugees" from Kiribati.

Education in Kiribati

When Kiribati became fully independent in 1979, six years of education were compulsory. More recently, the government extended the period of compulsory education to nine years, from ages 6 to 14. The system, which is administered by the Ministry of Education, Youth, and Sport, includes six years of primary school, three years of junior secondary school, and three years of senior secondary school or high school. As in many former colonies around the world, prior to indepen-dence many children were educated at mission schools run by the Roman Catholic Church, the Church of Jesus Christ of Latter-day Saints (Mormons), and other Christian groups. Some of these schools remain open, but the majority of Kiribati's children now attend public schools, which are free. I-Kiribati is used as the lan-guage of instruction for the first three years of primary school, after which English

This classroom is located in a primary school in the island country of Kiribati. Ongoing global warming and sea-level rise is endangering the future of Kiribati, most of the islands of which are only a few feet above sea level. Education is a key component in creating a sustainable future. (Lesley Xiao | Dreamstime.com)

becomes the language of instruction. The current literacy rates are unknown, although it is believed that the large majority of Kiribati's citizens are able to read and write.

The isolation of Kiribati's islands relative to one another has impeded the government's efforts to provide education to Kiribati's children. Although about half of the population live on the island of Tawara, many others live on isolated islands with small populations. For example, only about 10,000 people live on the three inhabited Line Islands, which are located nearly 2,000 miles east of Tawara. Thus, providing education to the relatively small numbers of children living on these isolated islands is expensive. Nevertheless, primary schools and junior secondary schools are located on most of Kiribati's inhabited islands.

It is believed that about 99 percent of Kiribati's children of primary school age attend primary school. However, secondary education is not available on some of the less populated islands, and students from these islands must travel to and board at schools in South Tawara in order to attend high school. In part because of the costs associated with transportation and boarding, it has been estimated that only about a third of Kiribati's children of high school age actually attend senior secondary school although it is believed that most Kiribati children do attend and complete primary school. In contrast to many less developed countries, girls attend secondary schools at higher rates than do boys.

Even for those who do complete secondary school, Kiribati's poverty and isolation contribute to high rates of unemployment. Many young adults who have completed secondary school leave Kiribati to work abroad, especially in Australia or New Zealand. In 2016, the government issued a four-year plan intended to promote economic development and improve the quality of life in Kiribati. The plan's vision statement reads: "Towards a better educated, healthier, more prosperous nation with a higher quality of life." Education has played an important role in the development and implementation of the plan.

Sustainability and Education in Kiribati

Environmental sustainability is of major concern in Kiribati. The threat of sea-level rise associated with ongoing global warming is of special concern, given that most of the country's land area is made up of low-lying atolls. An increase in sea level of as little as two or three feet could submerge a substantial portion of the country's land surface.

Even if the islands are not submerged entirely, it is expected that sea-level rise will cause substantial coastal erosion and increased salinity in the soil, making the land surface unfit for agriculture. The islands are threatened further by water pollution and marine waste, and it has been anticipated that sea-level rise could be associated with ocean acidification, salinization, coastal erosion, and flooding. Supplies of fresh water are also under threat. Each of these possible impacts of global warming and sea-level rise can have further impacts on Kiribati's efforts to remain a viable and sustainable country. Thus, sea-level rise could have significant impacts on agriculture, fishing, and other activities upon which Kiribati's economy depends currently.

Education has become recognized as a factor associated with creating awareness of sustainability and how Kiribati can survive in light of climate change and other environmental threats. In 2017, a booklet entitled "The Adventures of Vili" was prepared and distributed to every primary school student in the country. The goal of this project was to raise children's awareness of the environment and of sustainable practices, including consumption of healthy, locally grown foods. Various learning materials, including some that can be used in schools that lack access to the internet or even electricity, are also being provided. At the secondary level, a course on climate change has been added to the curriculum.

Further Reading

J. G. Federman, "Investing in Education in Kiribati," Borgen Project, April 29, 2017, https://www.borgenmagazine.com/education-in-kiribati/. Retrieved on January 24, 2019.

Government of Kiribati, "Kiribati development plan 2016–2019," 2016, http://www.mfed
.gov.ki/sites/default/files/Kiribati%20Development%20Plan%202016%20-%2019.
pdf. Retrieved on January 24, 2019.

Pacific Community, "World Environment Day," June 4, 2017, https://www.spc.int/updates
/news/2017/06/world-environment-day. Retrieved on January 24, 2020.

Sustainable Development Goals Knowledge Platform, "Kiribati," 2018, https://sustaina-
bledevelopment.un.org/memberstates/kiribati. Retrieved on January 24, 2020.

Kenneth R. Weiss, "Kiribati's dilemma: Before we drown we may die of thirst," *Scientific
American*, October 28, 2015, https://www.scientificamerican.com/article/kiribati-s
-dilemma-before-we-drown-we-may-die-of-thirst/. Retrieved on January 24, 2020.

NEW ZEALAND

New Zealand, which is located in the southwestern Pacific Ocean about 900 miles east of Australia, consists of two main islands, North Island and South Island, along with several smaller islands. The overall land area of New Zealand is about 103,500 square miles and the population was about 5.2 million as of 2022. Although South Island is slightly larger in land area, about three-quarters of the people live on North Island.

The first humans to settle in New Zealand were Polynesians, who are believed to have migrated southward from Polynesia to the islands in the thirteenth century AD and developed the Maori culture. The English mariner James Cook (1728–1779) circumnavigated the two islands in 1769 and claimed them for the United Kingdom. Migrants from the United Kingdom began to settle in the islands. As more and more English settlers arrived, many Maoris died from European diseases to which they had no immunity.

In 1840, the British government and several hundred Maori chiefs from throughout the islands signed the Treaty of Waitingi. The treaty granted Britain sovereignty over the islands. In theory, it gave Maoris the same rights as British settlers, but in practice, the Maoris were victimized by discrimination, and they forfeited the rights to many of their ancestral lands. The following year, the British made New Zealand a Crown Colony of the British Empire. It became a Dominion of the British Empire, with autonomy over its internal affairs, in 1907. In 1947, New Zealand's parliament passed the Statute of Westminster Adoption Act, asserting control over its defense and foreign policies and becoming fully independent. Although it is not as wealthy as Australia, New Zealand is recognized as a developed country. About 15 percent of New Zealanders are of Maori ancestry, and an increasing percentage of the people are migrants from island countries in the Pacific Ocean.

Education in New Zealand

After Europeans began to settle New Zealand, at first most schooling was provided by religious institutions. Missionaries began to teach the basics of the English language, reading, writing, and arithmetic to Maoris. These lessons emphasized the Bible, in efforts to promote the conversion of Maoris to Christianity.

Some of New Zealand's children of European ancestry were educated in private religious and secondary schools during most of the nineteenth century. In 1877, however, the Crown Colony established a system of state-run schools in New Zealand for the first time. At that time, education became compulsory for children between the ages of 7 and 13. However, the percentage of New Zealand's children who attended primary school at that time remained low. Secondary school was neither free nor compulsory, and it has been estimated that in 1900 only about 3 percent of New Zealand's teenagers were attending school. After the government made secondary education free in 1914, attendance rates began to increase.

Today, education in New Zealand is compulsory from the ages of 6 to 16. State-sponsored education remains free although parents are expected to pay for uniforms and school supplies. The system includes eight years of primary school followed by five years of secondary school. Children as young as one year old can attend preprimary schools, although these are not compulsory. Public education is administered by the Ministry of Education, which provides a national curriculum known as the New Zealand Curriculum. A parallel curriculum known as the Te Marautanga o Aoteroa is provided for Maori children. At the beginning of the twentieth century, English was the exclusive language of instruction. Children who spoke Maori at school were subject to punishment. Beginning in the 1970s, the Maori language was introduced in the curriculum. Today, Maori is the language of instruction in schools where Maoris represent the preponderance of the local population.

Sustainability and Education in New Zealand

New Zealand has been a leader in the development and implementation of sustainability principles. This leadership stems at least in part from local recognition of how humans have affected New Zealand's natural environment, especially since New Zealand became a Crown Colony. Because it is so isolated from major land masses around the world, New Zealand has a unique natural environment with large numbers of endemic species of animals and plants that are found nowhere else in the world. Many of these species have become extinct or highly endangered because of the introduction of nonnative species and because large amounts of once forested land have been cleared for agriculture and pasturing of livestock.

In 1991, the government of New Zealand enacted the Resource Management Act. The act promoted specifically the use of sustainability principles in the management of natural resources. The act was intended to provide a framework for "managing the use, development and protection of natural and physical resources in a way, or at a rate which enables people and communities to provide for their social, economic, and cultural well-being and for their health and safety while (a) Sustaining the potential of natural and physical resources (excluding minerals) to meet the reasonably foreseeable needs of future generations; and (b) Safeguarding the life-supporting capacity of air, water, soil, and ecosystem; and (c) Avoiding, remedying or mitigating any adverse effects of activities on the environment."

Students at Tauranga Girls' and Boys' Colleges in Tauranga, New Zealand, on Anzac Day in 2018. Anzac Day honors New Zealanders and Australians who served in "wars, conflicts, and peacekeeping operations." (Michael Williams | Dreamstime.com)

In implementing these principles, the act provided for a unified and integrated resource management system, replacing a large number of separate policies dealing with more specific aspects of the management of various resources. These separate policies had often been in conflict with one another. In establishing this unified regulatory framework, New Zealand became one of the first countries in the world to implement sustainability specifically.

Although the act provides a comprehensive and integrated framework for the management of New Zealand's unique environment and natural resources, it has been argued that the principles underlying the implementation of the act may not be sufficient to create a fully sustainable environment in New Zealand. Rather, it is argued that changes in individual attitudes toward and appreciation for sustainability are necessary. Education is seen as a key component of promoting these changes.

Sustainability education in New Zealand began in 1993 when a pilot program was undertaken in the city of Hamilton. This framework was expanded to many other districts beginning in 2002. In the following year, the Enviroschools Foundation was founded. The foundation's interpretation of sustainability "means living in a country where people work with positive energy to connect with each other, their cultural identity and their land, to create a healthier, peaceful, more equitable society. It means the regeneration of resilient, connected communities in which people care for each other and the environment. It means valuing indigenous knowledge and celebrating diversity so that everyone thrives."

Further Reading

Government of New Zealand, "Education for sustainability in New Zealand," 2010, https://www.educationcounts.govt.nz/publications/schooling/82841. Retrieved on January 31, 2019.

Nick Morrison, "How NZ could be a world leader in sustainability," Newsroom New Zealand, October 8, 2017, https://www.newsroom.co.nz/2017/10/05/51808/how-nz-could-be-a-world-leader-in-sustainability#. Retrieved on January 27, 2020.

Morgan Williams, "Sustainable New Zealand—The way forward," *New Zealand Geographic*, 70 (November–December 2004), https://www.nzgeo.com/stories/sustainable-new-zealand-the-way-forward/. Retrieved on January 31, 2019.

SWEDEN

The Kingdom of Sweden is located on the eastern half of the Scandinavian peninsula in northern Europe. It has a land area of nearly 174,000 square miles. As of 2022, its population was about 10.2 million, the large majority of whom live in the southern third of the country including the capital city of Stockholm.

Vikings occupied most of southern and central Scandinavia, including much of present-day Denmark, for several centuries beginning about 750 AD. Over the next several centuries, the Vikings expanded to the west, south, and east. The Vikings of present-day central and southern Sweden expanded eastward and southward to present-day Finland, Russia, Ukraine, and other Eastern European destinations. During the Middle Ages, the Swedish kingdom became powerful, especially after it ousted Germans from control of ports located on the south side of the Baltic Sea and was able to control trade through the Baltic Sea.

The Swedish kingdom was defeated by Russian armies in the Great Northern War, which was fought during the early eighteenth century. After this war, Sweden

---

Climate Change Education in Finland

As is the case with other Scandinavian countries, Finland has been a leader in promoting environmental sustainability. Finland is regarded as one of the most sustainable societies in the world, and Finnish educational authorities have recognized the importance of education in maintaining a sustainable society. In addition to being taught from textbooks, Finnish students are given hands-on training in sustainable practices such as recycling. Climate change, renewable energy, and other sustainability-related topics are integrated throughout the curriculum, and teachers are provided with learning materials involving environmental sustainability.

Source: David J. Cord, "Finnish schools emphasise climate change education," August 2019, https://finland.fi/life-society/finnish-schools-emphasise-climate-change-education/. Retrieved on March 21, 2020.

gave up its territories east and south of the Baltic. Sweden remained in control of present-day Finland until 1826, when it was ceded to Russia. Today, Sweden remains a constitutional monarchy. Sweden is recognized as one of the wealthiest and most developed countries in the world, ranking very high on most measures of social welfare and economic well-being. More than 80 percent of Sweden's inhabitants speak Swedish as their first language, although five other languages are also recognized by the government.

Education in Sweden

As in many European countries, until the nineteenth century education in Sweden was generally provided privately. During the Middle Ages, the Roman Catholic Church maintained school for the training of priests. After the Protestant Reformation, these were replaced by schools administered by the Evangelical Lutheran Church. The primary purpose of these schools was also to train the clergy. Meanwhile, the Swedish aristocracy arranged for their children to be educated by private tutors. In 1842, the government provided for four years of primary education, and this was extended to six years in the late nineteenth century. However, these schools were not always available in rural and isolated areas, and attendance was not obligatory until the government mandated seven years of compulsory education in the 1930s.

Education in Sweden today is compulsory for 10 years, from ages 6 to 16. The 9-year period of compulsory education is divided into 4 components. Education begins with *forskoleklass* or kindergarten. Many children attend forskoleklass for one year, but it is also available to children as young as one year old. In 2018, attendance at forskoleklass for one year became compulsory. Forskoleklass is followed by three years of lower elementary school, three years of upper elementary school, and three years of lower secondary school, all of which are compulsory. High school, or gymnasium, is available but is not required. Most Swedish children attend public schools, although private schools are available and are eligible for funding by the government.

Education is administered at the local level, although curricula and other aspects of school management are supervised closely by the national Ministry for Education and Research. Swedish is the language of instruction, although lower elementary school classes are conducted in areas where other languages are prevalent. For example, the Sami people represent a majority of the population of northern Sweden, and in these areas, primary education is provided in the Sami language. Literacy is virtually universal, although some immigrants from Africa and the Middle East who have moved to Sweden in recent years are illiterate.

Education and Sustainability in Sweden

Swedish society is recognized as very highly sustainable. In 2015, Sweden ranked as the most sustainable country in the world. This ranking was based on the degree to which each surveyed country adhered to the United Nations' Sustainable Development Goals. In a similar study conducted in 2018, Sweden ranked fifth in the world.

Several factors have contributed to the recognition of Sweden as the world's most sustainable country. Many Swedes purchase food and consumer products that have been labeled as eco-friendly. According to recent estimates, nearly 90 percent of aluminum cans and plastic bottles are recycled when empty.

Sweden has also committed itself to becoming fossil fuel-free by 2050. A short-term goal is to eliminate automobiles and other vehicles that are powered by fossil fuels by 2030. The government is investing intensively in other sources of energy including solar energy and wind energy. By 2015, more than half of Sweden's energy came from renewable sources. This percentage was the highest in the European Union. Sweden became one of the first countries in the world to initiate a carbon tax in 1995. And in order to promote the use of clean energy, Sweden levies heavy taxes on the sale of gasoline and other fossil fuels.

Education is playing an important role in promoting Sweden's sustainable lifestyle. Since the early twentieth century, the Swedish educational curriculum has emphasized the outdoors. In the 1960s, this tradition of outdoor education became linked to the environmental movement that developed worldwide, especially in Scandinavia, at that time. Sustainability has been a cornerstone of the curriculum ever since. While the concept of "sustainable development" has been controversial in many countries, the idea that a liberal market economy along with a generous welfare system can function only if and when coupled with environmental protection is less controversial in Sweden. That "sustainable development" is less controversial in Sweden as compared to other countries has been attributed to Sweden's emphasis on citizen participation in decision-making, as well as broad consensus among Sweden's leaders about the importance of environmental protection and sustainability.

In recent years, the focus of environmental education in Sweden has also changed. Historically, the purpose of environmental education was to transmit factual knowledge about environmental issues to students. More recently, this fact-based approach to environmental education has been replaced increasingly by a more participatory approach emphasizing communication between students and teachers along with the study of relationships among environmental protection, economic development, and social justice. This approach also involves teachers of geography, history, and economics and other social sciences as well as teachers of the natural sciences. Thus, students learn about sustainability via participatory engagement with the material, instead of reliance on the transmission of factual material.

How well has this participatory-based approach to environmental and sustainability education been working? Studies have compared levels of knowledge of sustainability and environmental issues between upper secondary students who have been educated using this participatory-based approach and those who were not educated in this way. Preliminary analysis, based on comparison of test results, has shown that levels of knowledge of students who have been exposed to the participatory approach were greater than those of other students. Supporters of the approach have claimed that students who are exposed to this approach will perpetuate and expand Sweden's ongoing emphasis on environmental sustainability as they transition toward adulthood.

Further Reading

Teresa Berglund, Niklas Gerike, and Shu-Nu Chang-Rundgren, "The implantation of education for sustainability in Sweden: Investigating the sustainability consciousness among upper secondary students," *Research in Science and Technological Education*, 32 (2014), pp. 318–339.

Johan Ohman, "New Swedish environmental and sustainability education research," *Utbildning und Demokrati*, 20 (2011), pp. 1–11, https://www.oru.se/globalassets/oru -sv/forskning/forskningsmiljoer/hs/humus/utbildning-och-demokrati/2011/nr1 /johan-ohman---new-swedish-environmental-and-sustainability-education-research. pdf. Retrieved on January 28, 2019.

Ben Wilde, "How Sweden Became the World's Most Sustainable Country: Top 5 Reasons," *ADEC Innovations Blog*, January 12, 2016, https://www.adecesg.com/resources/blog /how-sweden-became-the-world%E2%80%99s-most-sustainable-country-top-5 -reasons/. Retrieved on January 25, 2019.

UNITED STATES

In light of global climate change, pollution, and other environmental issues, Americans are paying more and more attention to environmental sustainability in the United States. On a global level, the sustainability of the United States is of special importance because of the degree to which the United States dominates the global economy and because Americans use more resources than are used in any other country. It is well recognized that efforts to promote sustainability in the United States are linked to effective education.

Discussion of sustainability education in the United States can be placed effectively in the context of environmental sustainability in American history. The history of the United States is one characterized by several centuries of large-scale environmental degradation, followed by more recent recognition of the value of environmental sustainability in recent years. With Americans becoming more concerned about preserving the environment, environmental and sustainability concerns have begun to develop within the American educational system.

Although estimates vary widely, many historians and anthropologists believe that between 2 and 10 million Native Americans lived in what is now the United States in 1492, before sustained European contact with North America. Thus, Europeans who moved to the present-day United States beginning in the early seventeenth century found a sparsely settled continent. The vast forests that had grown between the Atlantic coast and the Mississippi River prior to European settlement were cut down by the settlers, who converted much of the land to agricultural use. Over the next three centuries, Native Americans were driven away from most of the territory that they had occupied prior to European colonization. Many were exiled to reservations, where some of their descendants live today.

The first three centuries of European occupation of North America were characterized by steady expansion as the frontier of settlement moved westward and Native Americans were driven away. With westward expansion of the frontier came large-scale environmental destruction. For example, millions of bison or "buffaloes" (*Bison bison*) lived in central North American before the nineteenth century. During the nineteenth century, it is believed that humans killed as many as 50 million bison. By 1900, the bison had been hunted almost to extinction, and only a few hundred remained in the wild. Today, however, the bison population has recovered somewhat, although many bison have interbred with domestic cattle and/or live on ranches or in captivity. Similarly, human activity resulted in the extinction of the passenger pigeon (*Ectopistes migratorius*) and the Carolina parakeet (*Conuropsis carolinensis*).

By the late nineteenth century, most of the land within the 48 conterminous states had been occupied by settlers. In 1890, the U.S. Bureau of the Census announced that the frontier line, which had been defined as the line beyond which the Euro-American population was less than two per square mile, had been closed. The announcement of the closing of the frontier inspired the historian Frederick Jackson Turner (1861–1932) to examine the role of the frontier and its westward movement in American history. Turner argued that American culture, in contrast to the cultures of Europe, had been shaped and affected profoundly by the American frontier experience. In Turner's view, the frontier was a symbol of freedom and opportunity to Americans as they expanded westward.

Although the validity of Turner's arguments has been debated by historians ever since he first articulated them, the closing of the frontier and the recognition of the degree to which Americans had caused large-scale environmental damage and destruction induced many Americans to rethink relationships between American society and the natural environment. As it became clear that there were no longer additional lands available for settlement, efforts to preserve wilderness areas and prevent them from being developed began to be made. Yellowstone National Park was established in 1872, followed by Yosemite National Park in 1890. At this time, the conversation movement developed and continued through the first two decades of the twentieth century. Agencies including the National Park Service and the U.S. Forest Service were established and charged with managing natural resources. Conservation differed from environmental preservation, however, in that the conservation movement emphasized the management of the environment for continued human use. Recognizing the impact of the wanton slaughter of bison, limits were placed on the number of wild animals of other species that could be shot and killed legally each year in order to maintain the populations of these animals in the future.

After World War II, more and more attention began to be paid to environmental preservation. The publication of *Silent Spring* by Rachel Carson (1907–1964) was seen as a landmark event in that Carson called attention to the harmful impact of pesticides on the environment. In 1969, an oil well that had been drilled off the coast of Santa Barbara, California, blew out and leaked at least three million gallons of oil into the Pacific Ocean. The resulting oil slick was more than 800 square miles in area, and thousands of sea lions, seals, dolphins, and seabirds were killed in this disaster.

These and other events led to the celebration of the first Earth Day on April 22, 1970, with the intent of calling public attention to the issue of preserving the environment. The Environmental Protection Agency (EPA) was established in 1970. Several landmark laws including the Clean Air Act, the National Environmental Policy Act, the Endangered Species Act, and the Clean Water Act were enacted during the 1970s. Since that time, experts on environmental preservation have focused on the causes and impacts of air and water pollution, global climate change, habitat fragmentation, and other environmental issues. During the late twentieth and early twenty-first centuries, various environmental concerns became significant political issues, including the degree to which government should take an active role in environmental preservation.

Sustainability and Education in the United States

In the late twentieth and early twenty-first centuries, Americans have become more aware of the value and the importance of sustainability and environmental preservation. Practices such as recycling and use of renewable energy as opposed to reliance on fossil fuels came into common use, as did the use of solar panels and green building techniques. Education played an important role in creating and maintaining this awareness.

The roots of environmental and sustainability education in the United States can be found in the late nineteenth century, coinciding with the closing of the frontier and the conservation movement. "Nature study" was introduced into public school curricula during and after the 1890s. Nature study emphasized observation of the natural world as a significant component of teaching science, which had generally been taught from textbooks. One of the leaders of the nature study was Anna Botsford Comstock (1854–1930), whose 1911 book *The Handbook of Nature Study* was highly influential in training teachers in techniques of nature observation. Organizations such as the Boy Scouts and the Girl Scouts also emphasized nature study and observation.

In conjunction with the rise of the environmental movement in the 1960s and the 1970s, nature study gave way to a more integrated approach to the teaching of environmental issues. Ecology had emerged as an important field of study within the discipline of biology, and principles of ecology came to be linked with economics and the social science in order to teach about relationships between humans and the environment. In 1970, Congress passed the Environmental Education Act. The act authorized the U.S. Department of Health, Education, and Welfare to offer grants to develop environmentally oriented curricula and to establish teacher training programs.

Climate Change and Education in Alaska

Surface temperatures are increasing around the world, but rates of global warming in Alaska are among the highest in the world. Educators in Alaska are working to integrate knowledge of climate change and environmental sustainability in their classrooms, despite the importance of the fossil fuel industry to Alaska's economy. And as elsewhere, many teachers believe that they do not have time to teach environmental sustainability given other pressures and priorities. Encouraging students to keep weather records and collect other data about their local environments is one strategy that can help students become more aware of climate change.

Source: Elizabeth Jenkins, "How some teachers in Alaska are tackling the subject of climate change," *NPR*, April 22, 2019, https://www.npr.org/2019/04/22/716096487/how -some-teachers-in-alaska-are-tackling-the-subject-of-climate-change. Retrieved on March 21, 2020.

The original act was repealed in 1981, but it was revived in 1990 as the National Environmental Education Act. The revised act established an Office of Environmental Education under the jurisdiction of the EPA. The mission of the office was to "develop and support programs and related efforts, in consultation and coordination with other Federal agencies, to improve understanding of the natural and built environment, and the relationships between humans and their environment, including the global aspects of environmental problems." Thus, a key goal of the office was to promote environmental literacy and environmental awareness among Americans. Also, it illustrates the need for coordination among natural science, the social sciences, and humanities in teaching about sustainability. As Nicole Ardoin and her colleagues have observed, "By definition, environmental education encompasses approaches, tools, and programs that develop and support environmentally related attitudes, values, awareness, knowledge, and skills that prepare people to take informed action on behalf of the environment."

Over the past two decades, the effectiveness of environmental education programs has been monitored and evaluated. Results of these studies indicate, not surprisingly, that students' knowledge of environmental issues has increased. Also, such programs have been shown to increase student civic involvement, improve critical thinking skills, and promote environmentally friendly practices.

Some educators have argued that sustainability education should go beyond merely teaching about sustainability in the classroom. Perhaps following the development of nature study in the early twentieth century, these educators have advocated the construction and use of sustainable school buildings and facilities, including programs to promote the use of natural light, reduce energy use, and reduce water waste. In some schools, children participate directly in activities associated with sustainability and environmental awareness such as planting and cultivating gardens. According to one study, many children were more willing to eat vegetables that they had grown in these gardens compared to vegetables brought in from elsewhere. These factors are seen as enhancing the goal of teaching students to understand and act upon relationships between humans and the environment.

Further Reading

Nicole M. Ardoin, "The benefits of environmental education for K-12 students," North American Association for Environmental Education, n.d., https://naaee.org/eepro /research/eeworks/student-outcomes. Retrieved on February 3, 2019.

Nicole M. Ardoin, Alison W. Bowers, and Estelle Gaillard, "Environmental education outcomes for conservation: A systematic review," *Biological Conservation*, 2019, https:// www.sciencedirect.com/science/article/pii/S0006320719307116. Retrieved on February 3, 2019.

Rachel Carson, *Silent spring*. Boston: Houghton Mifflin, 1962.

Anna Botsford Comstock, *The handbook of nature study*. Ithaca, NY: Cornell University Press, 1986. Published originally in 1911.

Frederick Jackson Turner, "The significance of the frontier in American history," essay originally presented to the annual meeting of the American Historical Association in 1893, https://www.historians.org/about-aha-and-membership/aha-history-and-archives /historical-archives/the-significance-of-the-frontier-in-american-history. Retrieved on February 1, 2020.

References

Peter H. Diamandis, "A model for the future of education," *SingularityHub*, September 12, 2018, https://singularityhub.com/2018/09/12/a-model-for-the-future-of-education-and-the-tech-shaping-it/.

Edsys, "20 best education systems in the world," n.d., https://www.globalpartnership.org/news/infographic/what-makes-great-education.

Sean Fleming, "How can we prepare students for the Fourth Industrial Revolution? Five issues from innovative schools around the world," February 3, 2020, https://www.weforum.org/agenda/2020/02/schools-of-the-future-report-2020-education-changing-world/.

Germany Federal Ministry for Economic Cooperation and Development, "Education in developing countries," 2018, https://www.bmz.de/en/issues/Education/hintergrund bildungsituation/index.html.

Global Citizen, "10 barriers to education that children living in poverty face," 2019, https://www.globalcitizen.org/en/content/10-barriers-to-education-around-the-world-2/.

Global Partnership for Education, "What makes a great education" (infographic), January 24, 2019, https://www.globalpartnership.org/news/infographic/what-makes-great-education.

Google for Education, "Future of the classroom" (includes infographic), 2019, http://services.google.com/fh/files/misc/future_of_the_classroom_emerging_trends_in_k12_education.pdf?utm_source=web&utm_campaign=FY19-Q2-global-demandgen-website-other-futureoftheclassroom.

Katie Jones, "How technology is shaping the future of education," *Visual Capitalist*, February 17, 2020, https://www.visualcapitalist.com/how-technology-is-shaping-the-future-of-education/.

National Center for Education Statistics, "Program for international student assessment," 2018, https://nces.ed.gov/surveys/pisa/pisa2018/index.asp#/.

Nerdy Mates, "7 trends that will shape the future of education," n.d., https://nerdymates.com/blog/education-future.

Daniel Newman, "Top 5 digital transformation trends in education for 2020," *Forbes*, August 1, 2019, https://www.forbes.com/sites/danielnewman/2019/08/01/top-5-digital-transformation-trends-in-education-for-2020/#743339a85739.

Jack O'Sullivan, "Knowing how to learn is key in the information age," *Blog on Learning and Development*, May 9, 2017, https://bold.expert/knowing-how-to-learn-is-key-in-the-information-age/?gclid=EAIaIQobChMIu_jghvfR6AIVgbbICh3m9wYAEAAYAS ABEgJKpvD_BwE.

Kyle Pearce, "21st century education: Why we must completely reimagine learning," DIYGenius, July 25, 2019, https://www.diygenius.com/21st-century-education/.

Katie Puckett, "The Future of Education," *The Possible*, September 2017, https://www.the-possible.com/future-of-education-digital-campus-learning-teaching/.

Study International, "Here's how technology is shaping the future of education," February 14, 2019, https://www.studyinternational.com/news/heres-how-technology-is-shaping-the-future-of-education/.

Teachnology, "Gender inequities in education today" (includes links to other sites), n.d., https://www.teach-nology.com/litined/equity/gender/.

UNESCO, "Education and gender equality," 2015, https://en.unesco.org/themes/education-and-gender-equality.

UNESCO, "Education 2030: Incheon Declaration toward inclusive and equitable quality education and lifelong learning for all," 2015, https://unesdoc.unesco.org/ark:/48223/pf0000245656.

UNESCO, "Quality and learning indicators" (includes links to other resources), 2019, https://learningportal.iiep.unesco.org/en/issue-briefs/monitor-learning/quality-and-learning-indicators.

Ramya Vivekanandan, "Integrating 21st-century skills into education systems: From rhetoric to reality," Brookings Institute, February 14, 2019, https://www.brookings.edu/blog/education-plus-development/2019/02/14/integrating-21st-century-skills-into-education-systems-from-rhetoric-to-reality/.

World Bank, "The education crisis: Being in school is not the same as learning," January 22, 2019, https://www.worldbank.org/en/news/immersive-story/2019/01/22/pass-or-fail-how-can-the-world-do-its-homework.

World Population Review, "Education ranking by country 2020," https://worldpopulation-review.com/countries/education-rankings-by-country/.

Your Training Edge, "Five amazing digital trends to keep an eye on in 2020," November 21, 2019, https://www.yourtrainingedge.com/5-amazing-digital-education-trends-to-keep-an-eye-on-in-2020-and-beyond/.

Index

About the Author

Fred M. Shelley is professor emeritus of geography and environmental sustainability at the University of Oklahoma. He is author or editor of more than 20 books and more than 100 professional publications including ABC-CLIO's *Nation Shapes: The Story behind the World's Borders*; *The World's Population: An Encyclopedia of Critical Issues, Crises, and Ever-Growing Countries*; and *Geography of Trafficking: From Drug Smuggling to Modern-Day Slavery* (coauthored with Reagan Metz).

www.ingramcontent.com/pod-product-compliance
Lightning Source LLC
Chambersburg PA
CBHW080412270326
41929CB00018B/2994